DEBT

A · N · D

TAXES

DEBT

A · N · D

TAXES

JOHN H. MAKIN
AND
NORMAN J. ORNSTEIN

✦

AN AMERICAN ENTERPRISE
INSTITUTE BOOK

TIMES 𝕿 BOOKS

RANDOM HOUSE

Library of Congress Cataloging-in-Publication Data
Makin, John H.
    Debt and taxes: how America got into its budget mess and what to do about it/John H. Makin and Norman J. Ornstein.—1st ed.
    p.   cm.
    Previous ed. cataloged under: Makin, John H.
    "An American Enterprise Institute Book."
    Includes bibliographical references and index.
    ISBN-0-8129-2312-X
    1. Fiscal policy—United States—History.
I. Makin, John H.
II. Makin, John H. Debt and taxes.   III. Title.
HJ241.M36   1994
336.3'0973—dc20   93-30517

✦ ACKNOWLEDGMENTS ✦

This book had its genesis early in the Reagan presidency, when it became clear that difficulties over debt, taxes, deficits, and budgets would become the driving theme for the Reagan years, and likely of the presidencies to follow. As we watched the debate unfold (and frequently unravel), we began to ask some obvious questions: Is this really a revolution? Is this era truly different from others in America's past? Can the problem be solved by some combination of structural reforms? How much should we be concerned by deficits and debt—and how do they compare to past experiences and other countries?

Throughout the fiscal struggles of the 1980s, hyperbole abounded about the causes and consequences of our politics and economic policy. Books about the deficit, and about the Reagan presidency's approach to it, became a growth industry. What remained lacking, however, was context. The two of us, coming at the problem from very different backgrounds as, respectively, an economist and a political scientist, decided to try to provide some perspective—historical, political, and economic—to help inform the ongoing debate and provide grounding for the large group of interested observers and citizens who are not specialists in the budget process or fiscal policy.

The task proved to be daunting. The idea of a collaboration between an economist and a political scientist was appealing; the reality was that our different backgrounds and training, along with our different political outlooks, made the collaboration a regular debate over priorities, policies, and paradigms. In the end, we believe (and hope) that the book reflects a synergy —though it also undoubtedly reflects some of the tugging and hauling that took place between us over the years.

The Ford Foundation was instrumental in allowing us to get our project underway and provided encouragement and unstinting support for the several years that we worked on it; we are particularly grateful to David Arnold and Shep Forman. Our institution, the American Enterprise Institute, and its leadership, including Chris DeMuth and David Gerson, was itself wholly supportive and enthusiastic about our efforts. AEI's publications people, especially Ed Styles, Ann Petty, and Virginia Viega, deserve their own special thanks, as does Jim Bowman for his yeoman editing efforts and skillful suggestions.

As we worked on the project, which included a major conference and conference volume, *Balancing Act: Debt, Deficits and Taxes*, we were helped by the able assistance of David Zlowe and Mark Schmitt, along with Jim Haskell, James Chik, Kim Coursen, Lynn Hoverman, and Amy Schenkenberg. John Cavers, John Morgan, and Timothy Dickenson were sounding boards along the way and gave valuable advice and cautionary notes. Jonathan Rauch and Joe White deserve particular thanks for their willingness to read chapter and manuscript drafts and offer unvarnished criticism and helpful advice, putting in extraordinary time and effort—and improving a book whose remaining flaws are our own.

✦ CONTENTS ✦

PART THREE
FROM THE NEW DEAL TO THE NEW FRONTIER

PART FOUR
FROM THE GREAT SOCIETY
TO THE REAGAN REVOLUTION

PART FIVE
LESSONS

DEBT

A · N · D

TAXES

✦ 1 ✦

INTRODUCTION

In 1789, Benjamin Franklin wrote to Jean Baptiste Le Roy that "our constitution is in actual operation; everything appears to promise that it will last; but in this world nothing is certain but death and taxes." He might have added that, under American constitutional government, nothing is certain but debt and taxes. Franklin and his fellow framers of the Constitution were acutely aware of the massive debt accumulated by the Continental Congress during and after the Revolutionary War; they understood the need to levy taxes to pay interest on it and, ultimately, to reduce it to a manageable size. Failure to do so would have destroyed government, either through rebellion by citizens who only thirteen years earlier had taken up arms against taxation without representation or in the chaos of hyperinflation, the fate of governments (most recently the Soviet Union) that print money instead of collecting taxes.

This book is about the experience of Americans and their governments with debt and taxes. The national debt somewhat guiltily bequeathed from one generation to the next since 1789 has at times been a national obsession, even though other countries would rarely have considered the debt particularly large in relation to total national output. Often, the politicians who did most to create the debt, with the consent of the voters who elected and reelected them, have been most vehement in their denunciations of it.

The past decade has been such a period of debt consciousness. Between 1982 and 1992, during the Reagan and Bush administrations, large budget deficits symbolized to many America's inability to govern itself. The stubborn resistance of these deficits to all attempts by both the executive and the legislative branches to reduce them has no doubt contributed considerably

3

to the resentment, outrage, and alienation that a majority of Americans have expressed toward government and its leaders.

At the same time, the debt problem is not well or widely understood. According to common belief, the Reagan "revolution" created the deficits by substantially cutting tax revenues while greatly increasing defense spending and failing to cut other spending enough to make up the differences. Other popular beliefs are that these deficits are unprecedented in American history, certainly for peacetime; that their persistence and the failure of government to eliminate them have made this period unusual if not unique; and that the "divided government" characteristic of the decade—together with a misguided and out-of-control budgetary process—was partly responsible for the failure.

Each of these beliefs reflects some truth, but we should remember the fate of that other article of current wisdom through most of the decade: that the economy would collapse as a consequence of reckless, renegade fiscal policy, and that hyperinflation, recession, depression, or all three would ensue. But the sky did not fall. Indeed, it stayed sunny and a rather attractive shade of blue. As a result, rousing either the public or the politicians out of their torpor and into action against the debt and deficit problems became more difficult. In 1991–92, as deficits climbed once again to new records in dollars, 1980s-style alarm about them nearly disappeared, even among the gloomiest of economic prognosticators. But in 1993, spurred in part by H. Ross Perot and by President Clinton's first State of the Union message, deficits moved again to center stage.

Our purpose in this book is to look behind the popular excitement over debts and deficits and to ask why and how we got into this situation, how the struggles of the 1980s and early 1990s fit into historical patterns of political and economic thought concerning debt and taxes, and how much of the existing budgetary process is a real problem. In answering this last question, we give equal weight to political and economic considerations. Even large deficits may be of small consequence in purely economic terms, but where they loom large in a nation's political perceptions they can cause immense harm in other ways.

It is partly for this reason that historical perspective is so important. Despite periodic anxiety attacks—perhaps assisted by them—the U.S. record of dealing with public debt and taxes is a good one—especially compared with that of other countries. Debate about the moral and political consequences of government debt, the power to tax, and the role of government itself lay behind both the Revolutionary War and the establishment of the Republic.

What we know today as sound fiscal policy was central to the Founding Fathers' philosophical and practical struggle over the direction that the new nation was to take.

Throughout the nineteenth century, as politicians and policy makers struggled with taxing, spending, and debt, they had to balance their philosophies of government with protection of the economic interests of their own political bases and also with the interests of the economy as a whole. There was no fiscal policy as such at that time, just a series of separate policies on taxation, spending, and debt. This was more or less true until the Depression and World War II. The advent of modern economic science in the service of the modern industrial state promised relief from wild and uncontrolled swings of the business cycle and more stable and predictable economic growth. A coherent fiscal policy, together with other forms of government intervention in the economy, would presumably bring this about.

The 1980s brought solid and sustained economic growth—the longest continued peacetime expansion in history. But with that growth came a huge increase in federal indebtedness. The way in which the issues of taxing, spending, deficits, and debt arose in the 1980s differed significantly from both nineteenth-century and postwar economic patterns. One difference was the sheer size of the deficits—and their persistence during peacetime prosperity. Huge deficits at other times in American history had come with wars and depressions.

Another was the growing rigidity of the budget. Well before Ronald Reagan's emergence as a national politician, an increasing share of federal expenditures had become uncontrollable. Most of the budget during the 1980s was committed to obligations incurred in previous years. These obligations fell into three categories: entitlements, which were mostly transfer payments to the elderly; defense, which included heavy commitments to personnel and prior contracts that were difficult to change from year to year; and interest on cumulative debt.

These rigidities were mostly unintended consequences of a series of policy decisions made in the 1960s, 1970s, and 1980s for reasons other than fiscal policy—the determination in the early 1970s, for example, to index entitlement programs for inflation, or the seesawing decisions through the three decades to increase defense spending, then cut it back in the aftermath of the Vietnam War, then build it up again to compensate for Soviet aggressiveness and American weakness abroad.

Despite the extraordinary circumstances that have made fiscal policy in recent years seem so intractable, today's debate over debt and taxes exhibits continuities with earlier ones. When Franklin was writing to Le Roy, the argument was between two different strands of eighteenth-century Enlightenment thought: the British liberal tradition, which found its American expression in a deep-seated desire to minimize the size and role of government, and a more Continental belief in the power of rationally constituted governments to do good and to solve problems. In fiscal policy, this basic conflict was personified by Thomas Jefferson and Alexander Hamilton, and remarkably the lines of controversy adumbrated by them two hundred years ago have remained visible throughout American history.

Until recently, some version of the Jeffersonian philosophy of limited government has generally held the upper hand. Taxes were levied and debts (future taxes) accumulated when they were necessary in financing a war or in coping with an economic panic. Sometimes, as with the Civil War and the two world wars, the debt accumulation was huge. But nearly always when the crisis ended, the government "built down" the debt over the succeeding several years until it reached a more manageable level. Government grew in the process of responding to many of these crises, and its size rarely receded after a crisis. But this growth of government was less rapid than in other countries over the same period.

Since the election of Franklin Roosevelt in 1932, however, an updated version of Hamiltonianism—an activist central government to guide the nation's economic policy—has prevailed over Jefferson's vision of a decentralized, agrarian society. But Jefferson's legacy to the way in which America handles debt and taxes remains great, and his fear of large government is still found today, embedded deep in the American character. Yet his genius as president was to know when to sacrifice principle in the national interest. Jefferson broke from his abhorrence of government indebtedness when he permitted a sharp increase in the national debt to finance the Louisiana Purchase. His balance of ideology with pragmatism has served as a model for successful politicians.

Hamilton's economic brilliance and his lasting influence on the Republic have been no less impressive. He recognized that "a national debt can be to us a blessing" and single-handedly convinced a legion of skeptics in the first Congress, not to mention President George Washington, that his goals were right. Having successfully implemented his policy of a managed national debt and the reliable payment of interest on it, Hamilton was able to justify a larger and more powerful government and the accompanying taxes. Jeffersonianism, in the hands of less talented practitioners, subsequently reasserted itself—and eventually brought the country to the verge of financial collapse in the Civil War. But after that war the dominant Republicans' policy of high tariffs and protectionism owed much to the Hamiltonian precedent.

Governmental expansion lost its natural constraints, however, when government outgrew the revenues that nonruinous tariffs could generate and the income tax was introduced in 1913. The potential for abuse of power was as great as it had been before the Revolutionary War. Thus a new strain of Jeffersonianism began to evolve to define the limits on debt and taxes. Both Franklin Roosevelt and Ronald Reagan were Jeffersonians in this sense. As the powers of the executive branch grew along with the size of whole government, there were both risks and opportunities for neo-Jeffersonian presidents, and both Roosevelt and Reagan took them.

Conservatives, who see Roosevelt as a revolutionary ideological liberal, and liberals, who see Reagan as a revolutionary ideological conservative, will be shocked to see the two lumped together like this. But Roosevelt did not start with a master plan to expand the size and role of the federal government. He always responded to specific political and economic conditions. Reagan was more ideological in the beginning, but he found that the radicalism of his program for trimming the growth of government made it politically impossible to implement. Reagan's fundamental goal, of course, was to restrain and constrain the scope of the government. Fiscal policy was a means to achieve that goal, not an end. But his overall goal was simply not acceptable to enough politicians in Congress to make it work—thus, the attempt to use fiscal policy to force down the size of government failed. Reagan, like Roosevelt and Jefferson, ended up an improviser.

Reagan's Jeffersonianism and subsequent tax cuts produced a fiscal pattern that dominated the rest of his presidency and that of his successor. Because of this pattern of large deficits and the rhetoric of limited government, the usual processes for dealing with government borrowing and indebtedness were rendered less effective. The result was the extraordinary device of the Gramm-Rudman-Hollings Deficit Reduction Act, which proposed to cut through the political problems of reducing the deficit by an across-the-board sequestration of funds appropriated in excess of an annually shrinking borrowing limit.

It was not a great success. Its purpose was defeated every year with accounting legerdemain until it was jettisoned entirely in 1990 for the sake of an agreement to cut the deficit by raising taxes. That did not work either. Indeed, throughout the Reagan and Bush presidencies, every effort to reduce the deficit seemed only to increase it. This new kind of debt problem was caused not by crisis but by policy decisions made in peacetime prosperity, during a period of continuous divided government and uncertain party competition. The Clinton administration erased divided government and promised change, but the early lack of political strategy, policy crispness, and strong leadership created as much drift as decisive action. The gap between Jeffersonian rhetoric and the reality of large budget deficits only increased the frustration of politicians trying to rein the budgets in and communicated a message of failure to the electorate.

But Jeffersonianism differs in the huge and complex economy of a modern postindustrial state from what it was in the largely agrarian and preindustrial society of the post-Revolutionary period. One change has been the development and refinement of fiscal science and its use as a tool of government to manipulate the economy to achieve social goals. The "fiscal revolution in America," as economist Herbert Stein calls it, continued from the 1930s through the postwar period. It saw the creation of the President's Council of Economic Advisers and the Congressional Budget Office and the expansion of the Office of Management and Budget. With these developments came the belief that professional economists could manage the economy to produce desirable goals, such as full employment, while more or less removing fiscal issues from the arena of partisan conflict.

U.S. fiscal policy—taxes, spending, and the deficit that is the difference between them—has never been defined by a single principle or rule of thumb that government can apply systematically to changing circumstances. Nor has fiscal policy evolved steadily in one direction, not in the way that our courts, for example, have moved steadily toward a more expansive view of individual rights.

Fiscal policy is the sum of hundreds of other political and economic decisions, driven by forces usually beyond the control of individuals, so it moves in a herky-jerky pattern that is often clear only after the fact. Fiscal policy reflects the tensions between two radically divergent philosophies of government that have influenced all our politics since the time of Jefferson and Hamilton. Fiscal policy is redirected by crises, most often wars, but economic calamities as well. It is shaped by the intellectual debates about what government can or should do to promote steady prosperity. Political institutions shape the course of fiscal policy as they seek to balance voters' interests in government spending, low taxes, and, at rare moments, the deficit.

If these impersonal forces—philosophy of government, crisis, economic thought, politics—were all that went into fiscal policy, we might perceive a slow but steady trend, probably toward larger government, more spending, and more taxes, with the increase in taxes lagging behind the increases in spending. Many historians and economists, especially economists of the public-choice school, claim to have found such a mechanical trend toward ever-higher spending, taxes, and deficits. But these theories do not adequately explain fiscal policy in this century, especially in recent decades. That is because, at a few critical moments, fiscal policy has been influenced by more than the convergence of natural forces. At these defining moments, individuals elected to the presidency have taken on these forces, seeking to wrest control of the levers of fiscal policy and redirect it in radical ways.

Debt and taxes may be inevitable, but there is nothing inevitable about a Franklin Roosevelt, a Ronald Reagan, or a Bill Clinton. In their struggles with the larger forces, and the struggles of presidents who have tried but failed to redirect fiscal policy, we find the defining events in the development of fiscal policy.

In our own time the defining event was Ronald Reagan's confrontation with the federal government he was elected to lead in 1981. Reagan did not win every battle, and his eight-year administration certainly lost the war against big government and high taxes. But for one year he showed how a strong president could use the tools of fiscal policy to set one objective above others. His confrontations and accommodations with Congress, with ambivalent public opinion about spending and taxes, and with the bureaucracy's inevitable growth, would test the strength of these forces. Reagan's failures illuminated the areas where fiscal policy cannot be changed, and his successes brought us a new era in fiscal policy. In this era ever-increasing deficits and debt have come to seem as inevitable as taxes and spending became earlier in the century. By putting lower taxes above all other priorities in fiscal policy (including cutting spending, both domestic and defense spending), Reagan paved the way for a president who would have to put deficit reduction above all other priorities, including keeping taxes low.

Today's situation—political obsession with a $400 billion deficit, taxes that most Americans believe are still too high, a government that stubbornly will not shrink—has its roots in America's constitutional foundation, but we can trace it most directly to the politics of 1981, Reagan's first and most productive year.

This book, divided into five parts, begins with an account of the first year of the Reagan administration, which was, among other things, a response to the breakdown of Americans' confidence and which started the country's extraordinary focus over the past dozen years on debt and taxes, and asks, how revolutionary was the Reagan revolution? We then, in chapter 3, look at some of the ways in which changes in fiscal policy have come about in

American history and at the influence of governmental structures on those changes. In part 2, in two chapters of historical survey, we attempt to discover the roots and origins of American fiscal policy in the European background and the colonial period and to trace them through the constitutional debates to the birth of the modern nation-state during the Depression.

The next two chapters, in part 3, span the Roosevelt-to-Kennedy era. Here we look at the reluctant activism of Roosevelt, the contrasting reactivism of Harry Truman and Dwight Eisenhower, and the introduction of tax cuts to stimulate the economy for social-activist ends under John Kennedy and Lyndon Johnson. Part 4 examines the end of Jeffersonian liberalism. As the increased social spending and the costs of the Vietnam War created serious fiscal stresses, we see how the balance of power between the presidency and the Congress changed under the Nixon administration and how the seeds of our present fiscal situation were planted and grew under Gerald Ford and Jimmy Carter. After a chapter on the fate of Reaganism after the crucial year of 1981, we conclude part 4 with a recapitulation of the philosophical lessons of the American experience with debt and taxes since 1981.

Throughout this historical survey, we attempt to find the origins of the mechanisms of change and the belief in structural reform, of the competition between president and Congress, and of the philosophical and practical continuities, despite real and distinct changes, in public policy on taxing, spending, and debt. Finally, in part 5, we look at the likely result from the present situation and recommend some practical political ways of dealing with it.

We do not start from the belief that the American system has failed or that our fiscal problems are out of control and leading to disaster. Nor do we accept the thesis of James Buchanan and others of the public-choice school that our American brand of democratic politics leads inexorably to a government growing mindlessly out of control and that only constitutional reform can break the pattern. We are less panicked and more sanguine about where we have been, where we are, and where we are going, although we also have strong recommendations for change based upon the sound historical and philosophical base established in this book.

PART ONE

THE ELEMENTS OF FISCAL POLICY

✦

✦ 2 ✦

THE REAGAN
REVOLUTION
IN 1981

"If the mess is this bad, that's all the more reason why we're here."[1] With these words, two months after the 1980 election and just before he took office, Ronald Reagan declared to his aides that politics as usual was over—the most dramatic elements of the economic program he had laid out in his campaign would become the policy of his administration.

To all appearances, Reagan's first months in office were unusual, perhaps unprecedented in America's economic and political history. Reagan, like Franklin Roosevelt in 1932, benefited from one of the few American elections that expressed a clear mandate for change—change that, from the beginning, would involve a new approach to the domestic economy. As a spokesman for General Electric and afterward, Ronald Reagan's energies had been devoted to public advocacy of the view that only low taxes and small government make economic growth possible. Although his actions had not always matched his rhetoric—in California, government spending, adjusted for inflation, had grown at a record pace under Reagan[2]—his rhetoric had long since made him a bogeyman to the Democrats. He had also become a dreaded figure to the establishment of the Republican party just four years earlier, when he had sought to wrest its presidential nomination from incumbent president Gerald Ford—and in the process had helped elect the man he subsequently beat, Jimmy Carter. In four years, with only slight moderation of his views, Reagan had gone from being "unelectable" to being president.

REAGAN'S ELECTABILITY AND THE ECONOMY

What made this possible was not a transformation in Reagan but a series of nerve-wracking jolts to the American economy. The consumer price index had risen 12 percent in each of the two years before the election. Stagflation

—the unusual combination of inflation with economic stagnation—had challenged the economists' notion of a trade-off between unemployment and inflation; the jobless rate was more than 7 percent on election eve. The so-called misery index (the sum of inflation and unemployment percentages), which had been invented by Carter four years earlier, stood at more than twenty, or twice its level in 1976. The prime interest rate had risen to 21.5 percent after a roller-coaster ride through 1979 and 1980 that had nauseated and frightened Americans.

While the economic numbers did not approach the disastrous levels of 1932 (when unemployment was nearly 25 percent), and even though the economic record of President Carter over his full four years was, at worst, average for modern presidents, Americans were in no mood for generosity. In the post-Depression and postwar periods, Keynesian economics had promised an end to the wild swings of boom and bust that had characterized the economy throughout most of American history, and seemingly it had delivered. Economic problems and recessions had occurred, but the electorate still had a sense that the system was under control.

But the two years before the 1980 election shook that confidence and cast doubt on America's ability to control and regulate its own economic destiny. The general sense of fright, accentuated by energy crises in 1979 and 1980, was so pronounced that Ronald Reagan was able to appeal to it four years later as he repeated the Carter economic numbers time and again in his reelection campaign of 1984; George Bush did the same in 1988. To a considerable degree, three Republican presidential victories can be attributed to the economic conditions of 1980 and the subsequent recovery after a severe recession in 1982.

Reagan ran on an economic program that pledged to cut taxes, to raise military spending, to slash domestic spending, and to deliver a balanced budget by 1982. The last promise was a political necessity for any Republican, whose party had been advocating fiscal restraint and balanced budgets since well before Franklin Roosevelt's time. Questioning how Reagan could accomplish all these goals together, liberal Republican John Anderson, the congressman who ran as an independent presidential candidate in 1980, answered his own question: "With mirrors." But to the voters, the magic word was "change"; the specifics of change were less important.

Whether because of economic conditions and dissatisfaction with the performance of President Carter or because of the appeal of Reagan's promises, an unprecedented political perception produced Reagan's election. According to pollster Louis Harris, 1980 was "the first time in modern politics that a Republican has moved ahead of a Democrat on [the question of] how he would handle the economy."[3] In the Harris poll of October 1980, 43 percent said that Reagan could do the best job with the economy, 17 percent preferred Carter's economics, and 8 percent picked Anderson. Republicans who had won the presidency in the postwar era, Dwight Eisenhower and Richard Nixon, had run and won on foreign policy. Reagan certainly did all he could to exploit the burgeoning sense of national weakness, which had been exacerbated by the imprisonment of fifty-two diplomats in the American embassy in Iran for more than a year; but because he had had no experience in foreign affairs, he had little chance to win on this issue alone. To change public perceptions of the parties on economic policy, he needed to go beyond the traditional Republican call for fiscal restraint and a balanced budget—in short, to extend beyond politics as usual.

SEEDS OF AN ECONOMIC PROGRAM

To meet this need, Reagan had a philosophy in place; a neo-Jeffersonian distaste for both government intrusion in American lives and the heavy hand of government taxation. But this philosophical predisposition required a set of economic ideas to be turned into policy recommendations. He was fortunate to find, on Capitol Hill, in conservative think tanks, and in the editorial offices of the *Wall Street Journal*, a group of economic analysts whose thinking had been shaped by disgust with politics as usual and whose ideas meshed with his own inclinations.

Among them were David Stockman and Jude Wanniski. Both had written articles in the Spring 1975 *Public Interest* that marked a break with conventional economic theory.[4] It was a propitious time for new ideas, as stagflation and the moribund Great Society programs were presenting problems that could not be solved by such feeble political devices as President Ford's futile WIN (for Whip Inflation Now) strategy. Although they were both then unknown, Stockman and Wanniski held out to Reagan the possibility of an alternative economic policy that seemed to go well with his own instinct for low taxes and small government.

When he wrote "The Social Pork Barrel," Stockman was a fellow at Harvard's Institute of Politics and on leave from his job as executive director of the House Republican Conference—a post he had been appointed to through the patronage of John Anderson. Stockman's story is now well known, through his own book, *The Triumph of Politics* (1986), and through a controversial November 1981 article by William Greider in *The Atlantic*. It is a tale of his disenchantment with Reagan and with the dilution of his policy goals in the political process, which Stockman had observed as director of the Office of Management and Budget. After starting on the left and actively protesting against the Vietnam War, Stockman enrolled in Harvard's Divinity School, where he met the neoconservative scholar Daniel Patrick Moynihan, later a distinctively liberal senator. After coming to Capitol Hill to work for Anderson, Stockman was shocked by economic policy in the Nixon years, particularly the imposition of wage and price controls and the abolition of the gold standard, which had been engineered by Nixon's treasury secretary, John B. Connally, Jr. "The experience in John Connally's economics laboratory left me a born-again capitalist,"[5] Stockman wrote. With his ties to both the Left and the Right, he emerged as a purist more than a politician.

"The Social Pork Barrel," however, was not directly about economics or capitalism. Rather, it was a slashing attack on domestic government spending that exempted no one in the policy world except "the most extreme and idiosyncratic conservatives"[6] from the charge of conspiring in a "charade" to continue funding misguided or failed social programs at ever-higher levels. Over several pages Stockman demonstrated how inevitable deficits would be in coming years. His real quarrel, however, was not with deficits but with the way the government spent the public's money: on programs that were no longer needed; on programs that had failed; on programs intended to help the poor but with benefits so widely dispersed that they helped only the middle class. In general, he opposed government spending that benefited a narrow class of citizens but was funded by a tax burden on the much larger mass of Americans.

Stockman's thesis was in fierce opposition to the philosophy of federal involvement or spending in any except a few areas critical to national survival. Why, he wondered, should citizens of Michigan pay to build subways that were of benefit to the citizens of New York, if New Yorkers were unwilling to pay for them? What right did the federal government have to impose itself in this fashion in so many areas, from western water subsidies to economic development grants?

Despite his influential staff job in the GOP House hierarchy, Stockman's admonition seemed to come from outside the political system. He was in many cases harsher toward conservatives than liberals and believed that "conservative duplicity and liberal ideology both contribute to the dynamics and durability of the social pork barrel." His message to liberals was that if they did not pare down the miscellany of small social programs, larger goals such as national health insurance would always remain out of reach. Liberals might hope to gain enough revenue for such programs by eliminating tax breaks, but Stockman argued that any such effort would face a fierce backlash. And his message to conservatives was that they should stop pretending to oppose social programs that were "entirely incompatible with their basic beliefs" unless they were willing to "break with the system" and actively fight them.[7]

If Stockman's assault on politics-as-usual surprised readers of *Public Interest*, their sensibilities were further assaulted when they turned the page. "The Mundell-Laffer Hypothesis—A New View of the World Economy," by Jude Wanniski, presented one brand of supply-side thinking as a Copernican revolution in economics. Like Stockman, Wanniski began his career on the left and was not trained as an economist. After a successful stint as a reporter and columnist in Las Vegas, Wanniski had moved to the *Wall Street Journal* as an editorial writer. If Stockman was the stern midwestern minister, Wanniski was a pitchman promoting miraculous schemes for wealth.

Wanniski surely oversold supply-side thinking when he likened it to a Copernican revolution, but the supply-siders did have a point. After thirty years of trying to stabilize the economy just by managing the demand for output, the suggestion that government policy should be aimed at a positive endeavor —at politics that encouraged households and businesses to work more, to save more, and to invest more—was revolutionary. That meant lower marginal tax rates, elimination of the double tax on saving (sadly still extant), and incentives to buy more capital equipment. All these measures would increase output. That they initially lost revenue was not the end of their impact on budget deficits. If they increased output and thereby raised income, they could at least partly pay for themselves. As a candidate, George Bush missed this point when he called supply-side economics voodoo economics. He has never been forgiven by supply-siders.

Stockman wrote only of ideas; Wanniski also promoted people, in this case two iconoclastic economists, Robert Mundell and Arthur Laffer. The latter had lent his name to the Laffer curve, a reiteration of an old economic axiom, brilliantly promoted by Laffer and suggesting that lowering high tax rates would produce more government revenue, not less, because people would work harder and invest more. Laffer dropped the economists' usual cautious "could" for "would" and gave Ronald Reagan the intellectual basis for his promise of both lower taxes (not just lower tax rates), and a balanced budget.

Wanniski's *Public Interest* article was, in part, a plea for fixed international exchange rates and a gold standard; it referred also to Laffer's curve in a discussion of stagflation. A companion piece to Stockman, the essay shared Stockman's utter disdain for politics as usual—especially Republican politics —and for the efforts of economists to fine-tune the economy to produce growth and stability. "The pragmatic Republicanism of Richard Nixon shot into the twitching patient every antibody the economic doctors of Cambridge and Chicago prepared," Wanniski wrote. "And always the vital signs declined. . . . Deficits were run on purpose and deficits were run by accident."[8]

Neither Wanniski nor Mundell nor Laffer was destined to shape the economics of the Reagan administration from the inside, as Stockman was. Others whose tone was more moderate and whose ambitions were less sweeping, such as Norman Ture, Paul Craig Roberts, and Murray Weidenbaum, would take their places. Indeed, many of these more moderate planners would spend years trying to explain that the Laffer curve did not literally mean that tax cuts would pay for themselves, that, at most, they would partially pay for themselves.[9] Laffer and Wanniski "covered the supply-side movement with hyperbole," Roberts wrote. "It brought publicity to the movement, but criticism as well."[10]

Roberts, a strong supply-sider who became a top Treasury official in the Reagan administration, believed that the mainstream opposition to supply-side economics (he cites in particular a February 1981 editorial in the New York Times) emerged primarily because "unlike the Keynesian policy that it was displacing, supply-side economics came out of the policy process itself and not out of the universities."

In fact, neither Stockman's and Wanniski's early treatises[11] nor Reagan's economics, which owed so much to them, simply came out of the policy process. They arose out of a deep frustration and hostility toward the mainstream of that process as it had been functioning for decades. From the beginning, supply-sideism stressed its break with the past. It claimed to be an end run around the problems of traditional economics that were besetting the country in the mid-1970s. Most striking about Stockman's and Wanniski's articles was their particular anger at the Republicans, who both men contended were squandering a chance to offer the American people a new and different approach to spending and taxation. Within the rather hidebound and traditional-minded GOP, the supply-side doctrines did indeed find it rough going. In the same way, Ronald Reagan's greatest political challenge had been to divert the Republican mainstream rightward. Compared with his successful twelve-year effort to accomplish that task, winning the presidency was easy.

Both the Stockman and Wanniski pieces had another characteristic that appealed to Reagan: Stockman's was his eloquent hostility to an expansive federal role. Wanniski's was his ebullient optimism about the unlimited economic possibilities available to the United States if only it adopted a few basic and painless changes in approach. Even to old-fashioned Republicans raised on what came to be called the root-canal approach to deficits of traditional economics, the supply-siders with their claim of new and revolutionary ideas could also be seductive. And Ronald Reagan was one of those most willing to be seduced.

EARLY SUPPLY-SIDE ECONOMICS

From inside the policy process, supply-side economics at first looked less revolutionary than it became during the first Reagan administration. Led as expected by a few "extreme and idiosyncratic conservatives" in Congress, efforts to cut tax rates in the late 1970s also gained unexpected support from sympathetic Democrats. The first proposal for across-the-board cuts in the tax rates came February 23, 1977, from Republican Representative John Rousselot of California,[12] a member of the John Birch Society, who had been expected to offer a balanced-budget requirement. Coming during a sharp recession, Rousselot's surprising proposal was intended to substitute for a package of more conventional economic stimuli then under consideration. Opposing these old remedies—a onetime $50 tax rebate and an increase in spending programs that would swell the deficit to $70 billion from $50 billion —Rousselot argued that only a permanent tax-rate cut would "increase the reward to work, save, and invest." He was articulating a familiar axiom of economic theory, that the way least damaging to the economy to collect necessary tax revenues is to keep tax rates as low as possible. (Normally, this fundamental principle refers to collecting given tax revenues with the lowest possible tax rate on the broadest possible tax base—no loopholes—but the implied notion that high tax rates are damaging to economic performance is the same.)

Specifically, Rousselot's plan was to reduce each of the marginal tax rates by five percentage points. The top rate would fall to 65 percent from 70 percent and the lowest to 9 percent from 14 percent. Since this would give wealthy families a greater dollar savings on their taxes than poor ones, House Democrats, led by majority leader Jim Wright, declared it regressive and unacceptable. Representative Jack Kemp engaged Wright in a heated debate, frequently comparing the 5 percent cut to President Kennedy's tax reductions early in his term. Robert Giaimo, a Democrat and chairman of the House Budget Committee, turned around and attacked the Republicans for opposing the $50 rebate when that rebate had first been proposed by the Republican Ford administration. We can see Stockman's frustration: Democrats were referring to Republican precedents to encourage consensus, and Republicans who chose to break with the system were citing Democratic heroes in their rebellion. Rousselot's quixotic proposal lost by 110 votes, but Paul Craig Roberts, then a Budget Committee staff member, saw "victory nonetheless. The Republicans had accepted a new idea."[13]

Five months later, Kemp, a congressman from upstate New York who had been imbued with Wanniski's fervor both for the Laffer curve and for the gold standard, took up the cudgels for tax-rate cutting. With Republican Senator William Roth of Delaware, he proposed to cut personal income-tax rates by 30 percent in three years. A similar amendment proposed by conservative Democrat Sam Nunn of Georgia coupled tax cuts with a limitation on the growth of government spending to the inflation rate plus 1 percent. In October 1978, the Nunn amendment passed the Senate with just twenty dissenting votes but, despite strong support in the House, was killed in conference under the threat of a veto by President Carter.[14]

As a final measure of the degree to which Reagan's economics had been, if not endorsed, at least considered by those in the policy mainstream, the congressional Joint Economic Committee, led by Senator Lloyd Bentsen, in 1979 issued its first unanimous report in twenty years. Bentsen's introduction declared that "the major challenges today and for the foreseeable future are on the supply side of the economy." Greater investment and productivity were the only ways out of stagflation, the report argued, and a policy of restraint in federal spending and of cuts in tax and regulatory burdens was the way to achieve these goals. This report was signed by Senators Edward Kennedy and George McGovern, who were no more immune than their Republican counterparts to the political allure of tax cuts.

REVOLUTIONARY SUPPLY-SIDEISM

David Stockman had been elected to Congress by this time, and although he makes no mention of it in his book, he must have been amazed by the consensus of the Joint Economic Committee, apparently occasioned by the economic circumstances of the late 1970s. Just as he had suggested, Republicans had "broken with the system," and Democrats had joined them, since both had recognized that their goals would be unattainable in a permanently crippled economy. But when it came to presidential politics, Stockman held to the revolutionary view of supply-side economics, though he remained more frustrated by spending than concerned about marginal tax rates.

When he was asked to play the role of Jimmy Carter in the rehearsal with Ronald Reagan for his one debate with the president in 1980, Stockman gained an audience and an opportunity. After Reagan was elected, Kemp and Stockman began to plot ways to put Stockman in the cabinet. According to Stockman, Kemp promised "an Inchon landing" in which Kemp would get Stockman behind the lines of Reagan's key staff, most of whom were longtime aides from his days as governor of California, unfamiliar with Washington, and hostile to its institutions.[15] Stockman extended Kemp's metaphor into a memo, "Avoiding a GOP Economic Dunkirk," that won him the coveted job of director of the Office of Management and Budget (OMB).

The memo aimed to remind the Reaganites of the powerful combination of forces arrayed against them at the beginning of the new administration. The economic problems and threats were monumental, but at the same time new ideas and new politics empowered an entirely new direction for the government. Dramatic, even revolutionary, change had been made possible by dire economic conditions and by the political earthquake of November 1980. During the campaign, Reagan clearly advocated tax cuts; in "Dunkirk," Stockman aimed to show that tax cuts without accompanying budget cuts were more dangerous than no reform at all, whereas the two together would be a masterstroke, simultaneously accomplishing Reagan's philosophical, political, and economic goals. Not to combine tax cuts with budget cuts would court disaster, Stockman wrote:

> The preeminent danger is that an initial economic policy that includes the tax cuts but does not contain *decisive, credible elements* on matters of outlay control, future budget authority reduction, and a believable plan for curtailing the federal government's massive direct and indirect credit absorption will generate pervasive expectations of a continuing *"Reagan inflation."*

Not a full-fledged supply-sider, since he did not believe that tax cuts would pay for themselves, Stockman was still obsessed with the social pork barrel. He saw a 50 percent chance of a severe recession in early 1981 and warned that the government would have trouble responding. "The federal budget has now become an automatic '*coast-to-coast soup line*' that dispenses remedial aid with almost reckless abandon, converting the traditional notion of automatic stabilizers [like increased unemployment benefits and other safety net payments that rise during recessions] into multitudinous outlay spasms throughout the budget." Behind this baroque language lay an important truth. For when Stockman broke down the $36 billion growth in federal spending estimates between the June and September budget resolutions for fiscal year 1981, he was able to show that $26.1 billion was accounted for by automatic stabilizers. Uncontrollable budgetary outlays were prompted by higher unemployment, higher inflation, higher interest rates, and generally worsening conditions. To cut the government's spending and borrowing would thus take more than "legislated spending cuts in the traditional sense."

Instead, Stockman wanted Reagan to declare a national economic emergency. That would make it easier for him to demand from Congress the full Kemp-Roth tax cuts as well as cuts of 10 to 20 percent in public-sector capital spending, $10 billion to $20 billion in non–Social Security entitlements, and $8 billion from the $25 billion in programs that Stockman identified as low-priority. These cuts would be made in the budgets for fiscal 1982 and beyond and would require changes in the law governing outlays on some federal programs like Medicare and Medicaid. Of the $649 billion in estimated outlays for fiscal 1981, only about $80 billion could be touched directly by congressional budget action without changes in the law. Of that slice, Stockman wanted to cut about $13 billion. Once again, he warned of a squandered opportunity. If his warnings were not heeded, he said, "Washington will quickly become engulfed in political disorder commensurate with the surrounding economic disarray. A golden opportunity for permanent conservative policy revision and political realignment could be thoroughly dissipated before the Reagan administration is even up to speed. Congress, he concluded, would dissolve into "fire-fighting as usual"—in other words, the behavior that Stockman had so savagely criticized in 1975 and that he associated with the old-fashioned style of politics in 1981.

REAGAN'S ASSUMPTIONS

Reagan's economic policy brought about the most dramatic confrontation over the federal budget since the 1974 Budget Act established the process, but it was not the apocalyptic battle that Stockman foresaw and wished for. As in most budget confrontations, the assumptions about the future of the economy were at least as important as the choices among program areas, or "functions" in the terminology of the budget process. Reagan's choices were limited before he started by his pledge to accelerate the increase in defense spending ("Defense is not a budget issue," Reagan often insisted) and his repeated commitment not to touch Social Security. Changing the projections for economic growth, inflation, or interest rates by a few points can reduce a deficit instantly (and predict good news), while finding enough politically feasible cuts in domestic spending is a formidable task that inevitably involves screams of pain and outrage.

Reagan's economic assumptions had begun to take shape in the September before the election. At Wexford, a Virginia hunt-country estate, he met with advisers to hammer out a complete economic plan. The immediate goal was to counter the media's perception that Reagan was wavering in his support for successive 10 percent cuts in tax rates over the next three years. Some of the more orthodox economists at Wexford warned that with inflation so high already, tax cuts would be too risky, but Reagan insisted that he would keep his commitment. After the conference, Martin Anderson and Alan Greenspan (then a private economic forecaster) started work on a fact sheet detailing Reagan's economic plan. For their economic base line, they elected to use forecasts just released by the Senate Budget Committee. Other forecasts were available—from OMB, from Treasury, from the Congressional Budget Office, from other congressional committees, and from private forecasters—but the Budget Committee's predictions had both political and economic advantages. Because the committee was controlled by Democrats, its forecasts were credible, and because the forecast was more optimistic than most, it eased the task of predicting a balanced budget.

The economic assumptions that Anderson and Greenspan used, such as no indexing of tax rates for inflation, allowed them to predict dramatic government surpluses in coming years, as inflation pushed taxpayers into higher brackets and pumped up revenues. These assumptions allowed Reagan to figure in his cuts and still to predict a $23 billion surplus by fiscal 1983. According to Anderson, Reagan welcomed this strategy because as governor of California he had come up with a surplus in the state budget and returned it to the taxpayers as a rate cut.

Giving an existing surplus back to the taxpayers differs from giving a projected one in advance. Further, the economic assumptions were based on continued inflation; other parts of Reagan's economic plan, particularly in monetary policy, were intended to curb inflation and, as it turned out, were more successful than the forecasts accompanying his budget. Most important, the fact sheet prepared for Reagan's September 9, 1980, speech in Chicago did not emphasize drastic cuts in spending. From the perspective of the 1980 campaign, the deficit shot upward in 1983, when a surplus had been predicted, not so much because tax cuts were not matched by spending cuts as because the assumption of high inflation was not realized.

In Chicago, Reagan attacked "waste, extravagance, abuse and outright fraud in federal agencies and programs." He asserted that "billions of taxpayers' dollars" could be saved by cutting the fat from the budget. Specifically, he promised to cut 2 percent from the budget for fiscal 1981, escalating to 7 percent "of what would otherwise have been spent in fiscal 1985." The plan "does not require altering or taking back necessary entitlements already granted to the American people [but] *does* require restraining the congressional desire to 'add on' to every old program and to create new programs funded by deficits." This did not contradict the view of Congress expressed by Stockman in "The Social Pork Barrel" or in his "Dunkirk" attack on the "coast-to-coast soup line," but it was much narrower. Indeed, it meshed with American public opinion, which supported most existing government programs but wanted to cut back the federal government and eliminate waste, fraud, and abuse. Stockman had far more in mind than "waste, extravagance, abuse and outright fraud." In "Dunkirk," he argued forcefully that "a static, 'waste-cutting' approach . . . will hardly make a dent in the true fiscal problem."

The *Wall Street Journal*, in a September 20, 1980, editorial, criticized the Reagan economic plan as neither revolutionary nor supply-side.

> Ronald Reagan finally found some number crunchers to churn out an answer to the question of how he could cut taxes, increase defense spending, and balance the budget all at once. . . . if there are no tax cuts, taxes will increase sharply. . . . These built-in tax increases generate huge leverage—for increasing spending, reducing taxes, or reducing the government deficit. All you need to do is project the numbers out a few years, and combine the rising tax rate with modest fiscal restraint, and the supposedly impossible challenge to Mr. Reagan becomes child's play. . . . The supply-side analysis remains in Mr. Reagan's economic package, but has obviously been muted by the Nixon/Ford economic advisers who could provide numbers that would withstand attack. . . . Mr. Reagan has, in short, spelled out a prudent, gradual responsible reordering of economic priorities, not much different from the kind of thing Republicans have always offered.[16]

In later years, Senator Moynihan recalls, the columnist George Will would offer a free toaster to anyone who could name a single federal program that

Reagan had pledged to cut in his 1980 campaign. Will kept his toaster because there was none.[17] In a few cases, Reagan later did seek to eliminate entire programs, such as the Legal Services Corporation—which funds legal clinics for the poor—on fiscal grounds, but most were too small to produce much budget savings. In any case, Reagan's distaste was for the political orientation of the LSC, not for its funding.

Reagan's first year in office, 1981, was extraordinarily successful for the new president in his confrontations with Congress. He was aided by the clear mandate for change in his election, by the Republican majority in the Senate that accompanied that mandate, and by a surge of popular support after an assassin nearly took his life in March. It was a year devoted almost entirely to budget questions. More than two-thirds of the recorded votes in the Senate concerned the budget. A final key to Reagan's success, according to budget process expert Allen Schick, was his concentration on this one issue; he "did not have an ambitious legislative agenda; he wanted Congress to legislate less." As a result, the House and Senate recorded fewer votes than in any year since 1971.[18]

Reagan may have wanted Congress to legislate less, but in his battles over the budget, he did not make a concerted effort to force government to do less. Here again, the assumptions behind the budget played a crucial part. Both the White House and Congress started with what is called a current-policy (or current-services) base line for calculating cuts in the budget. When Reagan spoke, for example, of cutting 7 percent from "what would otherwise have been spent in fiscal year 1985," he was referring to cuts in the budgetary *increase* that would naturally have occurred if the government had continued to provide services at existing levels, with increases for inflation in all programs. In dollars, the budget for fiscal 1985 could be much higher than for fiscal 1981, but Reagan could still point to "cuts" by using a current-policy base line.

During the late 1970s, Republicans on the Senate Budget Committee had fought the use of the current-policy base line on the grounds that it automatically assumed expansion of government spending, especially in times of inflation. They preferred to use a current-law base line that would adjust only expenditures that, by law, increased with inflation, such as Social Security cost-of-living adjustments.

In 1981, though, Republicans in Congress as well as OMB welcomed the current-policy base line, despite its expansionary bias, for political reasons: it exaggerated the size of the cuts. With 10 percent inflation, for example, funding a $100 billion program at $105 billion for the next year could be claimed as a $5 billion cut. By using the current-policy base line, Schick writes, "the Republicans claimed more savings and the Democrats saved more programs, a happy combination for political institutions faced with difficult choices."[19] A household analogy to the current-policy base line would have a family planning to raise spending by 10 percent annually cut the increase to 5 percent and then congratulate itself on a "saving" even though its income remained constant and it had to borrow to finance 5 percent of its outlays.

Beyond this compromise on the assumptions about the definition of the budget, the Reagan administration made novel and aggressive use of reconciliation, a little-used budget procedure that allowed the president to press for changes after the first budget resolution had been passed. Reagan asked for $197 billion in reductions from the current-policy base line for fiscal years 1982 through 1984, and Congress agreed to all but $67 billion of those cuts. The administration was forced to back down on efforts to alter Social Security and in some cases resorted to "paper cuts," such as taking the expenses for the strategic petroleum reserve out of the budget.

On tax cuts, Congress not only accepted most of Reagan's proposals, it went even further than he had been prepared to go. As he promised, the president asked for 10 percent reductions in all rates in each of the next three years, so that the top rate on earned income would drop to 35 percent from 50 percent and the bottom rate to 10 percent from 14 percent. In addition to the Kemp-Roth cuts, the administration went along with a plan devised by Charls Walker—a business lobbyist from Texas and a prominent member of the Connally Treasury—to allow faster depreciation of investments in factories and equipment—in other words, to allow bigger deductions for depreciation in the first few years after an investment was made. Congress agreed to both proposals, except that it reduced the first year's tax-rate cut to 5 percent rather than 10 percent. But it also agreed to index tax rates to inflation starting in 1985 and accepted a proposal by liberal Democrat Bill Brodhead of Michigan to cut the top rate on unearned income to 50 percent from 70 percent—two proposals that the White House had actually held back because it expected congressional opposition. As in the late 1970s, cutting taxes proved not to be a partisan issue, and although Democrats were not as daring in their proposals as Kemp, for example, they were quite willing to accept and even extend Reagan's proposals to cut the federal government's share of the average paycheck.

The tax debate did revolve to some extent around supply-side premises, as Kemp and other advocates argued that additional revenues would more than make up for the tax-rate cuts. Some Democrats accepted that argument for the cuts in rates on unearned income because of their experiences in the mid-1970s with the Steiger amendment to cut capital gains rates. But the Democratic majority in the House did not accept the claims of the proponents of the Laffer curve; their own tax-rate cuts were put out as a *political* alternative, to save face and to secure for themselves at least some credit for tax cutting. The political maneuvering resulted in a bidding war, as the administration and the House Democrats each sweetened their tax packages with new cuts to attract votes. This process led to far more substantial cuts than anyone had expected. The early 1980s demonstrated a basic tax truth of American politics that had emerged in 1969–1970: whenever tax revenues climb to 20 percent of GNP, the public objects, and both parties try to outdo each other in cutting taxes.

Another set of economic assumptions became so well known that it was the subject of a feeble Washington joke: "Who is the highest-ranking woman in the Reagan administration?" "Rosy Scenario." For some months, the administration was torn by conflict between the advocates of different aspects of Reagan's economic program. Murray Weidenbaum, the first chairman of Reagan's Council of Economic Advisers, recalled: "It was a forced marriage. The supply-side people insisted on [forecasting] rapid growth in real terms and the monetarists insisted on rapid progress in bringing down inflation. Each of them would go along with a set of numbers as long as their own concern was satisfied."[20] These goals could not be reconciled with the sophisticated and standard model of the economy developed at the Wharton School, so the administration turned to a model tuned to supply-side economics that had been devised at the Claremont Economics Institute.[21]

Called the endogenous forecast model by econometricians who understood that models could be "tuned" to give any forecast desired, the new model produced the required rosy scenario, predicting real economic growth of 5 percent in 1983 and more than 4 percent in 1982 and 1984–1986. Growth at such levels would have represented a remarkable economic boom, generating higher revenues even with reduced tax rates. At the same time, inflation was predicted to decline steadily each year, down to 4.2 percent in 1986. Interest rates would be cut in half.[22] Mainstream economists attacked these assumptions as unrealistic and contradictory: they expected the tax cuts to produce higher inflation and could not imagine that growth of more than 4 percent could be sustained for five years. Both the mainstreamers and the supply-siders proved partly correct. Interest rates and inflation did come down, while the economy grew rapidly, especially in 1983 and 1984. But the drop in inflation cut revenues, while the palliative of current-policy base line budgeting kept spending growing. Deficits rose sharply.

Economic assumptions are central to any administration's fiscal policy, and no administration relied on them more heavily than Reagan's. Projecting unrealistically high growth and inflation levels was the only means it had to reconcile its conflicting pledges to cut taxes, to raise defense spending, and to balance the budget. As Schick noted early in 1982: "Unrealistic projections have more than a passive effect on the budget; they encourage budget makers to avoid difficult issues. Why consider whether the United States really can afford to lower taxes while raising defense expenditures when an expanding economy will satisfy both objectives?"[23]

STOCKMAN'S AGENDA

Stockman did not see it this way. He may have been influential in the choice of the pliable Claremont model over the Wharton method, but he was less interested in playing the assumptions game than in forcing a confrontation that would reduce federal spending. "I wasn't quite as sensitive to the degree to which the budget position, the deficit, was driven by economic assumptions," he told *Time* magazine's Laurence Barrett after he had left office. "Our assumptions were overly optimistic. I think everyone recognizes that. So, in a sense, they allowed us to fool ourselves into thinking that we had solved the budget gap after the tax cut."[24]

Stockman was insensitive to the centrality of economic assumptions not because he did not understand the budget but because his agenda was so broad and so different from that of other policy makers in the administration and Congress. Reviewing the administration's first year, Schick implicitly recognized a fundamental "feedback" problem encountered in modeling. He noted that in the 1970s

> the belief that the budget can shape the economy yielded to the frustrating notion that the economy shapes the budget. . . . The Reagan administration was determined to reverse the relationship between the budget and the economy. Rather than the budget nurturing the economy to vigor, the economy would restore the budget to balance.[25]

The economic assumptions, by this interpretation, were less important to Stockman than to others, because his intention was to break the federal budget loose from those assumptions, to free it from its imprisonment at the hands of unemployment, inflation, and interest rates—all of which forced up federal spending, in good times and bad. This was what Stockman had meant in "Dunkirk" by "coast-to-coast soup line." It was also what Wanniski had been referring to when he complained that "deficits were run on purpose and deficits were run by accident."

"The Reagan Revolution, as I had defined it, required a frontal assault on the American welfare state. That was the only way to pay for the massive . . . tax cut," Stockman wrote in *The Triumph of Politics*. [26] But Stockman's zeal for revolution met head-on with the American political system's roadblocks against major change; in 1981 the "crisis" in our political economy was not severe enough to tip the balance of change from substantial to revolutionary. Ronald Reagan had not defined his program in revolutionary terms when he spoke of cutting "waste, extravagance, abuse" without citing substantive programs; the voters did not define it that way when they gave Reagan his indisputable mandate; and Reagan's mainstream economists did not have it in mind when they fashioned an economic plan to "combine the rising tax rate with modest fiscal restraint."

The political coalition that had helped transform Reagan from the unelectable hero of the far Right of 1976 into the mainstream Republican nominee of 1980 supported a fiscal policy based not on dramatic cuts in federal spending but on reductions in tax rates—income-tax rates for most of the supply-siders and accelerated depreciation for the traditional GOP businessmen. Reagan's prime concern, too, was taxes. Stockman describes the battle for the tax cut as "one of the few things Ronald Reagan deeply wanted from his presidency. It was the only thing behind which he threw the full weight of his broad political shoulders." This made Stockman, as the real revolutionary, the odd man out. His concern was cutting spending to realize ultimately his Jeffersonian vision of a drastically limited federal government.

By the time of the big battle with Congress over the 30 percent, three-year tax cut, Stockman still considered himself a supply-sider, but he harbored no illusions about the Laffer curve. "I never believed that just cutting taxes alone will cause output and employment to expand," he recalls telling William Greider. [27] Stockman fought hard for the tax cut, which, he contends, "standing alone never had a chance." Support for it "was a mile wide, but convictions were an inch deep." [28] To many observers, including Senator Moynihan, Stockman seemed to think that tax cuts combined with Reagan's sharp increases in defense spending would push up deficits enough to force lower domestic spending.

To pass the 1981 tax bill, the administration had to enter a bidding war not only with the Democratic House leadership but also with boll-weevil Democrats, who had provided the margin of support for earlier budget cuts, and with Republicans. Because Reagan had drawn a line in the sand, threatening to veto anything less than a 25 percent tax cut (which is what he got), the currency in the bidding war was not reductions in the tax cut but additions to it—or what Stockman called the "ornaments" of concessions and deductions for specific industries. By Stockman's calculation, the ornaments increased the revenue loss of the tax bill by about 25 percent in the first few years and more in later years. "The straw that finally broke my back," as Stockman described it, "was the insistence by the leading boll weevil, Kent Hance, that the oil depletion allowance, a clear giveaway to the oil industry, be retained, at a cost of $4 billion annually.

By this point, Stockman says, he had realized that the tax cuts, far more than simple tax-rate cuts, were real revenue cuts that would be even more costly than Kemp-Roth alone and that he was unlikely to win the radical spending cuts needed to pay for the tax cuts. The administration was unconcerned, because "the whole California gang had taken [the Laffer curve] literally (and primitively)"[29] and assumed that lower tax rates would indeed increase revenues. Like the Whig Republicans of the nineteenth century who had high tariffs to pay for government programs, they thought that they would have the best of both worlds.

Not only were the tax-cut ornaments being traded away, so were future spending cuts. The vote of New York Democrat Mario Biaggi, for example, was bought with the promise that the administration would drop plans to cut a particularly vulnerable and costly provision: the minimum benefit for Social Security recipients. "One of the last votes for the tax cut was traded . . . for preservation of the first spending dollar that had to be eliminated. American government had come unhinged."

Stockman recalls Richard Darman, then the top aide to the White House chief of staff, James Baker, wondering, "Which is worse: winning now and fixing up the budget mess later, or losing now and facing a political mess immediately?"[30] The two briefly considered "calculated sabotage" of the tax bill, "but in the end, we chickened out."[31] Stockman was upset because of the additional lost revenue caused by the ornaments traded for votes, but he was even more concerned about Democrats who defected to Reagan's side for no clear payoff, such as Representative Norman Dicks of Washington, a "supporter of . . . a robust welfare state." To Stockman, Dicks's defection "didn't add up any more than our budget would" because "when it came time to perform the equally radical task of cutting the budget to fit the tax bill, those 236 congressmen who voted for our bill wouldn't be there."

Stockman fought hard for the tax bill; he did not want the votes that came with strings attached, because the strings were too costly, and he did not want the votes that came with no strings, because they were not committed to his assault on the welfare state. Moynihan and others have charged that Stockman deliberately ran up the bidding for the tax cut to create a deficit that would force congressional politicians to cut social spending. Stockman denies this, saying that "not six of the six hundred players in the game of fiscal governance in the spring and summer of 1981 would have willed this outcome [higher deficits]. Yet caught up in the powerful forces unleashed by the dangerous experiment of a few supply-siders who had gotten the president's good ear, they let it happen just the same."[32]

Of course, Reagan was not unconscious while all this occurred. He had frequently referred to his own "children's allowance theory," suggesting that Congress, like children, would be more penurious if they felt a fiscal discipline akin to being placed on an allowance—in this case, the "allowance" was to be limited by larger deficits.

The evidence suggests that while no grand strategy had been conceived far in advance, Stockman and others in the administration let the bidding war continue, once under way. When Stockman realized that Reagan's revolutionary zeal did not include much enthusiasm for cutting government out of people's lives, he came to believe that the only way to slash government spending was to force politicians to accept an unthinkable alternative: to slash spending or to preside over huge, unacceptable deficits. To his everlasting disappointment, their choice, and Reagan's, too, was deficits.

Stockman believed that he could forcibly initiate a conceptual linkage between taxation and spending in America. Tax cuts, as we have seen, were not revolutionary in 1981. Stockman draws a distinction between the basic Kemp-Roth proposal—"our supply-side stimulus to capitalists"—and the kind of tax cutting he calls "redistributionist political ornaments." But by 1981 partial endorsement of a supply-side approach by Senators McGovern and Kennedy (and after President Kennedy's heralded tax cuts proposed in 1961), neither type of tax cut was controversial or revolutionary.

Radical spending cuts, though, *were* revolutionary. Even regarding spending, Ronald Reagan was interested in little more than waste cutting and killing a few programs that he considered sanctuaries of left-wing social activism, like the Legal Services Corporation. Taxation and spending were considered separate domains—by Reagan, by Congress, and by almost everyone except Stockman. The budget process, as a once-a-year effort to bring the two together, can accomplish only so much. The American government cannot be forced to link spending with tax revenues in every action it takes, and it did not even before it turned to direct taxation to raise revenue. (Until 1913, most of the federal government's revenue came from tariffs, enacted for reasons unrelated to spending needs though they were exploited for that purpose.) Through two budget acts and several quantum leaps in our knowledge of how the economy works, taxation and spending had remained separate, each with its own political and economic calculus. American government had not "come unhinged" the day Biaggi traded his vote. The hinge had never existed.

Behind Stockman's desire to bond spending and taxation lay another revolutionary goal: to change the relationship between the budget and the economy. The economy was driving the budget, Stockman discovered, and he wanted the budget to drive the economy. But while the economy's domination of the budget may have expanded in the 1970s, it was nothing new. In 1946 the government explicitly recognized that federal spending should automatically adjust to stabilize the economy, but the two-way street connecting the economy and the budget had existed since the early days of the Republic. Every war, starting with the War of 1812, had produced an explosion in the size of the federal government that also affected the economy. Wars and the surge of spending of governments on war materials, financed largely by larger government debts, clearly influenced the economy. Prices and interest rates gyrated in wartime and afterward. The two-way connection between government budgets and the economy operates in peacetime as well, especially when tax rates are cut, as in 1981–1982. After Reagan, the economy continues to drive the budget, while still being influenced by it.

Today's deficit appears manageable, though troublesome, given current projections of continued economic growth, but the range for government action is narrow. One step off the narrow path by the economy or the government will throw the budget off course. Meanwhile, trying to cut the deficit too fast could be the very thing that pushes the economy off its path. The budget is as much a prisoner of the economy as it was in 1980, and for decades before, even though the economy is affected by the budget as well. Stockman tried to do more than mount a frontal assault on the American welfare state of the 1960s: he attempted to redefine the entire relationship of fiscal policy to politics in America. Stockman tried for a cut in government spending while the economy grew faster as a way of shrinking drastically the role of the federal government. If history is a reliable guide, his failure is not surprising.

The failure to bring about a revolution, though, did not leave us with either politics or economics as usual. Through the remainder of the 1980s—

through a deep recession in 1982 and then through more than seven consecutive years of economic growth—Congress and the president grappled with the politics of budget deficits larger, in dollar terms, than any in the past, and without the excuse of war or depression behind them. Throughout the Reagan years and the Bush presidency, American politics revolved around fiscal policy, not vice versa. Even if he wished otherwise, and even if his 1992 campaign focused on issues like "investment," "competitiveness," health-care reform, and welfare reform, Bill Clinton found that to be true in his presidency as well.

Faced with economic growth (fueled, ironically, by those Keynesian deficits), the public remained largely complacent. Politicians, though, became increasingly frustrated at their impotence to solve the deficit dilemma. They turned eventually, in 1985, to a radical structural reform, the Gramm-Rudman-Hollings Deficit Reduction Act, but they found that without sufficient political will, tinkering with fiscal structure did them little good.

The Reagan years showed us that some patterns of political economy long a part of the American experience would not be turned on their heads by a dramatic election, a visionary president, and a hard-driving ideologue of a budget director. But the policies that these factors produced *would* bring about a new and unusual dynamic in the politics of debt and taxes. We will analyze that dynamic and its implications for the future, but first we will look back, establishing some principles of, and a historical context for, the making of fiscal policy.

◆ 3 ◆

WHAT MAKES
FISCAL POLICY?

The federal government's policies on taxing, spending, and debt have evolved over time, and the size of government and the role it plays in American society have been determined by the political decisions of many generations. To a considerable degree, money drives policy in every political and economic system. But not all responses to this elemental pressure are identical. Fiscal policy in America has been shaped by our peculiar form of government and especially its system of separated and shared powers. The rigid division between the executive and legislative branches, in particular, has produced a considerable ambiguity about the exercise of power, which clever and determined politicians like Alexander Hamilton, the first treasury secretary, have been able to exploit to their own ends. Checks and balances have also had a powerful impact on the timing of policy and on outcomes. Most parliamentary democracies, for example, established income security programs, like social-security retirement insurance and government disability insurance, much earlier than our own presidential system did.

Every government has an implicit fiscal policy, but only since the Great Depression has the United States had an explicit one. As long as they have existed, governments have spent money to accomplish their ends and have raised money through a variety of means, including plunder and taxation. And as long as they have existed, governments have run deficits, gone into debt, and grappled with the consequences. But attempts to coordinate taxing, spending, and debt into a coherent set of policies that can help to govern an economy are not as old as the history of governments. Fiscal policy per se is only about fifty years old, while debt and taxes have been with us for millenniums.

THE HAMILTONIAN-JEFFERSONIAN DIALOGUE

In earlier periods of American life, the realities of war or economic crisis and decisions to buy territories, to build roads, or to protect manufactures through high tariffs determined government policies toward debt, taxing, and spending. Such events remain important, but in modern times there has also been an attempt to devise fiscal policies that would achieve economic goals and other public-policy objectives. Taxing, spending, and deficits, along with monetary policy, have been used to help attain full employment, to ease the boom and bust cycles in the economy, to lessen or to avoid recessions, to relieve poverty, and to accomplish other social goals.

We do not contend that fiscal policy now drives the economy and other public policy or even that fiscal policy has become an integrated whole, devised and implemented as a package. Indeed, a large part of today's deficit dilemma was caused by the passage and implementation of major spending and taxing policies without regard to their impact on the fiscal whole.

But the rationale behind fiscal policy has changed, and it has gained in comprehensiveness and coherence, in part because of the rise of professional economics, which has become an increasingly important factor in postwar American policy making. Nevertheless, factors that helped shape debt and tax measures in the eighteenth and nineteenth centuries remain important. American government has almost always been characterized by a struggle between two competing visions of society. Although they have changed and, to some extent, blurred as society has changed, the tension between them remains a driving force in our politics and economics. The debate between Jeffersonian and Hamiltonian conceptions of government has been sharp and peremptory since the first Congress, and the two strains of thought have taken turns in ascendancy. As each has gained the upper hand, it has naturally attempted to influence policy to bring its vision to life.

Among the many aspects to the Hamiltonian-Jeffersonian dialogue, different views of the size and scope of government, especially the federal government, were central. These differing views were an essential part of their broader conceptions of American society and also determined their differing approaches to public policy. Alexander Hamilton envisioned an America driven by a strong central government promoting and enhancing an international, industrial, mercantilist economy. Thomas Jefferson saw an agrarian and locally communitarian society with slight federal involvement in the lives of its virtuous and self-reliant citizenry, most of whom would live on family farms.

Let us consider each of these seminal figures. [1] Alexander Hamilton came to New York as an alien, without reputation or resources, but quickly made a name for himself. Endowed with compelling charm, wit, and brilliance, he became a leader in Whig circles before he was twenty-five years old, largely through sheer force of intellect.

Hamilton started with a fervent belief in the necessity of strong political authority, combined with an appreciation for the British aristocratic values that he had adopted as his own. Hamilton's friends and allies were bankers, manufacturers, traders, and other businesspeople. He had contempt for the agrarian way of life, for common folk, and for town-meeting democracy. Born in the West Indies, he was not as tied to a localized and decentralized society as many of his peers; he began with a nationalistic vision of a unified, vigorous, and powerful United States.

Hamilton believed that economic behavior, and the affairs of nations were best governed by the enlightened self-interest espoused by the Scottish philosopher Adam Smith. His political philosophy was close to that of Thomas Hobbes, who believed that a powerful state was necessary to control the disorderly passions of the masses. Hamilton acknowledged the need and desirability of a system of checks and balances, mostly to check the excesses of democracy. Thus, he was the most avid proponent among the framers of a strong executive. At the Constitutional Convention he even proposed the idea of a lifetime executive, with hereditary succession.

To be sure, it was not only Hamilton's distaste for the masses that engendered his belief in strong central authority. During the Revolutionary War, he had served as General Washington's aide, an experience that underscored for him the perils of a weak and indecisive Congress, which had trouble even supplying food or arms to its own troops. While Hamilton believed in the necessity of a strong government for protection from external threats, as treasury secretary he also had ambitious, even sweeping, plans for the American nation that required a strong and growing central government.

Jefferson started with a different set of premises about government and society. In contrast to Hamilton, Jefferson had a deep and fundamental fear of a big central government. His ideas about taxation, debt accumulation, and the functions appropriate to government came from the wellspring of his basic philosophy of governing, combined with his affection for the farmers, laborers, frontiersmen, and others who made up rural and agricultural life in America; many of these were debtors to commercial interests.

Jefferson's agrarian philosophy held that the only legitimate source of wealth was the earth or the sea, so he distrusted wealth obtained by other means. For Jefferson, who raised his own food, had his clothes woven, and saw to nearly all of his other economic needs at Monticello, middlemen like merchants or banks, who only bought and sold articles, were parasites who created nothing of value. By lending to a man the money to buy something that he could not otherwise afford, banks employed credit to inflate prices artificially. Always, the telltale residue of the "corrupt" practice of the creation of credit was debt, the waste product of excessive spending.

For Jefferson, the natural, and therefore the most desirable, order of things did not include large centers of commerce or the attendant use of credit. The specialization and resultant interdependence that brought forth mass production and a far higher standard of living for the population at large were, to him, unnatural, corrupt, and not worth the loss of independence.

Jefferson's view of the world affected his attitude not only to banks and credit but to the pace of development. He vastly underestimated the economic gains from specialization. The author of the Louisiana Purchase believed that it would take a thousand years for America to span the continent —and when it did, he imagined the continent would be dotted with hundreds of Monticellos. Jefferson's New World agrarian views represented a remarkably disparate combination of post-Enlightenment philosophy about the intrinsic rights of man and medieval notions about commercial intercourse. Jefferson's Declaration of Independence clearly recognized the intrinsic right of unjustly governed subjects to throw off their government.

Hamilton took his views, especially about the need for a modern, English-style mercantilistic economy shaped by government action, with him into his position as secretary of the treasury. From 1789 to 1795, he shaped and dominated American fiscal policy. Jefferson was appalled; when he had his turn in power, he tried to turn American policy around to fit his own conception of the appropriate role for the national government. Jeffersonian fiscal policies enjoyed considerable success until the War of 1812 made them impossible to follow.

VARIATIONS ON THE DIALOGUE

While there may be something primitive about the terms and substance of the debate Hamilton and Jefferson engaged in during the late eighteenth and early nineteenth centuries, the themes they articulated have persisted in the nation's political life with crosscurrents from other thinkers, in the 180 years since—up to and including the Reagan revolution. The role of the federal government in shaping society and the economy, the moral and the practical meaning of government debt, taxation as an instrument of fiscal policy, the role and the relative importance of workers and business people and of farmers and merchants and manufacturers—all these issues have been continuously at the center of the American debate over public philosophy. And all are rooted in the Hamiltonian-Jeffersonian dialogue.

While the difference between these two philosophies of government has been sharp and clear, the differences as they apply to policy and implementation have not always been marked by the same degree of clarity—and the American political system, like any other, has not often allowed ideological purity even when it was desired. Hamilton and Jefferson, in ways that foreshadowed more recent conflicts, fought for their distinctive visions primarily in the battle over the national debt. Indeed, throughout history, conflicts over debt and taxes have commonly been fought on more symbolic philosophical turf. Through most of America's two hundred years, for example, the idea of a balanced budget was a surrogate for the idea of a small and limited government. It became a highly charged symbol in American politics, and the focus for a wider but less well-articulated debate over the size and role of the federal government.

Thomas Jefferson's deep roots in the forerunner to the present Democratic party are proudly recalled today in the hundreds of Jefferson-Jackson Day events sponsored by state and local Democratic organizations. Other than at intermittent moments, such as the Taft presidency, the fundamental Jeffersonian principle of limited government did not consistently characterize the Republican party until Ronald Reagan became its leader and has characterized it less since he left the presidency. Through much of the nineteenth century, the Republicans' political program centered on a belief that high tariffs were necessary to promote and protect American industries and to enhance industrial expansion. When the tariffs also raised large sums of money for the Treasury, Republicans frequently used the surplus revenues to expand government services rather than lowering tariffs to reduce revenues and the size of government. Republicans became more attentive to limiting the size of government and keeping it efficient after the progressive income tax in 1913 replaced the tariff as the primary revenue source for the federal government.

This balance of the ideological and the practical is a reminder that even the finest-sounding political philosophies are usually developed out of somebody's narrow economic self-interest. Economic, and with them fiscal, policies are typically forged in the struggle of opposed economic interests. The clash between agrarian and industrial or commercial interests was a dominant cause of the regional conflict in American politics from the Revolution through the 1950s and was central to the Jeffersonian-Hamiltonian polarity. Jefferson believed strongly in the importance of protecting the agrarian interests (more particularly, the southern agrarian interest) from what he saw as the evil and rapaciousness of big central government. Such a government, he assumed, would be dominated by the interests of northern manufacturers and urban interests, whereas, in fact, rural and agricultural interests have always been amply represented in Congress.

By contrast, Hamilton's vision of an American mercantilist economic power had at heart the interests of the urban and industrial population. For them, a strong central government was necessary to promote industrial and commercial expansion. The Republican zeal for high tariffs reflected their protection of manufacturing interests at the expense of agrarian ones. Democrats, at least before the Civil War, took a different view as they treasured and protected the rural, agrarian way of life that dominated in the South.

Agrarian and industrial interests were not the only ones to clash in the creation of American fiscal policy. Around the turn of the century, the populist theme favored by the Democratic party and by the progressive wing of the Republican party challenged the business orientation of the conservative wing of the GOP and led to a debate over the merits of redistributing wealth from the haves to the have-nots in American society. Much of the country's subsequent tax policy has flowed from that clash, even though serious redistribution itself has never been politically viable.

POLITICAL REALIGNMENT AND FISCAL CHANGE

Philosophy, ideology, and special interests do not in and of themselves make and implement policy. Governing structures and mediating institutions are required. In America, ideas and interests have both tended to channel themselves through political parties, in a system that is cumbersome and unwieldy. There have been, however, sea changes during American history in policy toward debt and taxes. Usually, the major changes in economic policy and structure have been created by party realignments, though, as we show, not always in the way that theorists would have predicted. The major realignments of American history—1800, 1824, 1860, 1896, 1932—usually followed major crises—a war or a depression—though most began developing earlier. [2] In many cases, the crises provided the necessary but not sufficient condition for dramatic fiscal policy change, which also required political realignment.

What is a realignment? It is "a durable change in patterns of political behavior."[3] The realignments in the election years listed above resulted in massive changes in political loyalties among the electorate, with a single party coming to dominate the White House and Congress. In every case, this political hegemony lasted for a generation or more—long enough for the dominant party to bring about significant policy change. There are many different classifications of realignments, and many different causes, from sectarian and regional strife to slavery or economic collapse. What matters here is the changes that they brought about in fiscal policy.

Stanford political scientist David Brady has documented some of these changes, and the dynamics behind them. He suggests that in response to a national crisis or intense division in America, voters throw out an incumbent party and give another party both the presidency and new and large majorities in both houses of Congress.[4] Since the new members of Congress are elected because of a national problem or trends, they are less sensitive to localized forces in American politics. During such a period, heightened partisanship and a sharp turnover on key committees tend to remove inertia and other impediments to major policy action.

Consider, for example, the Civil War realignment, which "resulted in major policy changes in the scope of federal power over the individual states and in the expansion of the federal role in the economy. These major policy changes were enacted by the newly formed Republican congressional party." The changes included "aggressive national action through tariffs, expansionist banking policies, and internal improvements—mainly a transcontinental railroad and homestead legislation. The Civil War realignment resulted not only in the end of slavery, but also in a commitment to an industrial future for America."[5] Pragmatic big government flowered after the Civil War had illustrated, in a horrible way, the dangers of the Jeffersonian sanction of states' rights.

The Civil War realignment produced the highly protectionist Morrill tariff, passed in the newly Republican House of Representatives in 1859–1860, and other high tariffs passed in subsequent Republican congresses. Growing southern and western agrarian protests against the high tariffs and hard-money policies of this era, and a counterreaction by eastern bankers and businessmen to their populist, soft-money pleas, laid the foundation for the next realignment after the crash of 1893.

Although every partisan realignment in American history has coincided with a crisis of some sort, not all crises have brought about durable partisan political change. Most crises, however, have at least provided the impetus for important policy change. The American system moves slowly and incrementally, unless and until a crisis forces more sweeping change. When we do change in response to a crisis, the change usually outlasts the calamity— just as emergency rent control in New York City has lasted since World War II. The political system returns to incrementalism after a crisis, with unnecessary or even disastrous programs and mechanisms left in place. There may be some retrograde movement, but there is rarely a total reversion to the status quo.

WAR AND FISCAL CHANGE

The crises that have shaped American fiscal policies, at least through the 1950s, have been of two kinds: war and depression. Nearly every major policy or structural reform in fiscal decision making, from the income tax to the Budget and Accounting Act of 1921, has been brought about by the onset of a major war or enacted in its immediate aftermath, or it was initiated as a result of an economic disaster (they have sometimes gone together). And since the Civil War, each crisis has left the federal government permanently larger and more involved in the national economy than before.

Indeed, some theorists suggest that crises are at the root of most change in government. Author John Hughes, in a lively book on the inexorable growth of government control over the economy, noted:

> It is possible, by extended argument, to see the depression of the 1930s as a consequence of World War I and the failure of adjustment after- ward; to see the changes wrought by government control in the Second World War as a partial continuation of the New Deal; to see the post- 1945 economy as a combined legacy of the New Deal and the war; and then simply to trace out the continued expansion of government and its control powers and institutions under the impact of the cold war as merely linear extensions of recent American historical experiences. [6]

War has been a central factor in determining fiscal policy throughout history. Wars have been the source of nearly all the debt created by govern- ments and of the taxes levied to pay for these debts. America, created partly by a rebellion against the taxation generated by incessant warfare in Europe and shielded from potential enemies by broad oceanic buffers, came late to the debt and taxes that accompany a constant state of readiness for war.

The relationship between war, taxes, debt, and the size of government is a distinct and enduring one. Wars tend to generate common effects. In the first place, they always cost a great deal of money, and so they require large increases in tax revenues. To obtain these increases, not only more taxes but new ones are required. Even with new taxes, however, wars tend to escalate government spending so much that they inevitably swell a nation's debt. The deficits that lead to the debt and the necessity of financing debt and ultimately paying it off determine tax policies now as they have for centuries. In addition, the stress on the tax base caused by war debts and postwar spending tends to lead to major structural reform; in America, reforms in the Congress and the executive.

Major wars also lead to bigger government. Wars require bureaucracies to run them and to cope with the more centralized economies that they tend to call forth. These bureaucracies seldom disappear entirely when their reason for being does. Wars can generate the need for public improvements when battles occur on one's own soil. Above all, wars create veterans and promises to them. Keeping government promises to veterans about pensions, benefits, and general expectations can lead to political crises (various veterans' marches on Washington have resulted in violence) and always leads to larger government programs.

The expense of looking after a large number of aging and disabled veterans means that the costs of war to government can persist and expand for decades. One of the fastest-growing programs in the 1980s and 1990s has been the health care of veterans. The rapid expansion of this program has its roots in World War II; the more than 1 million veterans, most now in their sixties and seventies, are entitled to treatment at Department of Veterans Affairs hospitals for any health problem, whether service-related or not, and the number of ailments treated is increasing as they age.

As the Revolutionary War affected so profoundly the framing of the Republic and the governing philosophy and policies that followed, each succeeding war has had an impact. As treasury secretary, Alexander Hamilton used the post–Revolutionary War debt as an excuse to implement aggressive debt and tax measures over the bitter philosophical objections of Thomas Jefferson. Jefferson as president tried mightily, and with considerable success, to reverse those policies. During his presidency, thanks to surplus revenues from tariffs, Jefferson was able to eliminate the excise and other internal taxes and still reduce the debt sharply.

But the next war, in 1812, brought Jeffersonian parsimony to a halt, and ultimately reversed it. The expense of the War of 1812 required the government to reinstate the internal taxes that Jefferson had eliminated and to keep tariffs high. The debt skyrocketed. And since the increase in debt was in the form of short-term Treasury paper, the functional equivalent of paper money, inflation also skyrocketed, which in turn meant higher prices to carry out the war—and more debt to pay off.

After the war, high tariffs and other taxes created budget surpluses that paid off the debt and also provided revenue to pay for public improvements. While the federal government's postwar growth was not spectacular, the government was bigger and more expansive after the War of 1812, in large part as a result of the fiscal policies generated by the war.

The next major war, the Civil War, had a much more profound and lasting impact on the federal government and its management of debt and taxes. More than any crisis before it, the Civil War wrenched American political and economic institutions from their established patterns and altered forever the government's role in relation to society and the economy. Taxes rose sharply to pay for the war effort and at the same time moved well beyond the earlier dominant reliance on tariffs to include both income and excise taxes. This was not enough to stop the debt from soaring in an unprecedented way.

Civil War fiscal policies had both economic and social consequences. As political scientist James Savage notes:

> First, the high tariffs used to generate revenues to finance the debt created huge budget surpluses after the war. These surpluses enabled the federal government to expand its support for federal improvements and other expenditures far beyond the level permitted by the Jacksonian Americans in antebellum America. Second, the federal government's efforts to contract the greenback money supply and return to the gold standard sparked the Populist movement in rural America and the Democratic silver movement in the west . . . the reality of total war, the economic evolution of industrialization, and Republican party policies turned the United States from its preindustrial heritage. [7]

World War I again dramatically expanded deficits and debt, compounding the problem of debt accumulation after the depression of 1907. Taxes were increased sharply as a result of the war, and the newly implemented individual and corporate income taxes became the major vehicles for expansion. The war permanently transformed the income tax into a primary revenue source, with a progressive structure that promised a measure of income redistribution from rich to poor. The conduct of the war itself produced a federal government sharply expanded in size and scope. The federal government for the first time began to play an active role in agriculture and in other markets; it institutionalized, for example, the regulatory functions that had been put in place in the years just before the war.

World War II reinforced the growth and the centralizing tendencies of the federal government in even more dramatic fashion. The country mobilized to an unprecedented degree, and this mobilization required centralized decision making over far more than military strategy and action. Production, prices, industrial development, and the broader economy all became primary areas of federal concern. Even as battalions of American troops fanned out to the European and Pacific theaters, battalions of American bureaucrats occupied Washington and other cities to manage the nation's economy and society for the war effort. Most stayed in the permanently larger government after the war.

The war also created massive deficits, dwarfing in dollar amounts those of all previous wars combined. The resulting increase in individual and corporate income taxes dramatically expanded the base of income-tax payers while making the structure much more progressive.

The Korean War, though much smaller in scale than World War II, resulted in still more deficits and new taxes to pay for them, along with new agencies to regulate business and the economy. Most of the regulatory mechanisms remained in place after the war. [8]

The Vietnam War was an unacknowledged U.S. war, both politically and fiscally. The Great Society of Lyndon Johnson was piled atop the heavy fiscal commitment implicit in support of the war. President Johnson knew that the war was unpopular but hoped that the Great Society would compensate for it.

The main way to pay for both the guns and the butter, however, was through inflation, which amounted to a hefty tax on assets. In the cold February of 1968, during the New Hampshire primary, Senator Eugene McCarthy of Minnesota reminded LBJ of his errors, forcing him to forgo a reelection campaign.

The seeds had been sown, however, for heavier federal spending on a whole new set of government programs. Over the next four years, President Richard Nixon and the Congress enacted huge increases in Social Security benefits, and in 1972 they indexed those benefits to the rising inflation. Thus they put in place the sources of the surging budget deficits after 1982.

EFFECTS OF ECONOMIC CRISES

While the profound and far-reaching impact of war on government and society is in a class by itself, economic crises can be almost as momentous for fiscal policy. The U.S. economy—like those of other nations—has had peaks and valleys, periods of strong growth and deep decline. The times of severe economic turmoil—the panics of 1837, 1857, 1893, and 1907, as well as the Great Depression of the 1930s—have all been closely associated with changes in government policy on debt and taxes and with transformations in economics and politics.

The panic of 1837, in the era of Jacksonian politics in America, lasted longer than any other economic collapse save the panic of 1893 and the Great Depression. Caused by a massive credit collapse that reflected a failure of many state banks and exacerbated by domestic crop failures, the depression lasted seven years. During that time, federal revenues shrank from $50.8 million in 1836 to $8.3 million in 1843, as tariff income disappeared after the collapse of domestic demand for imports. Although it had been successfully liquidated in the early 1830s, the national debt made a comeback. It was never again to be entirely eliminated.

The 1837 depression brought about a movement in the states to pass constitutional provisions limiting their debt and curtailing their borrowing privileges. This impulse did not result in any dramatic shift in federal policy on debt and taxes; a full articulation of countercyclical fiscal measures by John Maynard Keynes and his followers was still a century away. The Jacksonians' move to assume the states' debts was resisted strenuously by southerners, led by John C. Calhoun, as federal co-optation and an infringement on states' rights.

But changes did occur after the 1837 depression. In state and federal government, the Democrats moved to decentralize the financial system, to increase state control over banks, and to implement a hard-money philosophy. The 1846 Independent Treasury Act, for example, required the Treasury to use only specie when conducting transactions and placed all federal deposits in decentralized "subtreasuries." Shaken by defaults, state governments cut back their activist economic policies; "laissez faire" became the watchword in the states.

These policies, in addition to the low tariff rates favored by Democrats, worked passably during the economic growth that lasted through the mid-1850s. But the panic of 1857 led to three consecutive years of large deficits and a decline in revenue that clearly contributed to the Republican takeover of the House of Representatives in 1858 and the highly protectionist Morrill tariff that followed in 1859.[9] After Republicans gained control of the Senate and took the White House in 1860, more protectionist tariffs followed, though these were not nearly enough to finance the Civil War. The shortage of revenues and the subsequent huge deficits led, as we see in greater detail in chapter 5, to profound changes in debt and tax policies.

The panic of 1893 had both fiscal- and monetary-policy roots, although the fact was hardly recognized at the time. In the 1880s, Republicans tried unsuccessfully to reduce the national debt sharply by means of the revenue earned from high tariffs. In addition, the Treasury sold gold to finance a buyback of federal securities that were paying much higher interest rates. In the short term, this policy reduced federal interest payments, but the Treasury's sale of gold was deflationary and resulted in a fall in inflation and interest rates. The value of the remaining high-yield government securities rose as they became scarcer, and the Treasury eventually began to lose money by paying a premium for its own paper. Meanwhile, the sharp contraction in the money supply resulting from the Treasury's sale of gold pushed the economy toward collapse, thereby reducing federal revenues and frustrating the Treasury's primary aim of reducing its debt.

At the same time, the free-silver movement, a successor to the Greenback party that arose after the panic of 1873, achieved a major legislative victory in 1890, when it traded support for the protectionist McKinley tariff bill for passage of the Sherman Silver Purchase Act. This legislation required the Treasury to purchase 4.5 million ounces of silver every month at the market price and with newly issued Treasury notes that were redeemable in either gold or silver. As a result—always the same when a gold standard is maintained with the price of gold set too low—both Americans and foreigners traded silver and paper money for gold. When the Treasury's gold reserves fell below $100 million in 1893, for the first time since the resumption of the gold standard fourteen years earlier, panic ensued. Bank credit and prices fell, and unemployment and interest rates rose.

The severe depression that followed (with a Democratic administration in power) led to the first income tax since the Civil War, through the Wilson-Gorman Act. But despite numerous experiences with an income tax throughout American history, a Supreme Court dominated by Republican appointees struck it down as an unconstitutional "direct tax."

Faced with a foreign withdrawal of gold (a legal and political necessity to maintain its gold payments), a massive reduction in revenue caused by the depression, and a court-ordered bar to raising new money with an income tax, the government had to borrow huge sums of money. And with the borrowed money, it had to buy large quantities of gold—a commodity it had only recently been eagerly selling. With depression and deflation, the official price of gold had become too high, so everyone was dumping it into the government's coffers. The debt ballooned, an unprecedented development in peacetime. From 1894 to 1896, the Treasury increased the debt 45 percent by issuing more than $262 million in new bonds to buy gold.

The debate over monetary policy was settled for a time in 1896, when William Jennings Bryan, the free-silver spokesman, was defeated decisively by William McKinley, a sound-money advocate. The official adoption of a gold standard with a fixed price of gold soon followed.

After the panic of 1893, a sense developed in American politics that wild economic swings and periods of economic collapse were in part a product of government inattention to coherent management of debt and taxes—and that efforts might be necessary to alter the structure of policy making. After the recovery from the 1893 depression, those feelings were reinforced by new deficits from the Spanish-American War of 1898 and the construction of the Panama Canal, which began in 1905. The depression of 1907, which followed another bank panic, stiffened the resolve of public and politicians to act when it produced deficits of $57 million in 1908 and $89 million in 1909: "The 1909 deficit shocked the Congress and the American people, for it was the largest peacetime deficit yet recorded in the country's history. Reaction to the deficit, subsequently produced reforms in the budgetary process . . . and reforms in the banking system."[10]

Banking reform came first. In 1913, Congress passed the Federal Reserve Act, in effect creating the modern-day Federal Reserve System. Budget reform germinated for a longer time. Stung by the large deficits, Congress in 1909 asked President William Howard Taft to investigate the budget process and recommend ways to improve its efficiency and to ensure balanced budgets. Taft created a presidential Commission on Economy and Efficiency, which recommended that the president institute the budget and that a new presidential agency centralize budget tasks. The recommendations were not acted upon, however, until after World War I, when, spurred by Woodrow Wilson and a disciplined Democratic party behind him, they were put into effect by the Budget and Accounting Act of 1921. The influence of these panics on fiscal policy was dwarfed by that of the Great Depression, which also had a far greater effect on the scope and involvement of government in the economy. (For a detailed discussion of its importance, see chapter 6.)

OTHER INFLUENCES

For most of America's history, attitudes toward debt and taxes and ideas about what to do with them changed in response to major events or crises. The crises also brought about political realignments out of which came the political coalitions that could implement policy changes. Each coalition's hegemony allowed the predominance of one set of ideas to fix major change in place. Beyond the formation of fiscal policy in response to events, however, governmental structures and policy processes, as subsequent chapters show, have also been immensely influential. Politics is doing what can be done with the means available. The materials its practitioners have to work with, including the established usages of governmental institutions, are often more important than philosophy or ideology. Americans, moreover, who have been taught to revere their Constitution, are perhaps more inclined than most people to believe in the efficacy of structural changes to overcome the vexing problems of taxing, spending, and debt.

The importance of the government's constitutional structure to fiscal policy therefore is a leitmotif of this book's generally historical approach and our main theme in the final chapter, which deals with the possibility of reform. If the Founding Fathers had decided to put the basic "powers of the purse" in the hands of the president rather than the Congress, we would almost certainly have had a different experience with debt and taxes: more than likely, a much larger federal government and more extensive federal presence in the economy.

Much of the anguished debate about the budget deficit in the 1980s was focused on structure and process, from the Balanced Budget Amendment to the Constitution to the line-item veto and from Gramm-Rudman-Hollings to the budget process reform. All the debate about structure, however, was really a diversion from the deadlock elsewhere in the system. With the paralysis of the political will, little could be done—except to hope that tinkering with structures would somehow save the day. It did not because it could not. Structural change matters. Ultimately, though, not structural change but the freeing of America's political energies, in one direction or another, is what moves the country forward. For that, we must first see how our political system got to this point; to do *that*, we must look where it started, as we do in part 2.

PART TWO

FROM COLONIAL TIMES TO THE CRASH

✦

⋆ 4 ⋆

ROOTS OF AMERICAN
FISCAL POLICY

As a new nation, America confronted the realities of war, debt, and taxes when it had to cope with the massive debts created by the Revolutionary War. In many respects, though, the origins of America itself lay in the relationship between war, debt, and taxes in seventeenth- and eighteenth-century Europe—and not only because the American colonists rebelled against the taxes that had been levied to pay for Britain's wars. Many of the colonists were descended from those who had come to America to escape from the costly, if not ruinous, wars fought in the name of religion and for territory that had been commonplace since the Reformation and the rise of nation-states in the sixteenth century.

SPAIN AND THE DUTCH REBELLION

A particularly instructive example of these wars is the Spanish subjugation of the Netherlands in the late sixteenth century.[1] Protestanism was by 1560 a major threat to the Holy Roman Empire. Britain, the Netherlands, the Scandinavian countries, and parts of Germany and France were becoming or had become Protestant. England and Holland were experiencing rapid economic development. Where Protestant governments came to power, they confiscated the lands of the Roman Catholic church.

The leader of the Catholic counteroffensive was Philip II of Spain, a sober, brooding fanatic who saw the Dutch Calvinists as a major threat to his vision of a Catholic and Hapsburg Europe. His assertion of Spanish authority in the Netherlands led to violent protests on their part, and to a brutal reaction by Philip and his henchman, the duke of Alva. The duke's Council of Troubles tortured, maimed, and beheaded many of the rebels to fulfill the "will of God."

This repression might have been effective, at least for a time, had the duke stopped with the torture of a few malcontents. Because he imposed a tax equal to a tenth of the value of all sales and a hundredth of every income, the duke of Alva made enemies and eventually rebels of almost all the Dutch. Without the tax, many of those who secretly objected to the excesses of the Calvinist rebels would have given him at least tacit support. But the hated tenth penny made enemies even of his few friends.

The Dutch Calvinists believed in hard work and believed, too, that the economic gain it brought was a sign of the grace of God bestowed on his elect. This religious spirit added a special fervor to the cries of outrage at the duke's tax, which had united the disparate citizens of the seventeen provinces of the Netherlands. William of Orange emerged at the head of the Dutch rebellion against Spanish authority; he was one of the Dutch noblemen whose estates had been confiscated by the duke of Alva's Council of Troubles.

In 1574, the duke of Alva laid siege to Leiden to gain control of Holland's most beautiful and prosperous city. To relieve the siege, William of Orange and his followers opened the city's protective dikes to flush out—literally—the surrounding Spanish forces.

After the dikes had been broken, the Dutch troops made an advance on Leiden, at times pushing and pulling their barges for miles over mud flats. The Spanish were driven off, and the siege of Leiden was broken, although six thousand citizens had died of starvation. William of Orange offered Leiden a choice of reward for refusing to surrender to the Spanish: relief from taxes during the city's annual fair or a university. The citizens chose a university. They reasoned, with considerable perspicacity, that taxes come and go in response to political considerations, but a university, once established, is a permanent benefit to a city and a nation.

The choice to retain a tax rather than to forgo a university (whose benefits Leideners continue to enjoy) demonstrated that the burghers of the Netherlands did not object to taxes as such. They opposed a tax assessed by a foreign king, a king alien in spirit, to enable him to continue to rule with little regard for the wishes or welfare of his subjects. Where a bourgeois population had the means to resist a central authority's exactions, as it did in the Netherlands in the sixteenth century, it insisted on mutual material benefits to justify taxes imposed by monarchs. This was especially true in the Netherlands, where so many subjects were, in varying degrees, remote from the ruler both in distance and in religious belief.

By 1576, Philip II had been largely bankrupted by continuous wars. He owed huge debts to merchants and was nearly two years in arrears on payments to his own troops, including those in Holland. So pressed, Philip received a dispensation from the pope permitting revocation of all promises "lest he should be ruined by usury while combating the heretics." Thus the king did not pay his army in the Netherlands; the enraged soldiers sacked Antwerp that year. This further atrocity by Spaniards moved the Dutch provinces into a closer confederation that ultimately drove Philip out of the Netherlands.

In issuing its dispensation, the Catholic church acted as an agent of monarchy over property rights and so hastened the day when royal absolutism could no longer survive. The king's authority was undermined not only among his creditors but also among the rest of his subjects, for whom subsequent tax demands seemed all the more arbitrary and unjust.

In 1581, at The Hague, the Calvinist party issued a call for independence with the oath of abjuration. The oath, a remarkably clear forerunner of Thomas Jefferson's Declaration of Independence, asserted that unjust government constituted forfeiture of the right to govern. Philip failed to recognize any of the rights asserted in the oath of abjuration and proceeded to offer a reward of seventy-five thousand guilders for the assassination of William of Orange. The sum proved too tempting to resist. After William was assassinated in 1584, the Dutch sought an alliance with Britain: they were unable to envision themselves unified without allegiance to another European monarch.

Philip, determined to break up the Anglo-Dutch alliance, finally sent the Spanish Armada to invade England. The well-known defeat of the Armada off the Scottish Hebrides in 1588 marked the end of Spanish primacy in Europe. But Philip's exertions on behalf of a Catholic counteroffensive in Holland and elsewhere had important ramifications for the history of other nations—including that of the American Republic.

TAXING BRITISH AMERICA

The role played by debt and taxes in the Dutch rebellion against Spanish rule was repeated two hundred years later in the American colonies during their revolt against British rule. Both the Spanish and the British had incurred heavy debts that strained the financial resources of their subjects, and both imposed harsh taxes and debased their currencies to manage their debts. Such impositions on the subjects of extended empires like the Dutch and the American colonies united those at the greatest distance from the center with a sense of common grievance. Thus, the pattern of debt, taxes, and revolution—*successful* revolution—appeared in America as it had in the Netherlands.

The American colonies fought the Revolutionary War primarily to avoid paying British taxes. Before this open conflict with Britain, the colonies had welcomed its might in the French and Indian War (1754–1763): the army and navy, financed by British taxes and British borrowing, drove the French out of America.

From Britain's perspective, the colonists were ungrateful louts. They showed their gratitude for British intervention by selling the French forces ammunition and other provisions for their battles against the British. After the war, the colonists showed their ingratitude by refusing to pay any taxes levied by a frustrated British Parliament to recoup some costs of defending and expanding the empire.

By the second half of the eighteenth century, the cost of defending and maintaining that empire had become too great to be borne by the home country alone. If its colonies did not yield sufficient revenues to pay for their own defense, the British empire would collapse.

By the end of the Seven Years' War, Britain's national debt had risen to £130 million, double its level just a decade earlier.[2] True, the war in Europe had contributed to the increase along with the cost of the French and Indian War, but the strain of fighting a war so far removed from its shores and managing it over long and costly lines of supply was great. Beyond that, Britain maintained extensive civil and military establishments in America at an annual cost of more than £350,000 in 1764, five times more than the cost fifteen years earlier.

Although the exact contribution of the colonies to defray Britain's costs of defense and administration is not known, the few available figures suggest that it was modest. A miscellany of debt payments, port duties, and other crude measures brought in about £2 million per year according to the British prime minister, William Pitt.[3] The heavy cost of the long war fought to protect the colonies from incursions by the French and Indians demonstrated clearly to the British Parliament and George Grenville, the chancellor of the exchequer, that more revenue had to be extracted from America.

The notion of taxing colonies in exchange for protection was hardly a novel one; neither Grenville nor Benjamin Franklin, the American envoy to Britain, expected trouble. The British were following standard practice by imposing duties on sugar (the Revenue Act of 1764) and fees on paper used for newspapers and commercial documents (the Stamp Act of 1765). Such imposts were an attempt to collect from British subjects in America the same taxes that were paid by British subjects in Britain.

The Stamp Act was unique in one important way. It was the first attempt by Parliament to impose a direct, internal excise tax on the colonies. It demonstrated that the British ruling class, having expended its blood and money to defend the colonies from incursions by other powers, viewed the colonists, at least for purposes of taxation, as the equivalent of British subjects living in Britain.

The Stamp Act was, to the British, a family affair and as such was levied without regard to its intrusive nature. It was not only direct but pervasive. It required the colonists to buy revenue stamps with specie (scarce hard money, not paper) and to affix the stamps to almost all documents including newspapers, licenses, commercial bills, notes and bonds, advertisements, pamphlets, leases, and numerous legal documents.

Parliament did try to soften the blow by specifying that American, not British, agents would collect the tax, although one suspects that few British agents were lining up to travel to the colonies to collect the tax. No doubt, had Parliament consulted with an experienced British excise man, it would have expected the ensuing trouble.

Not only was the Stamp Act especially intrusive, but its burden fell most heavily on the most powerful and articulate men in the colonies. The lawyers, merchants, journalists, and clergymen on whose stock-in-trade the stamps were to be affixed and paid for with hard currency were not prepared to pay annually the £60,000 that Parliament hoped to raise with the stamp excise; they were also in a strong position to resist it.

The direct British tax brought many thoughtful colonists face-to-face with a new reality. The British Parliament had not financed a war to defend them from Indian incursions and French limitation on their westward expansion without expecting in return some compensation, and control over that expansion. But even before the French and Indian War, the colonists were beginning to recognize the potential of the unsettled West and to be confident of their own abilities to manage expansion without Britain.

The colonists had an effective way to battle what they saw as the injustices of the Stamp Act and the Quartering Act, which forced them to shelter British soldiers. They boycotted British goods and tried to frustrate the agents of the Crown sent to America to distribute the stamps. In 1765, the Sons of Liberty, an organization of "respectable" men against the Stamp Act taxes, forced British stamp agents to resign, burned stamped paper, and incited attacks on individuals responsible for collecting the tax.

The Stamp Act was repealed by Parliament in 1766 under pressure from London merchants whose businesses were failing because of losses in the American market. The colonists had demonstrated their ability to deny to the British, for the time being at least, the economic benefits of empire. But by passing in the same year the Declaratory Act, which reasserted Britain's right to make laws for the colonials, Parliament signaled that the issue of taxation in the colonies was far from over.

The colonists also had to contend with the British Parliament's prohibition on their issuance of currency. The New England colonies had been restrained from issuing currency since 1751. The 1764 Currency Act extended the prohibition to the plantation colonies of the South. These laws meant that the colonies had no means either to collect seigniorage from printing or minting money or to devalue inflationary overissue of currency.

By prohibiting the issuance of currency and attempting to exact from the colonists taxes payable in scarce specie, the British Parliament was trying to squeeze the juice out of a cactus. Resentment and revolt were bound to arise because colonial governments, unable to issue money or to collect taxes, could not support their own legitimate undertakings. Indeed, their very existence must have seemed at risk if they were to bend to the British requirement that they pay over all customs duties or excise taxes in return for British protection.

Britain could only create hostility by trying to bring the colonists into line as contributing members of an empire that it had paid to develop and to maintain. Yet, in the eyes of the British, the taxes that they attempted to impose on the colonies were normal and justified, especially in view of the considerable costs that they had incurred in the French and Indian War— not to mention the additional costs incurred in the parallel Seven Years' War fought in Europe and elsewhere. Further, the British Parliament was influenced by a post-Enlightenment trend in Europe toward consolidation and centralization of control over empires.

CALL FOR REPRESENTATION

Beyond the direct unpleasantness following the British attempt to levy excise and other taxes on the American colonies, another problem helped to precipitate revolution. As the British Parliament, not the British king, was attempting to collect the taxes, the colonists expected Parliament, as a representative body, to be answerable to them or at least to be responsive to their concerns as British subjects. Both Thomas Jefferson and Benjamin

Franklin seriously considered the idea of an American sub-Parliament that could provide a link to the British Parliament for the colonies, while the colonists remained subjects of the king.

The leaders of the American Revolution might have accepted dominion status like that eventually granted to Canada and Australia had the British Parliament offered it. But Parliament, given the colonies' performance during and after the French and Indian War, did not consider them capable of responsible self-rule.

For their part, the colonists were not prepared to pay taxes levied by a representative legislature like the British Parliament in which they were not represented. Paying taxes to Parliament seemed to the colonists like paying federal taxes would seem today to Texans or Californians were they denied representation in Congress.

The American idea of representation as a necessary condition for taxation was a product of Enlightenment thinking that was perfectly clear to "radical" thinkers like Thomas Paine and Thomas Jefferson but not at all clear to an exasperated Lord North, who had become Britain's prime minister in 1770. Nor were such radical ideas clear to his colleagues in Parliament who had the misfortune to run afoul of a dangerous combination of American pragmatism and idealism.

On the eve of the Revolutionary War, the Americans possessed the two elements necessary for a revolution: a tangible impediment in the form of taxation without representation to "individual life, liberty and the pursuit of happiness" together with an ironclad principle—those who do not govern justly should not govern—to justify not paying taxes. Just government, for the American colonists, included the right to petition Parliament. Indeed, to them that was why Parliament existed.

Despite the anger of the American colonies at being taxed by Parliament without representation, the British might have avoided the American rebellion, or at least blunted its intensity, had they not ignored their own experience with excise taxes on life's necessities. In 1755, Samuel Johnson's famous dictionary had defined the excise as "a hateful tax levied upon commodities and adjudged not by the common judges of property but wretches hired by those to whom it is paid." These wretches were the excise men who were permitted to keep for themselves a portion of the taxes collected—and thus became pariahs in their communities.

By 1766, after the Americans had rejected the sugar and stamp taxes while continuing to evade British customs duties, they had become virtually free riders within the British Empire, enjoying its protection and other benefits without paying its costs. Thus, Parliament in 1767 imposed the Townshend duties, taxes on imports of essentials like paper, paint, lead, and tea. These taxes seemed to the colonists much like the hated excise taxes, since they were levied on life's necessities and had to be collected by a British agent who must have looked like an excise man to the colonists.

Again, a predictable American cry of protest went up; all duties were rescinded except for a symbolic tax on tea. Parliament seemed always to be frustrated when it tried to tax the colonists to force them to pay their dues for membership in the empire.

BRITISH FRUSTRATIONS

In retrospect, it may seem strange that the mighty British could not collect from the upstart colonists the taxes that they collected in the home country. But the British faced two basic problems in taxing the American colonies, and their inability to solve them led ultimately to an attempt to collect from the Americans contributions to the empire in a manner that precipitated revolution.

The first, and most frustrating, problem was that protection of their own territorial interests in North America required them to protect the colonists against the French as they had done during the Seven Years' War. British policy and presence in North America was part of a continuing European struggle for empire. Thus the eighteenth-century British defense umbrella over the American colonies was like the American defense umbrella over Europe and Japan after World War II. By spreading the umbrella over their own territorial interests, the British could not exclude the American colonies from also enjoying its benefits, just as America's policy of containing the Soviet empire in its own interests required it to defend Europe, Japan, and other regions.

Such a defense umbrella is a public good, like pure water or clean air, that a supplier cannot deny to those who have not contributed to maintaining it. Defense umbrellas are especially expensive public goods, and the British, like their American cousins two centuries later, tried hard to collect some of its expense from those beneath it. This was the eighteenth-century equivalent of burden sharing. That the colonies were part of the British Empire and not sovereign nations enjoying a free ride did not make it any easier for Britain to collect. The British could not separate from the pursuit of their own territorial interests the effective defense of the colonies against foreign incursions.

The second problem facing Britain in assessing the colonies for the cost of their defense was that the methods of tax collection in the eighteenth century were crude and especially ill suited to raising revenues from colonies located thousands of miles away. Since the British Crown had in 1698 relinquished inflation as a means of raising money by selling to a private corporation, the Bank of England, the exclusive right to issue legal tender, Britain had to rely solely on customs duties and excise taxes. Although the king was worse off for it, British subjects and the British economy were better off.

The reliance on selective taxes like customs duties on imports and excise taxes levied upon tea, tobacco, and other staples, which are difficult to conceal from the tax collector, meant that the tax rate must be high to yield adequate revenues. But throughout history, if the tax rate rises too high, efforts to avoid paying taxes increase to a point where raising the tax rate actually yields less revenue. (This insight was rediscovered with unusual enthusiasm by Arthur Laffer when the supply-side *Zeitgeist* and Ronald Reagan's quest for the presidency made lower tax rates the vogue.)

The colonists, like their British relatives, had become adept at avoiding high customs duties, particularly those destined for British coffers. But the alternative, the excise tax, was difficult for Britain to impose on the colonies. No excise man, paid well enough to compensate him for his unpopularity in England, would endure a lengthy and dangerous sea journey to try to collect taxes in the sparsely populated colonies with less protection against bodily harm than he enjoyed at home.

Because of this difficulty in collecting excise taxes, the British in the colonies were forced to fall back on high customs duties, which the colonists easily avoided by smuggling. The other logical alternative, an income tax, was not broadly applicable in the eighteenth century, since virtually all transactions were in cash and the considerable apparatus necessary to measure income and to assess such a tax was unavailable.

Unable to exclude the American colonies from their protection and unable to charge them for it, the British in 1773 hit upon a plan that was far too clever to succeed. The East India Company, the Crown corporation with exclusive rights to conduct trade with Asia (until Earl Grey broke the monopoly in 1833), had become saddled with a huge surplus of tea. Parliament decided to kill two birds with one stone. It would extract a contribution to the empire from the colonies while restoring a Crown corporation to financial health by granting to the East India Company the exclusive right to sell tea in America.

The many American tea merchants would have been ruined by this arrangement. Even if they had been able to supply some tea in the American market by subverting the East India Company monopoly, they would have had to accept a low price, since in disposing of its excess tea the British East India Company was, in effect, dumping tea on the American market. Furthermore, the intention of the East India Company to dispose of excess tea in America would depress the value of the considerable tea inventories held by American tea merchants and thereby compound their economic losses.

The British government was forced to help the East India Company dispose of its surplus tea because of its own incessant efforts to raise money through the sale of monopolies and customs duties. The East India Company had received its monopoly on the tea trade from the Crown, which then proceeded to tax tea so heavily that smuggling became profitable, and the value of the franchise sold by the Crown eroded. It is an old story. By the 1770s, tea smuggling had become so widespread in England that the East India Company's monopoly on the legitimate trade was nearly worthless. Why buy authorized tea at inflated prices when much cheaper tea is available through other channels? In effect, the Crown had devalued its grant to the East India Company by taxing tea too heavily and then failing to prevent smuggling.

To restore some of the value lost to smugglers operating on the British coasts, the Crown granted an American tea monopoly to the East India Company. Surely, thought Parliament, it could protect an American tea monopoly from smuggling. To do so was vital. Otherwise, the value of the Crown monopolies was in jeopardy, not to mention revenues from customs duties. To the British, the American tea monopoly was a critical test of their ability to protect vital sources of revenue. To the Americans, it represented a disastrous loss of valuable property rights to a Parliament in which they were not represented.

The prospect of a British tea monopoly and its ruinous implications for American tea merchants, not the residual Townshend duty on tea, precipitated the famous Boston Tea Party in which colonists disguised as Mohawks dumped British tea out of British ships into Boston harbor. The American merchants wanted less British tea available so that the price of their tea would rise.

OVERREACTION AND REVOLT

The exasperated British government overreacted by closing the port of Boston and rescinding the charter of Massachusetts. The port's closing threatened all American importers, not just tea merchants, with economic ruin. And rescinding the charter of the colony forbade the holding of town meetings to discuss such a disturbing prospect.

Thus, British reaction to the Boston Tea Party deprived American merchants in Massachusetts both of their livelihoods and of the means to address the problem at public meeting. In 1774, the Parliament excited further resentment among the colonists when it enacted the Quebec Act, which granted to the Canadian French the territorial rights in what are now the states of Wisconsin, Michigan, Illinois, Indiana, and Ohio. The Quebec Act was seen by Americans as an outrageously pro-French, pro-Catholic barrier to their westward expansion and completed a pattern of British oppression in which the economic interests of almost all of the American colonists— merchants, land speculators, farmers, frontiersmen, and common workmen —were undercut. The necessary preconditions for open rebellion were created.

Ultimately, the British fell back on an implicit decision to abandon the American colonies as a bad investment. Doing so involved them in immense financial losses, but the cost of attempting to maintain sovereignty, to continue administration and defense of the colonies, toward which the colonists could not be induced to pay anything, would have been even greater. But once they were freed from direct British control, the former colonists had to begin to provide for themselves in areas of defense and administration— meaning the Americans had to pay in full for what they got. That required taxes and borrowing.

By the time the American revolutionaries faced the problem of levying taxes, they had been quarreling with Britain for years over questions of tax justice and held strong and well-defined ideas about fair and prudent taxation. But pragmatism was also necessary if they were to deal with the enormous debt incurred during the War of Independence. They had fought a war to avoid British taxes and the burdens of British debt, yet, in the process, they had acquired a debt of their own equal to more than two-fifths of the new nation's income. To service it, they had to resort to taxes themselves— largely in the form of customs duties.

America's constitutional deliberations in the 1780s revolved around these two economic realities: resentment of British taxation and the heavy debt that had been incurred to end it. The power of the purse became a dominant theme for the framers of the Constitution, who devoted much time and energy to the specification and division of economic powers. From the beginning, America's political leaders saw the importance of keeping economic policy in the control of a democratic political structure. But the war debts, both of the Union and of the states, loomed over the debates at the Constitutional Convention, as did the aftereffects of wartime inflation.

Financing the Revolution had been a major headache to the Americans. With no power to tax, the Continental Congress had been forced to finance the war effort by borrowing, both abroad and at home, through voluntary loans. When these resources proved insufficient, it borrowed involuntarily through the issue of fiat money. Foreign and domestic bonds, which had to be issued at a high rate of interest to find lenders, accounted for less than one-fifth of the wartime revenues of the government. The rest, well over $225 million in an economy that generated barely $200 million in annual national income, came from the issuance of paper money. Not surprisingly, severe inflation resulted.

At the currency depreciated rapidly, Congress attempted monetary and fiscal reform to stabilize it. Robert Morris, a Philadelphia businessman and member of Congress, was appointed superintendent of finance in 1781. He imposed budgetary controls and pushed Congress to charter the Bank of North America, the nation's first commercial bank, to serve as the government's fiscal agent. For reasons of ideology and politics—factors we will consider shortly—Morris was not entirely successful, and he failed to achieve his major objective, which was to secure taxing power for the post-Revolutionary national government.

PAYING OFF THE REVOLUTIONARY DEBT

Nevertheless, the Revolution and its economic consequences gave a larger role to the national government than it had ever played in the former colonists' affairs. After the war, American leaders needed to cope with the crushing debt it left—nearly $75 million or 42 percent of the national product—and an interest burden that consumed more than half of the meager federal revenues. (By contrast, interest on our $3 trillion national debt today takes up less than 15 percent of federal revenues.)

Alexander Hamilton's view of an expansive role for the federal government, discussed in chapter 3, influenced management of the debt when Hamilton became George Washington's secretary of the treasury. Hamilton's

Report on the Public Credit, issued on January 14, 1790, as the First Congress prepared for its second session, contained a detailed plan to pay off the debt by refinancing it.

Hamilton wanted to fund the debt through its capitalization and consolidation, to build strong American credit, and to turn the debt from a liability into an asset. More broadly, though, he saw the legitimization of the debt as a way to build a growing market economy. Debt financing would thus be accompanied by centralized coinage and banking, new sources of federal revenue, and a policy of systematic protection and promotion of American manufacturing.

The first treasury secretary saw the war debt as an opportunity for the new nation to establish a sound credit rating, to create a respectable name for America, and to cement the Union. The consequence of a "properly funded" national debt, as he saw it, would be more capital, better agriculture and manufacturing, more trade, lower interest rates (with more money), and easier and cheaper borrowing. To achieve his goal, Hamilton suggested that the federal government move beyond consolidating the national debt and assume all the states' debts. Hamilton thus became the first and most pervasive advocate of a close involvement of the national government in the national economy.

It would not have been difficult for Hamilton to settle with creditors for lower interest, extended repayment, or devaluation of the debt's principal (the United States then was better positioned than Mexico is today in the debt market). But he insisted on a consolidation scheme aimed at full repayment of previously contracted debt obligations that was to build a national reputation strong enough to take care of the country's capital needs over the long run.[4]

Debt was not the only vehicle that Hamilton had in mind for American expansion. Taxes, in the form of tariffs, were also part of his program. He saw in tariffs the dual benefits of enhanced commerce and revenue. Hamilton had not absorbed the writings of David Hume on the benefits of free trade and saw no problem in the government's pursuing an industrial policy —by cultivating some branches of trade and discouraging others, by assisting infant industries, and by opening new sources of trade. His views on industrial policy, therefore, complemented his need for revenues with which to pay for the rest of the federal government and to advance American industrial expansion.

The First Congress accepted his plan and passed the Tariff Act of 1789 as one of its first actions. It was signed into law by President Washington on

July 4. This act was explicitly designed to protect and defend American manufactures and to assist American shipping interests. Passage of the Tariff Act of 1789 reflected a basic decision to make import duties the primary source of federal revenues—a decision that was scarcely altered until the imposition of the income tax more than a century later.

There were few other reasonable alternatives at the time. Not surprisingly in the light of pre-Revolutionary experience with heavy-handed British efforts at levying excise taxes, internal taxes were not popular. Moreover, without a money-based market economy throughout the new and geographically diverse Union, most internal taxes were nearly impossible to collect. Hamilton, however, needed more revenues than tariffs provided to pay the interest on the debt, and persuaded the Second Congress to impose an excise tax on distilled spirits. The result was the Whiskey Rebellion—an outcry against a tax on a corn by-product that could be stored and shipped to market by small farmers, for whom distilling was a profitable sideline.

Another of Hamilton's projects was the establishment of the Bank of the United States. An important feature of Hamilton's vision of the bank was the way it could provide for use of the public debt as the basis of the nation's currency. Stock in the bank was sold to investors, who could pay for as much as four-fifths of their stock in government securities at par. The convertibility of securities into bank stock both increased the market value of the securities and provided, without a large injection of specie (gold or silver), the ability for the bank to circulate $10 million in notes that would become the country's major currency equivalent.

As Forrest McDonald has written:

Basing the currency on bank notes instead of gold and silver had profound consequences. The crucial characteristic of banking currency is that it is money created in present, not out of past savings but out of the expectation of future income. Furthermore, because it was inherent in Hamilton's system that money and capital were interchangeable, the government could create capital as well as money by institutionalizing future expectations. This meant that the nation's economic development could be financed on credit without the need for collateral.[5]

As Hamilton recognized, his scheme would work only if the credit was sound, that is, only if the new American government invariably honored its debt obligations.

Madison and Jefferson opposed the national bank because of Jefferson's strong philosophical opposition to the use of credit and the implied expansion of the role of the federal government. Hamilton won the argument in the First Congress, which by its acceptance of the Hamiltonian vision of the roles of debt and taxes chose his form of political economy. "The United States would be built under a government-channeled, government-encouraged, and sometimes government-subsidized system of private enterprise for personal profit."[6]

While Hamilton and his philosophy of an economically activist government won a number of early rounds, Jefferson had a turn to implement his vision of America under a more limited government when he became president in 1801. The financing of the American Revolution on credit pained Jefferson. He, like Hamilton, wished to consolidate state debts with the debts of the Continental Congress, but Jefferson's aim was to pay them off as quickly as possible to eradicate what he saw as a symbol of corruption within the new American government.

Unlike Hamilton, Jefferson believed that debt weakened the social fabric and provided an opening for the corrupting influence of big and powerful government. In the twelve years of the Washington and Adams administrations, the debt had grown from $75 million to more than $83 million. When Jefferson assumed the presidency, he set about single-mindedly to reduce the role and scope of the federal government by eliminating the national debt. He was remarkably successful, as the debt dropped from $86 million in 1803 to just $45 million in 1812.

But despite views of political economy different from those of Hamilton, Jefferson as president found himself working within the existing Hamiltonian political and economic structure. Although he did not approve of an activist, tariff-based industrial policy, he was more intent on eliminating the internal taxes on alcohol, slaves, houses, sugar, and lands that had grown up since 1789 than he was on reducing tariffs. In fact, the handsome revenues that were flowing into federal coffers from the customs duties allowed him to reduce the other taxes and the debt at the same time.

Jefferson's philosophy did not mean in practice a rigid adherence to one basic principle. He was not averse to geographical expansion through the federal government's buying of land, as the Louisiana Purchase shows. Jefferson used the Hamiltonian tariff not only to cut taxes and to reduce the debt but also to pay for public improvements in education and transportation. He did not mind paying for new public works if it could be done at the expense of the rich. As he commented in a letter written in 1811 to Pierre-Samuel Du Pont de Nemours:

We are all the more reconciled to the tax on importation, because it falls exclusively on the rich, and with the equal partitions of intestate's estates, constitutes the best agrarian law. In fact, the poor man in this country who uses nothing but what is made within his own farm or family, or within the United States, pays not a farthing of tax to the general government but on his salt; and should we go into that manufacture as we ought to, he will pay not one cent. Our revenues once liberated by the discharge of the public debt, and its surplus applied to canals, roads, schools, etc., the farmer will see his government supported, his children educated, and the face of his country made a paradise by the contributions of the rich alone, without his being called on to spare a cent from his earnings. The path we are now pursuing leads directly to this end, which we cannot fail to attain unless our administration should fall into unwise hands.

IMPACT OF THE WAR OF 1812

Few hands could have been less unwise than those of Jefferson's successor, James Madison. But with the War of 1812, this rosy vision of the future had to be deferred. Jeffersonian policies on debt and taxes were reversed; to pay for the war, internal taxes were reinstated while tariffs remained high. The war required so much money that the debt, reduced so sharply in the first decade of the nineteenth century, jumped to 20 percent of GNP. From 1812 to 1816, the national debt increased from $45 million to $127 million, though the increase was restrained by huge tax increases that boosted revenues. Most of the increase in debt was in the form of short-term Treasury paper, the functional equivalent of paper money. This sharp increase in money equivalents, a substitute for more debt, meant skyrocketing inflation, which in turn meant higher prices to carry on the war—even though the earlier debts incurred by the government to pay for the war were devalued. Inflation also devalued the American government's credit rating and led to stringent measures to restore it once the war was over.

After the war, the high tariffs and other taxes that it had demanded created budget surpluses that paid off the debt and also provided revenue to pay for public improvements. While the growth of the federal government had not been spectacular, it was bigger and more expansive after the War of 1812, largely because of the wartime tax measures.

Interest on the national debt at the end of that war consumed a share of total federal revenues three times as large as the share consumed during the "massive" budget deficit years in the 1980s. As a result, the federal government's credit was shaky, to say the least. Jeffersonian scruples notwithstanding, it is little wonder that in February 1815 Madison, the Republican, called for Federalist-sounding measures such as direct internal taxation, a protective (revenue-yielding) tariff, a new national bank, and more military forces. The last measure was no doubt expected to reduce the probability of another costly war.

In 1816, the Congress enacted a large tariff increase primarily aimed at British imports. As always with tariffs, the temptation to kill two birds with one stone was irresistible: Uncle Sam could pay for a war against the British with a tax on British goods, which, not incidentally, made American goods look more attractive. Indeed, the end of the war against the British in 1815 was a turning point for America away from European goods, toward establishment of its own industries behind high tariff walls. The war reestablished for a time the thrust of the Federalists' initiatives for a stronger central government and reinforced the temptation to use the multipurpose tariff. The latter was particularly attractive to northern manufacturers and, from their perspective, came with the bonus of disadvantaging the South, which depended on goods imported from Britain.

Henry Clay and John C. Calhoun, nationalist leaders in Congress, aimed to establish an "American system" to bind the nation together with a new web of roads and canals financed by high protective tariffs. Calhoun saw the tariff protection as an appeal to self-interest that would "form a new and most powerful cement" to unite in common self-interest the diverse parts of the nation.

Tariffs, taxes on imported goods, were the overwhelming fiscal reality in nineteenth-century America before the Civil War. Tariff revenues paid off the Revolutionary War debt. The 1816 tariff increase was meant to generate revenues to pay off the debt from the War of 1812. After 1820, American industries grew ever more rapidly in the northeastern United States behind the wall of protective tariffs and with the benefit of a rapidly growing national market for the products of American manufacturers, free from outside competition. The tariff benefited American producers mightily but at considerable expense to American consumers, who were cut off by it from much of what a thriving nineteenth-century world economy had to offer.

For Hamiltonian Federalists, high tariffs meant the best of both worlds. Tariffs protected the industries that they wanted protected, while providing enough revenues to pay for ambitious and aggressive (for the times) government programs—buying territories, building roads, bridges, and canals— that meant an enlarged national governmental presence.

The role of the federal government in the early nineteenth century did not approach its extent today. Tariffs ranging from 40 percent to 60 percent of the value of imported goods were needed to generate revenues equal to 2 or 3 percent of national income. In 1992, federal tax rates no higher than 33 percent applied to a much broader income-tax base yielded revenues equal to a fifth of national income. Still, the nineteenth-century tariff revenues constituted the main source of financing for federal projects and supported construction of roads and canals, maintenance of defense forces, and payment of veterans' pensions until the Civil War.

· 5 ·

FROM THE CIVIL WAR
TO THE
GREAT DEPRESSION

On the night of October 16, 1859, John Brown, dreaming of an abolitionist republic in the Appalachians, led a small force of thirteen whites and five Negroes and seized the federal armory at Harpers Ferry, a small town in what was then Virginia. A day later, Colonel Robert E. Lee arrived at the head of a company of U.S. Marines and arrested Brown and his men. On December 2, 1859, after a trial in Charles Town, Virginia, John Brown was hanged for treason against the Commonwealth of Virginia.

DIVERGING NORTH-SOUTH ECONOMIES

Brown's famous raid had not come out of the blue. America's expansion into its new western territories had raised the issue of whether new states would be free or slave. The states' rights position, increasingly synonymous with that of the southern states, was that new states should determine whether they would be free or slave. The conflict between southern and northern states, however, was bound up with economic and fiscal issues as well.

During the 1850s, an east-west trade axis developing between the industrial northeast and western farmers, who relied increasingly on new machinery to replace labor, had begun to make the old plantation agrarianism of the South increasingly irrelevant to the emerging national economy. By the middle of the century, not only slavery but the labor-intensive southern agriculture had come to symbolize the growing alienation between two American nations. On the one side was the agrarian South, with its attachment to Jeffersonian principles of small federal government and self-reliance. On the other side was the industrial North, with its attachment to the trappings of enterprise and the Hamiltonian belief in big government buttressed by a strong central bank to expedite commerce and to help manage debt. To northerners, these institutions were no longer merely optional for states that wanted them but essential to a modern economy, which was growing ever more specialized and therefore interdependent.

Once slavery had become economically redundant, the moral dimension, especially in northeastern and western states, became more pronounced. Though moderates condemned John Brown's act of extremism against slavery as injudicious, even for a noble cause, the poet Ralph Waldo Emerson spoke for growing numbers in the North who believed that the "new saint" Brown would in death "make the gallows glorious like the cross."

The increasing political and moral pressure against slavery that finally helped bring about the Civil War grew partly out of the very Jeffersonianism that was invoked by the southern slaveholders. Thomas Jefferson's vision of a self-sufficient agrarian America with a minimal federal government and an emphasis on states' rights, together with its influence on James Monroe, James Madison, and Andrew Jackson, had retarded the growth of strong federal institutions that might have been able to bring together the economies of the North and the South. The Civil War was, in the context of our central story about debt and taxes, a symbol of the inadequacy by 1850 of Jefferson's utopian vision for America as the basis for a coherent nation-state.

The economic wedge between North and South cut deeper as the nineteenth century progressed. Northern manufacturers benefited from the high level of protection afforded by high tariffs against competing British manufacturers. The expansion of capital-intensive output by the textile mills and manufacturers in the Northeast enhanced the return on their machines and buildings.

While the high tariff protected northern manufacturers and enhanced their profits, it forced southern states to buy most of their manufactured goods from the North by making most imports—like those from Britain, the South's favored trading partner—prohibitively expensive. Beyond that, for southerners both the tariff-financed federal government and tariff-protected northern economic strength grew at their expense to threaten states' rights and their way of life, which was based on the sale of agricultural products to Britain in exchange for supplies of the trappings of southern gentility. The attachment of both Jefferson and Hamilton to tariffs as ideal revenue sources would not have been well received in the southern states at mid-century. Indeed, from the South's perspective, they smacked of the taxation without representation over which the War of Independence had been fought just seventy-five years earlier.

Unsurprisingly, then, a major aim of the newly established Confederacy was to make New Orleans, Charleston, and Savannah low-tariff ports. Through these ports would pass goods that could be shipped to the new western states (today's Midwest) at prices that would undercut the price of manufactured goods produced in the Northeast. The superior European goods that entered through southern ports would also, of course, be available in the southern states at lower prices than those resulting from the galling tariffs that protected northern manufacturers.

The Confederacy's low-tariff ports were a threat not only to the primary source of federal revenues but to the existence of America's manufacturing industries in the Northeast. The moral, antislavery side of the Civil War may have been primary in the debate, but at least as important in the policy formation was the opposition of northern business enterprise to a move by the southern states toward what today would be called free trade. The Confederates, however, had not read and absorbed Ricardo's famous treatise on comparative advantage, the best early statement of the advantages of free trade. Rather, they simply realized that a tariff-financed federal government was anathema to their own interests and indeed to their very survival.

The election of Lincoln was the death knell for the United States as it had existed since the Revolution. During his debates with Stephen Douglas in the 1858 campaign for the U.S. Senate, Lincoln had eloquently set forth his view that states' rights did not include the right of a state to choose between slave or free status. In so doing, Lincoln lost the senatorial seat to Douglas, but gained a key boost for the White House. In the presidential election, Lincoln carried every free state but New Jersey, which he lost on a divided vote. In southern states, he received not a single electoral vote.

Lincoln's victory tied the North's economic interest in high protective tariffs to its moralism about slavery. As in the Revolutionary War, moral principles on both sides—opposition to slavery in the North and abhorrence of taxation without representation in the South—brought the nation to war. But these moral issues overlay the self-interests. The continuation of tariffs would eventually have ruined slave-based agrarian agriculture, yet their rescission would have severely disadvantaged northern manufacturers and eliminated the major source of federal revenue.

Lincoln had been chosen president by the northern states with the realization that states of the Deep South, at least, might well secede from the Union. The Confederacy, too, seemed eager for the war to begin. The opening shots of the Civil War were fired by Confederate forces at Fort Sumter, a garrison for federal troops acting as support for U.S. customs officers on an island in the harbor of Charleston. No doubt the act of firing on the agents of the hated tariff gave special pleasure to the soldiers of the Confederacy, then America's incipient free-trade republic. The four staff officers sent by Confederate General P. G. T. Beauregard to demand the surrender of Fort Sumter declined a request by the fort's commander, Major Robert Anderson (who had been Beauregard's star artillery student at West Point), to surrender with honor after two days, when the garrison's food would be exhausted. Instead, they gave, on their own responsibility, orders to fire. On April 12, 1861, at 4:30 A.M., the Civil War began.

DEFINING AMERICA

The Civil War would be the defining event of two centuries of American life —in fiscal as much as in political and social history. The financial demands of the war resulted in the sharpest increase in the national debt in the nation's history before World War II. It resulted in much higher tariffs and the creation of a national central bank, the forerunner of the Federal Reserve System. It was also a decisive repudiation of Jefferson's moral-agrarian view of America, and it established the preeminence of industry over agriculture in America's economic future.

With the huge increase in interest-bearing national debt fed by the war effort, massive issues of greenbacks—paper money—were used to supplement the Union's tremendous need for cash to reclaim the Confederacy. The Confederacy, too, relied heavily on the issuance of paper money to finance its war effort. After the war, Confederate money was worthless, and southerners suffered the common fate of losers in wars financed by printing money. A similar policy in Germany during World War I resulted in hyperinflation—1,000+ percent increases in prices—that wiped out the assets of the middle class after this war was lost.

Economic events just before the Civil War confronted the federal government with especially pressing fiscal problems. The panic of 1857 resulted in the following three years in large deficits, which grew because of the modest revenues accruing to the federal government under the Democrats' policy of low tariffs. When Lincoln confronted this problem and the prospect of the massive debts to be generated by the war, he and his treasury secretary, Salmon Chase, were forced to formulate a new series of fiscal policies and to restructure the nation's financial arrangements to give the federal government more flexibility and control over them. The policy change began with the 1861 Morrill Act, which put into effect the new and higher tariffs generally favored by Republican policies. But the high tariffs did not generate surpluses, as they had in previous decades; they merely slowed slightly the massive increase in debt that the war engendered.

Tariffs high enough to finance wars contained the seeds of their own destruction, for they eventually became counterproductive. As American manufacturers became better able to compete in world markets, high tariffs impeded the movement of their goods into European markets. Governments in England and on the Continent were not inclined to admit American goods freely if two-way trade was impossible. By 1860, narrowly based tariffs had been clearly exposed as a primitive form of taxation. The broadly based income tax, which generated far more revenue than high tariffs with low tax rates, was the wave of the future.

One response of Treasury Secretary Chase, albeit a delayed one, was to turn to internal taxes—both a progressive income tax and an inheritance tax. Before that, however, the administration suspended specie payments, distributed paper money—greenbacks—to pay for the war through three legal-tender acts, and relied on huge direct enforced borrowing from banks and the public. To protect the currency and to limit hoarding of specie, the administration left the gold standard in 1861. The government also recentralized the banking system through the National Banking Act. This created a system of federally chartered national banks that were in competition with local banks and were able to issue national bank notes.

These policies, which Congress agreed to only because of the horrendous costs of the war, had far-reaching consequences after the war. As James Savage notes:

> First, the high tariffs used to generate revenues to finance the debt created huge budget surpluses after the war. These surpluses enabled the federal government to expand its support for federal improvements and other expenditures far beyond the level permitted by the Jacksonian Democrats in antebellum America. Second, the federal government's efforts to contract the greenback money supply and return to the gold standard sparked the Populist movement in rural America and the Democratic silver movement in the west. Third, the national banking system developed into the Federal Reserve System. . . . The reality of total war, the economic evolution in industrialization, and Republican party policies turned the United States from its preindustrial heritage.[1]

Between 1861 and 1866, the national debt grew from $90 million to $2.75 billion. That remarkable thirtyfold increase in just five years increased the ratio of debt to national income from 2 percent to more than 50 percent. The twenty-five-fold increase in the ratio of debt to national income was the most rapid ever to occur in American history and, along with rising inflation, produced enormous upward pressure on interest rates.

The share of federal spending devoted to interest payments on the national debt jumped from 8.9 percent in 1860 to almost 25 percent in 1866. This was the highest proportion since the 50 percent plus level in 1789. The ratio of national debt to GNP was nearly ten percentage points higher in 1866 than in 1789, when the new federal government took on the Revolutionary War debts. Even though federal taxes during the Civil War amounted to an unprecedented 10 percent of national income, the debt increased even faster.

Even World War II produced a less dramatic drain of federal revenues into interest on the debt. The ratio of debt to GNP slightly more than doubled from about 50 percent in 1942 to 122 percent in 1945. But thanks to the mighty income tax—together with tax withholding from paychecks, which had begun during the war—federal revenues jumped from just over 7 percent of GNP in 1941 to 23.5 percent of GNP in 1945. This figure was well above the postwar average of about 18 percent. After World War II, however, and despite its huge increase in government debt, the share of federal revenue going to pay interest on the debt actually fell from more than 13 percent in 1941 to less than 10 percent in 1945 because of the massive wartime revenue surge and the interest-rate ceilings on government bonds.

NEW PATTERNS OF FEDERAL SPENDING

The federal government was never the same after the Civil War. Its aftermath vindicated Jefferson's fears that high taxes (tariffs and excise taxes) would lead to ever-growing government, more government officials, and more and more people, including pensioners, on the government payroll.

Just as the states' rights legacy of Jefferson had by 1860 been stretched until it threatened the Union, so after the Civil War was the Republican policy of high protective tariffs stretched to its limits. After sixty years of financing pensions, public works, and a growing list of projects undertaken to buy off opposition to them, tariffs proved inadequate to their task. Federal obligations had become so extensive that only a federal income tax could provide enough tax revenue to meet them.

Before the war, federal outlays had risen as high as $65 million. After the war, they never dipped below $240 million, through Republican and Democratic administrations and Congresses. Spending went up in almost every category, and some new categories were introduced. Spending increased sharply on rivers and harbors, bridges, roads, public buildings, and lighthouses. Before the war, there had been no federal role in railroad development; after the war, the federal government introduced subsidies and other policies to encourage railroad construction and expansion. Army pensions also accounted for a significant share of the increase in federal spending. Before the war, pensions were a tiny share of the budget. By 1880, pensions accounted for 21 percent of the total federal budget. They mushroomed to 34 percent in 1890. Even in 1900, four decades after the war, they came to a full 27 percent of the federal budget.

The stresses and strains in the governmental process caused by these new and increased federal expenditures eventually brought about major congressional budget reform. The budgetary and spending power hitherto wielded by the House Appropriations Committee was decentralized and parceled out to several authorizing committees.

After the Civil War, the Whig Republicans inaugurated what today would be called a tax-and-spend policy. This change was intended partly to rationalize the protective tariff and partly to undertake new public works and capital improvements. During the Civil War, tariffs were sharply increased along with excise taxes to help pay for the war. The average tariff rate on dutiable imports in 1861 was about 19 percent. By 1865, it had risen to 48 percent. This high level of duty was retained for a number of years after the war to help pay the large accumulation of debt. But the Republicans were also anxious to maintain high protective barriers behind which the war-vitalized industrial North planned, more actively and consciously than Clay and Calhoun ever had, to expand into a huge national market behind high tariff walls.

In 1883, the economist Henry George wrote, "We are spending great sums on useless 'public improvements' and are paying pensions under a law which seems framed but to put a premium upon fraud and get away with public money. And yet the great questions before Congress is what to do with the surplus."

George wrote at a time of structural change in Congress that sharply decentralized spending authority, from a penurious Appropriations Committee to substantive committees that chafed at the vast power concentrated in one committee, and were eager to spend burgeoning federal revenue surpluses, and more. It started in 1877, when the House Commerce Committee reported the rivers and harbors bill; instead of referring it to the Appropriations Committee, as in other years, Representative John H. Reagan of Texas moved to suspend the rules and pass the bill. Suspension of the rules, used for noncontroversial measures, required a two-thirds vote, normally unavailable for anything as important and precedential as bypassing the appropriations process. But there was a wider appeal for this approach than Appropriations Committee Chairman Samuel Randall imagined—after all, it avoided "the dreaded pruning knife of a disinterested arbiter."[2]

The precedent of allowing the Commerce Committee to usurp the Appropriations panel on rivers and harbors appropriations was repeated the next year, and then, over the next several years, extended to other areas, including agriculture in 1880, and a slew of areas, from army, navy, military-academy, and Indian affairs to the post office, postal roads, and consular and diplomatic appropriations, in 1885. The Senate followed this pattern fourteen years later. It took the momentum of the First World War and the need for severe budget restraint in its aftermath, to return to a more centralized, and disciplined, spending approach in Congress.[3]

The Civil War marked an end to the Jeffersonian traditions on which spending grew only during wartime and shrank again in peacetime, when government functions would be expected to consume only about 2 percent of national income. Yet the post–Civil War Republican consolidation would not altogether have pleased Hamilton or other eighteenth- and early-nineteenth-century Whigs. America in the last three decades of the nineteenth century was becoming economically and therefore politically isolationist. American business contemplated the growth of a huge national market in which there was no need to consider restrictions on trade as limits to economic growth, as England had. The symbol of the new great national market was the completion of the transcontinental railroad at Promontory Point, Utah Territory, in 1869, when the Central Pacific came eastward from California to join the Union Pacific line, moving westward from Nebraska. The first American transcontinental rail line initiated the world's greatest customs union, the continental United States of America, with no customs barriers between and among its states and high (40 to 45 percent) customs rates protecting its producers from foreign competition.

Jefferson's image of an unspoiled, agrarian America composed of many self-sufficient farms had held sway from 1800 until the Civil War, with a brief interruption during and immediately after the War of 1812. After 1865, it was replaced by the vision derived from Hamilton and adopted by the Republican party: an America dominated by American business enterprise, which bought from and sold to other Americans. The buying and selling flowed smoothly across state boundaries behind high tariff walls that impeded entrance into the American market by goods from the rest of the world. America's common language, currency, and transport system, augmented in 1869 by the new transcontinental rail system, created a massive common market a century before the Europe version.

Eventually, the high tariff walls, designed to shield American producers in the world's first common market under a single government, became unsustainable. The high tariffs helped American manufacturers at the expense of American consumers. For a time, the tariff's unpopularity with this group was limited by the expanding public works and pension programs it made possible. Many American workers were also willing to pay higher prices to protect their own jobs, even though, as they discovered after World War II, these would have been unaffected by more open markets. Tax-and-spend was invented at the federal level by nineteenth-century Republicans anxious to buy off resistance to high tariffs. Their belief in limited government was compromised by their perceived need for the tariff, and with the introduction of the income tax, which became inevitable as a fiscal tool. As more and more Americans became affected by or dependent upon federal programs financed by high tariff revenues, the demands on federal revenue even began to outgrow tariff rates of 45 percent.

The source of the pressure for the income tax was twofold. First, there was the desire to continue and to expand government programs, which had begun to generate their own growth, just as Jefferson had feared. Second, huge fortunes were amassed by the owners of American capital, who were protected by high tariffs and able to sell into a huge captive marketplace as the transcontinental railroad opened a great land mass. These fortunes were to become the target of an income tax tied to a reduction in tariffs.

The high tariffs of the nineteenth century were especially burdensome on lower- and middle-income taxpayers—the workingmen and -women they were supposed to protect. The 45 percent duty is almost incredible when compared with today's duties of 3 to 5 percent. The tariff amounted to a selective consumption tax, levied at a high rate on imported goods, which enabled American producers to charge higher prices for their goods. In the same way, import quotas today on foreign steel and autos push up prices of American automobiles and steel. Spending on dutiable items comprises a larger share of the income of lower- and middle-income individuals than of the wealthy, so the effective tax rate created by import duties is higher for lower-income individuals. This meets the definition of a regressive tax.

The regressive nature of tariffs and excise taxes employed to raise federal revenue during the nineteenth century was intensified by their disparate effects on labor and capital. Since most of America's protected industries were capital-intensive manufacturers, output of manufactured goods in the United States was greater than it would have been without the tariff. This created an extra demand for capital, as the capital-intensive manufacturing sector was artificially expanded. The tariff-induced extra demand for capital enhanced the return to the capital owned by higher-income Americans while the tax burden on higher-income Americans was reduced by the tariff.

Thus, just as the tariff had a double impact on the South before the Civil War, the tariff and the artificial expansion of manufacturing production created a double tax burden on lower- and middle-income taxpayers relative to the wealthy after the Civil War. But the twin burdens of the tariff were for some time too well hidden to provide Democrats with a political issue to use against Republicans.

By 1890, fiscal policy was caught in a vicious circle. The steady growth of federal spending—undertaken in large part to justify high tariffs—led to higher deficits which in turn created the need to finance rising federal spending with higher tariffs. One result was the McKinley tariff, under which the average tariff rate rose toward 50 percent. The cycle of tax, spend, and tax some more was completed.

Partly in reaction to the double burden of higher tariffs on the poor and the middle class, the Democratic administration of Grover Cleveland in 1894 introduced the Wilson-Gorham tariff, which cut tariff rates and provided for an income tax. The cry of soak the rich was applied both to individuals and to corporations; the Wilson-Gorham bill levied a 2 percent tax on all incomes above $4,000. The bill passed the Congress but was declared unconstitutional by the Supreme Court in 1895.

In parallel with the economic developments acquainted with tariff and tax-and-spend policies, other economic effects resulted from the unusual era of deflation in the United States after the Civil War. In 1869, Congress enacted the Public Credit Act, which in effect returned the United States to the gold standard. Greenbacks—$356 million in paper used in Civil War financing—were left in circulation, but no more were printed. As the economy grew, the money supply did not. The resulting scarcity of money caused prices to fall for most of the two decades after the Civil War.

The hard-money practices of the Republicans after the Civil War and the insistence on convertibility of paper money into specie, together with the limitation on the issue of bank notes, produced a paradoxical Jeffersonianism. By pegging the price of gold and limiting the issue of money, the Republicans were following policies that a hard-money advocate like Jefferson would have approved. But by pegging the price of gold too low and thereby causing the supply of money to contract, Republican policies caused a deflation that hurt the indebted agrarian sector. The return to the gold standard and the slowdown in the availability of new gold meant that the money stock grew slowly, if at all, during the 1870s and 1880s. A long period of deflation, punctuated by the bank panic of 1873, and a severe depression from 1873 to 1879—the longest recorded economic contraction in American history—created pressure to expand the money supply.

Demand for more money took the form of movements either to allow convertibility between gold and silver at a price that would put more silver into circulation or to break away from the gold standard altogether. This pressure originated in the real burden placed on debtors, mainly in the agrarian Midwest and South. Just as debtors benefit from inflation by repaying their loans in cheaper dollars, the debtors who had contracted to pay back their loans in dollars at the beginning of this deflationary period found that falling prices added to the real burden of their debt. They had to pay back in dollars that were worth more than they had been when the debts were contracted.[4]

POPULISTS AND PROGRESSIVES

The economic hardship caused by deflation and the increasing value of real debt in some agricultural areas gave rise to the Populist movement. Its central prescription was to follow or to restore policies to end deflation and to push prices back up. The movement was also based on resentment of bankers and the rich in general, since the positive impact of deflation on lenders at the expense of borrowers compounded the regressive effects, in terms of income distribution, of the high-tariff policies throughout the late nineteenth century.

The Populist movement peaked in 1896, when William Jennings Bryan ran against William McKinley for the first time. Bryan had shot to prominence in 1896 with his famous "cross of gold" speech to the Democratic National Convention. The target of his anger was the burden that deflation and, by implication, the gold standard imposed upon his strongest supporters in the Midwest and South. But Bryan lost twice to McKinley. In 1901, a year after his second victory, McKinley was shot by an anarchist at the Pan-American Exposition in Buffalo; Teddy Roosevelt, a leader of the Progressive Republicans, became president, representing a sharp change from Whig philosophy.

With its social upheaval, massive deficits, and federal victory over states' rights, the Civil War had brought about dramatic and enduring change in the nation's political equilibrium. The Republican party had decimated the Democrats, and its "New Whiggery," as historian Louis Hartz characterized it, of high tariffs, huge budget surpluses, major public expenditures, and greenback money blurred some of the original Jeffersonian-Hamiltonian distinctions. Again, Savage:

> Like Hamilton, the Republicans sought to promote and protect industries, chiefly located in the North and Midwest, through a system of high tariffs. These tariffs were not always popular, as they were considered by many small merchants and farmers—regardless of political affiliation— to be a direct subsidy for the wealthy manufacturing interests which provided them with an unfair advantage in the marketplace. To . . . legitimize the need for high tariffs, the Republicans dramatically increased public expenditures in the late nineteenth century. By spending at such a rate that the government might be forced into running deficits, tariffs were made to appear as a national necessity for providing revenues to balance the budget and to retire the national debt.[5]

What made this Whiggery new? In contrast to old Whigs like Henry Clay and Daniel Webster, the postwar Republicans used the Jeffersonian philosophy of limited government to promote the tariff-based industrial policy of Hamilton. The new Whigs' political hegemony from the Civil War to the Great Depression institutionalized Hamiltonian policies, which were justified with Jeffersonian rhetoric.

The period from 1861 to 1932 saw additional growth in the federal bureaucracy, a permanent system of protective tariffs, centralized banking, federal funding for internal improvements, and the use of budget deficits and surpluses for economic and political ends. The new Whigs promoted and protected the manufacturing industry, often at the expense of agrarian interests, and used huge budget surpluses produced by high tariffs to increase government spending without being vilified for unbalancing the budget. Their policies, dominant for seventy years, were entirely consistent with the goals outlined by Hamilton in his *Report on the Public Credit*.

Around the turn of the century, however, new Whig Republicanism was challenged, and for a time superseded, by Progressive Republicanism. The Progressive movement affected both political parties, but it most clearly altered the Republicans. Emerging in the 1870s, as industrialization took off, progressivism took root as a Midwest-based reform movement in cities such as Detroit and Toledo, where reactions against slum-based poverty and political machines and unsafe factories emerged as a major political force in the 1890s. Robert La Follette's term as governor of Wisconsin (1901–1906) was a model for the ideas and philosophy of progressivism; the La Follette administration passed political reforms (an antilobbying law, a direct primary law), economic reforms (state banking control), and antibusiness reforms (higher taxes on corporations, a rate-setting railroad commission).

Progressives railed against the excess power of trusts and corporate wealth, which they saw as Hamiltonian capitalism run rampant, and found themselves in constant conflict with conservative or Whig Republicans. The Progressives' only president, Theodore Roosevelt, managed to implement a substantial share of the movement's program, including antitrust laws, railroad regulation, and food, drug, and meat inspection; he advocated a progressive income tax. But every step of the way, he fought with a Congress dominated by conservatives of his own party, who were led in the House of Representatives by speaker Joe Cannon.

Progressives distrusted big business and regular party politics, but unlike the Jefferson-Jackson Populists, they were not at all uneasy about a strong federal government. They believed that the influences of corrupt practices and machine politics could be purged and that the power of government could be harnessed for such socially useful ends as curbing the power of the trusts. The ideal of the Progressives was a clean government, free of the taint of trusts or bosses, run by the spirit and science of administrative efficiency, the new science of public administration.

Theodore Roosevelt was succeeded in 1908 by his vice president, William Howard Taft, whose disdain for the Progressives led Roosevelt to challenge him four years later as an insurgent candidate of the progressive Bull Moose party. The Republican split resulted in the election of the Democrat Woodrow Wilson. But even the conservative Taft had embraced the ideal of administrative efficiency; spurred by the Progressives, he created the Commission on Economy and Efficiency, which resulted in major budget reform in 1921.

The Progressive movement also helped to bring about the permanent income tax. In 1909, conservative Republicans tried a tactical maneuver to sidetrack a corporate income tax by promoting as an alternative a constitutional amendment for a general income tax. Many believed that the long ratification process in the states would doom it. The amendment passed Congress, and when Progressive Republicans and Democrats gained control of many state legislatures in 1912, the amendment was soon ratified. The progressive income tax, along with antitrust reforms, the secret ballot, and the direct primary, became the legacies of the Progressive movement, which faded as a serious threat to the two-party system soon after the Bull Moose uprising in 1912.

CRACKS IN THE ECONOMY

The early twentieth century witnessed the development of large cracks in the high-tariff, deflationary regime of late-nineteenth-century America. The panic of 1907 revealed the need for a central bank to control the total level of credit in the economy. In 1909, the federal budget deficit reached $89.4 million, the largest peacetime deficit in nominal dollars up to that point. By this time, the income redistribution implicit in high tariff rates was obvious; tariffs could no longer be used to meet the ever-escalating revenue needs of a federal government that continued to depend, into the twentieth century, on the tax-and-spend policies of the nineteenth century.

The 1907 economic disaster led, as has so often been the case, to major structural reform. In 1913, as we have noted, Congress passed the Federal Reserve Act to create a central bank. That same year saw both the Underwood tariff, which smashed the Republican protective tariffs that had been in place since 1861, and the ratification of the Sixteenth Amendment to the Constitution, by which an income tax was introduced to replace and to augment the lost tariff revenue.

The 1913 reforms were precipitated by new president Woodrow Wilson, whose Democratic party had taken full control of Congress even as he swept into office to become the first Democratic president in sixteen years. Wilson's worldview dictated his domestic economic policy; his assertive internationalism called for sweeping reductions in tariffs, but Democratic party ideology required some replacement for the forgone revenues. Thus the Underwood-Simmons Tariff Act included a progressive income tax, targeted at the rich.[6] Separately, responding to unease after the economic crisis, the Wilsonian Democrats created the Federal Reserve System and, the following year, reformed the Sherman Act to stiffen antitrust laws, while creating a Federal Trade Board to regulate interstate business except for railroads.

These changes reflected a dynamic, progressive orientation that was closer in some ways to Theodore Roosevelt's approach in the 1912 campaign than to Wilson's—and certainly was a sharp departure from the traditional Republican view of William Howard Taft. The changes defined Wilson's first term in the area of domestic policy, at least, while polarizing the minority Republican party, isolating its Progressive wing and leaving the traditionalists basically in charge. In a broader way, the policy and process changes of the Wilson era signaled a clear end to the deflationary, high-tariff period that followed the Civil War.

During that period, the Republican strategy had been to tax with tariffs and then to spend the proceeds to justify the high tariffs. Once the income tax was in place, this strategy was quickly abandoned. Clearly, an income tax would provide any additional revenues that were needed over and above the reduced revenues available from tariffs. The burden of tariffs was still high by later standards, as the Underwood tariff set the average rate at about 30 percent. With one grave exception (the Republican Hawley-Smoot Tariff Act signed by President Herbert Hoover on June 17, 1930), further growth of federal spending would be financed by income taxes levied more heavily than tariffs had been on wealthy Americans and on corporations. The 1913 income tax called for graduated taxes of 1 to 6 percent on incomes of $4,000 or more for both individuals and corporations. The new emphasis of the Progressive Republicans was a balanced budget as a symbol of the efficiency of government. Progressive tax burdens made for Progressive Republicans, dedicated to paring federal spending, though not necessarily the federal role in the economy. The Republican aim now was to constrain progressive income taxes, not to rationalize higher protective tariffs. Still, many traditional Republicans never got over their attachment to the protectionist aspects of higher tariffs, and when the going got rough in 1930, Representative Willis Hawley and Senator Reed Smoot reverted, with disastrous consequences, to form.

For the Progressive Republicans, the commonsense concept of a balanced budget, made politically appealing by frequent analogies with family finance, came to replace the pre–Civil War, Jefferson-Jackson theme of corruption from big government as the cornerstone of their philosophy of fiscal responsibility. At the same time, ideological resistance to big government weakened. Federal spending was viewed as all right as long as it was efficiently administered. The convenient corollary for the Republicans was that too much spending led to inefficiency, a theme rejuvenated by the Grace Commission during the 1980s. But Republicans lacked an effective Jeffersonian antidote to big-government policies until Ronald Reagan articulated the supply-side case for lower tax rates in 1980.

World War I dramatically expanded deficits and debt once again and compounded the problem of debt accumulation after the depression of 1907. Taxes were increased sharply because of the war, and the newly implemented individual and corporate income taxes became the major vehicles for expan-

sion. The personal income tax expanded in scope and also changed in substance. As political scientist John Witte notes:

> The First World War had an important impact on the income tax, trans-
> forming it from a highly contested but insignificant form of revenue into
> a major tax. Rate and provision adjustments made over several years
> turned what was almost a proportional tax into one with a highly progres-
> sive nominal rate structure.[7]

Tax rates were raised to previously unimaginable heights—as great as
77 percent for incomes over $1 million—although as Witte adds, "the tax
never reached the majority of citizens." Nevertheless, by the end of the war,
after the corporate tax was augmented with an excess-profits provision and
personal income-tax rates and exemptions were adjusted, the resulting revenues had made the twin income taxes the source of more than half of all
federal revenue.[8] Spending went up as taxes went up, but spending went up
far more. In fiscal 1916, the federal government spent $713 million while
raising $761 million, for a surplus of $48 million. In fiscal 1917, the federal
government's revenues went up to $1.1 billion—but spending climbed to
more than $1.9 billion, for a deficit of $853 million.

At the peak of the war's effects on America's finances, in 1918 and 1919,
the deficits reached what were for the time gigantic proportions, even though
revenues, especially from income tax, soared. Revenues were $3.6 billion in
1918 and more than $5 billion the next year; expenditures in the two years
were $12.6 billion and $18.5 billion, respectively. Thus in only two years a
deficit of more than $22 billion was created, and public debt increased by
more than 800 percent. The ratio of debt to GNP rose from 4.9 percent in
1917 to 30.3 percent just two years later. Still, the rise in tax revenues was
sharp enough to keep interest on the huge debt increase from absorbing
much more than 20 percent of GNP.

Management of the war effort also expanded the size and scope of the
federal government. For the first time, for example, the federal government
began to play an aggressive role in agriculture. The Food Administration was
created in 1917 and placed under the direction of Herbert Hoover; it guaranteed a minimum price on wheat through government-coordinated purchases
and sales and acted to raise the production of hogs by fixing the price at a
higher level.

In a more general way, World War I forced the government to use a series
of precedents for federal control of the economy that had been established

after the 1907 depression. Interventionist legislation in place before the war, like the Clayton Act, the Federal Trade Commission Act, and the Federal Reserve Act, was employed to an unprecedented degree during the war. And after the war, things did not change dramatically. In 1920, during the period of "normalcy" that followed, Treasury Secretary David Houston noted:

> The first impulse of many was to turn to the Government and especially to the Treasury, as the sole instrumentality for full economic salvation. This disposition, well developed before the war, was reinforced during hostilities by practices of the Government which became necessary for the successful prosecution of the war. It is this disposition, rather than self-aggrandizing efforts of Federal departments to extend their functions, which is the main explanation of mounting Federal budgets and of centralizing tendencies frequently criticized.[9]

Nevertheless, there was a certain amount of normalcy in America's postwar return to isolationism and business as usual. The big difference, compared with the prewar period, was the American discovery of stock ownership. Americans, in a nation that had become rich seemingly without the effort that had always been required throughout history, indulged themselves in a collective fantasy that owning stocks meant owning Park Avenue apartments and country estates in only a few years for anyone with a little market savvy. Unfortunately, reality reasserted itself in 1929.

THE 1929 WATERSHED

The stock market crashed in October 1929. The crash's devastating effects on the economy were exacerbated by the Federal Reserve. Although put in place to prevent the compounding of financial panic in the private sector, the Fed did exactly the reverse. It cut the money supply instead of increasing it. The Fed's confusion about how to avoid compounding a massive erasure of the paper wealth that had been administered by fickle security markets, together with financial collapse in Europe, brought on the Great Depression. Fortunately, the Fed did not repeat the error of the early 1930s in the wake of the stock market crash of October 1987.

As if the Fed's bungling was not bad enough, the Republican party's reaction to the prospect of larger federal deficits was to revert to its nineteenth-century form and to pass the Hawley-Smoot Tariff Act in June 1930. That measure not only produced the negative effects—higher prices and regressive tax burdens—already associated with high tariffs but led to retaliatory measures abroad, all of which added to the length and depth of the Depression. Incredibly, tariff rates that had hovered around 38 to 40 percent during the 1920s rose to almost 60 percent with the Hawley-Smoot tariff. The disastrous effects on trade were obvious, yet little effort was made to reduce tariff rates until after World War II. Probably the extreme isolationism after World War I was aggravated by the Depression, which in turn led to more isolationism. Only when the cost became all but ruinous to the country did people wake up.

Despite the cycles of war and recession that led to an expanded scope for government, the federal government in the watershed year of 1929 was closer to its scope and size in 1800 than to its position twenty years later, after a depression and another world war. These events transformed the government in Washington, D.C., into a true national government, hailed by some as the architect of great economic and social progress and bitterly opposed by others as the major impediment to the same ends. The high point of the federal government as a primary mover in economic and social policy was Lyndon Johnson's Great Society, which he superimposed on what proved to be America's most hated war, Vietnam. The reaction to what postwar America had come to see as too much government was the credo stated in Ronald Reagan's 1981 inaugural address: "Government is not the solution to our problem; government is the problem."

From the Revolutionary War until the onset of the Great Depression, American fiscal policy was dominated by competing appeals to morality and pragmatism. The Hamiltonian tradition established early in the life of the new American Republic the tendency toward strong central government, justified on practical grounds; the usefulness of a well-managed policy of federal debt accumulation and reduction; and the need for a strong central bank. Equally, the Jeffersonian, agrarian, moral tradition was established as the alternative. This eschews large federal government as essentially corrupt, allows for debt accumulation only to finance wars necessary for the survival of the Republic, advocates strongly the rapid extinction of debt, and shuns a strong central bank. Jefferson believed that no generation had the right to encumber another generation with its debts and therefore felt that a span of twenty years was appropriate to extinguish them.

The fifty years after the Civil War were dominated by Hamiltonian policies that would have been anathema to Jefferson, yet the fact that these were Republican policies seems strange to us in the light of subsequent events. Republicans provided the foundations of the modern, behemoth state with a tariff policy that increased federal spending; Republicans introduced the income tax, which served as the basis for much further expansion of government in the wake of the Depression and World War II. Yet when this expansion reached the point when some limits had to be reasserted, the nation turned to Republicans for a new Jeffersonianism. Instead of a reasoned and philosophical approach to the ideal scope of government, followed by a discussion of the tax levels needed to support it, Ronald Reagan reversed the order and cut taxes to limit the scope of government.

Thomas Jefferson, the spiritual father both of the modern Democratic party and of recent attempts to limit the size of government, would be stunned by the contemporary American polity so largely defined by the New Deal of Franklin Roosevelt and the Great Society of Lyndon Johnson. Thanks to the income tax, Roosevelt had the means for an immense expansion of the federal government into American life—which he carefully justified in terms of Jeffersonian principles. It took Ronald Reagan, the man who spoke like Jefferson and acted like Hamilton, to remind Americans that limits on federal power, if loose ones, are in fact presupposed in the American political tradition.

PART THREE

FROM THE NEW DEAL TO THE NEW FRONTIER

◆

⋆ 6 ⋆

FROM FDR
TO EISENHOWER

Although the United States had suffered economic turmoil during the panics of 1837, 1857, 1873, 1893, and 1907, none had so severe an impact on debt and taxes—and on the scope and size of government—as the Great Depression of the 1930s. The economic devastation and political changes it wrought over many years combined with new Keynesian ideas to create dramatic and long-lasting changes.

The Depression produced large budget deficits, unprecedented levels of unemployment, bank failures, and crashes of stock and commodity markets. Under President Herbert Hoover, the government responded to the stock market crash and ensuing economic problems with policies that had contradictory effects. The president, for example, pushed for more federal public works. Federal spending grew from $3.3 billion in 1929 to $4.7 billion in 1932. But Hoover was also determined to erase ballooning budget deficits. Herbert Stein has noted that Hoover was not an inflexible budget balancer; he recognized that the budget need not be balanced every year and hoped to implement tax cuts to stimulate the economy, even if they resulted in a temporary imbalance in the budget.[1] But as the Federal Reserve Board was pursuing a tight-money policy, Hoover felt that the federal borrowing required to achieve a tax cut would limit private-sector borrowing and cut off any recovery. He had an instinctive fear of crowding out, today's term for the pressure on credit markets arising from large federal deficits. Hoover therefore pressed Congress for a tax increase to cut budget deficits.

If Hoover was no reflexive balancer, Franklin D. Roosevelt was no automatic Keynesian. On the campaign trail in 1932, and in the White House in 1933, he also called for a balanced budget and tried to reduce federal spending in 1933 by cutting veterans' benefits and federal salaries. While Roosevelt clung to the dogma of budget balancing for several years, the relentless pressures of unemployment and economic turmoil led policy in other directions. The basic federal response to the Depression was a broad expansion of government's presence in society and the economy, including the creation of the Federal Deposit Insurance Corporation (FDIC), the Works Progress Administration (WPA), and the other so-called alphabet agencies. The federal regulatory role was expanded with the creation of the Securities and Exchange Commission and the Federal Communications Commission. Social Security was arguably the most significant program in American history in terms of fiscal and social policy.

The upshot was a dramatic increase in the federal government's share of the economy. Discussing the Great Depression, economist Sidney Ratner and his colleagues note, "In that one decade of minimal economic growth the share of total goods and services purchased by government nearly doubled, while the share of government transfer payments more than tripled."[2]

The Depression permanently institutionalized the deep federal involvement in all aspects of the economy; it also created a direct role for economic theory, and economists, in creating and implementing what has come to be known as fiscal policy. Stein has called this the "fiscal revolution" in America, though we argue that the necessary conditions for a comprehensive fiscal revolution were not in place until after World War II. Still, the Depression moved America away from changes in policy or expansion of government largely as a response to crisis and toward a major role for government in the economy and in everyday life. In short, the Depression set the stage for government policy to expand or to change without the impetus of a major war. To some, the potential scope for government involvement in the economy seemed limitless. It remained for neo-Jeffersonians to define and to constrain that role.

Initially, simple inertia limited the growth of government. Depression-inspired policies, as part of a watershed era, seemed far more radical prospectively than they seem to today's analysts looking back over half a century. In 1928, four years before Roosevelt's election to the presidency and one year before the 1929 stock market crash, the federal government resembled what it had been in 1800 more than the institution it would become by 1948. Indeed, 1928 may have been the last year when an expanding role for government did not seem the normal way of responding to an emergency. The events after 1928 seemed to reinforce the notion that a market economy was too unstable to survive without being balanced by what was known at the time as big government. The dividing line, however, was much further from big government than from laissez faire during the four years before Roosevelt —and, indeed, during most of Roosevelt's presidency—than it was in 1980.

In the 1932 campaign, Roosevelt, representing the party of Jefferson, tried to reconcile the philosophical legacy of the previous seventy years with the modern realities of an industrialized society, the need to deal with desperate economic conditions, and his own instincts for action. FDR could not embrace Jefferson's deep distrust of centralized government—but neither did he want to identify his activist administration with the principles of Hamilton. Roosevelt grappled directly with this dilemma, finding refuge in the Jeffersonian themes of individualism and equality, while drawing on the Populist and Progressive movements that had shaped his political environment.

Roosevelt's approach to America's problems suggested a reliance on Jefferson's philosophy of equality of opportunity, linked to a faith in the competency of individuals. In Jefferson's day, anyone who wanted to earn a living was able to do so. Jefferson advocated a balance between government power and individual liberty. The government was charged with, and limited to, protecting that liberty—together with private property rights—while ensuring equality and opportunity.

But Roosevelt had to react against the growth of Hamiltonian-style government that had accompanied America's industrialization in the late nineteenth and early twentieth centuries. A stronger federal government, increasingly dominated by the interests of business, had in Roosevelt's eyes distorted government power into an instrument of social and economic inequality. The power of capital took precedence over the rights and liberties of common men. A strong but enlightened administration could provide a counterbalance to this tendency, Roosevelt suggested, eliminating the inequality and privilege fostered by Hamiltonianism and restoring Jeffersonian ideals.

By stressing what could be construed as the class conflict implied in the Hamilton-Jefferson dichotomy—business and the princes of privilege versus the common or forgotten man—and not the issue of the size and role of centralized government (and by continuing to preach the value and necessity of a balanced budget), Roosevelt rationalized his policy with the philosophical legacy of his party, even if what we might call his new Jeffersonianism was at best a hybrid. Still, his need to rationalize or to explain his own philosophical approach in these terms demonstrates clearly the power of ideas in the making of American public policy—a power that was to be demonstrated fifty years later by Ronald Reagan.[3]

A NEW DEAL IN ECONOMICS

Roosevelt's inauguration in March 1933 and the famous One Hundred Days that followed marked the beginning of the modern federal government. Roosevelt's conduct of tax, budget, monetary, and regulatory policies was critical to the operation of the economy as a whole and affected specific industries and firms operating within it.

The emergencies that had created the crisis had come quickly during the presidency of Herbert Hoover. Hoover was ill equipped to deal with them, partly because of his close attachment to economic policies that sprang from political necessity and were inadequate to changed characteristics and partly because of the modest resources at the disposal of the federal government. The stock market crash of October 1929, the Hawley-Smoot tariff of June 1930, the abandonment of the gold standard by Britain in 1931, and the subsequent abortive attempt by the Federal Reserve to defend the dollar's link to gold until suspension of the gold standard in March of 1933—all constituted a massive cumulative shock to the American economy. Their impact was reinforced by the policy architects' lack of understanding of the nature and severity of their errors—errors that had caused a series of self-reinforcing negative pressures on America's banks and factories. These events seem to have preordained a deep and long depression; yet viewed retrospectively, the Great Depression was anything but an ever-lurking menace waiting to waylay the economy. On the contrary, it required an almost incredible stream of wrongheaded, harmful policy moves before it could happen.

In the face of these economic calamities, largely the result of mistakes in monetary policy, the question of whether the federal government should or could try to right the economy with offsetting budget or tax policies was irrelevant. The federal fiscal presence was far too small to have much of an effect. In 1931, almost twenty years after the passage of an income tax, federal revenues were about 4 percent of GNP, or a fifth of their level in the 1970s and 1980s. And a fifth of that went not to pay for government services but to pay some of the federal debt accumulated during World War I.

In 1917, the federal debt stood at just below 5 percent of GNP, while interest on the debt consumed about 7.5 percent of federal revenues. Just two years later, the ratio of federal debt to GNP had jumped to more than 30 percent and interest on the debt consumed more than 20 percent of federal revenues. More than a decade later, in 1931, the ratio of federal debt to GNP had fallen to 22 percent, but, in large part because of the nature of monetary policy and its effects on interest rates, interest still consumed almost 20 percent of federal revenues. This made interest on the debt almost a third more burdensome on the public purse than it was in 1988, at the end of Ronald Reagan's presidency. Without the benefit of modern economics, the Republican President Hoover, with a large budget deficit in prospect in 1931, felt he had little choice but to propose a large tax increase despite high and rising unemployment.

Roosevelt's response to the symptoms of chronic inadequate demand was scarcely the kind of countercyclical Keynesian fiscal policy that is sometimes attributed to him. While the tax base eroded, he struggled to maintain revenues by instituting sharp increases in federal tax rates. Roosevelt and the Congress raised the effective federal tax rate by 700 percent between 1932 and 1939.[4]

The tax increases fell on rich and poor alike. A large part of the tax increase on lower- and middle-income groups came from the payroll tax instituted in 1935 to finance the Social Security System. The 1935 Wealth Tax Act raised income-tax rates on "the rich" and corporations. Roosevelt further harried the well-to-do with new taxes, including one on undistributed corporate profits that proved so unworkable, both politically and administratively, that it had to be abandoned. The initial strong political appeal of "soak the rich" taxes on undistributed profits left unaddressed the problems of average people who owned small amounts of stock and who found that even though they did not have incomes large enough to owe tax, the tax reduced their dividends before they received them. Their voices, however, stayed muted.

Clearly, Roosevelt's policies were motivated less by the need to stimulate stagnant demand than by an abhorrence of deficits and of attendant increases in the national debt. Yet it was precisely the prescription of anti-cyclical fiscal demand-management policy that both should rise when the economy was contracting. Fortunately, Roosevelt found it impossible to stick to his fiscal policy. During much of the 1930s, while tax rates rose sharply, tax revenues were flat or down. Meanwhile, the program of the New Deal meant that federal expenditures and deficits both rose sharply.

Of course, there was a third factor—simply "relief" rather than "stimulating demand." The desire to provide relief, the immediate, personal-income effects of policy, as opposed to theoretical and broad economic effects, was sharp and clear—not dramatically different from the present, when the equivalent of "relief" is "entitlement."

In short, the deficit financing of the New Deal was not part of a conscious effort to spend the economy out of a recession. Rather, it was forced by the need to respond in an ad hoc manner to the unprecedented economic difficulties that came with a world economic depression. The view about deficits and debt expressed in 1932 by Milwaukee's Socialist mayor, Daniel Hoan, that governments "are choking themselves to death by the borrowing habit" was, to judge by his policies, shared by Roosevelt.[5]

The market crash and subsequent bank failures had wiped out the life savings of a new and comfortably well-off middle class whose stocks and homes had appreciated during the decade after the war and who had become far better off than they had expected to be. By 1934, one-third of all home-owners were delinquent in their mortgage payments, and in 1933, by some measures, nearly one-third of the labor force was unemployed.

Along with these grim statistics, Roosevelt sensed a profound feeling of unease among common people and elites alike that the economic basis of western society was eroding. The British historian Arnold Toynbee put it this way: "The year 1931 was distinguished from previous years—in the 'postwar' and in the 'prewar' age alike—by one outstanding feature. In 1931, men and women all over the world were seriously contemplating and frankly discussing the possibility that the western system of society might break down and cease to work."[6] The critic Edmund Wilson said it more succinctly in 1931: "With the present breakdown we have come to the end of something."[7]

In the face of such questioning, Roosevelt had to do something. He put together a program whose outlines are clearer in retrospect than they were in prospect. The era of activist federal government policy had just begun; the intense effort devoted to packaging, like that devoted to Ronald Reagan's five-point program for the economy in 1980–1981, had not begun to appear in 1933. Roosevelt had to grope toward a set of policies that would contain and then correct the conditions that many feared would bring a total economic collapse.

Roosevelt's policies included a program aimed at increasing jobs, real incomes, and profits. The first step was to devalue the dollar against gold. This meant raising the official dollar price of gold from $22 to $35 per ounce, as was done after the United States left the gold standard on March 6, 1933, two days after Roosevelt was inaugurated. But for the most part, a genuine countercyclical reflation was avoided in favor of artificial price supports. The general supposition was that, because rising prices were characteristic of prosperity, all one had to do to get prosperity was to raise prices.

The result was the National Industrial Recovery Act, aimed at encouraging business organizations to form cartels to promote "fair" competition or, more specifically, improved wages and working conditions. Although most of its measures were declared unconstitutional by the Supreme Court, the National Recovery Administration was the paradigm for numerous federal regulatory agencies. These formed the nucleus of the "big government" against which the Reagan revolution reacted half a century later. Farm policy was designed to raise prices for farm products just as the NRA aimed to raise the prices of industrial products.

In 1933, there was a compelling case for countercyclical deficit spending and the reversal of perversely tight monetary policies, yet Roosevelt's fiscal policy consisted of only lukewarm expansion of federal spending financed by sharp increases in tax rates. This was testimony to the strength of America's moral abhorrence of government debt. Instead of fiscal policy, the administration concentrated on measures like "soak the rich" taxes on dividends, high individual incomes, and corporate incomes, along with deposit insurance and Social Security. Bank-deposit insurance was opposed by Hoover and initially by Roosevelt but was finally passed by Congress in 1933: after the bank holidays and closures of the early 1930s, few individuals would be prepared to put their money into private banks without some government guarantee on the value of their principal. The objection of both presidents to deposit insurance was that "the weak banks would pull down the strong."[8]

Ironically, Roosevelt, the greatest leader of the party of Jefferson in the twentieth century, provided the decisive rejection of ideas so dear to Jefferson: a weak central government and the immorality and inadvisability of increasing debts of the government during peacetime. Roosevelt understood that Jefferson's rejection of a strong central government was part of a vision of the world that had been irretrievably lost since the Civil War. Jefferson's moral-agrarian belief in a laissez-faire nation of small self-sufficient farmers was an anachronism that Roosevelt to his great credit recognized could no longer guide America. The Hawley-Smoot tariff of 1930 had been a last desperate effort to recapture the Jeffersonian ideal of self-sufficiency, even though it was perpetrated by Republicans. It was as if they thought that since high tariffs had been part of the prosperous era following the Civil War, high tariffs could somehow restore to the world of the twentieth century, transformed as it had been by world war, the prosperity of the late nineteenth century.

America in 1930 was no longer a nation of self-sufficient farmers for whom high tariffs were not a direct burden. Instead, the economy was dominated by powerful industries, of which ordinary Americans had become suspicious. Foreign competition could constrain these industries only if tariffs were kept low. Moreover, America's financial system, especially after Britain's ill-advised return to the gold standard in 1926, had become precariously tied to the financial fortunes of Europe.

After World War I, America eagerly extricated itself from the affairs of Europe and prepared to pursue economic prosperity on its own, behind high tariff walls if necessary. But America was playing in an economic game that it did not understand well. After 1926, Britain attempted to overvalue its currency in terms of commodities by returning to the pre–World War I gold standard. This meant that the Bank of England, the closest thing to a world central bank at the time, in a repeat of the deflationary American move to a gold standard after the Civil War, had to keep drawing liquidity out of the world financial system. A combination of less money and lower prices was the only way to validate a gold standard that started off requiring too few pounds and too few dollars to buy an ounce of gold.

The tie to gold meant that America, too, had to withdraw money from the system at a pace that was neither anticipated nor appropriate in view of the needs of a growing economy. The strain thus created in the system began to appear in October 1929 with the stock market crash and the disastrous events, already chronicled, that followed and exacerbated the downturn. The events that led up to the era of Roosevelt and the New Deal showed not so much that the economy was not taking care of itself as that governments, possessed of new tools to control the money supply, taxes, and expenditure, were desperately ill informed as to the proper use of those tools.

Central to the Keynesian revolution was the idea that governments could conquer unemployment, which was articulated by Lloyd George in 1929 at a meeting of Liberal candidates. Historian A. J. P. Taylor writes of the meeting: "This was a dramatic event: the moment when the new ideas toward which economists were fumbling first broke into public consciousness." Prosperity was to be generated through public works paid for by a deliberate deficit, which would ultimately absorb the expenditure; according to Taylor, this was the outline of the New Deal that Roosevelt applied with some success in the United States.[9]

While Taylor may err in characterizing the New Deal as a classic application of nascent Keynesian economics, he understands clearly the problem of converting sophisticated new ideas into public policy and provides an insightful description of how such objectives may fail to be achieved. In writing of Keynes's efforts to refine his theories during the early 1930s, Taylor adds:

Where experts lagged, ordinary men were bewildered.

The new ideas underlying Lloyd George's program were difficult to grasp. It seemed common sense that a reduction in taxes made the taxpayer richer, and paradoxical to argue that individuals benefited more from increased public spending. The lessons of the War were all drawn one way. Nations were supposed to have been ruined by the vast expenditure. No one pointed out that they had also prospered while the war was on and had benefited afterwards from its capital creations. Again, it was accepted doctrine that British exports lagged because costs of production were too high; and high taxation was blamed for this about as much as high wages. Thus there began in 1929 a cleavage between informed opinion and the assumptions of ordinary men which has lasted almost to the present day. The cleavage existed in many fields. Einstein, like Keynes, was incomprehensible where Newton, like Adam Smith, had been neat and obvious. The concertgoer could hum the themes of Mozart and Beethoven, not those of Stravinsky. He never learned to hum the themes of the new economics.[10]

With the New Deal, Roosevelt produced a hodgepodge of classical ideas about sound government finance and a few stabs at what was to become known as Keynesian (as distinct from Keynes's) anticyclical policy. The Keynesian approach to demand management—as opposed to the elegant economics of Keynes, which, fully comprehended, would not have created the supply-side, anti-Keynesian revolution of the Reagan years—dominated the American government's fiscal policy in its initial coherent manifestation from 1945 to 1980.

If, during the Great Depression, there existed a conflict between the language, goals, and themes of the new economics and the norms of American people, it did not deter policy makers from trying to apply Keynesian economics to the modern American economy. While Keynes was not the guru of Franklin Roosevelt as the president tried to lift America out of depression in the 1930s, the economist was the mentor of a generation of American economists who came to FDR's Washington in the 1940s to mobilize for World War II and the massive job of restructuring, regulating, and coordinating the wartime economy. In the war's aftermath, the new economics took firm root in the machinery and substance of federal fiscal policy and pushed forward yet again the fiscal revolution.

There has always been fiscal policy, that is, spending, taxing, and debt management, in government. But the idea that policy makers could by their manipulation of fiscal or monetary policy influence the paths of GNP, employment, inflation, or interest rates took hold only during the late Roosevelt era and did not become formally rooted in the policy process until the Republican administration of Dwight Eisenhower.

Three conditions had to be met before proactive economic measures could actually be tried by a president or Congress. First, macroeconomic theory had to be developed, as Keynes and his colleagues were doing at Cambridge University. By 1945, the second stage was reached: the theory had become sufficiently compelling both to affect economic thinking and to move macroeconomics from the theory stage to the action stage on both sides of the Atlantic. Finally, the role of the federal government in recovery had to become pervasive enough for the new theoretical, anticyclical policies to operate on it. The last condition was fulfilled by the requirements of financing World War II.

WORLD WAR II

During World War II, the country mobilized to an unprecedented degree. This mobilization required centralized decision making over far more than military strategy and action: production, prices, industrial development, and the broader economy all became primary areas of federal government concern. Even as battalions of American troops fanned out to the European and Pacific theaters, battalions of American bureaucrats occupied Washington and other cities to mesh the nation's economy and society with the war effort. The federal civilian work force stood at 1.1 million people in 1940. In 1941, it went to 1.6 million; in 1942, to 2.7 million; and in 1943, to 3.2 million. During that four-year period, as the government's civilian payroll tripled, the number of federal employees actually based in Washington more than doubled, reaching nearly 300,000.

The massive war effort also created massive deficits, dwarfing those of World War I. In fiscal 1941, before America's involvement in the war, the gross federal debt stood at $57.5 billion (the deficit that year was $4.8 billion). The ratio of debt to GNP after the years of deficit spending in the Depression and *before* America entered the war in 1941 stood at 45 percent, well above its ratio at the *end* of World War I and close to the ratio attained at the end of the Civil War. Five years later, the gross federal debt had nearly quintupled, to $271 billion, or a staggering 130 percent of gross national product. This was by far the highest level this ratio ever attained in American history. But the capacity of the federal government to collect taxes had improved so dramatically that revenues ballooned, reducing the interest burden as a share of government. The share of federal revenue consumed by interest on the debt actually fell from 13.2 percent in 1941 to 9.9 percent in 1945. America spent massively on World War II, but even more impressive than the gush of military equipment purchased and thrown into battle was the ease with which it was paid for. By the end of the war, the American production machine, then the heart of the American economy, had become the marvel of the world. It was admired and envied far more by those outside America than by the fortunate souls within. As André Malraux, the French statesman and author, once said to Richard Nixon: "The United States is the first nation in history to become a great power without trying to do so."

Despite America's economic might, special measures were required to pay for the war's huge cost. The first option considered by the Roosevelt administration was an excess-profits tax. It had been the first option as well in World War I. In 1940, a hasty, limited excess-profits tax was enacted. In 1941, when war was on the horizon and expenditures were increasing as a result of America's lend-lease program with Britain, Treasury Secretary Henry Morgenthau testified before the House Ways and Means Committee in favor of a new tax bill that would increase all major sources of taxes. The administration's goal was to pay for two-thirds of the war's expenditures with taxes and the remainder through borrowing, Morgenthau said; in the end, taxes accounted for three-fifths of the federal government's wartime expenditures, compared with two-fifths for World War I and one-fifth for the Civil War.[11]

By 1942, the demand for more war-related spending meant an intense need for massive new revenues. The revenue act that year increased corporate and individual income taxes, refined and broadened the excess-profits tax, broadened the base and reduced the progressivity of the personal income tax, and imposed a flat 5 percent victory tax to be collected from everyone with gross incomes over $624, regardless of whether they paid income taxes.

The 1942 act sharply changed tax policy in the United States. The income-tax base more than doubled in size, as the number of taxpayers increased from 13 million to 28 million, while 50 million were paying the victory tax.[12] In 1943, yet another new tax bill introduced Americans to tax withholding for the first time.

By the end of the war, millions of new taxpayers had been drawn into the tax net, and individual and corporate income taxes accounted for three-quarters of the nation's federal tax burden—up from less than 40 percent before the war. Before the war, about 7 percent of the public paid some income taxes; at the height of the war, 64 percent of the population did so. Four million Americans were income-tax payers in 1939; the number rose to 43 million by 1945. Income taxes had by 1945 become almost as inevitable as death for Americans, as they had already become for the citizens of many other countries.

The changes persisted even after the war. While income taxes had declined considerably following World War I, and excise and customs taxes had regained their prewar prominence, no such pattern followed World War II. Income taxes continued at or near wartime rates. They also were much more progressive, albeit more widespread, than in the prewar era and were part of a much more complicated and multilayered tax structure.

The war also transformed government and the economy. Numerous federal agencies were created during the war, including the Office of Price Administration, the National War Labor Board, the War Production Board, the War Resources Board, the War Industries Board, the War Trade Board, the War Food Administration, and the War Manpower Commission. Primacy over the economy moved from the private sector to the federal government and its new agencies. Their efforts, along with the draft, reduced unemployment from 14 percent before the war to less than 5 percent during it and affirmed a large, permanent role for the federal government in managing the economy. Postwar legislation solidified that larger role. Douglas Higgs comments:

> As victory came into view almost everyone demanded an end to the galling restraints of the garrison economy, and a rapid if incomplete dismantling of the administrative apparatus of control ensued. But a host of legacies remained: all the government-financed plants and equipment and the military-industrial complex to continue operating them; important postwar legislation inspired by wartime practices, including the Employment Act, the Taft-Hartley Act, and the Selective Service Act of 1948; the GI Bill and the new middle class it fostered; a voracious and effective income tax system; a massive foreign-aid program. . . . Most significantly the war moved the prevailing ideology markedly toward acceptance of an enlarged governmental presence in the economy. At last, even the majority of businessmen had come to accept, and often to demand, Big Government.[13]

Unsurprisingly, war-weariness, together with the wrenching conversion from wartime mobilization to peacetime pursuits, to be expected after a major war, brought with it the desire for other changes. In Britain, the voters unceremoniously dumped Winston Churchill and his wartime government as soon as they had a chance. In 1946, the American electorate threw out the Democratic majority that had controlled the Senate for fourteen years and the House of Representatives for sixteen. Two years later, President Harry Truman characterized the new and hostile legislature as the "Do-Nothing Congress."

THE TRUMAN YEARS

But in 1946, perhaps even more important changes were taking place in the bureaucracy. The war had brought to Washington a flood of experts from academia and business who had managed the war effort, from war production to central economic management. When the war ended, many of these experts stayed. Along with them lingered a strong sense that economic expertise could be used to solve systemic economic problems and not simply to minimize the damage when the nation's economy stumbled into a crisis.

The Employment Act of 1946 was one result of this new thinking. The initial thrust of the act was to find a way to achieve full employment as a formal goal of the federal government, an ambition that had gained consensus during the war. As Herbert Stein has noted, "Full employment became the flag around which everyone could rally."[14] The act explicitly made the federal government responsible for this goal and set up the expectation that it would be pursued by the vigorous application of fiscal policy.

Partly for the sake of achieving full employment, economic expertise was institutionalized in the federal government through a new economic arm, the President's Council of Economic Advisers. Despite the existence of this council and the broad influence of Keynes's economic theories, the Truman years were to see no major anticyclical policies either on the fiscal or on the monetary front.

The postwar Truman years between 1946 and the early 1950s were dominated by the economic symptoms of demobilization after the massive war effort of 1941 to 1945. Prices spurted upward as Truman and an uncharacteristically cooperative Congress began to remove the most onerous wartime excise taxes and price controls. The price increases, which had been expected in view of pent-up demand for goods and pent-up savings to pay for them, were nevertheless short-lived. The consumer price index, which the government began compiling in 1946 as it became more aware of the deficiencies in its data gathering for decision making, rose 18.1 percent from the end of 1945 to the end of 1946. During 1947, however, it rose by 8.8 percent and during 1948 by only 3 percent. In 1949, it actually declined by 2.1 percent. Part of the reason for the slowdown in inflation was a slowdown in the economy. After sluggish growth during 1946 and 1947, the economy bounced back and grew at 3.9 percent during 1948—but then it did not grow at all during 1949.

The economy was far more robust in the postwar period than many economists had expected. The severe economic slowdown that had followed partial mobilization during World War I was expected to be repeated with a vengeance after the far more lengthy and profound mobilization for World War II. In fact, demobilization and reconversion to a peacetime economy were relatively smooth, bearing out the economic axiom that an event too widely anticipated will often fail to occur precisely because it is anticipated.

Virtually every economist in 1946 feared a postwar depression, and yet the Truman administration contemplated virtually no countercyclical measures. A predepression, pre-Keynesian mentality still governed the thinking of Washington's most powerful men more than a decade after the New Deal. Because the Federal Reserve was until 1951 constrained to keep at a low level the interest rates on the massive government debt accumulated during the war, easy money was the rule. This easy-money policy provided a stimulative underpinning for the economy, but it was less the result of any conscious anticyclical policy than a by-product of the desire to minimize the cost of servicing a national debt that had risen by the war's end to more than 100 percent of GNP. The debt managers in Washington had not failed to notice the seriousness of a debt-GNP ratio that was more than twice what it had been after the Civil War and three times what Washington and Hamilton had faced in 1789, before the debt accumulated during the Revolutionary War had begun to be reduced.

Nevertheless, by 1946 massive wartime tax increases had swelled federal revenues so much that paying the interest on the huge debt was far less of a strain than it had been after those previous wars. Interest on the national debt consumed 53 percent of federal revenues in 1789, 25 percent in 1866, 20 percent in 1919, and 37 percent in 1933, at the bottom of the Depression. By 1945, the federal government's interest bill was just under 10 percent of its revenues, well *below* the 13.2 percent level of 1941.

The war-inspired tax system that had created this windfall to the government was left essentially intact by Truman and his successors. At the end of World War II, the top tax rate on personal income was 94 percent, and even for the lowest bracket, on incomes of less than $2,000, the rate was a hefty 23 percent—more than four-fifths of 1992's *top* bracket. After the war, government spending plummeted to a postwar low of $33 billion (13 percent of GNP) in 1948 from its height of $98 billion, or 46 percent of GNP, in 1945.

Meanwhile, federal revenues *increased* during this period in dollar terms; as a proportion of GNP, they shrank only to 16.8 percent from 20 percent of GNP at the end of the war. Despite—indeed, because of—the efficient revenue machine created by tax measures enacted to finance World War II, it was becoming incumbent upon government to define the limits on its tendency to go on gathering in a large fraction of all income in peacetime.

While Truman and his administration did not put into place any sophisticated countercyclical economic policy, both they and their Republican counterparts in Congress were beginning to see the postwar tax system as an opportunity to fine-tune the economy and to help particular industries—although the ideas of Democrats and Republicans about what direction the politics should take were usually diametrically opposed. Some of the fiercest ideological battles of the Truman years were fought in the partisan struggle over taxes.

Just weeks after the Japanese surrendered, Truman asked Congress to cut revenues by about $5.2 billion, or about 12 percent of the total, by eliminating a 3 percent "normal tax" (a remnant of the 5 percent victory tax) on all income and by repealing the excess-profits tax—which by that time had reached more than 90 percent on any corporate profits above a prewar base. Congress kept the 3 percent basic levy but cut all individual and corporate tax rates by about four percentage points.

Truman claimed that "removing barriers to speedy reconversion and to the expansion of our peacetime economy" was the purpose of his tax-cut proposal. But the cuts could not be deep because a $30 billion deficit was projected for 1946. The version passed by Congress cut revenues by more than Truman had asked and was attacked both for giving "the lion's share of tax forgiveness to those who don't need it" and for removing about 12 million people from the tax rolls. Nonetheless, it passed overwhelmingly. The 1945 bill was controlled by events, including the obvious need to pare back wartime tax rates to avoid stifling the recovery. Set against this imperative, however, was Truman's wish for a balanced budget after sixteen consecutive years of federal deficits.

The Republican Eightieth Congress brought with it the fiercest battles over tax policy ever fought in Washington until the Reagan administration. Twice in 1947, Congress sent Truman general tax-reduction bills; he vetoed the versions Congress enacted. The first bill, a flat 20 percent cut in all income-tax rates, was pushed through by the new Ways and Means chairman, Harold Knutson of Minnesota, on traditional grounds that it would free funds for business investment. Knutson allowed only two days of hearings on the proposal, but the House altered the plan to make the cut more progressive. The standard Democratic alternative was an increase in the personal exemption. A more complex Republican bill, with five stages of cuts rather than four, passed the Senate.

Today, a struggle between GOP tax cutters and Democratic taxers may seem normal, but 1947 differed in two ways from the present. Democrats focused on the need for debt reduction, and the public largely agreed. Truman vetoed the first 1947 bill on the grounds that it would worsen inflation, leave too little surplus for debt reduction, and disproportionately benefit the rich. His position was supported by a Gallup poll showing that 53 percent of the public preferred to use the surplus to reduce debt rather than to lower taxes. (Gallup asked this question only once, unfortunately.) Knutson reintroduced the bill; again, it survived Democratic attempts to concentrate its benefits in the lower brackets, and again Truman vetoed it. This time, the House voted to override, but the motion fell five votes short in the Senate.

Ultimately, in 1948, Republicans succeeded in cutting tax rates; their measure reduced effective rates by 17 percent at the low end and 9.75 percent at the top, increased and broadened the personal exemption, and gave all couples filing jointly the right to split their income. By combining the preferred Republican form of tax reduction (across-the-board rate cuts) with the Democrats' preference for removing the poorest taxpayers from the rolls entirely, Congress was able to beat Truman's veto by forty-five votes in the House and nineteen in the Senate.

Despite the tax cut, the tax code in 1949 differed little from the wartime structure. The bottom bracket was down to 16.6 percent from 23 percent at the end of the war, and the top bracket had fallen to 82 percent from 94 percent. These were small decreases for a government whose expenditures had fallen by two-thirds, and they affected revenues only enough to turn a small surplus into a small deficit. While congressional Democrats gently pursued a more progressive method of tax cutting, Truman's main interest apparently was to maintain tax rates that would preserve the surplus. In 1948, he acknowledged that the surplus was "one of the most powerful anti-inflationary factors in our economy" but urged that tax rates be kept high "until inflation has been stopped"—although a postwar spurt of high prices had ended six months earlier and the economy appeared to be slowing. The principles of postwar adjustment that Truman had accepted in the employment act two years earlier did not extend to his attitude about taxation, where he was indistinguishable from a doctrinaire low-inflation, balanced-budget Republican.

Before the Korean War broke out in 1950, Truman began the year with a new tactic in his continuing effort to keep taxes at levels that would maintain a surplus: an attack on "loopholes." The word entered our political vocabulary at this time, and closing loopholes was to become a useful tactic for politicians with various objectives. Without the Korean War, the assault on loopholes might have brought Truman more success with Congress in 1950. It was both a useful political tool and a natural product of the far greater complexity of the tax code and of the higher tax rates resulting from insufficiently repealed wartime measures. More loopholes had been created by the political compromises that went into the 1948 bill, and along with them had come opportunities for both politicians and special interests to further their goals through the tax mechanism.

Chief among the loopholes was the oil depletion allowance, which Truman tried to cut to 15 percent from 27.5 percent at the same time he asked for comparable cuts in other mineral depletion allowances. No loophole was "so excessive" as the depletion allowance, Truman said, citing one beneficiary who had built up a tax-free income of $5 million. But both the House Ways and Means Committee and the Senate Finance Committee deleted Truman's cut in the depletion allowance in 1950 and again in 1951.

America's relief that the economy did not collapse after the war was tempered by its increasing alarm over the spread of communism in postwar Europe. The Cold War had begun as the Iron Curtain fell over Eastern Europe. Government's role in the world would have to be substantial.

After the Depression and victory in World War II, the American view of the federal government as a can-do institution was running high. The government was seen as willing and able to deal with issues of welfare, economic stabilization, international financial arrangements, and a myriad of other matters that previously had been seen as largely outside its sphere.

A government that could beat Adolf Hitler, Benito Mussolini, and the Japanese warlords certainly ought to be able to run the economy. The expectation grew within the government and among the governed that the United States was now a world leader, a defender and rebuilder of democracy worldwide, and fully able to monitor price levels and employment and to make adjustments if worrisome signs appeared.

Most Americans felt good about themselves and their nation. Pocketbook issues dominated individuals' concerns. Indeed, it would have been difficult to find articles in major newspapers and magazines about the national budget, tax-reform proposals, or economic policy, even if readers had been interested in such topics. Prices rose for a time, but at least rationing had been lifted. In 1948, unemployment was a modest 3.8 percent of the civilian work force. The mild recession in 1949 raised the unemployment rate to nearly 6 percent, but the federal government took modest action, and few observers saw a return to the Depression in the offing.

In the midst of the anxiety about demobilization and possible economic calamity, President Truman was more interested in the technicalities of budget preparation than in any sophisticated notions of economic policy or countercyclical measures. He paid close attention to the budget not because he thought of it as a balance wheel for the economy but because he had a deep interest in the technicalities of budget preparation and execution. Truman was rather like an accountant, less concerned with the bottom line than with getting to it by employing sound accounting principles.

Truman's view of the budget, like Roosevelt's, was closer to Hoover's than to John Kennedy's or even to Dwight Eisenhower's. Truman, Roosevelt, and Hoover were not only pre-Keynesian presidents; they were preeconomics presidents. For all three, what little they had to say about economics was based on analogies with sound household finance, such as "a penny saved is a penny earned" or, when it came to budgetary matters, "neither a borrower nor a lender be"—unless you get into a war, in which case you have to be a borrower. Thereafter, the need to repay is urgent.

Truman's views on spending were outdone in their penuriousness by Congress's. The House, especially, cut back the spending requests of the president consistently in every area save the FBI. The Senate proved more generous, but not by much. As a result, and despite the formidable possibility of a "peace dividend" after the war, there was no rise in domestic federal spending spurred by legislative initiative or by any pent-up demand from the public.

To be sure, government's economic expertise was expanding. The Employment Act of 1946 created a joint congressional committee (subsequently named the Joint Economic Committee) to receive the mandated yearly economic reports of the president, which had been drafted by the new Council of Economic Advisers, and to review them in terms of the policy goal of full employment. But in the late 1940s, the committee was barely getting under way.

Under Truman, the Council of Economic Advisers did not play a key role in formulating economic policy concerning the comprehensive path of the economy. This was not so much because the economists on the council were outsiders in the Truman White House, though in fact they were, but because they lacked a consensus on economic measures to keep the economy on an even keel.

For his part, Truman stubbornly continued to focus on technical budget issues. His economic policy command to the CEA was to keep the GNP at about $200 billion, and he would do the rest. For him, economy still meant the virtue of saving money rather than the complex interactions between gross national product, employment, interest rates, and prices.

More aggressive economic plans would have been put on hold in any case when the North Koreans invaded South Korea in late June 1950. The economy had to be mobilized for war; production had to be increased drastically and shifted away from consumer to military needs. The federal budget went from surpluses of $9.2 billion in 1950 and $6.5 billion in 1951 to deficits from 1952 through 1954 of $3.7 billion, $7.1 billion, and $6.0 billion.

Coming as it did just five years after World War II, the Korean War reminded Americans that America's new position as leader of the free world and the apparently aggressive nature of communism were going to test their can-do government. Again, as after the Depression and World War II, the growth of government in response to a national crisis proved to be permanent. There was no commensurate reduction in its size afterward. From the Korean War onward, Cold War demands replaced "hot" war demands, shaping spending and revenue requirements even as other programs, notably entitlements, grew unnoticed beneath the surface.

EISENHOWER'S FIRST TERM

Eisenhower came into office attacking Truman's "wanton extravagance and inflationary policies," promising to balance the budget and to cut taxes. Unlike Reagan nearly thirty years later, however, Eisenhower put a much higher priority on balancing the budget than on cutting taxes: "Reduction of taxes will be justified only as we show we can succeed in bringing the budget under control," he said in his first State of the Union message. Eisenhower slashed the budget for fiscal 1954 by $4.5 billion, but he also asked for an extension of the excess-profits tax and repeal of a scheduled cut in the normal corporate tax back to 25 percent, promising "a completely revised program of taxation" for the next year.

The Eisenhower years began with the White House and Congress both under GOP rule, but the situation changed after only two years. For the remainder of his presidency, the Republican president had to govern with the help of a Democratic Congress. Although partisan conflict over budget and tax priorities was often high, it never reached the level of bitterness that prevailed between Truman and the "Do-Nothing" Eightieth Congress. The political dynamics were different in other ways as well, especially after the

1958 election brought a huge Democratic majority to both houses of Congress. This majority, which had been swollen by large numbers of northern, liberal Democrats, began to prod Eisenhower on domestic policy. Congress sent up to the White House progressive but expensive programs designed to improve highways or education, and the tightfisted Eisenhower would resist. In the end, however, he often managed not only to support them but even to take credit for them.

Eisenhower's fiscal policies were constructed under these political dynamics, but they were also a reflection of his own operating style and the drive of his chief economic adviser. Under Eisenhower, the role of the Council of Economic Advisers as a center for economists' policy making began to take on new prominence—largely because of the personality and talents of its chairman, Arthur Burns. Burns's professorial appearance did not create high expectations of success among his White House colleagues. Sherman Adams, Eisenhower's chief of staff, reports about his first meeting with Burns:

> When I took my first look at Burns, on the day he came to my office before I was to take him in to meet the president, I had a sinking sensation. If somebody had asked me to describe the mental image I had of the type of New Deal official we were in the process of moving out of Washington, this was it—a glassy stare through thick lenses, peering out from under a canopy of unruly hair parted in the middle, a large pipe with a curved stem: the very incarnation of all the externals that were such anathema to Republican businessmen and politicians. I wondered if we both would be thrown out of Eisenhower's office.[15]

Despite Adams's erroneous initial impression, Burns was no off-the-wall academic. Although a professor of economics at Columbia University, he was pragmatic, eclectic, and hardheaded, neither Keynesian nor classicist nor part of the then-nascent University of Chicago monetarist school. Burns was primarily interested in monitoring the state of the economy and in creating a stable, predictable, but limited role for government in mitigating the business cycles that he had spent much of his professional career studying.

Burns's practical and down-to-earth habit of mind apparently appealed to Eisenhower. The rapport and respect that grew up between the president and Burns probably saved the CEA from extinction and helped to institutionalize the role of modern professional economics in presidential decision making. Burns, who was always able to command the attention of a roomful of people, educated Eisenhower, an amateur in economic policy, in the difficulties and challenges of managing the economy. Eisenhower, observers noted, paid rapt attention when Burns held forth on economic principles and options. Adams continues:

> To me, Arthur Burns turned out to be a pleasant surprise. He and Eisenhower got along fine. They shared the same outlook and philosophy. Far from being the abstract and impractical professor, Burns had his feet planted solidly on the ground and had no difficulty in more than holding his own in arguments at the Cabinet table with such hardheaded protagonists as Secretary of the Treasury George Humphrey and Budget Director Dodge. As soon as the 1954 downturn began to appear, Eisenhower set aside ample time at Cabinet meetings so that Burns could discuss the economics of the situation. These periods lasted often as long as thirty minutes and Eisenhower listened to him with fascination. . . . One morning after Burns had finished a detailed outline of contributions that various government departments could make toward strengthening the economy, Eisenhower said to him admiringly, "Arthur, my boy, you would have made a fine Chief of Staff, overseas, during the war." Eisenhower, a lifelong Army man, could offer no higher compliment.[16]

Eisenhower the general was comfortable depending on Burns as an expert on something he himself knew little about. And at first, economic issues were not critical. The 1952 election did not focus on them, and Eisenhower was not comfortable pretending to any knowledge of economic matters. He was at his worst when commenting on such matters extemporaneously.

Burns's first challenge, and opportunity, emerged in August 1953, when the economy began to slow as Korean War expenditures wound down. A number of the leading economic indicators—which Burns had identified as predictors of the path of the economy when he was at the National Bureau of Economic Research—began to point to a slower economy.

Burns, unlike the CEA chairmen under Truman, had the attention of the president. If Eisenhower was no expert on economics, he understood its political consequences. A recession early in the first Republican administration since 1932 would have raised the specter of Hoover and would have been much more of a political disaster for the Republican party than an economic disaster for the nation. Publicly, Eisenhower stuck to his Republican principles and faith in a free economy, resisting heavy pressures for federal inter-

vention from labor unions and from a newly activist Joint Economic
Committee led by Senator Paul H. Douglas, a distinguished economist from
the University of Chicago.

In private, Eisenhower was more concerned. As Adams recalls:

On the morning of September 25, 1953, when Burns gave the Cabinet a
long and detailed report on the Council's view of the economic situation,
together with specific recommendations to combat further recession,
Eisenhower, observed that he was ready, if it became necessary, to use
the full resources of the Government to prevent "another 1929" as the
Republicans had pledged during the 1952 campaign, but he made it plain
that he was not wavering in his economic creed that the best way to
combat a depression, in his view, was to spur the individual on to greater
and freer economic activity.[17]

Burns kept his cool, observing that the looming recession was not likely to
be deep or prolonged but that its onset could be prevented or at least mitigated by allowing some of the tax cuts that Eisenhower had hitherto been
resisting. That meant putting aside the stated objective of reducing the following year's budget deficit.

Besides the tax cuts, Burns suggested that some provision be made for the
old standby of increasing public-works projects as a countercyclical measure
—although he saw that such a course would not sufficiently stimulate the
economy. Nevertheless, he granted that public works would generate jobs
and help to sustain growth. Overcoming a natural Republican reluctance to
push public works, Burns noted that the conditions of the economy and
society were particularly susceptible to stimulation through highway construction and improvements. He pointed out that highways encourage shopping center construction, subdivision development, and other secondary
benefits. Not accidentally, his view meshed well with Eisenhower's own. His
management of Allied strategy in Europe during World War II had acquainted him with the military need for fast roads. Doubtless, Eisenhower
appreciated Hitler's autobahns, the long ribbons of expressway that allowed
speedy vehicular travel across Germany. The main support for the subsequent 1954 Federal Aid Highway Act came from the Defense Department,
which saw the military necessity of rapid land transport of its troops for
mobilization. Beyond this, the initial section of the interstate highway system
was to be a four-lane stretch, today known as I-270, that provides direct and

rapid access from Washington, D.C., halfway to Gettysburg, Pennsylvania, the location of Eisenhower's country retreat.

Burns admitted that highways were not the exclusive road to economic recovery. Automatic stabilizers, too, would have some effect as lower incomes cut tax collections and unemployment insurance kicked in to help out many families. Few of Burns's economist colleagues thought that recession would lead to a depression, though many feared that it might lead to a political depression for Republican candidates in the next election.

Burns supported a modest tax cut as an insurance measure, taken in a timely manner to contain and perhaps to avoid a recession. Politically, he bet that the Republican fear of a recession outweighed the force of fiscal orthodoxy. Politicians and their advisers, deeply ingrained in such orthodoxy, would have been horrified by the idea of a tax cut in the teeth of the growing budget deficit that was to be expected in an economic slowdown. The combination of Burns's sagacity and the Republicans' political fear of recession produced a countercyclical tax cut of the sort, if not the size, envisioned by Keynesian economists. The idea was to stimulate spending —demand—and thereby induce more production, more hiring, and lower unemployment. Burns was not a committed Keynesian, but he did not want to miss the chance to demonstrate to the president the value and usefulness of timely economic advice. As a result, he got a Republican administration faced with a budget deficit to support for the first time in American history the principle of tax reduction as a countercyclical measure.

The tax cuts together with some modest increases in federal spending mitigated the recession. The unemployment rate stayed below 6 percent, save for one month during 1954, and by mid-1954, the recession was over. The Republicans could breathe a sigh of relief at having come through their first recession since the catastrophe of 1929 without severe harm in the eyes of the nation. (Their relief was not quite so palpable in the aftermath of the 1958 recession.)

Though not so dramatic as the fiscal measures that were later to be undertaken during the Kennedy administration of 1961–1963, the 1954 Burns-Eisenhower maneuvers to avoid recession were both unconventional and successful, and they therefore came to be seen as an effective use of fiscal policy to control the painful swing of the trade cycle. Some observers, such as Neil Jacoby, have called the 1954 tax cut the first deliberate application of compensatory fiscal policy. According to the conventional historical wisdom, a dynamic, innovative Roosevelt pioneered in the use of anticyclical fiscal measures to fight a depression. Actually, however, that policy was innovated twenty years later by a "do-nothing" Republican president who faced and knowingly exacerbated a budget deficit by cutting taxes. Eisenhower was anxious not to have a serious recession, the Republican disease, reappear on his watch and was prepared to undertake bold and risky measures to avoid it. While he was not the conservative revolutionary that Reagan was, prepared to jettison the balanced-budget orthodoxy altogether, Eisenhower was pragmatic enough to deal with the challenge facing him by temporarily abandoning his strongly held fiscal views.

Eisenhower's public rationale for his tax-cutting policies was not derived from Keynesian economics. Instead, he spoke of closing loopholes, reducing the more glaring inequities, promoting economic growth, and striving to "make the law simpler and surer." With the addition of simplification as a goal, Eisenhower had perfected the full complement of political nostrums that would figure in all subsequent debates over tax policy: closing loopholes (fairness or equity), removing obstacles to investment (growth), and simplification.

The congressional debate in 1954 resembled Truman's battles, as Democrats attempted to replace some of the changes with an increase in the personal exemption and accused Eisenhower of practicing the "trickle-down" economics of Andrew Mellon. But the changes they proposed were so many, and individually so minor, that the debate is not so illuminating as it was in earlier years. With no sharp partisan split or pointed debate over fiscal policy per se, only in retrospect can we see the significance of the tax cuts for future fiscal policy.

EISENHOWER'S SECOND TERM

Burns resigned as chairman of the CEA after the 1956 election. The remainder of the Eisenhower years did not bring much expansion of Keynesian fiscal policy or any other major innovations in economics. Despite an unanticipated surplus in the boom year of 1956, Eisenhower, reverting to form, declared that more tax cuts would have to wait until the next year and urged that "we be mindful of our enormous national debt and of the obligation we have toward future Americans to reduce that debt whenever we can appropriately do so. Under conditions of high peacetime prosperity, such as now exist, we can never justify going further into debt to give ourselves a tax cut at the expense of our children."

Once again, the corporate and excise rates were extended, this time with little debate. In 1957, Eisenhower again put off tax reduction, warning that "in a prosperous period, the principal threat . . . is inflation."

With a recession in 1958, Paul Douglas and other Democrats pushed for a sizable tax cut, but this time Eisenhower resisted. The difference from 1954 was that he was now secure in his political standing after a landslide reelection victory in 1956 and that the political and economic counsel of Arthur Burns had been relegated to the outside through occasional letters. In 1958, Eisenhower kept his priorities focused on keeping down inflation and balancing the budget, not on ameliorating the recession.

Herbert Stein has noted that the postwar consensus on fiscal policy had two main prescriptions for a recession:

First, there should be no attempt to offset the deficit that would automatically result from the decline of revenues. Second, in a serious recession, more positive steps should be taken, notably a temporary reduction of tax rates. The first prescription was followed in 1958, as it had been in 1949 and in 1954. . . . But the potentially largest step, and the one receiving the most attention—tax reduction—was not taken.[18]

Why not? Besides Burns's absence—outside the administration, he made frequent speeches advocating a tax cut—one reason was the growing feeling that no tax cut could be temporary; the politics of a Republican president and a Democratic Congress, each looking for political advantage, would make every tax cut permanent. Second, the consensus fiscal policy assumed that, in Stein's words, "recession and inflation were distinct conditions that would not exist simultaneously."[19] In 1958, though, it appeared that we were indeed having both at the same time. "In the circumstances," says Stein, "a choice had to be made, and the Eisenhower administration made it on the side of continuing the fight against inflation while making the minimum concessions to ending the recession."[20]

After the recession, Eisenhower promised tax reduction again: not the next year, but "in the reasonably foreseeable future." Aside from the sixth extension in corporate and excise taxes, the only major legislation of 1959 increased the gasoline tax to 4 cents from 3 cents per gallon to retain the "pay-as-you-go" principle of the costly Highway Trust Fund.

Eisenhower and Reagan were similar in their rhetoric—which called for balancing the budget and cutting taxes to promote growth—but the differences in their priorities made for remarkably different experiences. Eisenhower gave his first priority to balancing the budget and, except for 1954, consistently postponed tax cuts; Reagan gave his first priority to cutting taxes and year after year postponed balancing the budget. Under both presidents, the federal government remained as big and as costly as it had become under their predecessor, but under Reagan the result was a growing deficit, while under Eisenhower deficits occurred only during recessionary periods. In that sense, the Eisenhower years were the end of the era in which balanced budgets were closer to reality than theory.

✦ 7 ✦

THE NEW PROMISE
OF ECONOMIC GROWTH

On October 4, 1957, the Soviet Union launched its first satellite, *Sputnik I*. A month later, it launched *Sputnik II*, which weighed 1,120.29 pounds, into an orbit that was 1,056 miles above the earth. *Sputnik II* even carried a dog, named Laika, on board. These stunning technological feats by the Soviets came when the U.S. Navy was hoping to launch a tiny, 21.5-pound satellite into an orbit barely 300 miles above the earth with a rocket that produced a thrust equal to one-tenth of that of the rockets that launched the Sputniks.

Sputnik became the symbol of a decisive loss of American postwar dominance in military, scientific, and economic endeavors. The world had looked, at least to Americans, more benign and certainly more secure than it had for decades. Indeed, the period between the signing of the Korean Armistice on July 28, 1953, and the launching of *Sputnik I* in the autumn of 1957, has been called by William Manchester, somewhat inaccurately, the Eisenhower siesta.[1]

But Sputnik abruptly ended a period of complacency that had lasted from the victorious conclusion of World War II until the beginning, amid unprecedented prosperity, of the second Eisenhower administration. The sense of shock was deep. While President Eisenhower said that he was not worried "an iota," Senator Henry M. Jackson urged the former general to proclaim "a week of shame and danger." Writers and politicians bemoaned an America gone soft, an America that had neglected education and basic research.

Charles E. Wilson, Eisenhower's secretary of defense, was berated for his downgrading of basic research. Wilson, the man who became famous for telling the Senate Armed Services Committee in 1952 that "what is good for General Motors is good for the country."[2] had mocked scientific research as an essentially frivolous investigation of "what makes grass green and fried potatoes brown." The anti-intellectualism seemed somehow typical of the pre-Sputnik 1950s, but it was blown away by the cries for more and better education and more spending on research, which followed upon the news of the Soviet satellite. These cries were being heard again in the late 1980s— this time in response not to a Soviet military threat but to the Japanese economic challenge.

Sputnik's blow to America's feeling of security was severe. Although few had noticed it at the time, the blow was foreshadowed six weeks earlier, on August 26, 1957, when the Soviets reported the first successful launch of a multistage rocket that carried an intercontinental ballistic missile. Jubilant about the success of the Soviet ICBM, Nikita Khrushchev, first secretary of the Soviet Communist party, said, "The U.S. does not have an intercontinental ballistic missile: otherwise it would also have easily launched an earth satellite of its own."[3] He added that the West might as well scrap its B-52s and abandon its airfields: "If you study our latest proposals you will no longer find any mention of control posts [radar installations] or airfields. It is useless to create control posts to watch obsolete airplanes."[4]

The two Sputnik launches dramatically demonstrated to the West, and to the rest of the world, a decisive Soviet technological superiority that could not be hushed up as the launch of the ICBM had been. The most significant characteristic of the ICBM, so far as Americans were concerned, was the rocket's ability to cross, in a matter of minutes, the broad oceans that had done so much to ensure American security for nearly two hundred years. American schoolchildren started hearing from their teachers the pathetic instruction to "dive under your desks if you see a bright flash." The teachers failed to add that if they saw a bright flash, they would be incinerated almost instantly, either above or beneath the desk.

Before the development of the Soviet ICBM, America and its allies had enjoyed the protection of a formidable deterrent to the Soviet threat in Europe. America's nuclear capability was an almost costless cement that held together the Western alliance. Sole possession of nuclear capability by the United States until 1949 had meant that its allies enjoyed the benefits of that deterrence without any additional cost to America. Nor did America have any desire to exclude its allies from the benefits of its nuclear shield, since the alliance was its instrument to contain the spread of communism.

Even after the Soviets developed their own nuclear devices, the American deterrence was highly credible in view of its capability to annihilate the Soviet Union from European bases without the fear of itself being annihilated.

Plenty of real firepower backed up America's power-based strategy for maintaining Western security. In 1954, the first hydrogen bomb was exploded by the United States. It was one hundred times more powerful than any previous weapon. In the same year, Eisenhower's secretary of state, John Foster Dulles, declared that America's defensive strategy was to be shifted from an emphasis on containment of the Soviet Union (the Truman Doctrine) to one of massive retaliation in the event of a Soviet attack on the United States. Nevertheless, when Dulles enunciated the doctrine of massive retaliation, the likelihood of a Soviet attack seemed remote.

But once the Soviet Union had demonstrated the feasibility of ICBMs four months before the United States was able to do the same, the power and the credibility of American deterrence through massive retaliation were sharply diminished. And absolute deterrence—the ability to annihilate the Soviets without fear of ourselves being annihilated—was swept away by the existence of Soviet ICBMs.

THE FRUITS OF OVERINDULGENCE

The Sputnik episode and the recriminations in its aftermath provide a vivid reminder that periodically since World War II, America has wrestled with the notion that its power and its global prominence are on the wane. The signs of alleged decline have come in both military areas and economic areas. The Sputnik shock came together with the 1957–1958 recession and the mild stroke of the once-vigorous Eisenhower in November of 1957 to reinforce the feeling among Americans that their nation had to get moving again. That feeling, coupled with the vigor, the energy, the youth, and the great personal magnetism of John F. Kennedy was enough to elect him president of the United States in 1960.

Apart from the emotion and the appeal of renewing the sense of national identity, numerous strands of thought were involved in Kennedy's election. His campaign had been built around the central theme of reinvigoration and growth after the stagnancy revealed by the Sputnik shock, but the new president was also surrounded by liberal intellectuals who were impatient with the fundamentally conservative Truman and Eisenhower administrations. They viewed the decade and a half after 1945 as an interruption of what they saw as the thrust of the New Deal away from laissez-faire capitalism. This was taking Roosevelt at the valuation of his conservative enemies. As we have seen, the supposed turning away from capitalism was no part of the real New Deal. Instead, it was a retrospective inference, founded on the hostility of the Right and the wishful thinking of the Left. Nevertheless, Kennedy was seen by many as having taken up the Rooseveltian legacy.

John Kenneth Galbraith's *The Affluent Society* set the tone for the Democrats.[5] Published in 1957, it coincided with the distress over American decline that followed the Sputnik launch. For Galbraith, America was an affluent society in which the private sector was gorging itself on consumption while government, especially national defense, was starved for resources.

The symbol of liberal disgust with overconsumption in the late 1950s was the Edsel, a redundant and particularly unattractive automobile introduced in the 1958 model year by the Ford Motor Company. Ford had spent three years and $250 million (about $1 billion in 1990 dollars) developing a $3,500 car that no one wanted or needed—while the Russians developed ICBMs and Sputniks.

America's sense of indignation about its own sloth and overindulgence in the late 1950s—the feeling that the nation was getting soft—created a sense of crisis less enduring but as sudden and in some ways more urgent than the crises of the Depression and World War II. Though the immediate consequences were less tangible than those of Japan's attack on Pearl Harbor, the sense of vulnerability inspired by Soviet ICBMs was greater than that occasioned by an all-out Japanese effort that barely reached a remote American military outpost halfway across the Pacific. Conditioned by the can-do responses of government to Depression and war, America was ready for something new on the policy front. It came from a group of young economists in Cambridge and New Haven who had been advising John Kennedy when he was still a senator from Massachusetts.

As part of the post-Sputnik spasm of liberal criticism of Eisenhower-era policies, academic economists like James Tobin of Yale University were bemoaning the "missile gap" that became a big issue in the 1960 Nixon-Kennedy debates. In the March 1958 *Yale Law Review*, Tobin published an article, remarkable by today's standards for someone calling himself a liberal, that was highly critical of the Eisenhower administration's low defense spending. Invoking the theme of the affluent society, he cited a *New Yorker* cartoon in which "a middle-aged, middle-class wife" comments to her husband: "It's been a great week for everybody. The Russians have the Intercontinental Ballistic Missile and we have the Edsel."

Wrote Tobin of the cartoon:

The major economic and political foreign policy of the administration could not be more succinctly expressed. The response of the administration to the news in August of 1957 of Russia's success with missiles was a continuation of the vigorous effort to reduce the rate of spending of the Defense Department by about $4 billion a year . . . at a time when the world situation cried out for accelerating and enlarging our defense effort.[6]

For Tobin, the outmoded economic ideology of laissez-faire capitalism was the major underlying problem for America: "The policies [it has] dictated have cost the United States and gravely threatened its survival as a nation." Tobin and many of his liberal Democratic colleagues sought to lay the blame for America's loss of vigor and its tendency to favor consumption over saving and hard work on what he characterized as laissez-faire capitalism—even though this was virtually indistinguishable from Jeffersonian limited government. Tobin described what he opposed as the view that "government intervention in economic life—spending, taxing, borrowing, regulating—is an evil to be minimized: man's needs are best accommodated and progress is most rapid when private enterprise flourishes unfettered by government regulations and unburdened by the dead weight of government activity."

In fact, with changes far more modest than those called for by Tobin and others, some of America's best growth years came in the decades after 1958. Real per capita income in America rose 86 percent between 1958 and 1988. That meant an average annual growth rate of real per capita GNP of 2.1 percent, which was more than one-third faster than it had been during the previous thirty years.

KEYNES AND THEN SOME

A revolution in economics and its impact on the economy came during the 1950s—supposedly the era of America's intellectual torpor—from economists who came to Washington in the 1950s and 1960s. Their ideas were essentially Keynesian, but they went well beyond Keynes. Keynes's major contribution had been to suggest that changes in government spending might be necessary to offset changes in private spending to eliminate the business cycle, or at least to mitigate its most adverse effects. Keynes's young American disciples, however, believed that Keynesian demand management could be used for more positive economic ends.

The essence of Keynesian economics was to suggest that when private spending—especially investment, its most volatile element—falls, government spending ought to be increased to maintain something close to the previous level of total demand for goods and services. More stable demand would lead to more stable production schedules, and employment as well. This concept was beginning to enter the economic orthodoxy of the time, but the young liberal economists around Kennedy were interested not just in avoiding depression and unemployment. They began to see Keynes's ideas as the basis for a magic formula that could be used to create growth and prosperity by government fiat.

On one level, Keynes's theory had been an attack on the laissez-faire notion that economies would eventually return to full employment on their own through flexibility of wages and prices. Faced with the persistent unemployment in the United Kingdom and the United States during the Depression of the 1930s, Keynes created a theoretical system that allowed for the observable persistence of unemployment. Part of his theory relied on the notion that prices were "sticky" downward and failed to fall rapidly enough to ensure that all labor would be hired and all goods bought even if prices and wages fell. Pre-Keynesian "classical" economists presented sophisticated models suggesting that if prices fell far enough the purchasing power of the money held by individuals in the economy would rise by enough to push spending back up. The Depression, however, seemed to be powerful evidence that any "real balance effect" operated too slowly to maintain full employment—something that the Employment Act of 1946 had made for the first time the responsibility of the federal government.

The next intellectual step for committed Keynesians in the 1950s was to suggest that government policies could actually affect the growth rate of the economy. At the time, growth theory was an esoteric, highly mathematical branch of economics, but it was beginning to be seen as a dynamic extension of Keynesian principles. The idea was not just to dampen business cycles but perhaps to alter the trajectory—the growth path—of the economy. That involved discovering ways to accelerate capital formation and thereby to increase growth, real wages, and income per capita. To many young economists of the era, it appeared that Keynes had discovered the philosopher's stone that could turn base metals into gold.

Part of the impatience of liberal economists with the Eisenhower administration stemmed from their view that by clinging to balanced-budget orthodoxy and rejecting the latest developments in economic science, the growth rate of the U.S. economy was being held well below its potential. If a 2 percent growth rate could somehow have been a 3 percent growth rate, then about $60 billion worth of income (in today's dollars) was being lost in a year.

The theories of growth developed by Robert Solow and Edmund Phelps and extended by James Tobin and others played a significant role in the tax policies that emerged during the Kennedy administration. They also meshed with Kennedy's well-chosen rhetoric about "getting America moving again." Although this was partly an antidote to America's Sputnik-induced feeling of flaccidity, it also led Kennedy to what he regarded as a more dynamic fiscal policy. Moreover, since some growth-enhancing measures amounted to sharp reductions in the tax rate on purchases of capital by business, they helped to soften Kennedy's antibusiness image.

Early in the 1960 campaign, Kennedy assistant Ted Sorensen put together a team of economic advisers for Kennedy—mostly professors at Harvard, Yale, and MIT, including Solow, Paul Samuelson, Galbraith, and Tobin—who provided both academic legitimacy to Kennedy's positions and a substantial education in economics for the candidate. Because of his background and inclinations, however, together with the realities of the campaign, he did not take tax-cutting or deficit-tolerating positions. Kennedy ran as a fiscal conservative and an old-fashioned budget balancer.[7] He decried budget deficits, saying that they could be justified only under conditions of national emergency or serious recession.

The Democratic party platform, reflecting Kennedy's campaign rhetoric, said that while the country required more spending to meet social needs, "except in periods of recession or national emergency, these needs can be met with a balanced budget, with no increase in present tax rates, and with some surplus for the gradual reduction of our national debt."[8]

As Stein notes, there is no reason to believe that Kennedy emphasized the importance of a balanced budget and the desirability of a surplus as an election tactic; his position reflected the conventional wisdom both of his party and of its intellectuals. But that wisdom was changing, even as the campaign unfolded, in part because of the growing feeling that the economy was stagnant.[9]

KENNEDY'S INVESTMENT TAX CREDIT

When Kennedy took office in January 1961, the economy was in recession; unemployment was 6.7 percent, up by nearly one and one-half points from the previous January. But Kennedy and his economic advisers, including Walter Heller, the chairman of the CEA, and Samuelson, were more concerned with the longer-standing lifelessness in the economy. In his State of the Union message, Kennedy commented, "The present state of our economy is disturbing. We take office in the wake of seven months of recession, three and one-half years of slack, seven years of diminished economic growth, and nine years of falling farm income."

But the concern about stagnation did not spur Kennedy to recommend dramatic measures at first; those measures—particularly the tax cuts that became such a valued precedent for Ronald Reagan's Republicans in 1980— were not put together into proposals until late in 1962. Neither did the Kennedy administration simply decide to rest with the economic status quo. The desire to do something to get the country moving, while also acknowledging the importance of the business sector, led to the investment tax credit.

The investment tax credit was the major new idea in the tax plan proposed by Kennedy in April 1961, just three months after he took office. It was designed to stimulate the purchase of new capital equipment and showed a detailed grasp of the new Keynesian growth theory as it related to tax policy. The plan focused quite narrowly on investment incentives, although it also included measures to close loopholes on "expense-account living" and repealed the partial tax exemption that dividends had had since 1954. The idea was precisely to channel investment where it would be most productive, not just to give a break to businessmen or those who lived on dividends. Kennedy also proposed that dividends and interest should be subject to withholding, which raised howls of protest both from investors and from retirees, who counted on interest and dividend checks as much as workers counted on salary checks.

This investment tax credit, Kennedy's most revolutionary proposal, was aimed precisely at new investment, not all investment. The proposal to accelerate economic growth by inducing the increased purchase of specific forms of capital represented a remarkably rapid adoption by government policy makers of ideas that had appeared only five years earlier in esoteric economic journals. While it had taken nearly twenty years after the publication of Keynes's general theory to apply the countercyclical fiscal policy ideas embodied in that major work, the growth-enhancing ideas of the mid-1950s appeared specifically in Kennedy's first major tax message. Said Kennedy: "Inevitably, capital expansion and modernization—now frequently under the name of automation—alter established modes of production. Great benefits result and are distributed widely."

No doubt the sense of dynamism implicit in government measures designed to excite faster economic growth served as an appealing antidote to the national feeling of having "gone soft" that had emerged in the late 1950s. Faster growth, like the idea of modernization, carried with it a satisfying sense of national rejuvenation. Democrats liked it because the government was making it happen. To them, it was an application of the successful Roosevelt formula of liberal pragmatism and beneficent government action. Republicans, after some initial grousing, came to like it, too. Lower taxes on investment could not be all bad, especially if government could satisfy its growing appetite for revenues from a larger national output instead of from taxing more things at higher rates.

As always when theory makes the transition to practice, there was a danger that the potential of the ideas of the growth theorists would be exaggerated and perhaps abused by politicians. The notion that the growth of the economy can be accelerated and thereby yield future increases in tax revenue by the politically attractive method of cutting taxes is a heady one for politicians. Indeed, Ronald Reagan's supply-siders in 1981 referred to the ideas of Kennedy's economic advisers, which were really the prototype for supply-side economics, though they were packaged differently.

The attractiveness of pro-growth tax policy in the form of accelerated-depreciation measures or, as it was further developed by Kennedy's advisers, the investment tax credit, is tied up with the enchantment of most politicians and the public, especially businessmen, with the notion of something magical about capital formation and something even more magical about faster capital formation. This notion has also attracted a strong following in the U.S. Congress, where members are always on the lookout for ways in which the country can seem to eat its cake and have it, too.

Investment—the purchase of capital or, more tangibly, of the machinery and buildings that combine with labor to produce output—is commonly considered the key to economic growth for a number of reasons. First, although standard growth theory shows that the growth of output comes from the growth of the labor force, the growth of the capital stock, and technological change—which is merely a catchall phrase for the part of growth that cannot be precisely attributed either to labor or capital—not all of those variables are equally controllable. Population growth determines the growth of the labor force and is difficult to affect in the short run. And since technological change is essentially the part of growth that cannot be explained, then the part of growth left over for adjustment through policy measures is capital formation.

The second appeal of enhancing capital formation is tied to its tangibility. Capital formation suggests building for the future: factories, machinery, smokestacks (at least in a preenvironmentalist era), and all the outward manifestations of production go naturally together with workers rolling up their sleeves and walking into busy factories to produce more and better goods and prosperity for everyone. These things are part of the image of a nation moving ahead. Such imagery probably got its biggest boost during World War II, when the government was mounting propaganda campaigns exhorting Americans to increase the production of weapons. It was a relatively easy transition to more gentle forms of encouragement for the production of more goods and services for domestic consumption.

The third, and perhaps most potent, reason for encouraging capital formation derives from the possibility that building new machines to replace existing ones carries with it an extra, almost magical, growth bonus. In the process of using a machine, workers and management may think of better ways to work with it and suggest modifications in its design to increase its productivity. This kind of embodied technological change suggests that the more rapidly machines can be replaced and ideas for better machines incorporated into the production process, the more rapidly the economy will grow. The development of computers during the 1970s and 1980s is an example of this process.

With these reasons to think of tax policy as desirable, government planners can use tax policy as a means to accelerate the rate at which machines are replaced. Accelerated depreciation, which allows businesses to take larger depreciation allowances before calculating taxes, and the investment tax credit, which gives them a credit toward their tax for purchasing a new machine or other piece of capital, are the tax measures designed by economists to speed up capital formation and growth. If the turnover of the capital stock can be accelerated under the embodiment theory, the government can increase economic growth.

An even more attractive possibility exists. If the measures are effective enough, the revenue given up through investment tax credits and accelerated depreciation may be less than the revenue gained through taxes on the larger income created by a higher rate of economic growth. This is the 1960s version of supply-side economics. In the 1980s, supply-side economics coupled the assumption of growth from capital formation with the further assumption that labor could be excited to further effort and production by lower tax rates on income. The lower tax rates on income would produce enough additional work by individuals—work performed in return for the prospect of higher after-tax earnings—so that the tax cut would actually lead to higher revenue. The consequences of this additional assumption we see in chapter 11.

In his drive to win bipartisan support for his new tax policies, Kennedy emphasized loophole closing along with the classic supply-side notion that, because of the growth-enhancing properties of the investment-tax-credit proposals, such tax cuts would be self-financing. In an April 20, 1961, message to Congress, the president said: "The elimination of certain defects and inequities as proposed below will provide revenue gains to offset the tax reductions offered to stimulate the economy. Thus no net loss of revenue is involved in this set of proposals."[10]

Kennedy represented his initial foray into tax reform as part of a necessary transition away from the remnants of the tax system that had grown up during World War II, but he also set the tone for tax reformers for many years to come. Recalling the large expansion in the coverage of the income tax during the war, Kennedy noted, "So many taxpayers have become so preoccupied with so many tax saving devices that business decisions are interfered with and the efficient functioning of the price system is distorted."[11]

While investment tax credits had by the 1970s, and more than ever in 1981, come to be viewed as considerably probusiness, the initial response of the business community to these credits was less than enthusiastic. But the critics of the Kennedy tax initiative focused on attendant measures of taxation of foreign income, limits on expense accounts, and the withholding tax on interest and dividends. A few days after the Kennedy tax plan appeared, Morris Peloubet, a certified public accountant specializing in depreciation issues, was quoted in the *New York Times*: "Compared with proposals put forward by recognized authorities in Congressional hearings and embodied in legislation already introduced in both houses it [the Kennedy proposal] is vague, uncertain in application and its effect on revenue is doubtful and unpredictable."[12]

Republican response was not enthusiastic either. A Republican member of the House Ways and Means Committee, Bruce Alger, called Kennedy's tax message "a mishmash of muddled goals and uncertain generalities that will tend to have a disturbing impact on economic recovery and progress."

The negative reaction to the initial Kennedy tax proposal was no doubt due partly to nervousness in the business community about what Kennedy and his crew of Harvard economists were up to and partly to the newness of the ideas to tax professionals who were constantly working at the problem of minimizing taxes for businesses and wealthy individuals. To them, the investment tax credit sounded like a gimmick. When it was eventually adopted after Kennedy's death, the economists' idea to aim the tax credit only at new investment was replaced by an investment tax credit on all investment, a measure that the designers of the original tax credit proposal decried. Spreading the investment tax credit over all investment and not just new investment lost more revenue, while taking away much of the vigor of the proposal's ability to add new capital.

EARLY KENNEDY CONCERNS

That a new president would venture so aggressively into what must have seemed to be experimental growth-enhancing measures is testimony to the importance he attached to dissolving what he thought was American lassitude, if not paralysis, in the wake of Eisenhower and Sputnik. Using the tax code to stimulate growth, Kennedy laid himself open to criticism from business that he was meddling in decisions that should be left to the private sector, but his activist fiscal measures could look to the precedent established during the early experiments by CEA economists under Arthur Burns. Once Republicans abandoned strict fiscal orthodoxy, accepting activism to help GOP constituencies, the way was open for Democrats to try out some of their own medicine.

Kennedy was concerned with maintaining both the perception and the reality of U.S. global leadership in the face of increasing competition from the Soviet Union. On April 12, 1961, slightly more than a week before Kennedy's tax measure was proposed, the Soviets succeeded in launching the first man into space. Yuri Gagarin, a twenty-seven-year-old Soviet air force major, went aloft in a 10,395-pound space vehicle and achieved orbital flight before returning safely back to earth.

Comparisons with the initial U.S. effort to put a living being into space were not favorable. A few months earlier, on January 31, 1961, America had lobbed a chimpanzee named Ham into space. Ham rode for eighteen minutes in a rocket that reached a maximum altitude of 150 miles before dropping into the sea off Cape Canaveral. The huge gap between popping a chimpanzee into space and orbiting a Soviet air force major around the earth was wide and painfully obvious. Even Alan Shepard's fifteen-minute nonorbital flight into space on May 5, 1961, did little to close it.

Kennedy, anxious to keep his promise to get the economy moving again, was aware that a higher rate of economic growth, if achievable, would enable him to continue aggressive competition with the Soviets' military and space technology, while still allowing him to entertain the idea of expanding the social programs being pushed by the liberal activists in his administration. Because of the economic measures that Kennedy initiated, the real guns-and-butter president, Lyndon Johnson, was able to pursue simultaneously the Vietnam War and the Great Society. Unfortunately, the ability to undertake such ambitious spending programs was contingent on 4 percent sustained American growth, a goal that was achieved for a few years during the 1960s before 1967, but not after.

Unlike Johnson, Kennedy had to learn a lot to get new legislation like his 1961 tax initiative adopted. Momentum for new tax measures is almost never great in the Congress, since new measures always disturb a tax code that has been delicately balanced to include provisions dear to the constituents of the key tax-writing committees. Kennedy sent only his tax message to Congress, not a draft bill, an omission that communicated to the Congress a lack of urgency on Kennedy's part. He also did not do well at marshaling support from outside the Congress. The hearings on tax reform, held in open and closed sessions for several months by the House Ways and Means Committee, revealed Kennedy's weak links with business. Although the reform, particularly its more dynamic segments, was ultimately in the interest of business, Kennedy found few friends among business leaders. Howard Peterson, speaking for the Committee on Economic Development, said that the ITC was "the most novel, the most arbitrary, and the most objectionable feature of the [Kennedy tax] proposals. We believe that the proposed investment tax credit involves too much arbitrary inequity, and the liberalization of depreciation charges is a better balanced approach to the encouragement of investment."[13]

When he put forward his initial tax proposals, Kennedy made clear his intention of submitting a more sweeping tax package in 1962. In the meantime, Wilbur Mills, chairman of the House Ways and Means Committee, could go on pushing his long-held dream of reforming the tax law by broadening the tax base. He wanted to give the benefits to individuals instead of to corporations, as Kennedy's proposal appeared to do. The expectation in Mills's mind that bigger and better things could be done, coupled with the lack of an enthusiastic response for Kennedy's innovative tax proposals, led the Ways and Means Committee on October 23, 1961, to postpone action until 1962, while it adopted a far less ambitious tax package for 1961.

In September, Treasury Secretary Douglas Dillon asserted that, although the administration wanted to present a tax-cut proposal in its 1962 tax-reform package, defense needs caused by the Berlin crisis made such a cut difficult. The Berlin Wall had gone up in August 1961, and the administration's focus returned to the terrestrial, from the space race with the Soviets. Further, with little support for tax reform for the sake of reform, more ambitious tax-reform proposals were unlikely to pass in 1962.

Whatever the ultimate outcome, Kennedy needed passage of part of his initial tax package to show strength to Congress, to the tax lobbyists, and to the public. While he and his advisers put off any substantial tax-reform proposals, like those ultimately passed after his death, they did push to have the investment-tax-credit package passed. Clearly, if Kennedy was unable to push through such a targeted reform, then he would not stand much chance of getting a broader overhaul of the tax system. The administration was also anxious to set a precedent by sounding the tax message to Congress from the executive branch—a precedent that was to prove immensely valuable to Ronald Reagan twenty years later. This would establish that the initiative for broader tax reform, lower tax rates, and base broadening lay with the enlightened Kennedy technocrats and not with the political hacks in Congress. Thus, whether by accident or design, the success or failure of the Kennedy administration's experiment with tax policy over the remainder of its term was limited to the success or failure of the investment tax credit.

MODIFIED POSITIONS

In 1962, Kennedy was willing to accept the watered-down version that came from the House Ways and Means Committee and the Senate Finance Committee, reasoning that some bill was better than none at all. While the original Heller-Kennedy investment tax credit called for three stages of deductibility (6 percent, 10 percent, and finally 15 percent) to encourage investment in new plants and equipment over and above what would normally be spent, effectively the final bill allowed a tax credit of 7 percent on the purchase of any plant or equipment, even if the expenditure was made only to replace existing assets.

The broadening of the investment tax credit was not a surprising development. Among the representatives of business, the more narrowly focused tax credit on new investment seemed capricious and likely to favor only limited segments of industry. The broader measure carried the appeal of something for everyone and therefore found sufficient support to pass the tax committees in Congress. The economists' arguments about the importance of encouraging additions to the stock of plant and equipment were lost in the shuffle. Rather, another idea vaguely underscored by the embodiment theory was born: more investment per se was a good thing. What kind of investment —on extra equipment or a replacement for existing equipment—did not matter.

Business executives began to support the investment tax credit and some of the other provisions in the 1962 tax bill once they became familiar with all its implications. It became clear that, along with the investment tax credit, a revised depreciation schedule was offered, allowing faster write-offs of business assets. Treasury Secretary Dillon acknowledged that this change alone would be a $1.5 billion ($14 billion in 1993 dollars) tax break for business in the first year. The change in depreciation schedules was made July 11, 1962, by executive action, one month before the Senate Finance Committee reported the amended investment-tax-credit bill to the full Senate. After business had what it wanted, if the president wanted an investment tax credit as well, that was fine with business interests. Faster depreciation and investment tax credits—a combination that can result in negative tax rates or actual subsidies on the use of specific forms of favored investment—became linked together in yet another pattern that was to be repeated by Ronald Reagan's supply-siders two decades later.

With primarily the change in depreciation, Kennedy hoped to woo the business community and soothe the wounds opened when, in an attempt to hold down rising inflation in April 1962, he had forced the steel industry to rescind a round of price increases. But with the economy recovered by early 1962 from the 1960 recession, there was little appetite for more sweeping tax reduction. In February 1962, Kennedy commented at a press conference, "For the present time there is not a chance of tax reduction." By June 1962, though, after a dramatic drop in the stock market on May 28, the chances had changed substantially. Worried for the first time about the possibility of a Kennedy recession, the president and his economic team decided that it was time for a bold move to stimulate the economy. That became the Kennedy tax cut, announced June 7.[14]

Government could stimulate the economy in two main ways: by raising government expenditures and by cutting taxes. Kennedy opted for the latter, more Jeffersonian route because of a belief that Congress would not accept a significant increase in nondefense expenditures. Either course, predictably enough, would lead to an increased budget deficit, but Kennedy believed, correctly, that business would not object to a budget deficit caused by a tax cut. It wanted tax reduction too much for that.

He also saw that, in general, the shibboleth in American politics about the sanctity of a balanced budget was no longer as potent in 1962 as in the 1950s and before. Dwight Eisenhower's 1958 budget deficit of $12.4 billion had taught voters and politicians alike that deficits per se did not cause economic havoc.

Kennedy declared that the economy's central problem was that "our present tax system exerts too heavy a drag on growth, that it siphons out of the private economy too large a share of personal and business purchasing power, that it reduces the financial incentives for personal effort, investment and risktaking."

Although Truman and Eisenhower had been aware of the role that tax policy played in economic growth and spoke of it in their annual promises of tax reduction, neither ever acted on it. Kennedy not only acted, he brought a more sophisticated economic rationale to bear on the subject. He emphasized a productive capacity, unused since 1957, to demonstrate the drag on the economy. The choice, Kennedy said, was "between two kinds of deficits: a chronic deficit of inertia, as the unwanted result of inadequate revenues and a restricted economy, or a temporary deficit of transition, resulting from a tax cut designed to boost the economy, increase the tax revenues and achieve a future budget surplus."

The Kennedy tax cut was not defined in June, either in amount or in specific elements. While most observers expected a cut of around $3 billion, the president's promise for tax cuts for lower-income taxpayers, middle Americans, and corporations meant that such cuts would likely amount to much more—probably upward of $10 billion unless they were accompanied by stiff (and unpopular) provisions to close loopholes.[15]

Working within guidelines established by Wilbur Mills, Douglas Dillon's Treasury came up with a package that included net tax reductions of $10 billion, based on $13.6 billion in tax cuts and $3.4 billion in new revenues from loophole closings and other reforms, to be phased in from 1963 to 1965. The authors of the package also promised to keep the fiscal 1964 budget under $100 billion in expenditures and to keep the deficit below the $12.4 billion that it had reached under Eisenhower in 1959.

Announced in detail by the president in January 1963, the tax-cut package was not enacted for more than a year, in large part because of public and congressional opposition to the "reforms" that raised countervailing revenue. These limited, for example, itemized deductions to those exceeding 5 percent of income, a provision that incensed so many people that the final package kept the tax cuts and dropped the reforms. The result was a larger net revenue loss than Kennedy had proposed or expected.

The tax cut that was finally enacted in February 1964, three months after Kennedy was assassinated, amounted to about $14 billion and reduced income-tax rates across the board. Most drastically, it slashed the top marginal tax rate from 91 percent to 70 percent and cut corporate rates from 52 percent to 47 percent (a "normal" rate of 22 percent and a surtax of 25 percent).

AN EVALUATION

Partly because of the inevitable political dynamics of crafting tax policy, the experiments with supply-side economics in the 1960s—just like those in the 1980s—had mixed results. The 1960s experiment with accelerated depreciation and investment tax credits did produce an increase in investment, but as the theorists who put the ideas forward knew, and as the politicians who applied them chose to ignore, the incentive effects for higher investment that flowed from tax changes were largely temporary. Accelerated depreciation or investment tax credits said that businessmen should increase the number of machines and other capital they owned. And, indeed, businessmen did so after the introduction of tax incentives in 1964. Once the new machines have been bought, however, the incentive effect of the tax measures to increase investment is largely over, although some persistent positive effect on growth may follow embodiment effects and a larger stock of machinery and more depreciation, which in turn requires larger purchases of machinery just to keep the enlarged stock of machinery intact.

The existence of a secondary effect on growth, whereby the act of buying more machines and replacing machines more rapidly accelerates the rate at which new ideas are embodied in the capital stock, was and continues to be difficult to detect. The concept of embodied technological change continues to excite the imagination of economists and lobbyists who are seeking to obtain tax preferences for the businesses that they represent. While embodiment is theoretically possible, its reality will probably never live up to the expectations of lobbyists when they talk about the magic of incentives for capital formation.

Kennedy's experience with innovative tax proposals was not atypical of his experience with his other legislative initiatives. Outright victories, even with a Democratic-controlled Congress, were few. Typically, powerful congressional committees watered down Kennedy's plans. The same southern Democrats who opposed civil rights legislation in the early 1960s also opposed other liberal, progressive proposals on welfare, economics, education, and Medicare. And these Democrats were often the chairmen of the powerful congressional committees with which the White House had to deal.

Moreover, a conservative coalition between southern Democrats and Republicans could command a winning majority in both houses of Congress. As a result, in 1962 Congress killed Kennedy's proposals for Medicare, college aid, urban affairs, civil rights legislation, and extended unemployment compensation. In view of the membership of congressional committees, it is surprising that Kennedy moved as far as he did with innovative tax legislation.

Like most presidents, Kennedy was often placed in the position of having to respond to actions over which he had limited control. His battle with the steel industry over price increases is only one example. He inherited the Bay of Pigs invasion plans from the Eisenhower administration and did not have adequate information on the situation in Cuba. He went nose-to-nose with the Soviets over missiles in Cuba during October 1962. Earlier, in August 1961, the Soviets forced the Berlin Wall onto Kennedy's list of crises, which interfered with his own sense of priorities.

The Kennedy administration finally proposed civil rights legislation on February 28, 1963. The proposal was criticized in Congress as "thin" by liberals of both parties. It was seen as an affront by southern Democrats in Congress. The resulting mass civil rights demonstration in Birmingham on April 3 spawned others nationwide. Television viewers took a break from their usual "wasteland" programming to watch dogs and water hoses being used against the demonstrators. Only after Kennedy's hand had been forced in this way did he submit an expanded civil rights bill on June 11. The initiative was not in Kennedy's hands as much as it was in those of the protestors. The march on Washington two months later, during the hot August of 1963, underscored the fact that Washington was reacting to popular pressures for civil rights rather than controlling them.

It is odd, in view of Kennedy's posthumous reputation, that a careful reading of the legislative initiatives of the first two years of his administration shows that its ideas on tax policy were far better articulated than its ideas on civil rights. Other social programs fared no better than civil rights. There were failures to move legislation on school aid, area-redevelopment funds, mass-transit aid, a youth-employment bill, an overhaul of unemployment compensation, and minimum-wage increases. The Great Society was not even a speck on the horizon.

Beyond legislative initiatives, Kennedy's efforts to get the economy moving again met with limited success. GNP growth, which stood at about 2.2 percent during 1960, the last year of the Eisenhower administration, rose only to 2.6 percent in 1961. Meanwhile, unemployment rose from 5.4 percent of the labor force in 1960 to 6.5 percent in 1961, while black unemployment rose from 10.2 percent in 1960 to 12.4 percent in 1961. Among Kennedy's economists at least, these difficulties fueled the push in 1962 for the investment stimulus package.

While Kennedy and his economists struggled to get new economic measures adopted, unemployment stayed high by postwar standards, even as growth picked up. In 1962 and 1963, about 5.5 percent of workers were unemployed. By 1964, the rate had dropped to 5 percent. In 1962 and 1963, economic growth jumped more than 4 percent. After the effects of the 1964 tax cut began to take hold, the unemployment rate dropped to 4.4 percent, while economic growth rates averaged more than 5.5 percent from 1964 through 1966.

Kennedy's experiment with growth economics, not put into play until after his death, did much to create the belief that the U.S. economy could sustain long-term growth at above a 4 percent annual rate. Kennedy's successor, Lyndon Johnson, was left with a tremendous growth bonus that ended up squandered on the twin vacuums of the Vietnam War and the Great Society.

PART FOUR

FROM THE GREAT SOCIETY TO THE REAGAN REVOLUTION

✦

· 8 ·

THE END OF
JEFFERSONIAN
LIBERALISM

In 1971, Doris Kearns, one of Lyndon Baines Johnson's most sympathetic biographers, discussed the Great Society with the former president. Johnson compared the Great Society to a young girl who "had a real chance to grow into a beautiful woman . . . and when she grew up I figured she'd be so big and beautiful that the American people couldn't help but fall in love with her, and once they did, they'd want to keep her around forever, making her a permanent part of American life, more permanent even than the New Deal."[1]

The Johnson presidency started not with the Great Society but by picking up the Kennedy legacy wherever he and Congress could. That included especially the big tax cut, which had been moving toward enactment when JFK was assassinated; LBJ added another, smaller cut in excise taxes on his own in 1965. But while tax cuts occurred in the Johnson years, they were far more identified with Kennedy. Johnson's expected legacy to the country was not fiscal policy per se, but rather social policy to flow from the fruits of fiscal policy—the "Great Society."

"Great Society" was a term coined by President Johnson and defined in a speech at the University of Michigan on May 22, 1964:

The Great Society rests on abundance and liberty for all. It demands an end to poverty and racial injustice, to which we are totally committed in our time. . . .

The Great Society is a place where every child can find knowledge to enrich his mind and to enlarge his talents. It is a place where leisure is a welcome chance to build and reflect, not a feared cause of boredom and restlessness. It is a place where the city of man serves not only the needs of the body and the demands of commerce, but the desire for beauty and the hunger of community.

. . . But most of all, the Great Society is not a safe harbor, a resting place, a final objective, a finished work. It is a challenge constantly renewed, beckoning us toward a destiny where the meaning of our lives matches the marvelous products of our labor.

If the term was LBJ's, the programs that defined it included many that had been bubbling in the policy process going back to the Truman administration —such as federal aid to elementary and secondary education, and Medicare —and some that had been bottled up in Congress in the Kennedy years— like the tax cut and civil rights.

For LBJ, the linchpin of the Great Society was his own "War on Poverty," which included ten programs under the umbrella of the Economic Opportunity Act of 1964, including the Job Corps and VISTA. Added to the poverty cluster to encompass the Great Society agenda was Medicare, along with Medicaid, the Partnership for Health program, scholarships for college students, aid to elementary and secondary education, consumer-protection laws, and welfare reform.

Despite his moving and flowery rhetoric about the meaning of the Great Society, and the obviously large ambition driving his vision, President Johnson did not foresee that his programs would eventually grow to become a large share of the budget, crowding out other budget elements, or have a significant, independent impact on the economy. But they did, and not just because of the guns-and-butter imbalance.

As Herbert Stein pointed out in *Presidential Economics*, the Great Society program "reflected a misconception of the long-run budget situation, if not a total neglect of the long run. The new spending measures were launched in an atmosphere still colored by the notion of the fiscal dividend." In other words, the administration expected that as the economy grew—and grew robustly—revenues would increase sharply; indeed, it was necessary, went the thinking, to use those revenues, injecting the money into the economy to keep it from getting depressed.[2]

The optimism of LBJ's economic advisers was evident in their 1966 *Economic Report to the President*:

The strength of the advance in 1965 was exceptional and surpassed expectations. The Council's Annual Report of 1965, which contained one of the more optimistic forecasts at that time, estimated a gain of $38 billion in GNP for the year—the midpoint of a $33–44 billion range. In contrast, the actual gain was a record $47 billion.

Of course, the economy did not grow as LBJ's economic team had envisioned, especially after 1973, and the revenue dividend never materialized. But the programs continued to grow, particularly in the post-LBJ years. As Stein documents, "In 1965, the last year before the Vietnam War dominated federal finances, social programs cost $30 billion, 25 percent of the budget and 4.5 percent of the GNP. By 1980 these programs cost $280 billion, 48 percent of the budget and 11 percent of the GNP. In constant dollars, the increase was 310 percent, more than five times as large as the percentage increase of real GNP."[3]

The largest engine of growth was in the health-care programs, Medicare and Medicaid. Increased life spans, increased use of medical care spurred by its ready availability, and increased demand for services, fueled by the lack of direct cost to the beneficiaries, all contributed. At the same time, other Johnsonian social programs grew in the post-LBJ era, spurred on by his example and rhetoric.

Ironically, despite LBJ's focus on the War on Poverty, most of the money did not end up going to the poor. In the post-Johnson era, the Great Society programs were expanded to include ever-greater numbers of people, stretching well past the poverty line, as political demands and opportunities to do something for the vast bulk of the electorate, especially the likely voters, intervened. Again, Stein:

> Between 1965 and 1980, federal expenditures targeted on poor people and requiring a demonstration of need to qualify for benefits rose from 4 percent to 9 percent of the federal budget. In the same period, federal benefits not targeted on poor people and not involving a test of need rose from 24 percent to 40 percent of the budget. In 1980, only about 20 percent of federal benefit payments went to raise people who were otherwise below the poverty line toward it or to it. The remaining approximately 80 percent went to people who even without it would have been above the poverty line.[4]

The Great Society push and ethos thus set into motion the sharp expansion of entitlement programs which, as we shall recount, dominated the fiscal impact of the Nixon years and beyond by generating a massive transfer of resources mostly within the middle class, mostly from younger, working people to older people. It was paid for partly by inflation, partly by budget deficits, and partly at the expense of defense in the post-Vietnam years.

In his State of the Union message in January 1966, President Lyndon B. Johnson declared, "This nation is mighty enough, its society is healthy enough, its people are strong enough, to pursue our goals in the rest of the world while still building a Great Society here at home." Thus, LBJ directly made the link between Vietnam and social programs, between guns and butter.

That link, of course, created a series of ripple effects on the economy and the government that reverberated for decades. Prime among them was the encouragement of inflation, which had already begun to show warning signs of advancement in 1965. The president's economic advisers saw the signals and told the president. CEA Chairman Gardner Ackley sent a memorandum to the president in December 1965:

If the budget is $115 billion, there is little question in my mind that a significant tax increase will be needed to prevent an intolerable degree of inflationary pressure. With a budget of $110 billion the question is more difficult. My tentative opinion is that a tax increase would probably still be necessary.[5]

At the same time, the Federal Reserve, worried itself about incipient inflation, raised the discount rate. President Johnson invited Fed Chairman William McChesney Martin down to his ranch to talk—and the discount rate increase was postponed.

Throughout 1966, Ackley, Budget Director Charles Schultze, and a consensus of outside economists pushed the president to take anti-inflationary steps, especially a tax hike; he strenuously resisted. After the disastrous midterm elections, the president relented, recommending a 6 percent tax surcharge in the January 1967 *Economic Report to the President*. But the president did not follow through with a tax message to Congress. The desire to avoid the unpleasant reality that more guns and more butter meant more taxes pushed LBJ to reject the strong advice of a phalanx of economic advisers—and to pay the inflationary price.

Many parts of the Great Society did endure, although in forms vastly different from what Johnson had envisioned. By the late 1970s, nearly all the programs had lost their ability to infatuate Americans—and indeed were used by Republican presidential candidates as prime exhibits of the failure of big government. Lyndon Johnson had meant the Great Society to go far beyond the more modest goals and accomplishments of the New Deal. But with the prime exception of Medicare, most of its programs, including the War on Poverty, the Job Corps, VISTA, and Community Action Programs, never caught on like Social Security, the core of the New Deal and the expanded role of government that it stood for, and a program that continues to command near-universal approval from Americans.

The sweeping Great Society vision of Lyndon Johnson floundered for a number of reasons. The programs were struggling to take root while the nation was being drawn further and further into the bitter conflict in Vietnam. And the continuing robust growth of the economy that would make their effortless expansion possible simply did not occur.

Indeed, had the American economy grown at a 4 percent rate from 1966 through 1989, rather than the actual 2.8 percent rate, the actual level of 1989 federal spending would have resulted in a budget *surplus* of $163 billion, just enough to restore the remnants of the Great Society programs to their envisioned level of about 5.5 percent of GNP (about $282 billion) instead of the 3.8 percent of GNP (about $206 billion) that materialized. After closing that $76 billion gap, there would still be about $87 billion left over to apply to the S&L bailout and the Social Security bailout.

It is fair to say that, if Americans have abandoned Lyndon Johnson's utopian Great Society vision for America, the federal government has still firmly tied its spending programs to Kennedy's hope and Johnson's assumption of 4 percent growth. Persistent deficits and a rising national debt are steady, though not constraining, reminders that growth has only proceeded at a rate equal to just 70 percent of the ambitious target of 4 percent. Seen in this way, persistent deficits may be looked upon as a result of economic underperformance, though such an interpretation might be questioned in view of the fact that no mature industrial economy has ever sustained 4 percent growth for more than a few years. It almost seems that optimistic presidents can push federal spending to a level consistent with an optimistic view of the economy and not suffer—at least for a decade—from the fact that the economy can't deliver 4 percent growth.

If a portion of the Johnson legacy was sluggish growth coupled with inflation—stagflation, as it came to be called—another, inadvertent part of the legacy was the beginning of the entitlement revolution. It was Medicare and Medicaid far more than the War on Poverty that endured well beyond the Johnson presidency itself, to the applause of the American people, but to the detriment of sound fiscal policy. From the Nixon years onward, entitlements became the engine of growth in the federal budget, increasingly moving budget decisions away from the standard appropriations and budget processes toward automatic, uncontrollable increases set by population, demographics, and inflation.

If poverty programs symbolized uncontrolled government growth to many Americans by the time of Ronald Reagan's election, they were, in fact, only a minor part of the federal budget. It was the universally popular entitlement side of the Great Society that should have been the target of voters' wrath—but was not.

Not many of these facts were clear in 1968, when the impact of the Great Society was overshadowed by the assassinations of Robert Kennedy and Martin Luther King, riots, and protests over Vietnam.

Eugene McCarthy emerged after the 1968 New Hampshire primary as a candidate who supported a liberal domestic agenda while condemning the war in Vietnam. Lyndon Johnson departed the presidential race, and the extreme bitterness within the Democratic party spilled over at their convention in Chicago in August of 1968. The democratic nominee, Hubert Humphrey, was never able to recover from the ugly television images that were part of the Chicago convention. Those images included Chicago policemen beating anti–Vietnam War demonstrators with nightsticks while, inside the convention hall, Chicago Mayor Richard J. Daley and his Chicago henchmen, in front of nationwide television hookups, cursed and insulted Connecticut Senator Abraham Ribicoff as he attempted to address the convention.

Deeper societal conflict led to the independent candidacy of George Wallace, and a genuine, three-way race for president. Richard Nixon emerged triumphant, albeit with a bare popular vote plurality of 43.5 percent and an electoral vote majority of 302 of the 538 votes. He entered office to confront continued division over race and Vietnam, along with the Johnson fiscal legacy.

ECONOMIC SHOCK WAVES

Johnson's withdrawal from the 1968 presidential race made way for the presidency of Richard Nixon and four more years of the national obsession with the Vietnam War—which were followed by three years of obsession with Watergate. While the highest levels of government trained their attention on these twin tragedies, one level down, where policies of lasting impact are set, a series of economic events was taking place: these would transform the U.S.

economy from a high-growth, low-inflation model to a low-growth, high-inflation model. Economic dislocations due to the quadrupling of oil prices during the 1970s, together with the double-digit inflation that they had helped create by the end of that decade, spawned the budget crises and major tax reform of the 1980s—which, in turn, ballooned the debt burdens of the 1990s.

Economic shock waves from the Vietnam War outlasted the formidable political and social upheavals that it caused. The effort to pay for the war without an increase in taxes produced a surge in money growth and subsequent inflation. That inflation spurred six Persian Gulf nations to threaten an oil-production stoppage unless Aramco, the consortium of twenty-three Western oil companies that dealt with them, increased annual payments for oil by $10 billion. On February 14, 1971, after three years during which inflation averaged nearly 6 percent, Aramco agreed to the demands by the Persian Gulf nations that made up the core of the Organization of Petroleum Exporting Countries.

Aramco's problems with OPEC's initial muscle flexing were far from the mind of Richard Nixon as he struggled with the national nightmare of Vietnam. As subsequent events were to demonstrate, fear that his presidency—like Johnson's—might fall victim to it led him to extreme measures on both economic and political fronts.

In February 1969, Nixon appointed Arthur Burns chairman of the Federal Reserve, succeeding the formidable William McChesney Martin, Jr., who had been chairman since 1951. A mild recession that began late in 1969 and ended a year later, in part the by-product of a General Motors strike, was followed by a modest slowdown in inflation. Burns quickly pushed money growth to the double-digit level. The first result, as usual, was a sharp recovery in economic growth, which helped set the stage for Richard Nixon's reelection in 1972. But by the end of 1973, inflation reached 8.4 percent, and OPEC, provoked by the Yom Kippur War in Israel, quadrupled oil prices in October 1973.

The first oil crisis of the 1970s was, in a sense, the result of Vietnam. Without Vietnam, Johnson would probably have been unbeatable in 1968. Without the continuation of Vietnam, Richard Nixon might not have found it necessary to press so hard for the inflationary policies that ultimately created the 1970s oil crises.

Vietnam and then Watergate helped to cause—and to divert attention from—fundamental economic and political changes that were to lead to unprecedented budgetary and tax measures more than a decade later. The

1971 resurgence in U.S. money growth brought about in August 1971 the end of the Bretton Woods system of fixed exchange rates, which also affected the budgetary, and inflationary, environment of the 1970s and 1980s.

After inflation, the real problem faced by Americans in the global economy was how to devalue the dollar, which had been the linchpin of the Bretton Woods system of fixed exchange rates. In May 1971, some turbulence in the foreign-exchange markets, followed by some modest reevaluations of European currencies, hinted at some heavy pressure on the dollar. President Nixon took his economic team to Camp David and, after two days of discussion, articulated the New Economic Policy on August 15, 1971. Domestic aspects of the NEP included a ninety-day freeze on wages and prices, an investment tax credit, and an end to the excise tax on automobiles.

The object of the NEP, no doubt attributable to the perceived success of Keynesian policies of demand stimulation followed in the Kennedy-Johnson years, was to keep a lid on wages and prices while increasing capital formation and growth. Its effect, typically, was merely to hold back the upward pressures on wages and prices in the short run only to make them stronger in the long run. The result was inflation in the prices of petroleum and everything else when the controls were lifted during 1973 and 1974.

The international parts of the NEP were the most significant, as they decoupled the United States from the more cautious economic policies of Europe and Japan. The NEP imposed a 10 percent tax on the value of all imports and, most important, formally ended the convertability of the dollar into gold—even for foreign governments. The dollar was floated: the United States offered neither to buy nor to sell its currency on foreign-exchange markets but allowed exchange rates to seek their own level or be set by the intervention of other governments. Floating the dollar was a necessary policy for a nation which, plagued by a costly and divisive war, also had an ambitious domestic agenda and elected to finance the extra costs by printing money rather than by cutting other forms of spending or by raising taxes.

The world's economic managers made a brief attempt to return to fixed exchange rates from December 1971 through February 1973, but the continued inflation in the United States made a stable exchange rate between the dollar and the currencies of less-inflationary Europe and Japan impossible. Given the heavy stresses placed on the international financial system by the oil price shock of 1973, the return to floating exchange rates was as fortunate for the global trading system as it was expedient for the United States.

Richard Nixon can perhaps be forgiven some neglect of substantive domestic policy after his reelection in view of the deluge of problems that confronted the White House in 1973—a year that was to prove momentous not only for his presidency but for the Middle East and the world economy as well. By January 1974, oil prices had quadrupled, and inflation was well on the way toward the 14 percent it reached at its peak in 1979. By that time, there had been two recessions, an oil crisis, fundamental changes in the budget procedure, and huge increases in Social Security benefits that were to transform both budget and tax policies in the 1980s and beyond.

Nixon's problems in 1973 seemed to reach a critical mass in October of that year, after a summer of Watergate hearings had seriously questioned the sustainability of his presidency. On October 6, Egypt and Syria launched an attack on Israel, which began the Yom Kippur War. While that conflict was boiling in the Middle East, Nixon's legal problems with Watergate became acute. Spiro Agnew was replaced as vice president by Gerald Ford.

On October 16, 1973, OPEC raised oil prices by 70 percent and five days later embargoed oil shipments to the United States in protest against U.S. support for Israel in the Yom Kippur War. No doubt sensing the extreme pressure on the White House, Soviet Premier Leonid Brezhnev on October 24 sent the embattled U.S. president a message that Soviet intervention in the Yom Kippur War in support of the Egyptian and Syrian forces could come without warning.

The embattled Nixon turned management of the Middle East crisis over to Secretary of State Henry Kissinger, who, along with the rest of Nixon's cabinet, drafted a stern reply to Brezhnev. Nixon underscored U.S. determination to contain the crisis in the Middle East on October 27, when he placed U.S. troops on a worldwide alert to counter the Soviet threat. Simultaneously, he canceled a news conference on the Watergate affair, prompting some congressional critics to claim that the crisis in the Middle East with the Soviets had been engineered to divert attention from his legal problems. A justifiably outraged Henry Kissinger characterized such charges as ludicrous in the face of the hostilities in the Middle East and the gravity of the Soviet threat.

The events of 1973 were followed by an unsettled and unsettling 1974. On January 2, President Nixon established a national speed limit of 55 miles per hour to remind Americans that gasoline was no longer in abundant supply. Gas lines and frequent disruptions of supply, however, made such reminders unnecessary. The 70 percent OPEC price rise in October 1973 had been followed by another increase of 128 percent on December 23. A quadrupling of oil prices in less than a year threw the U.S. economy into a severe recession—accompanied by the nation's first double-digit inflation since the end of World War II. Stagflation and recession, gas lines, and, by summer, the end of the Nixon presidency made 1974 into an unprecedented disaster for America.

By July, opinion surveys showed that inflation had replaced the energy crisis as the chief concern of most Americans—and both of them had eclipsed Watergate. Forty-eight percent of those surveyed cited the high cost of living as the chief problem facing them, while 15 percent cited a lack of trust in government, and 11 percent cited Watergate.

The survey results were telling, inasmuch as they suggested that by mid-1974, Americans were no longer as concerned about the availability of gasoline and heating oil as they were about their cost. The message had sunk in that OPEC meant not to deprive the West of oil but merely to supply it at a much higher price.

The oil prices and accompanying inflation reinforced in everyone's mind the warnings, like that of the Club of Rome in 1972, that the world was running out of natural resources (a warning that the following decade proved rash). But in 1974, the oil crisis and the resulting inflation created an obsession with scarcity that was to manifest itself a few years later in a flight from financial assets into tangible ones like houses, oil, coins, ceramics, gold, and silver. Such behavior always accompanies a surge of inflation—and this surge was not to end until it had destroyed the political career of Jimmy Carter six years later.

THE POLITICAL DYNAMIC AND THE FEDERAL AGENDA

Despite Vietnam and Watergate, policies toward debt and taxes in the Nixon years were perhaps more influenced by less obvious political realities—realities that were to have huge impact on later decades. One of the most important factors was the political dynamic. Nixon had won the White House in 1968 in an unusually divisive election. In a three-way race with Hubert Humphrey, at the head of a badly divided Democratic party, and George Wallace, Nixon captured only 43.5 percent of the popular votes cast. The Democrats managed to retain firm control of both houses of Congress. Nixon tried at his inauguration to build support and momentum with a conciliatory attempt to "bring us together," but early in 1969, the political division between the increasingly liberal Democratic Congress and the combative conservative Republican president clearly was growing sharper.

Vietnam was certainly the catalyst; it had, after all, driven a wedge of distrust and animosity between the Democratic Congress and Nixon's Democratic predecessor, Lyndon Johnson. But divisions over education, welfare, and the rest of domestic policy were now prominent, along with the palpable sense in Congress that Nixon was far more directly hostile to its role and power than Eisenhower, his mentor and the last Republican president, had been.

While issues mattered, the question of political control, over both the agenda of the federal government and the future of both parties in upcoming elections, was central. One of the major battlegrounds became policy toward the elderly, especially as it focused on Social Security. Social Security had been a hot political issue at the time of its creation in 1935, but by the mid-1960s, as Martha Derthick noted in *Policymaking for Social Security*, it was perhaps the most popular and least controversial program in government. When Democrats claimed that Barry Goldwater had questioned the premise of the program in the 1964 presidential campaign, that candidate had been greeted by a torrent of denunciation and staunch support for the program from all sides of the political spectrum.[6]

At different times in the 1960s, liberal economist Paul Samuelson pronounced Social Security the most successful program in the modern American welfare state, while conservative economist Milton Friedman called it a sacred cow that no politician dared criticize. The program had no real problems, politically or administratively, added economist Otto Eckstein.[7]

The program thrived because it generated support and satisfaction from workers and recipients. Satisfaction levels had continued to rise: the political process had evolved a system of periodic, ad hoc adjustments in benefit levels and conditions for retired workers and their survivors, as Congress tried to compensate for the effects of inflation by establishing a formula for benefits based on a percentage of current monthly wage rates. The system of ad hoc increases in Social Security benefits enabled enough adjustment to satisfy recipients while allowing members of Congress to claim credit for increasing benefits. Because the procedure gave Congress some leeway over budget decisions, both Congress and the president had time to consider both economic and budgetary effects before making decisions to change the Social Security program.

From 1952, when the ad hoc system of adjustments went into effect, until 1971, Congress raised benefit levels seven times without increasing taxes, leaving recipients with higher purchasing power and the system with a surplus. Troubles began to appear, however, in the late 1960s. Social Security reemerged as a controversial political issue when the elderly, as their number grew, gained strength as a major lobbying force.

In the late 1960s, senior citizens' lobbying groups began to complain with increasing fervor that the public pension system was failing to meet the basic needs of an increasing number of its recipients. They pointed to the high poverty rate of the elderly: in 1970, 25 percent of them fell below the poverty line, compared with 12.6 percent of the population as a whole.[8] The figures, they said, understated poverty among the elderly, disguising an estimated additional 1.6 million "hidden poor" who would have been below the poverty line if they had not lived with their children.

Nelson Cruikshank, president of the National Council of Senior Citizens, stated the lobbyists' case at a Senate Finance Committee hearing in January 1972: "Rarely do we see the hardship and suffering of the millions of the elderly who are the poorest of the U.S. poor. The elderly do not parade their poverty. As a matter of pride, they do their best to hide it."[9]

Poverty among the elderly was exacerbated by growing inflation. By the time Lyndon Johnson left office, after trying to finance both the Vietnam War and the Great Society out of growth and only raising taxes in his final year, inflation had risen to about 5 percent and showed no signs of subsiding. Inflation became the rallying point for those dissatisfied with the Social Security System because their benefits were being eaten away. Protecting Social Security recipients from the ravages of inflation became a major political objective.

From Nixon's arrival at the White House in 1969 onward, the Democratic Congress and the Republican president competed over who could be more sensitive to the needs of the elderly. Nixon in 1969 proposed indexing Social Security benefits to inflation, a process that had long been favored by the ranking minority member of the House Ways and Means Committee, John Byrnes. This was not at first a partisan issue: indexing had been endorsed by both party political platforms in 1968. In an address on September 25, 1969, Nixon stated:

> The impact of an inflation now in its fourth year has undermined the value of every Social Security check. . . . the way to prevent future unfairness is to attach the benefit schedule to the cost of living. . . . By acting to make future benefit raises automatic with rises in the cost of living, we remove questions about future years; we do much to remove this system from biennial politics; and we make fair treatment of beneficiaries a matter of certainty rather than a matter of hope.

In addition to proposing the indexing of benefits, he recommended the indexing of the payroll tax base—and a 10 percent across-the-board benefit increase to offset the loss of purchasing power caused by previous inflation.

While there was bipartisan backing for indexing, there was not unanimity. Organized labor, especially the AFL-CIO, favored general expansion of Social Security but argued that the Nixon measures fell far short of what was required to meet the financial needs of the elderly. Labor wanted a much larger benefit increase first, before indexed cost-of-living adjustments were built in. Business, conversely, was wary of the whole idea of indexing, fearing that it would not stop at Social Security benefits but would inevitably spread to the wage structure itself, worsening the already serious inflation problem.

THE POWER OF WILBUR MILLS

Dissent from labor and business, however, was not the administration's major concern. The White House was more worried about one key Democratic player, not only in the Social Security arena but in virtually every area of domestic policy of interest to Nixon: Wilbur Mills, chairman of the House Ways and Means Committee. Daniel Patrick Moynihan, then a key Nixon domestic policy adviser, wrote of Mills: "[He] was in this period generally held the second most powerful man in Washington, following only the president." [10]

Mills had come to the House from Arkansas (via Harvard Law School) in 1938. His intelligence and "youthful audacity" brought him to the attention of Speaker Sam Rayburn; Mills received a coveted seat on Ways and Means in only his second term. [11] By 1958, he became chairman of the committee. Over the next decade and a half, he carefully and diligently built his influence in the House. When Nixon became president, the Ways and Means Committee consisted of fifteen Democrats and ten Republicans. Representative Byrnes worked closely with Mills in a bipartisan and centrist atmosphere. Political scientist John Manley said of the committee: "Its Democrats were liberal, but not fervid; its Republicans were conservative, but not unyielding; its Southerners were moderate by standards of the racially aroused South." [12]

Mills had tried to make the committee roughly representative of the House as a whole, and he used his unparalleled knowledge of taxes and other matters that came before it to give it (and himself) enormous power over any matter that involved revenues. Mills did not dictate to his committee; he forged unity by forging consensus, bringing together Democrats and Republicans. With a united committee and the use of closed rules on the House floor—rules that allowed no amendments—bills from Mills's committee nearly always prevailed in the House. In his first ten years as chairman, Mills lost only twice on the House floor on important legislation. *Time* magazine called him "Never Miss Wilbur."

From revenue sharing and welfare reform to taxes, health, and Social Security, the Nixon administration had to deal with Mills, and the dealings were not easy. As writer Murray Seeger noted in the *Atlantic Monthly* at the time,

> It is Mills's legendary record as a successful legislator that has given the Republican White House so much trouble. Unlike many committee chairmen, Mills is not susceptible to ordinary horse trading with the White House—a new dam or post office in return for a bill, for instance. He has such firm control over his committee, with influence extending to the Republican side, that the White House cannot muster a majority against him . . . no Administration can afford to alienate him completely.[13]

The tension and competition between Nixon and Mills became evident early in the first Nixon term on the issue of trade. Following up a campaign promise to southern voters, Nixon in his first year in the White House crafted a bill to establish quotas for textile imports. The bill died in the Senate, and subsequent direct negotiations with the Japanese also foundered. With tough, protectionist talk on the rise, Mills, a free trader and an opponent of mandatory quotas, stepped in with a proposal for voluntary restraint by the Japanese for three years, which they embraced. An embarrassed administration accused Mills of interfering with official negotiations but could not disguise the fact that the Ways and Means chairman had worked out an agreement where it had failed—an agreement that avoided the unpalatable path of mandatory, legislated quotas.

Trade was not the only issue on which Nixon and Mills competed. On tax reform, revenue sharing, Nixon's family-assistance plan, and all other major components of the Nixon domestic agenda, Mills had his own ideas and the power to reshape the political and legislative landscape. But the competition became most pronounced on Social Security. Beginning with benefit increases, Democrats competed with Nixon to show generosity and sensitivity to the elderly. In both 1969 and 1970, Mills added generous Social Security benefit increases to veto-proof legislation, in each case sharply raising the administration's ante: from 10 to 15 percent in 1969 (supported 400 to 0 in the House) and from 6 to 10 percent in 1970.

The Mills-Nixon tension increased over the indexing of benefits. While Nixon, Byrnes, and most Democrats pushed indexation, Mills opposed it. He did not want to lose congressional—and committee—control over an important question like benefit increases, and he felt that Congress was already adjusting benefits to the cost of living through its year-to-year actions, so that automatic adjustments were unnecessary.

But Mills lost the battle on this issue in 1970, though he won the year's war. The House used a parliamentary maneuver to bypass the closed rule, then overrode Mills's opposition and passed an indexation provision by a vote of 233 to 144. Republicans on and off the Ways and Means Committee joined liberal, northern, non–Ways and Means Democrats to defeat Mills's coalition of southern Democrats and his Ways and Means colleagues.[14] The Senate also approved indexing. The House vote, however, came so late in the session—December 29—that Mills was able to keep a conference committee from convening, and indexing was not enacted into law.

In the spring of 1971, another key policy shift occurred. The Advisory Council on Social Security recommended that the assumption of a constant level of earnings used to determine tax revenue be dropped in favor of a more dynamic model based on the assumption that incomes were increasing annually. The dynamic model was closer to reality, but it also resulted in projections of big increases in Social Security revenues without any payroll-tax increases. Forecasts of a huge surplus in the system's reserve fund offered an irresistible temptation to politicians to spend the excess.

Surprisingly, the first prominent politician to come forward with a plan to do so was Mills. Without consulting even his own committee, he proposed a 20 percent increase in Social Security benefits for 1972. As Derthick commented, "From a man who had always stood for 'fiscal soundness' and who moved cautiously when he moved at all, this sudden, seemingly reckless stroke came as a great surprise."[15]

What had gotten into Wilbur Mills? There were two explanations. First, Mills expected Richard Nixon, preparing for his reelection campaign, to announce a similar benefit increase. The move was to preempt him and prevent the president from getting political credit. Second, Mills himself harbored presidential ambitions.

In 1971, Mills had begun to put together a presidential campaign for 1972. These ambitions were never realized—or even given any hope. To presidential campaign operatives and veteran political reporters, his attempt seemed ludicrous. Mills had no experience in national party or presidential politics, no base of delegate support, no team of experienced and proven advisers.

His support came from a group of about thirty colleagues in the House, who themselves were not major players in national Democratic party affairs. Mills's legendary reputation and his power in the corridors of Congress were virtually unknown outside the Beltway and his native state of Arkansas. His owlish, bespectacled appearance made him something less than an ideal candidate for the television age.

Nevertheless, Mills declared an exploratory candidacy, while staying low-key about it through the winter of 1971. In late January 1972, however, he appointed a New Hampshire coordinator for a statewide write-in campaign; on February 11, less than one month before the New Hampshire primary, Mills entered the race. In late February, right before the New Hampshire primary, he began a media blitz in the state and announced his support for a 20 percent increase in Social Security benefits.

The Nixon administration was dismayed by Mills's proposal. Facing a $25.5 billion budget deficit for fiscal 1973, it did not relish adding $6 billion in increased Social Security payments to it. Nixon countered with a proposed increase of 5 percent in Social Security benefits and once again called for indexing. While Congress could not resist the siren song of a generous boost in benefits, indexing seemed an ever more attractive escape from the bidding war that had developed over Social Security. Not surprisingly, Congress attached both the benefit increase and indexing to a bill raising the ceiling on the national debt. Nixon felt forced to sign the bill.

The indexing provision did not take effect immediately; it was delayed for two and a half years. This enabled politicians to claim credit for the immediate 20 percent boost in benefits while offering some consolation to fiscal conservatives with the knowledge that at least a few years would pass before inflation indexing pushed up benefits even further; after the massive 20 percent increase in benefits, Congress made two further adjustments. It increased benefits 5.9 percent in July 1973; then, in December, after the Arab oil embargo sent inflation soaring, it superseded the July increase with a two-step increase of 17 percent beginning in March 1974, followed by an additional 4 percent in June.[16]

Nixon had finally achieved indexing of Social Security—but only after benefit levels had been increased by more than 40 percent in just three years. In the fourteen years between 1952 and 1965, Social Security benefits increased by 45.6 percent, an average of 2.7 percent per year. In the five years from 1967 to 1972—most of that time with a Republican president and a Democratic Congress competing in benevolence—benefits increased by 71.5 percent. That represented an annual average increase of 14.3 percent, or more than twice the rate of inflation.

Unfortunately, indexing took effect just as high inflation was beginning. Because of the double-digit inflation from 1979 to 1981, benefits increased by another 40 percent, while earnings rose by only 16 percent. This surge in benefits eventually necessitated the Social Security reforms of 1983. These imposed a huge increase in payroll taxes so that by the late 1980s, two-thirds of American families paid more in payroll taxes than they did in federal income taxes. Before long, indexing was applied to other federal benefit programs, including veterans' and civil service pensions, which also increased sharply during the inflationary period.

CONTROL OF PRIORITIES AND THE BUDGET

The politics of Social Security increases and indexing gained much attention during the Nixon presidency, but their significance was not yet recognized, and they were overshadowed at the time by other areas of domestic conflict between Nixon and Congress, including welfare reform and revenue sharing. A second occasion of political strife, however, did not go unnoticed. That was the harsh and increasing conflict between the two branches over spending and budget priorities, which led ultimately to landmark budget reform.

From the beginning of his presidency, Nixon clashed repeatedly with Congress over spending priorities and budget control. Congress's suspicions about President Nixon's motives in budgetary matters were aroused early in his first year, when the president created an Advisory Council on Executive Organization. This was known as the Ash Council, for its chairman, Roy Ash, who had been the head of Litton Industries.

The Ash Council recommended creating a Domestic Council in the White House, as well as moving the Bureau of the Budget from the aegis of the Treasury Department to the Executive Office of the president and transforming it into the Office of Management and Budget. The Domestic Council would formulate new initiatives, while OMB would coordinate the operations; both planning and management would be under the direct control of the president.

Sound administrative theory or not, the effect, as Congress saw it, was to politicize an impartial and professional Bureau of the Budget. Congress's suspicions were reinforced as the president vetoed numerous appropriations measures, usually accompanying the veto with a tough attack on Congress. Congress, in turn, used the appropriations process to score political points against the president, portraying him as indifferent to education, poverty, and other social needs.

The tensions intensified in the presidential election year of 1972. Trying to distance himself from Washington insiders, Nixon went on the offensive and accused Congress of reckless spending and fiscal irresponsibility. On July 26, he proposed that Congress impose a $250 billion spending ceiling for fiscal 1973; a defensive Congress, stung by the attacks, went along.

Nixon's verbal assault on Congress was accompanied by specific actions. In 1972, the president vetoed sixteen bills, most of them regular authorizations; twelve of the vetoes came after Congress had adjourned, when there could be no override.

Nor did the 1972 election end the budget wars between president and Congress. After his reelection, Nixon vetoed the Federal Water Pollution Control Act Amendments of 1972, despite an expected override. The president publicly denounced the act, threatening to exercise his presidential prerogative to withhold spending funds even if it became law.

After Congress overrode his veto, Nixon impounded $6 billion of water-pollution-control funds and later increased that to $9 billion. He impounded $18 billion in congressionally appropriated funds—not only for water pollution but also for subsidized housing programs, disaster relief, rural and community development projects, and agricultural programs.

Though a traditional presidential prerogative, the impoundment power had been used only in small doses and for small amounts of money. It was usually employed because circumstances had changed since the appropriations had been enacted or because the money simply could not be spent before the end of the fiscal year. But Nixon's impoundment of $18 billion went far beyond what any previous president had done and seemed a clear political use of a previously benign power. As Allen Schick commented, "Under the guise of merely restraining expenditures, the Nixon Administration undoubtedly was trying to curtail some programs that were at variance with its own priorities."[17]

In 1974, Congress passed a budget act that, although it was ostensibly intended to impose a more orderly framework on federal budget making, also attempted to wrest some budgetary power away from the president, into the hands of the Congress. The budget act of 1974 established the framework within which the budget battles of the 1980s were to be fought. The periodic review of the budget as it moved through Congress every year ensured that increased public attention would be paid to the budget-making process. This, coupled with the large deficits of the 1980s, made the federal budget and its implications a focus of much of the debate over domestic economic and social policy during that decade.

Impoundment of funds by Nixon provided the excuse for budget reform in Congress, though lawmakers also realized that their process was not working well. Spending priorities were set only in a haphazard fashion. Overlapping jurisdictions, both substantive and procedural, were becoming a growing problem in Congress, because of the turf battles that they led to and because of the lack of policy coordination that they engendered. The result was not a real budget but a set of separate decisions about funding, formulas, and authorizations with no comprehensive authority or organizing principle. In addition, Congress was increasingly stung by criticism that it was falling behind its deadlines and work schedule. It was becoming common for it not to complete all its appropriations bills before the new fiscal year began on July 1 and to rely on continuing resolutions to get around the deadline.

The budget act was an attempt to resolve these problems and to assert more congressional control over the power of the purse. First, Congress changed the fiscal year to give itself more time to complete its money decisions. Previously, as the president's budget was submitted in January, shortly after the new congressional session began, there had been fewer than six months to complete work in both houses of Congress on all thirteen separate appropriations bills, then send them on to the president for signature. Changing the start of the fiscal year to the end of September would give Congress nearly nine months. This, the reformers believed, would end the problem of missing deadlines and getting by with continuing resolutions.

Next, Congress agreed to create two new committees, budget panels for the House and the Senate. Their task was to coordinate the actions of the several committees in each house that could appropriate funds. The budget committees totaled the appropriations approved by other panels and issued a budget resolution to serve as an internal blueprint for economic and budget priorities. A first budget resolution was to be approved early in the spring to set broad spending and revenue targets. A later resolution, to be passed only two weeks before the fiscal year was to begin, would bind the committees to spending ceilings and revenue floors. Continuing resolutions were to be eliminated, and the whole budget process was to follow an orderly and timely procedure guided by new rules to be enforced by the budget committees and the discipline of Congress itself. At the end of the yearly budget cycle, Congress left a two-week period for reconciliation of existing laws and formulas that might conflict with the second budget resolution.

Concern about growing presidential power over the public purse took budget reformers in two directions. First, the executive's impoundment power was sharply curtailed. The president would need the acquiescence of

Congress for purely managerial deferrals of spending and the direct, active vote of approval of Congress for policy-related rescissions of program funding. Second, to counter the growing impact and policy role of the Office of Management and Budget, Congress created its own counterpart, the Congressional Budget Office (CBO), with a staff of more than two hundred economists and other budget professionals. The Congressional Budget and Impoundment Control Act was adopted one month before President Nixon resigned.

Entitlement indexing and the budget act remain the two most enduring fiscal legacies of the Nixon era. But many other changes, such as revenue sharing with the states, occurred in the fiscal area, despite Nixon's lack of interest or zeal about budget or tax policy. Under Nixon, we saw some significant restructuring of the budgetary priorities. In general, the Nixon era was a time for big cuts in defense as a share of the budget and of the GNP, combined with equally large increases in entitlements and other mandatory spending. In fiscal 1968, just before Nixon's presidency, defense spending was a full 9.6 percent of the gross national product. In nominal dollars, defense was not cut, but it declined steadily thereafter as a share of GNP; when Nixon left office, defense spending was down to 5.7 percent of GNP, a stunning drop in only a seven-year period. The trajectory of defense spending was almost the mirror image of entitlements, which went from 6.2 percent of GNP in fiscal 1968 to 10.3 percent in fiscal 1975. Discretionary domestic spending stayed roughly the same.

On taxes, Nixon had to deal throughout his presidency with the conflicting demands for an end to the Vietnam tax surcharge implemented by President Johnson and the increasing demands for tax reform heard throughout the political process; both issues were caught up in partisan competition. Realizing early in his presidency that there would be no peace dividend, Nixon decided to ask for an extension of the surcharge. To win votes for an extension in the Democratic Congress, though, he had to agree to a series of "tax reforms" that hit at business and the wealthy. These included an end to the Kennedy-era investment tax credit and implementation of a minimum tax to prevent the wealthy from not paying any taxes at all. He also had to accept costly tax relief for lower- and middle-income taxpayers through an increase in the personal exemption.

On balance, the 1969 tax bill lost substantial tax revenues in future years by providing new benefits to the bulk of the taxpayers. Nixon was unhappy about that but still signed the bill, trading the revenue he wanted for 1970 in return for undesirable revenue losses down the road.[18] Within two years, however, Nixon became concerned about stimulating the economy and creating jobs and shifted to support for new tax cuts, including renewal of the investment tax credit. By the end of his presidency, he had shifted once again, to more vigorous attacks on the growth in domestic spending in the budget. This was what Herbert Stein calls "the old-time religion phase" of the Nixon presidency.[19] But at a time when his effectiveness was fading under the cloud of Watergate, he was unable to hold down the explosive entitlement growth.

Soon after the 1974 Budget and Impoundment Control Act was passed by Congress, Richard Nixon left the presidency. His successor, Gerald Ford, who had served many years in the House of Representatives, had to pick up the pieces, including a new budget process that he had opposed because of its attack on presidential prerogatives and a Congress far more assertive in fiscal areas and far more suspicious of presidential motives and actions than it had been, before impoundment and Watergate, when he was House Republican Leader.

Ford and Congress wrangled constantly over spending and priorities, leading to frequent vetoes of congressional initiatives and appropriations. In the Ninety-Fourth Congress (1975–1976) Ford vetoed thirty-seven bills; eight were overridden by Congress. But despite the partisan and ideological struggles, or perhaps because of them, few significant changes were made in budget direction, or budget priorities. The trends continued toward higher entitlement spending and reduced defense spending as shares of the budget.

STAGFLATION AND FORD

Ford was plagued also by confusion over how to handle the phenomenon of stagflation, with its higher inflation and slower growth. During the postwar period, the federal government had gradually come to accept that most cycles were caused by movements in demand. Under that assumption, faster inflation meant too much demand and a need to tighten monetary policy and to clamp down on federal spending. The oil shock of 1973–1974 introduced into the system what came to be called supply shock. The term reappeared in 1980, transformed as "supply-side economics." The oil shock meant simply that America could produce less, other things being equal, when oil cost $30 a barrel than when oil cost $10 a barrel. The 1974 oil price increases translated into a negative supply shock, which meant higher prices and less output—or stagflation, as it came to be known.

When inflation was running more than 12 percent, Ford, searching for some guidance in the turbulent early weeks of his presidency, called an inflation summit for September 27, 1974. This was attended by eight hundred economists, businessmen, and financiers. The summit delegates, stunned by the oil shock and influenced by the inflation numbers and by public-opinion polls, concluded that inflation was the nation's number-one problem. A week and a half later, on October 8, the president announced a "Whip Inflation Now" (WIN) program. WIN buttons were issued for government employees and other interested parties, and a 5 percent income tax surcharge was levied on taxpayers, who were already groaning under the weight of the $68 billion that had been added to America's annual oil bill. October 8 was also the day the Franklin National Bank was declared insolvent, an event that evoked memories of the deflationary policies of the 1930s.

October 1974 marked more than the beginning of the WIN program. It was also the beginning of the severest U.S. recession in postwar history to that point. The depth of the drop had not been foreseen by any significant group of economists or forecasters. Within six months, unemployment rose to 9.2 percent—a full two percentage points higher than it had been at any previous time in the postwar era. By the beginning of 1975, the Ford administration, along with many other observers, had changed its focus, perceiving that recession, not inflation, was the biggest problem facing the nation.

The negative-supply shock administered by the quadrupling of oil prices required tax reductions and steady monetary policy. The policies imple-mented at the beginning of 1975 included a temporary tax cut combined with a rapid increase in the money supply. The idea was to give the economy a boost out of the doldrums but to roll back the tax reductions before they pushed up budget deficits or caused further inflation. This example of "ex-treme fine-tuning," in Stein's phrase, actually had some impact.[20] The 1975 budget deficit reached 4.3 percent of GNP, a figure comparable to budget deficits in the 1980s—although, adjusted for the business cycle and inflation, it was merely 0.9 percent of GNP. Inflation fell from 11 percent in 1974 to 9 percent in 1975 and to less than 6 percent in 1976. But the belated turn-around from restrictive to expansionary policies was insufficient to rescue Gerald Ford from the aftermath of Watergate and the unforgivable sin of pardoning Richard M. Nixon.

CARTER'S PROMISE OF LEADERSHIP

Jimmy Carter, elected president in November 1976, was determined to bring to America the moral leadership that had been lacking during the years of Vietnam and Watergate and was determined also to get the economy moving after the Ford doldrums. During the 1976 campaign, Carter had hammered away at Ford for his high "misery index," defined by Carter as the sum of the unemployment and inflation rates. His criticism was particularly strong about unemployment, as was traditional in the Democratic party; indeed, the major domestic initiative of Democrats at the time was the Humphrey-Hawkins bill, which set reducing unemployment to 4 percent as the top policy goal of the country.

Carter was right in his belief that the American citizenry needed healing after the shocks of the previous decade. But he also missed some serious problems, including the steady upward climb of inflation, still a great concern to most Americans, together with the Social Security time bomb that had been planted at the time of the huge increases in benefits and their indexing. In effect, an inflation crisis produced a budget crisis when the largest portion of federal outlays was indexed to inflation.

By the end of 1975, the industrial world was beginning to adjust to the oil shock. Fears that OPEC would buy up the rest of the world, which would bankrupt itself trying to pay for oil, had disappeared; two economists from the Brookings Institution concluded in a study on higher oil prices that OPEC was "no significant threat to living standards or economic growth." One coauthor in the Brookings study was Charles L. Schultze, who a year later became chairman of Jimmy Carter's Council of Economic Advisers.[21]

Meanwhile, the first economic summit for the six major industrial countries had gathered at Rambouillet, an elegant chateau thirty miles southwest of Paris, to provide a framework for quiet, informal discussions. (Canada was later included to make up what was called the Group of Seven, or the G-7.) The outcome of the Rambouillet economic summit was inconclusive. The six countries that had led the industrial world into stagflation declared that they would not accept another burst of inflation. By then, they had begun to realize that it was oil-induced supply starvation, not demand pressure, that was plaguing the industrial world. In addition, there were the usual pledges to avoid "beggar thy neighbor" protectionism and the commitment to accelerate trade negotiations under way in the Tokyo round of the General Agreement on Tariffs and Trade. Finally, there were pledges to aid the non–oil-providing third world as it faced the pain of higher oil prices.

The general background surrounding the economic summit of the mid-1970s was sometimes likened to the onset of the Great Depression. Writing about Rambouillet, the London *Economist* left little to one's imagination:

There is greater reason to fear that the 1975 slump might prove to be another mishandled convulsion like that of 1929–35. The sequence could run from stock-market crash (1929 and 1974) through financial crises (1930–31 and 1974–??) to aborted recovery (1930 and 1975–76). If there is an abortion of the recovery over the coming twelve months, politicians might over-react and produce a great unstable boom in 1977.[22]

"A great unstable boom" led by the inflationary policies of the new U.S. president is exactly what did follow. What the *Economist* missed was that although the symptoms of 1974–1975 superficially resembled those of 1929–1930, the disease was different. The major clue was inflation. Prices were sagging in the 1929–1933 period, while they were soaring in 1974–1975. The surge of inflation excited the appetite to move out of financial assets and into real assets, while simultaneously reducing the drag of the large (4.3 percent of GNP) deficit in 1975. Broadly viewed, the Depression era provided a poor analogy. Keynes's great *General Theory of Employment, Interest and Money* had revealed a flaw in Say's Law, whereby supply created its own demand. But while supply does not necessarily create its own demand from quarter to quarter or from year to year, and some demand management can smooth the path of the economy, neither does demand create its own supply, especially when more costly oil is making other goods scarcer.

The powerful demand stimulation of the Carter economics team in 1977 and 1978—provided through another double-digit growth surge of easy money—pushed inflation to unprecedented levels by 1978. At the same time, the U.S. dollar, which was floating against other currencies and being talked down by Treasury Secretary Michael Blumenthal, depreciated so rapidly that the leaders of France and Germany were beginning to talk about a European monetary system lest the U.S. dollar become an unstable and unusable international unit of account.

The economic policy of the Carter years was characterized by mixed signals and abrupt changes in focus. At the beginning of his term, Carter tried to stimulate the economy by pushing a temporary fifty-dollar tax rebate for all Americans, by increasing the budget deficit, and by expanding the money supply. The fifty-dollar rebate was controversial, and ridiculed in many quarters, but Carter worked hard to enlist the reluctant support of Democratic congressional leaders like Speaker of the House Thomas P. "Tip" O'Neill of Massachusetts. But then, just as the rebate was to be debated in Congress, Carter abruptly withdrew it in a move that caused anger and hostility among his allies and undermined confidence in his judgment. The other parts of the program, however, were implemented: the budget deficit indeed did rise significantly in 1977, and the money supply, as noted, grew enormously through 1979.

A BORN-AGAIN FISCAL CONSERVATIVE

But by 1979, the rocketing inflation that was fueled by Carter's easy-money policy had clearly changed the political scene as well as the economic. Inflation had greatly increased entitlement growth, which in turn had made more likely the prospect of a disastrous deficit in 1980 and had wreaked havoc with interest rates and financial markets. Carter, joined by his Federal Reserve Chairman Paul Volcker, responded by altering his basic approach to economic policy.

Carter became, in effect, a born-again fiscal conservative. He put the strongest emphasis on the goal of a balanced budget, using rhetoric that, with the possible exception of Truman, no Democratic president had employed since Roosevelt in the 1932 campaign. Carter aimed at serious restraint on domestic spending, calling for a 50 percent cut in its annual rate of increase from 1979 through 1983. He foreswore any tax reduction and projected a budget surplus by fiscal 1982. Carter also moved for severe restraint in money growth and made no vigorous protest when Volcker employed even more restraint than expected.

Carter's budget policy outraged many traditional, liberal Democratic constituencies and more than anything else brought about the challenge to his renomination by Senator Edward M. Kennedy, which greatly damaged the president's political standing. Bringing restraint to domestic spending growth itself required extraordinary governmental measures; in 1980, reconciliation, a previously obscure and unused process built into the budget act of 1974, was employed for the first time to implement domestic budget cuts. Even so, the deficit grew significantly in Carter's last year, to a nominal $66 billion, or more than 3 percent of GNP.

At the same time, the high levels of inflation generated substantial tax-bracket creep; by 1981, revenues had reached nearly 21 percent of GNP, their highest level in the postwar period, which made the budget deficit even more striking. Efforts begun in 1979 to rein in the double-digit inflation had failed by 1980, the year of the Carter-Reagan contest for the presidency. Although economic growth had begun to slow during 1980, inflation remained high. High unemployment and high inflation enabled Carter's Republican opponent, Ronald Reagan, to use the same misery index that Carter had used so effectively against Ford in 1976. It was even more effective against the hapless Carter.

The continuing trauma of American hostages in Iran helped to topple Carter from the presidency. But the single image that remains most potent from the 1980 campaign is Ronald Reagan, in the October debate, asking the American public, "Are you better off than you were four years ago?"

Ronald Reagan was elected by a landslide in November 1980 with a mandate to get the economy under control—to take whatever actions were required to stem runaway inflation and to bring back stable economic performance and growth. Two decades of attempts to fine-tune fiscal policy and to bring modern economic science to bear on the national economy had, in the end, bred stagflation and economic turmoil, along with less, not more, control over the federal budget. A reaction against these policies had set in even during Carter's presidency—a reaction signaled by his change in monetary policy under Volcker and by the unprecedented use of reconciliation as an extreme measure to bring the budget under control in 1980. But it was Ronald Reagan who was given the mandate for change, a change that his supporters and his detractors alike thought could be revolutionary.

⋆ 9 ⋆

FISCAL POLICY
IN THE REAGAN YEARS

As we saw in chapter 2, the first year of the Reagan administration brought with it dazzling political triumphs for the president on the budget and on taxes. But genuine policy revolution did not follow. The conflicting goals expressed by Ronald Reagan, which John Anderson had said contemptuously during the 1980 campaign could be reconciled only "with mirrors," were not being reconciled at all. In their comprehensive look at the deficit debate in the 1980s, Joseph White and Aaron Wildavsky have noted that "as soon as the reconciliation and tax-cut battles ended, the deficit panic began."[1]

Long before Reagan's second year, it was apparent that the administration's deficit projections had been based on wishful thinking and that the president's promise of a balanced budget by 1984 was not likely to be fulfilled. The consensus in the private sector was that the federal deficit for fiscal 1982 would surpass Reagan's target of $42.5 billion by perhaps $20 billion. Further, the Congressional Budget Office predicted that the president's promise of a balanced budget in fiscal 1984 might fall $50 billion short. Lester Thurow represented the pessimistic consensus of economists when he said, "With the resulting structure of taxes and expenditures [after the 1981 tax cuts], the President is not going to be balancing the Federal budget in 1984 or any other year . . . budget deficits are going to be bigger, not smaller."[2]

The administration's forecast of February 1981 soon became known as Rosy Scenario. Arnold Moskowitz of Dean Witter Reynolds summed up Wall Street's initial reaction to the president's economic program: "The new supply-side view is that deficits don't matter. We [Wall Street] think that they do—deficits are simply not the hallmark of good economic management."

Reagan responded by urging patience: "Some people are frustrated because we don't see instant recovery, but we never promised it would be easy, and we never promised it would be quick."[3] While the president called for calm, he was warned by his advisers that something had to be done to reassure the markets. David Stockman, the budget director, advocated a $30 billion cut in the defense budget over the next three fiscal years. Reagan reluctantly agreed to a $13 billion cut over the same period, saying, "If it comes down to balancing the budget or defense, the balanced budget will have to give way."[4]

The president's campaign promise of a balanced budget had quickly been subordinated to his other goals. In mid-November 1981, roughly one year after being elected on a platform calling for a balanced budget, the president said, "I did not come here to balance the budget—not at the expense of my tax cutting program and my defense program. If we can't do it in 1984, we'll have to do it later."[5] Reagan's fiscal 1983 budget proposal, his second as president, moved the target date for a balanced budget from FY 1984 to FY 1987.

PLANS FOR THE 1983 BUDGET

The budget process for fiscal 1983 began in a much different manner than that of the preceding year. President Reagan's FY 1983 budget proposal was the first of a series to be declared dead on arrival by Democrats in Congress. Early in the year, it was obvious even within the administration that the Reagan plan of relying on spending cuts alone to restrain the deficit would not work; the fiscal 1983 deficit was clearly headed over $100 billion. Reagan's rhetoric held—he called for cutting both discretionary spending and some entitlements while increasing defense expenditures—but his proposal also included tax increases, which the administration insisted on referring to euphemistically as revenue enhancements.

Congress began to take matters into its own hands. When plans proposed by prominent Republicans as well as Democrats on Capitol Hill made it clear that even Reagan's precious 1981 tax cut was in jeopardy, he adopted a strategy different from the hard-line, take-it-or-leave-it approach of early 1981. He gave his staff the go-ahead to negotiate with congressional leaders. The full-scale bipartisan negotiations that followed were conducted by a handful of key leaders from the White House, the Senate, and the House of Representatives, who became known as the Gang of Seventeen. Meetings were held at both ends of Pennsylvania Avenue, in many different settings. But the negotiations of the Gang of Seventeen ultimately collapsed amid mutual mistrust and charges on both sides of political manipulation.

What followed became a kind of model for the budget process over the succeeding several years. Acrimonious debate in the Senate was accompanied by chaos in the House. In late May, the House rejected seven different budget proposals. The first six included a Reagan-backed budget offered by Minority Leader Robert Michel (Reagan's first budget setback), a moderate bipartisan alternative offered by Democrat Les Aspin, a pay-as-you-go plan offered by Democrat George Miller, a liberal plan offered by Democrat David Obey, a package put together by the Congressional Black Caucus, and a conservative Republican plan that called for a balanced budget in fiscal 1983.[6] After defeating those six, the House finished its handiwork by rejecting the plan that had been approved by its own Budget Committee.

After a few more weeks of political maneuvering, both the House and the Senate finally passed their own budget resolutions. Final congressional passage of a joint resolution did not take place until June 23, nearly six weeks after the May 15 deadline imposed by the 1974 budget act. No one rejoiced. Despite some $6.5 billion in projected spending cuts and nearly $21 billion in revenue increases, James R. Jones, chairman of the House Budget Committee, commented, "I feel very strongly we are underestimating where the deficit is going to be."[7] The projected fiscal 1983 deficit stood at $104 billion.

While 1981 had been characterized by the high-stakes, high-visibility battle to cut taxes, 1982 was characterized by the effort to raise taxes. The resulting Tax Equity and Fiscal Responsibility Act (TEFRA) was a product of the political shrewdness of Senate Finance Committee Chairman Bob Dole, but its passage, in the end, required a hard push by the antitax president.

What turned Ronald Reagan from the fierce champion of tax cuts into first the compliant accepter and then the energetic proponent of a substantial tax increase? In part, he was following a pattern—established when he was governor of California—of holding firm to a principle until it was no longer tenable, then compromising and declaring victory. Reagan was convinced by his advisers that this tax increase was really a matter of shoring up tax-code compliance, or correcting mistakes in the tax code. The president was also convinced that he had gotten a good deal. He was under the impression that for every one dollar in new revenues, the budget plan would give him three dollars in outlay savings.

It is not entirely clear where Reagan got that idea, but it was an inaccurate one. "When eventually someone told Reagan the Congress did not give him any three-for-one, the president felt betrayed. Believing the administration had been 'snookered' . . . on TEFRA, Reagan, Regan and Meese became very suspicious of other compromises."[8]

For the rest of 1982, the budget debate was characterized by bickering within Congress and between Congress and the White House. A major dispute over a supplemental appropriations bill resulted first in a veto, then in an angry veto override by Congress.

In the span of two years, the battle over fiscal policy had traveled a long way. In his first year, the president won big victories for all his policies, including large defense increases, large social cuts, and a massive tax cut. In his second year, when he was defensive over the ballooning deficit and the faltering economy, Reagan still fought for maintaining planned defense increases and more cuts in spending on domestic programs; he achieved only modest success.

But as his second year and the FY 1983 budget process came to a close and the midterm election neared, Reagan found himself acceding to a tax increase—which showed how far the politics of debt and taxes had devolved from the high point of Reaganomics in mid-1981. Passage of TEFRA and the override proved that as the Ninety-Seventh Congress was coming to a close, the budget playing field was being leveled. Democrats were now able to assert themselves on budget matters, and the promise of the Reagan revolution was suddenly transformed into trench warfare over deficits.

Stung by criticism over the persistent deficits, Reagan decided to seize the initiative by advocating a constitutional amendment that would require a balanced budget. In an April 19, 1982, television address, the president commented: "Once we've created a balanced budget—and we will—I want to ensure that we keep it for many long years after I've left office. And there's only one way to do that . . . only a constitutional amendment will do the job."[9]

To Reagan, the amendment was a way to underscore his continued ideological commitment to a balanced budget, even if his policies signaled a different set of priorities. The Republican-dominated Senate passed the amendment with the two-thirds majority required for constitutional amendments, but after an acrimonious debate, the proposal failed in the House. Although defeated, the president saw that the issue kept the Democrats on the defensive, and he continued his crusade for a balanced-budget amendment throughout his presidency, supplementing it in his second term with the call for a line-item veto. The balanced-budget amendment was not to surface again in a serious way until a decade later, in June 1992.

The 1982 congressional elections did not provide any dramatic breakthrough to transform the fiscal debate or to signal a public consensus. The Democrats gained twenty-six seats in the House, a gain large enough to return the balance of power from the boll-weevil–Republican coalition to mainstream Democrats. In the Senate, the Republicans picked up one seat, that vacated by Independent Senator Harry Byrd of Virginia, to hold a majority of fifty-four to forty-six.

DEBATE IN 1983

The budget debate in Reagan's third year reflected the post-1982 political alignment. The president's budget proposal was not embraced by Congress, but it was not rejected out of hand. For once, there was a feeling that the White House, recognizing the new reality in the House, had made realistic assumptions about the economy. But that did not mean that a new, smooth, and timely budget process was in place. The pattern of the 1980s had been set, and months of bickering and wrangling—both between parties and within parties, both between institutions and within institutions—now seemed inescapable.

Reagan's budget called for a 10 percent, inflation-adjusted increase in defense spending and at the same time imposed an across-the-board freeze in domestic expenditures. Because of inflation, this freeze amounted to a cut in real social spending. Despite the freeze, the budget still projected triple-digit deficits for the next five years, including a FY 1984 deficit of $188.8 billion. President Reagan also called for a contingency tax increase to take effect in FY 1986 if deficits remained above 2.5 percent of GNP. When it was presented, Reagan called his proposal a "sweeping set of fiscal policy changes designed to reduce substantially the mounting Federal deficits that threaten the renewal of economic growth."[10]

After examining the specifics of the president's proposal, the Democratic leadership in Congress wasted no time in offering its opinions. House Speaker Tip O'Neill declared that he could not truthfully conceive of a freeze on domestic spending. Republicans, too, were doubtful. Senate Majority Leader Howard Baker commented that he expected "a real donnybrook . . . a ferocious debate" about defense.[11] Republican Representative Denny Smith added that "the President's plan isn't going anywhere."[12]

Exercising their newly reacquired control, House Budget Committee Democrats took one day to pass a fiscal 1984 budget resolution, by a straight party-line vote of twenty to eleven. The absence of Representative Phil Gramm, a maverick Democrat who was soon to switch parties and who had been removed from the committee by the Democratic leadership, simplified the Democrats' task.

The House Democrats' budget plan demonstrated the differences between their priorities and the president's. The House plan sought to increase domestic spending by roughly $33 billion, mostly by increasing funding for domestic programs that had been the victims of cuts in FY 1982 and FY 1983. Defense spending was limited to a 4 percent, inflation-adjusted increase. The plan also called for $30 billion in additional revenues in FY 1984, a provision that placed in jeopardy both the third installment of the 1981 tax cut and the indexing provisions intended to prevent bracket creep. One week later, after the Republicans failed to offer an alternative, the full House passed the committee-backed resolution 229 to 196. Having switched to the Republican party, Representative Gramm called the house resolution "the most irresponsible budget that has ever been proposed during my four years in Congress."[13]

While the Democratic majority in the House was easily able to pass the resolution, the Republican majority in the Senate had great difficulty in forging a consensus. Republican members of the Senate Budget Committee were divided. Some GOP senators felt that deficit reduction should come only in the form of spending cuts, while others were willing to discuss tax increases.

The disarray of Senate Republicans over the budget in 1983 dramatized the turnaround since 1981, when congressional Republicans showed unwavering support for Reagan's economic policies. House Speaker O'Neill, watching with his Democratic colleagues from the sidelines, gleefully commented: "For two years the Senate voted in lockstep to support the Reagan program of big spending for the Pentagon and big tax cuts for the wealthy. Today, the Senate refused to go any further."[14]

As the Senate continued to drag its feet, the possibility of no congressional budget resolution became real. In mid-April, word was leaked that Defense Secretary Caspar Weinberger had told the president that the administration might be better off without a congressional budget. White House spokesman Larry Speakes, when asked whether Reagan would prefer no budget resolution or increased taxes, replied, "No budget resolution!" Observers could not help noticing that the budget process that had enabled Reagan to score such resounding victories at the outset of his term had quickly become the object of much disdain from the administration.

Despite the divisions and difficulties, a budget resolution was eventually passed in late June, enabling the real and serious issues to be debated and compromises to be forged. The main battleground in 1983, not surprisingly, was taxes. Democrats in Congress were reluctant to pass a tax-increase bill without the president's endorsement. The president, however, expressed his adamant opposition to any deficit-reduction measure that included tax increases: "We don't face large deficits because Americans are not taxed enough. We face those deficits because the Congress still spends too much. . . . And I am prepared to veto any tax increases . . . no matter how they arrive."[15]

By August, Senate Finance Chairman Bob Dole was willing to acknowledge the need for new revenues, saying, "We will have to raise taxes, but we will have to cut spending first." The Kansas Republican added that "the time is fast approaching when we will have to decide whether this Congress is a serious deliberative body or not. [The budget deficit] ought to be at the heart of our legislative agenda. Instead it is sort of a sideshow. . . . It seems we are drifting into an aimless stupor." That drifting did not go unnoticed by the media and the public.[16] In September, *Time* reported, "After many months of bitter wrangling . . . Congress and the Reagan Administration have at last reached a tacit understanding about what they will do . . . to reduce those gargantuan $200 billion budget deficits. In a word, nothing."[17] *Time* was right —but while they did nothing, they spent an enormous amount of time and energy to reach that end.

Much of the action came from infighting within the administration, some of it over the significance of the federal deficit. Treasury Secretary Donald Regan challenged the notion that large deficits make interest rates go up. In trying to play down the seriousness of the deficits, Regan rejected the notion that taxes should be raised, insisting that the only meaningful solution to the deficit problem was to reduce spending. In support of his contention, Regan cited a Treasury study that had surveyed the academic literature on deficits and interest rates and found little solid empirical evidence for any connection. Meanwhile, Martin Feldstein, chairman of the President's Council of Economic Advisers, ventured his contrary opinion: "The reason for the very high level of long-term real interest rates is undoubtedly the unprecedented level of the budget deficits that are now predicted . . . if no legislative action is taken."

Feldstein's call for what he termed necessary tax increases upset many members of the administration, including President Reagan. But some on Wall Street agreed with Feldstein. *Fortune* quoted a "highly regarded Wall Street economist" as saying, "Don Regan is pretty close to being the most dangerous man in America. It's incredible that the Secretary of the Treasury . . . can go around implying that deficits don't matter."[18]

The intense criticism of large budget deficits during the fall of 1983 lacked coherence for a simple reason: interest rates were stable or falling relative to their record high levels during the early 1980s. In October 1983, long-term interest rates were about 11.5 percent, well below the 13.5 percent rates that had prevailed a little over a year earlier during the summer of 1982. Interest rates continued to fall during the years of the budget debate in the mid-1980s, reaching a low of about 7.5 percent in mid-1986. Although much of the fall in interest rates was due to lower inflation, and the decline was more nominal than real, the steady drop undercut the urgency of calls for deficit reduction by undercutting the traditional claim that bigger budget deficits meant higher interest rates.

Division in the administration was matched by division and disarray in Congress, perhaps partly because of the strong economy and falling interest rates. Despite the arrival of the new fiscal year, neither chamber considered a deficit-reduction package. In October, the House Ways and Means Committee reported a bill that would have increased taxes by $8 billion. Three weeks later, on November 17, the House effectively rejected the bill. In response, the Senate suspended action on its deficit reduction, which included $13.4 billion in tax increases. Thus "for the first time since passage of the Congressional Budget Act in 1974 Congress failed to enact deficit reduction measures required by its own budget plan."[19] *Time* reported that

> On Capitol Hill last week, the ballooning federal deficit was being treated more as a conversation piece than an urgent problem. Despite a few genuine efforts to do what everyone knew had to be done—raise revenues and reduce spending—the week ended with a blizzard of babbling and fruitless finger pointing between Congress and the White House.[20]

As with any political issue, the finger pointing went in many directions. Senator Dole said: "There are two stumbling blocks. One, Ronald Reagan; the other, Tip O'Neill. Unless we have the two giants in this town on board, we're not going to put together a deficit-reduction package." On the day that the House failed to consider the deficit-reduction measure approved by the Ways and Means Committee, Speaker O'Neill commented, "The next time I see Republican crocodile tears about the deficits, I will ask them where their party was today." *Time* magazine reported that "Reagan's unyielding resistance to any tax increases at all this year and his refusal to join in the search for solutions to the deficit mess have contributed heavily to the inability of the legislature to act on basic economic issues."[21]

As Congress adjourned for the year on November 18, members were left to reflect on their failures—and in time-honored fashion, to flagellate themselves and their institution. Representative Barber Conable said, "If any of us said we were going home with our heads held high, we'd be kidding ourselves."[22] Dan Rostenkowski of Illinois, chairman of the Ways and Means Committee, summed up public sentiment toward the Congress: "As we leave Washington, word of our impotence will precede us. We have put special interests on notice that we can be pushed around. We have confessed to an already doubting nation that we are ruled by political fear, rather than economic courage."[23]

Despite this perception, the remarks of Representative Leon Panetta in September 1983 may have been more accurate. He said: "The public does not translate the deficit into something that really bites them. We are going to have to get public support for action on the deficit."[24]

The continuing, robust economic recovery seemed to support Panetta's assertion. The October 31, 1983, issue of *Business Week* reported increases in industrial output, employment, personal income, and retail sales. Analysts were upgrading estimates of the leading economic indicators. The sky was not falling from huge deficits; why should the public be alarmed?

ENDING THE FIRST TERM

The year 1984 would prove to be another strange and tumultuous one for the budget process. It began with what had become the usual fashion—the president's budget was rejected on delivery. Before the year ended, the Senate abandoned the budget process set out in 1974, refusing to consider a budget resolution for FY 1985 until it enacted deficit-reduction legislation. The House, conversely, damned the torpedoes and proceeded full speed ahead, as the Democrats were able to forge a budget consensus with relative ease. Then the usual bickering took over; ultimately, Congress would pass a budget resolution on October 1, the first day of fiscal 1985 and more than four months after the statutory deadline.

Separate deficit-reduction legislation—that trimmed deficits by a projected $149.2 billion over the next three fiscal years—also passed. This figure included $50.8 billion from increased tax revenues, $58.3 billion from curbing projected increases in defense, $12.2 billion from savings in entitlements, and $3.9 billion from reductions in nondefense discretionary spending. And after all of this, the deficit was projected to reach nearly $208 billion in fiscal 1987!

As Ronald Reagan's first term drew to a close, he could look back on a series of paradoxes. When he ran for the presidency in 1980, the deficit stood at $60 billion, and he promised to balance the budget by 1984. Four years later, the deficit had nearly tripled, to $175 billion, and was projected to rise, not fall, through the first two years of his second term.

While Reagan had cloaked himself in budget-balancing rhetoric, from the start he clearly was far more intent on reducing the size and the scope of the federal government than on doing anything else. Here, too, was a paradox: during Reagan's first term, federal spending had gone from 22.4 percent of GNP in 1980 to 23.5 percent by 1984, a startling increase in peacetime. This happened despite Reagan's having brought about the largest spending and tax cut in the nation's history. True, the increase had come largely in entitlements, defense, and net interest, while discretionary domestic spending had been held down, but nothing could disguise the swelling of the federal government that Reagan had campaigned against but had acquiesced in during his first term as president.

Candidate and president Reagan had also run and governed on a vociferous antitax pledge and had followed through on it with the large tax cut of the Economic Recovery Tax Act in 1981. But in each of his subsequent years, if the 1983 Social Security reforms are included, Reagan signed into law sizable tax increases. Still, by 1984, federal tax revenues had fallen to 18.1 percent of GNP, well below the 20.1 percent level that had prevailed in 1981, when Reagan took office.

In 1981, President Reagan dominated the budget process and Congress as few presidents had ever done. But he became increasingly reactive thereafter. Hugh Heclo has said: "The White House found it increasingly difficult in 1982 and 1983 to dominate the agenda with its budget proposals. Indeed what had been a president-led budget process in the first year had become virtually a presidentless and stalemated process by 1984."[25]

While the weak state of the American economy had been a major theme and the most effective weapon in Ronald Reagan's campaign armory in 1980, the strong state of the economy was an equally major theme in his reelection bid in 1984. Democratic challenger Walter F. Mondale sought to capitalize on public concerns about the burgeoning federal deficit but found, as Leon Panetta's earlier comment might have suggested, no real public audience. The public's indifference to the deficit, combined with its aversion to tax increases and the inescapable reality of a booming economy, doomed Mondale to a landslide defeat by the triumphant president.

CONTROL OF THE BUDGET

The Reagan administration set out in 1981 with an agenda that in a historical context might have been revolutionary in conception. But from that ambitious start, the Reagan years became ordinary and predictable when the administration encountered the political process in Congress. The failure of the president and Congress to reduce the deficit became a problem because they had failed to exercise control over the federal budget and fiscal policy. In contrast, Paul Volcker and the Fed had succeeded with monetary policy, managing to bring down interest rates and inflation and fostering a strong economic recovery.

When Reagan took office in 1981, 72 percent of Americans named inflation as the number-one problem facing the nation; 8 percent were most concerned about unemployment. In a speech on February 5, 1981, Reagan declared: "We don't have to choose between inflation and unemployment—they go hand in hand. It's time to try something different." By the time he left office, the strong U.S. economy had proved that, indeed, we did not have to choose between inflation and unemployment. By late 1988, inflation stood at 4.4 percent, and the unemployment rate, at 5.4 percent, was below the 6 percent level that many economists had come to think of as its natural minimum. This time the problem that Americans identified as the worst our nation faced was the deficit, although it was not clear why they thought it was bad. Certainly, the deficit did not carry the negative political repercussions of inflation or unemployment, which was fortunate for Reagan, since it was harder to eliminate.

Whatever Ronald Reagan's intentions about budget deficits—whether he aimed, as some of his advisers clearly did, to use them as a political tool to force deep cuts in domestic spending or whether they grew as an unintended consequence of other policies and policy objectives—there was at least one clear objective that Reagan and his team were coming to see as truly revolutionary: control of the budget. All those holding power shared David Stockman's view that domestic spending was constantly, almost inevitably, increasing, driven largely by the growth of spending on entitlements, the outlays for Social Security and government health programs that were set by law and not included in any deficit-reduction proposals.

Ronald Reagan and David Stockman were both working to promote the most Jeffersonian vision of the role of the federal government in American society that had been seen in national politics since 1932. But to realize their Jeffersonian ambitions, they had to employ Hamiltonian means. The massive change required to cut the federal government required a strong federal government; continuing the drift toward a government of even more massive size was much easier. Moreover, when Stockman in the heat of the battle with Congress in 1981 encouraged a bidding war on tax cuts to force bigger cuts in spending, he inadvertently produced the sort of budget deficits that would have scared even Hamilton and would have made Jefferson drop dead with fright.

Stockman saw the goal in philosophical terms, but he waged the war along tactical lines. There were two battles to be fought before the Reagan team could remake the federal budget to its liking. The first was political, the second economic. First, the Reagan team had to break the broad consensus by which discretionary social programs had grown without significant opposition in the 1970s. This battle was effectively won in 1981, though much of the credit must go to members of Congress who helped shift the focus of economic stimulus from the spending side to the tax side and began moving spending from discretionary domestic programs to defense.

The object of the second battle was to make the budget drive the economy, rather than letting the economy drive the budget. An increase of a single percentage point in inflation would automatically trigger $3 billion in federal spending, the Congressional Budget Office found in 1981.[26] Various benefits were tied to the unemployment rate, and numerous federal loan and loan-guarantee programs became more costly when interest rates rose. All three rates were increasing in 1981. Slowing the growth of federal spending, then, would require far more than simply putting together working majorities in Congress to cut "waste and fraud" from programs. It would require an attack on the entitlement programs that established benefits by statute rather than by appropriations and were deliberately made immune to attack. The most costly entitlements were—and still are—the much-expanded contemporary version of Franklin Roosevelt's modest Social Security program (along with other retirement benefits, such as veterans' pensions) and Medicare and Medicaid, Lyndon Johnson's efforts to match or surpass FDR's legacy.

By the end of 1982, the second battle was clearly lost. The economy was driving the budget just as much as it had driven it in the 1970s, and the Reagan administration's effort to pretend that this could be otherwise had apparently made things worse. Specifically, Reagan's budget and tax cuts did not immediately restore the economy to health; instead, in 1982, a teetering economy plummeted into the deepest recession in decades and left the budget $127 billion in deficit. That unprecedented figure was already double Reagan's projections, and it would almost double again. At $208 billion, or

6.3 percent of GNP, the 1983 deficit was the largest since the recession of 1976. That was the year in which Stockman, Wanniski, and others had begun to complain that the federal budget was hostage to the economy. Even though these conservatives had taken firm political control of the presidential budget by 1982, they were unable to overcome the fact that in shaping the federal budget, political decisions about taxing and spending cannot be made without the closest attention being given to fluctuations in economic statistics. Why waste the political capital to cut $3 billion from the federal budget when a 1 percent increase in inflation could wipe out the cut?

Reagan's aides, including Stockman, White House Chief of Staff James Baker, and Baker's deputy, Richard Darman, had come to recognize that economic conditions so dramatically different from the original rosy projections demanded a different approach. The Republican leadership in Congress, which had never been committed to the supply-side vision anyway, was even more blunt: five GOP senators, including Paul Laxalt of Nevada, a close Reagan friend, visited the White House at the end of 1981 in an attempt to change the direction of the administration's economic policy. Senate Majority Leader Howard Baker outlined the political consequences of the deficit, arguing that "cutting alone isn't going to do it"—not even if the administration attacked entitlements.

FOCUSING ON SOCIAL SECURITY

The battle to gain control of entitlements, and therefore of the budget process, focused on Social Security, the largest of them and the one that has become almost synonymous with the word "entitlement." That single program, with numerous peripheral benefits tacked on between the 1930s and the 1980s, accounted for 21 percent of federal outlays in 1981. Franklin Roosevelt might almost have had Reagan in mind when in 1935 he answered advisers who criticized as regressive the payroll tax that funded the system: "No damn politician can ever scrap my social security system."[27]

Reagan and his aides had no intention of scrapping Social Security (even if some had no real aversion to doing so). They wanted to cut discretionary domestic spending, which they believed was largely wasted. But the Reagan White House did ask Congress, just days after the administration's first great triumph on a budget-reconciliation bill, to make enough changes to eliminate the growing gap between income and expenditure in the Social Security System's trust fund. The gap had developed because in the early 1970s, Social Security had been made an entitlement that was tied not only to demographics (as more Americans attained the age of eligibility, more had to be paid out) and income (if Americans made less, the trust fund would take in less) but also to price fluctuations by the creation of automatic yearly cost-of-living adjustments (COLAs) for beneficiaries.

In theory, this system might have been workable—inflation, for instance, would have a net effect of zero on the trust fund if higher incomes offset benefit increases. But the cost-of-living adjustments were based on the consumer price index, a measure that significantly overstated the inflation rate in the 1970s because of a combination of technical difficulties with the index and the way it estimated housing costs. This had caused benefits to increase much faster than wages. Together with the new features that Congress had been tacking on through the 1960s and 1970s (generous benefits for college-student survivors of beneficiaries, for example), COLAs were driving the Social Security trust fund quickly into the red in the early 1980s. The fund had a long-term, unfunded deficit of $1.8 trillion (the difference between its projected payouts and its projected receipts over seventy-five years), and, more significant for policy makers, a short-term cash crunch that seemed likely for 1983. The more immediate crisis necessitated a small benefit cut, a small tax increase, or a slight delay in issuing checks, but the prospect of such adjustment led to widespread alarm that the system was "bankrupt."[28]

Both the short- and long-term Social Security crises stemmed from the extension of Roosevelt's determination to isolate the system from any "damn politician." A similar purpose had been in the minds of those who had wrested control of discretionary benefit increases away from Congress and insisted on indexation in the early 1970s. Set in motion by a Republican president who wanted to avoid looking bad every year when he had to fight Congress to hold down excessive benefit increases, this mechanism merely ensured that the political circumstances surrounding its construction and implementation would come back to haunt all subsequent presidents and Congresses—and that they could then do nothing about them. Indexation was not an apolitical solution; it was merely politics fossilized and loaded onto the shoulders of future generations.

It was also the trump card in the game of get all you can. The result of twenty years of discretionary increases and ten of automatic increases in Social Security was, according to Murray Weidenbaum, that "the average retiree on Social Security [had] a higher income than the rest of the population."[29] The result for government and for taxpayers, however, was less happy. To the extent that Social Security was a large and uncontrollable portion of the federal budget, it ensured that the budget would continue to be driven by, indeed determined by, the economy instead of the other way around. And the attempt to depoliticize it had merely ensured that politicians would be, to an increasing extent, impotent to do anything about its budgetary consequences.

Reagan declined to make a direct attempt to detach Social Security outlays from their tendency to outgrow, during periods of inflation, the wage base that financed them. Modification of the cost-of-living adjustment was never even considered at the White House. When, early in the 1981 hearings of the Senate Budget Committee, Chairman Pete Domenici suggested a more modest investment in COLAs, Reagan abruptly shut the door. But soon thereafter, Richard Schweiker, health and human services secretary, offered, on behalf of the president, a package that reduced benefits for those retiring before age sixty-five, cut the minimum benefit, and trimmed benefits for those retiring after 1986. These changes would have saved more money than was needed, allowing the administration to promise eventual cuts in the payroll tax. They also would have had the effect, as economist William Niskanen has pointed out, of changing Social Security from "the nation's primary provision system" to "a floor on real retirement income."[30]

In any event, the political response to these proposals was so swift and decisive that, to Niskanen, it seemed "almost an anticlimax." The Senate promptly passed a resolution condemning the president's action, ninety-eight to zero. This happened despite the fact that Democratic Congressman Jake Pickle, chairman of the Social Security subcommittee of Ways and Means, was about to come out with recommendations not all that different from Reagan's. The Social Security issue was handed over to an independent commission, chaired by Alan Greenspan, that eventually abated the crisis by raising the payroll tax and phasing in a slightly higher retirement age over many years.

Although the commission more or less solved the immediate crisis with Social Security, its creation was the Reagan administration's first admission that its political mandate would not give it control over the federal budget. The budget was still driven by the economy, and even the mildest attempts to detach it ran up against political forces, such as those embodied in the ninety-eight-to-zero vote, that could not be overcome.

THE ERA OF MASSIVE DEFICITS

With the budget still tied to the economy, as the economy entered a severe recession in 1981, the era of Stockman's massive $200 billion deficits "as far as the eye can see" began. The economy recovered from the recession; the federal budget did not, or did not do so completely. When, in 1988, a Republican gave Reagan credit for the longest economic expansion in postwar history, Democratic vice-presidential candidate Lloyd Bentsen responded that producing an economic expansion is easy if it can be done by writing "two trillion dollars in hot checks." Bentsen's comment clearly delineated the debate on the Reagan years. True, they had been prosperous, but the prosperity had been borrowed from future generations by the heavy borrowing of government, businesses, and households. The 1990s became a decade of trying to pay back debts accumulated in the 1980s.

The 1981 rebuff of Reagan's attempt to control the increase in Social Security outlays came just after the administration's triumph on the budget resolution that generated most of the largest spending cuts of the 1980s. The vote to declare Social Security effectively off-limits to the president marked an early end to Reagan's notable successes in forcing Congress to accept his spending priorities. That period of success did not last long after his landslide victory and the attempt on his life in March 1981. The early budget successes were, as political scientist James Pfiffner notes, "the result of advance planning, singleness of purpose and speed of execution." The strategy was, in Pfiffner's words, first "to cow the opposition and stampede as many members of Congress as possible onto the winning band wagon" and second "to make it seem as if programs benefiting all segments of society, rich as well as poor, were being cut alike."[31]

Though successful at first, this political strategy began to fail as early as late 1981, when Reagan asked for $13 billion in additional cuts and Congress granted only $4 billion. The administration's attempt to meddle with the popular Social Security program, which provoked cries of outrage that Reagan was trying to "balance the budget on the backs of the elderly," also challenged the president's aura of success. Few people were impressed by David Stockman's claim that the administration wanted to cut "weak claims" rather than "weak claimants."

But even without these setbacks, neither the Reagan administration's political support nor its economic forecast could withstand the 1982 recession. The administration had predicted a $45 billion deficit for 1982. The recession increased federal outlays by $30 billion and decreased revenues by $23 billion,[32] so that the total 1982 deficit suddenly reached $128 billion. That record-breaking figure provided such a shock that beginning with the 1983 budget, debt and deficits became the central concerns in fiscal policy. After the recession, when inflation apparently had been wrung out of the economy, the deficit became the political-economic bugaboo of the 1980s.

While the administration began to see the limits to its ability to cut domestic spending and entitlements as early as May 1981, it did not adjust its spending strategy accordingly. It continued to ask for—though it did not receive—8 percent annual real growth in the defense budget and projected that nondefense spending would fall by the same percentage in real terms in the budget for 1983. Reagan also rejected the idea of raising any personal income tax rates.

Although things did not go entirely according to plan when the politically powerful President Reagan took his tax and budget proposals to Congress in the spring of 1981, by the next summer the political situation was far worse. The unique combination that had enabled Reagan to get even half of what he wanted the year before—and as the disillusioned Stockman might later have argued, half of what he wanted might have been worse than none—was now missing. "Last year, the White House could reach out to the public with new ideas," Republican Congressman Ralph Regula of Ohio noted at the time. "This year, Members [of Congress] are fragmented and more sensitive to constituent interests. There is also less devotion to the President's cause."[33]

At this point, the White House's yearning for mastery over the budget process only accelerated the collapse of Stockman's effort to make the budget drive the economy. "A high White House person told me they are more concerned about control of the process than [budget] numbers," Representative Tom Tauke of Iowa said during the fight over the 1983 budget. "What people ignore is that we are incredibly close on the numbers."[34] Although the White House won some important concessions in the 1983 budget process, particularly on Social Security, no concerted effort was made to strip the federal budget of unnecessary spending. Like the subsequent budgets of 1984 and 1985, this was, to use the description of William Niskanen, a member of Reagan's Council of Economic Advisers, a "housekeeping" budget.

With these budgets, a deficit in the range of $100 billion to $200 billion became a permanent feature of the American economy for the rest of the decade. By the end of 1982, in its proposals for the FY 1984 budget, even the administration was acknowledging that the deficit would not disappear but would remain at or above $150 billion through 1988. It was becoming clear that there was more to this deficit problem than just a crisis—the recession —since the deficits produced by every previous crisis in American history had evaporated within a few years.

The Reagan administration's response to the sudden permanent deficit and the failure of Stockman's attempt to bring the budget under its political control was to move to ensure that the deficit did not become a political liability to the president. With a reelection campaign just around the corner, Reagan turned to dreams of a balanced-budget amendment and thus to a purely rhetorical strategy on fiscal policy.

For Reagan, actually passing the balanced-budget amendment does not appear to have been a top priority. According to the *Congressional Quarterly*, he made only four or five phone calls to lawmakers in the days leading up to the dramatic vote.[35] And there were good reasons—at the time and in retrospect—to say that the amendment would not have been particularly sound policy. After all, the goal of the budget process at that time was to get the deficit down from the $100 billion-plus stratosphere, or at least to keep it from accelerating further, not necessarily to bring the deficit to zero immediately. But for Reagan, the proposed balanced-budget amendment served as an excuse to evade the political consequences of the persistent deficit. Although he did little to get it passed, Reagan mentioned the amendment in every subsequent State of the Union message, coupling it with the proposal that the president be allowed to veto individual line items in spending bills.

Neither proposal had much chance of passing Congress—especially the line-item–veto, which would sharply limit the spending power of Congress. Both proposals substituted new and inflexible mechanisms for the political will that was lacking, both in Congress and in the White House, to cut back on entitlements or defense spending or to raise taxes. Reagan's critics said that to evaluate them as policies or even as legislative proposals missed the essentially political point of the balanced-budget amendment and the line-item–veto proposal: to allow Reagan to claim, as he did time and again, that "the President can't spend one dime. . . . Congress does all the spending."

Reagan and his aides had exaggerated the political damage that would be caused by the persistence of $100 billion deficits. The deficit itself would never be so acute a concern for voters as the tangible miseries of inflation and unemployment; but it was reasonable at the time to think that since the Republican party had for years presented itself as the party of the balanced budget, to have broken that promise so overtly would mean political ignominy. Voters, however, were really no more interested in a balanced budget per se than members of Congress had been during Stockman's heady first months. In the wake of the tax revolt of the late 1970s that had swept Reagan into office, voters were almost single-mindedly interested in lower taxes, and as long as politicians at least promised not to raise them, they were little concerned with whether the funds came from borrowing or from reduced spending. The Democrats' attempt to steal the intuitive appeal of the idea of a balanced budget without giving up their party's historical commitment to social programs failed largely because they failed to recognize this monomania of the voters. Walter Mondale signed his political death warrant when he said, "Mr. Reagan will raise taxes, and so will I."

Although the 1988 Democratic nominee, Michael Dukakis, had learned from Mondale's grievous error, Reagan's successor, George Bush, took the lead in attacking tax increases as the only alternative to deficits. Once again, the Democrats were stymied in their attempt to slide over and become the party of the balanced budget. Further, the deficit made it impossible for Democrats to propose any new or expanded social roles for government, since to do so would be to raise the question of how to pay for them; new taxes or more deficit spending were the only answers. Instead, the Democrats wound up standing for nothing, and the deficit became a Republican device for perpetuating the party's hegemony in presidential politics.

Senator Daniel Patrick Moynihan, who was most perceptive in recognizing Stockman's flawed second agenda of forcing down spending by cutting taxes in 1981, was also among those who recognized early the political value of the deficit for Republicans. But in early 1983, hardly anyone saw it that way. The deficit appeared to be Reagan's political Achilles' heel. As a result, the administration's purpose shifted subtly but significantly from one of taking political control of the deficit to one of avoiding political responsibility for the deficit.

GRAMM-RUDMAN-HOLLINGS

Although the balanced-budget amendment and line-item–veto proposals were not expected to be implemented but rather were intended to provide political cover for the deficit, they had a significant impact on the kinds of policies that were adopted to cope with the budget crisis. While the deficit had grown largely because of the "automatic government" (in political scientist Kent Weaver's phrase) created by the indexation of entitlements, the reaction of Congress in the mid-1980s was to seek out more, not fewer, automatic mechanisms with which they hoped to reduce the deficit. The balanced-budget amendment was only the most drastic among such automatic proposals, in that it assumed that legislators would under no circumstances be able to make sound choices about short-term deficit spending. Although that proposal was too unacceptable to get the two-thirds vote needed, Congress was not averse to another automatic plan, one that also assumed that legislators did not have the political courage to cut the deficit on their own.

This was the Gramm-Rudman-Hollings system, put forward by a coalition of senators that included a stalwart conservative who, as a Democratic member of the House had been a leader of the boll-weevil advocates of Reagan's 1981 tax and spending proposals (Phil Gramm), one of the leading moderate Republicans (Warren Rudman), and a crusty moderate, southern Democrat who had run for president in 1984 on a platform calling for an across-the-board budget freeze (Ernest Hollings).

After Reagan had rejected the bold deficit-reduction plan pushed by the Republican Senate for the fiscal 1986 budget, the three senators put forth in September 1985 a proposal that set a timetable for reducing the deficit to particular target levels each subsequent year: $172 billion in fiscal 1986, $144 billion in fiscal 1987, and so on, until it reached zero in fiscal 1991. The plan appeared to have a doomsday device that would force Congress to achieve the targets. If the deficit could not be cut to the prescribed levels, something called sequestration would take place: federal spending would be cut a fixed percentage across the board to get to within 10 percent of the targeted deficit. Virtually all entitlement programs, plus the interest on the federal debt—about 60 percent of spending—were exempt from sequestration; the cuts would fall most heavily on defense spending, which Reagan at the time was still trying to increase. But they would also fall on Congress itself, and on the domestic discretionary spending to which many congressmen were particularly attached. Therefore, neither the president nor the Congress was considered likely to see sequestration as an acceptable method of cutting the budget.

Whatever its virtues, the Gramm-Rudman-Hollings plan meant that the majority of the budget outlays that had been most responsible for the deficit —the automatic half, or entitlements—constituted the portion that would be exempt from the automatic cutting mechanism. But because politicians seemed unable to respond with courage and compromise to more conventional political imperatives, it was thought necessary to force them to act responsibly by holding the ax of automatic cuts above their heads.

Passing Gramm-Rudman-Hollings, though, was for some members an easier move than actually confronting the 1986 budget and bringing the deficit down right then and there. "Members realize that we have a whale of a problem that we've all been saying that we're going to solve," said Democratic Representative Phil Sharp of Indiana. "And here's this highly visible solution and the day of excuses is long over."[36] The attractiveness of the measure was evident: the bill swept through both houses and reached Reagan's desk in barely three months.

In some ways, Gramm-Rudman-Hollings was an ideal response to Stockman's effort to cut spending by creating a fearsome deficit. As economist Michael Boskin has written: "Gramm-Rudman-Hollings is an example of deficit phobia forcing substantial pressure for spending reduction. Whether the process will work will be seen in the next few years."[37] Writing in 1987, Boskin was being overgenerous, as it was already becoming apparent that the automated process was no substitute for conscious, confrontational cuts in spending—or tax increases if spending cuts proved impossible. By 1988, Senator Hollings had already renounced the process, and the chairmen and ranking Republican members of both congressional budget committees had declared that it did not work.

Gramm-Rudman-Hollings, rather than creating "substantial pressure for spending reduction," instead created substantial pressure on the ingenuity of accountants, who were called on to put federal spending even further beyond political control by making various programs, such as the rescue of the savings and loan industry in 1989, exempt from the deficit targets or, worse, to set whole programs off budget. Off-budget financing was a device invented shortly after the development of the unified federal budget in 1969. In 1970, just $9.6 billion—most of it related to federal credit programs—was segregated from the $200 billion federal budget. By fiscal year 1989, $211 billion in federal spending was not recorded in the $926 billion budget. This figure included the liabilities of various quasi-governmental corporations such as the Federal National Mortgage Association and the Student Loan Marketing Association, which basically enjoyed a line of credit at the U.S. Treasury. But the bulk of the increase resulted from the decision, when Gramm-Rudman-Hollings was instituted, to take the Social Security System's receipts and disbursements off the budget.

The trick of taking so much spending off-budget was made because the Social Security trust fund began to generate a surplus as a result of the 1983 Greenspan commission reforms, described above. That surplus was counted toward satisfaction of the Gramm-Rudman targets. By 1990, although the deficit excluding Social Security surpluses had not really decreased substantially since 1985—it was still more than $200 billion—the deficit as reported for Gramm-Rudman purposes was below $135 billion and shrinking. At this point, it would be fair to say that the government was not "balancing the budget on the backs of the elderly," to recall that potent phrase from the early Reagan years, but was attempting to balance it on the backs of the younger workers who paid a heavy proportion of their earnings—more than 15 percent—in the regressive Social Security tax and stood to get back a far lower return on their payroll taxes than either their parents or their grandparents.

Finally, Gramm-Rudman was obsolete by 1990 because the negotiations that it envisioned generating between the branches had become irrelevant. If defense spending was going to go down anyway, as it did after 1986 and especially after Reagan launched a new round of major arms-control agreements in 1987, there was no incentive for the executive branch to avoid the automatic cuts. Indeed, even in years when the budget agreement should have been relatively achievable, such as 1989, sequestration went into effect, at least temporarily until the political process found ways to negate it. The automatic cuts of the Gramm-Rudman system were so carefully targeted, in contrast to the sledgehammer effect of a balanced-budget amendment, that it managed to be at once impotent (after a few years) and dangerous (for the off-budget spending complexity that it generated).

As the 1980s dawned with Ronald Reagan's election, they presented the possibility of a remarkable era for American fiscal policy, one in which ratcheting up of federal spending and the tax burden could be replaced with political choices about spending and the deficit. At any rate, this was a possibility that Stockman envisioned at the time. Clearly, this could not occur along the lines of Stockman's scheme, and perhaps it was never a realistic possibility for the decade. But the country ended the Reagan years, and the decade, with a system for making federal fiscal decisions that was more automatic, further beyond political control, and more vulnerable to the ebbs and flows of the economy than it was in the period when Stockman first observed the process at work, fifteen years earlier.

· 10 ·

TAXES AND THE DRIVE
FOR NEUTRALITY

If, in early 1987, you had traveled to the beautiful desert town of Sedona in northern Arizona, you might have stayed at an inn where the luxury might have reminded you of an English country house or a French chateau. There among the striking red rocks that had been the backdrop for a number of Western films, you could forget the rugged landscape all around you in the incongruous surroundings of expensive French fabrics and exquisite furniture. But you would have found that the inn was in receivership. The investors for whom it had been built as an income-tax write-off under the old dispensation had been unprepared for the loophole-closing provisions of the 1986 tax act, and now they were about to take a real loss.

If you had then chartered an airplane to take a better look at the countryside around Sedona, you would have seen a beautiful and dramatic landscape, broad patches of dry desert on which little other than sagebrush could survive. But in the midst of this huge brown desert, you could have made out a green rectangle, one to two miles long on each side, which the locals would have been able to tell you was a Christmas tree farm. They would also have been happy to inform you that it was for sale.

Only a few months before, the Christmas Tree Farmers' Association had joined a host of other special-interest groups in testifying before the House Ways and Means Committee. It had assured the committee members that if the special provisions encouraging the raising of Christmas trees were removed from the tax code, Americans would either have no Christmas trees or would have to buy their Christmas trees from Canada. They were careful not to mention that the tax code had become so ridiculous that it had made the raising of Christmas trees in the Arizona desert into an attractive financial proposition.

When the reform went through despite their warnings, it was hard luck for the ranchers whom the old code had rewarded for using otherwise unused land in original ways. These people had a complaint: if the tax code encouraged them to plant Christmas trees in the desert, it should not be changed so that they would be forced to sell their property at a loss. Nevertheless, somebody had to question whether the national interest was served by a tax code that made it profitable to raise Christmas trees in the desert.

In 1986, after a long period of political cowardice before the bullying of lobbyists, officials in Washington were finally asking that question. If money flows to enterprises that never would exist without tax incentives, it flows away from enterprises that might survive on their own and therefore are intrinsically more beneficial to the economy. This undeniable truth had made itself heard despite many competing shouts of outrage in the process leading up to the tax-reform act—which finally came about because people were forced to recognize that Christmas trees should not grow in the desert.

An income tax like the one that yields more than half the revenue of the federal government and an even higher share of the revenue of most states requires two things: a high degree of literacy among the taxpayers, if we are to judge from the complexity of U.S. tax forms, and an ample supply of cheap paper, if we are to judge from the huge number of those forms. Before these two conditions were met, governments were forced to levy taxes on tangible things. Excise taxes have been levied on a broad range of objects including windows, liquor (a great favorite), tea, coffee, cattle, and even on one's own head, the so-called poll tax.

The primary purpose of levying taxes has always been to pay for the necessary and sometimes not-so-necessary activities of governments, everything from national defense to the provision of roads and bridges. Tax policy for socially desirable ends—that is, using the method of collecting taxes to alter social behavior in ways that seem appropriate to the policy makers—has long been a part of the debate over how people should be taxed, even though it is a subject on which the state of our knowledge is uncertain. In the days before income taxes, heavy excises on liquor or tobacco were justified as a means to curb the "excesses" of people given to overusing spirits, stimulants, or other pleasurable diversions. Tariffs or taxes on foreign goods, which were the primary source of U.S. government revenue until 1913, were sometimes justified as necessary to encourage domestic industry in the face of competition from "cheap" foreign goods or, alternatively, to discourage dependence on "unreliable" foreign sources of supply.

AN ISSUE OF FAIRNESS

All these arguments, to varying degrees, remain with us, as does the most popular argument regarding the use of the income tax: if tax rates increase with incomes, those more able to pay the tax will pay more of it. More broadly, with the introduction of the income tax came the idea of equity, the belief that the tax system could and should be used to achieve a more "fair" distribution of income. "Fair" meant that those with higher incomes, by paying over a higher share of their income as taxes, should pay a great deal more tax than those less well off. Having established this notion of fairness, those anxious to raise more tax revenues have been tempted to flatter the largest possible portion of the population by describing those with higher incomes as rich.

Walter Mondale, for example, tried to nominate families earning more than $60,000 per year for inclusion in the "rich" club during his 1984 campaign for the presidency. Mondale's gambit backfired when millions of voting Americans earning more than $60,000 asked themselves if they were really rich. John Adams, a Los Angeles advertising executive, captured some of the negative response to Mondale's initiative in the "My Turn" column in *Newsweek* in the fall of 1984. Wrote Adams:

> Me rich? Good lord, I live in a three-bedroom house in a nice but hardly chic neighborhood. Our family car is a '79 Mercury station-wagon. The children attend private schools, but to offset part of that cost my wife, Penny, keeps a sharp eye out for sales and shuts off the air-conditioner on all but the worst summer days to save on energy expenses. I inherited nothing from my parents when they died, did not attend a "money" college with an old boy network and have basically worked like a Trojan to get where I am and own what I do. Comfortable, even affluent? Sure. But rich?[1]

By the 1984, election, when Mondale promised to raise taxes to deal with deficits, it became clear that, at least during the mid-1980s, the old "soak the rich" rationale for higher income taxes had run its course among American voters.

Unlike in many class-driven societies, most Americans did not dislike the rich, or want to take their wealth away; they aspired to be rich themselves, or to allow their children the chance to attain affluence. But Americans also share a passion for fairness, including the necessity of each paying his fair share. What American voters really did not like was the loophole-ridden American tax code that left many people in neighborhoods like Mr. Adams's wondering whether their neighbors were paying any taxes at all. Middle-class cocktail parties routinely included discussion of someone's latest tax shelter. The existence of high tax rates appeared to have challenged otherwise rational individuals to go to extraordinary lengths, sometimes actually losing money in the process, to generate the feeling, if not the reality, that they were not being ensnared by Uncle Sam's 50 percent–plus tax rates.

In 1984, there were tax reformers both in the Republican and in the Democratic parties. The basic idea behind fundamental tax reform—closing loopholes and using the revenue to make possible lower tax rates—happened to combine a politically appealing idea with a sound approach to tax policy. The need to collect taxes always distorts economic behavior, since people will try to arrange their activities to minimize the taxes that they must pay. Indeed, if tax rates get high enough, the incentive to avoid tax becomes so great that tax revenues fall rather than rise with tax rates. Beyond that, taxes affect incentives. If individuals know that for an additional dollar earned, say from working overtime or building up a business, they will get to keep only twenty-five cents, the tax system discourages work and penalizes economic performance. Likewise, high and variable tax rates on income from capital tend to discourage investment and can thereby slow economic growth.

REAGAN AND REFORM

Anticipating that the Democrats might make good use of the tax-reform issue in the 1984 presidential campaign, President Reagan proposed in his 1984 State of the Union message a basic tax-reform program to achieve a triad of fairness, simplicity, and economic growth. Democratic Senator Bill Bradley had already proposed a loophole-closing, rate-lowering tax plan, as had Republican Congressman Jack Kemp and Republican Senator William Roth.

The Democrats cooperated fully with the president's strategy on taxes. In his July 1984 speech in San Francisco accepting the Democratic nomination for president, Senator Mondale promised to raise Americans' taxes. He tried to soften the blow by talking about reform as taxing the rich, but he could not help confirming what most Americans believed anyway: that this tax reform was simply a wedge to pry open the door to raising taxes. Ronald Reagan, meanwhile, simply held off enumerating any specifics about his tax plan until after his decisive victory in November.

But Reagan was serious about tax reform. More particularly, he was serious about lowering the top tax rates, at least to 35 percent. To get tax rates down, he was willing to close a lot more loopholes than many of his advisers, not to mention many of his major financial supporters, liked.

When the president's tax plan appeared on November 28, 1984, just a few weeks after his election to a second term, it created quite a sensation. The response at the press conference during which Treasury Secretary Donald Regan discussed the plan was so lively that he was pressed into saying that the whole plan was "written on a word processor"[2]—that many of the provisions were for discussion only and could be changed. The November tax-reform plan was labeled the Treasury Department's proposal, not the president's proposal, to allow some redrafting of its more controversial provisions.

The Treasury's proposal was a remarkable document from the point of view of most tax specialists. It eliminated fourteen tax brackets, with rates ranging from 11 to 50 percent, and replaced them with a simple, three-bracket system in which the only tax rates were 15, 25, and 35 percent. It also removed low-income Americans from the income-tax rolls—although as they all discovered once tax reform was finally in place two years later, they were still subject to the ever-present payroll tax that finances Social Security and is the primary tax burden for more than two-thirds of Americans.

The loophole closings that were proposed by the Treasury to pay for the lower tax rates raised many eyebrows around Washington. The sacrosanct deduction for home-mortgage interest, for example, was retained only for a taxpayer's principal residence. Real estate developers pressing forward with plans for communities of vacation and retirement homes were apoplectic. The exclusion from taxable income of health-insurance benefits, part of the cherished package of fringe benefits for most American workers, was retained but capped at $70 per month for individuals and $175 per month for families. While the Treasury claimed that the change would affect only about 30 percent of all employees, the notion that tax breaks for health insurance could be tampered with caused panic in many circles, including the well-financed health-care lobby in Washington.

Perhaps the biggest stunner in the Treasury's proposal was the repeal of itemized deductions for all state and local taxes. To economists unconcerned about political theory and states' rights, this proposal made a great deal of sense. If federal tax reform were to provide comprehensive tax relief, there had to be some cap on state and local taxes. Ending the deductibility of those taxes would increase political resistance to their increase or imposition and therefore make states and localities far more dependent on the federal government for revenues to provide for state and local services. Further, the states and localities that levied especially high taxes, such as New York, Wisconsin, and California, might stand to lose out to lower-tax states if the burden of high local and state taxes was not eased by deductibility. But the idea of double taxation enraged the states and localities.

American business was in for the biggest shock when it looked over the Treasury's proposal. The basic idea behind the package on capital and business income was to treat all forms of business activity equally, a sharp contrast to the existing tax code, which attempted to identify winners and give special tax breaks to particular forms of activity. The good news was that the Treasury Department's proposal reduced the corporate tax rate from 48 percent to 33 percent. Then came what seemed to many of America's captains of industry the bad news. The capital gains tax rate that had been lowered to 20 percent by the 1981 tax act was to revert to the tax rate applied to ordinary income. That inflation gains were excluded from tax and that capital gains continued to enjoy the substantial benefits of deferral until gains were realized provided little consolation. The differential or preferential capital gains tax rate of 20 percent had been taken by many—especially traditional country club Republicans—as a symbol of the federal government's commitment to faster growth and a more competitive America. That little empirical evidence links a long series of impositions and removals of a differential tax rate on capital gains with either faster growth or more competitiveness was of little importance to those convinced that the capital gains tax preference was the key to all that was good about America.

As if the loss of the capital gains tax rate would not be enough, the Treasury proposed revoking the ever-popular investment tax credit and modifying the accelerated-cost-recovery system. These provisions had produced negative tax rates on companies' acquisitions of equipment after both were enacted in 1981. Many businessmen—along with influential economists such as Martin Feldstein, former chairman of the President's Council of Academic Advisers—thought that ending the investment tax credit would be a serious blow to economic growth. Feldstein won many friends in the business community by testifying frequently before Congress on the severe dangers to the economy if the investment tax credit were done away with—a credit which, after all, had begun with the Kennedy administration.

To compensate for the loss of a lower rate on capital gains, the investment tax credit, and accelerated cost recovery, the Treasury proposed eliminating the double taxation of corporate dividends. Corporate dividends were (and still are) taxed once as corporate profits and then again when received by shareholders as dividends. The Treasury's proposal to eliminate the double taxation of dividends was far more valuable than most business leaders bothered to discover. Many corporate executives preferred to stay with double taxation of dividends, since that measure provided a handy excuse not to pay dividends, but instead to retain cash and to "reward" investors with capital gains that received better tax treatment.

The Treasury's proposal also included the elimination of some sacred cows, such as the full write-offs from tax of intangible drilling costs and other measures particularly favored by the oil industry. Furthermore, the Treasury's tax plan curtailed many of the tax shelters that had proliferated under the loophole-ridden tax code born in an era of 70 and 90 percent tax rates. Taken all together, the Treasury's tax plan as proposed in November 1984 would actually have provided substantial systemic benefits to the economy. The more balanced treatment of different forms of income, the indexing of capital gains taxed as ordinary income, and the elimination of the double taxation of dividends were important steps, part of a coherent economic argument about growth, endorsed by many economists.

Further, the Treasury proposed indexing interest income and expense so that savers would be taxed only on the real or noninflationary portion of interest earnings, while borrowers would be able to deduct only the real or noninflationary portion of interest expense. In effect, the Treasury was removing a subsidy to overborrowing that had gone a long way toward creating excesses in the commercial real estate market during the 1970s and 1980s. These measures would likely have provided considerable additional incentives to more saving and investment by lowering market interest rates and thus reducing the uncertainty among borrowers and investors caused by variable inflation rates. They might also have helped to curb the excesses of high-flying savings and loan operators.

The Treasury's tax plan was not entirely devoid of political compromises. It left untouched the full—that is, not inflation-indexed—deductibility of mortgage interest on a homeowner's principal residence. This opening was later exploited by the many among both borrowers and creditors who wanted to retain full deductibility of all interest expense.

The Treasury's proposal was an economist's income-tax reform plan, not at all a plan that would have been put together by a politician. It offended too many powerful interests; while it had the political appeal of "taking the poor off the tax rolls," it also smacked of favoring the rich by virtue of its low 35 percent tax rate for the top bracket. Never mind that the real benefits for the rich came from the special provisions of the tax code that the Treasury proposal eliminated. In the view of most of the smart money in Washington, the general public was too unsophisticated to understand these fine points and after examination of the Treasury proposal, many declared that tax reform was dead.

SUPPORT FOR TAX REFORM

Washington insiders who were skeptical about tax reform overlooked two things. First, they underestimated the president's determination to lower tax rates so that additional effort by individuals and entrepreneurs would not be penalized. The president's experience with the 90 percent tax rates at the top during the 1950s was often repeated. After working on just a few movies as an actor, Ronald Reagan took the rest of each year off because the federal government took virtually all of his additional earnings, and he was opposed to seeking out tax shelters. Second, the tax-reform skeptics overlooked the support for tax reform in Congress, especially among powerful Democrats. Senator Bill Bradley, coauthor with Representative Richard Gephardt (D-MO) of the well-known Bradley-Gephardt plan for tax reform that pushed top rates down to 30 percent and eliminated virtually all tax shelters, had an experience similar to Ronald Reagan's. On becoming a professional basketball player after a stint as a Rhodes scholar, Bradley discovered the hypocritical "tax planning" required to retain a significant portion of his high salary and deplored the fact that, under the tax code, he was a "depreciable asset," a major tax break for the New York Knicks. He, too, became a determined tax reformer.

But more important than Bradley's support was the inclination toward tax reform of the powerful chairman of the House Ways and Means Committee, Dan Rostenkowski. All tax legislation must originate in the Ways and Means Committee, and basic tax reform would have been almost impossible without active support from the chairman and key members of the committee.

Rostenkowski sensed, even before the intense heat of the presidential campaign in the fall of 1984, that the president was serious about tax reform. During the summer of 1984, Rostenkowski's chief of staff, Joseph Dowley, asked two think tanks in Washington, the American Enterprise Institute and the Brookings Institution, to put together a tax retreat at which experts would discuss basic aspects of tax reform for the benefit of the Ways and Means Committee members. Rostenkowski was careful to balance the conference with scholars of both conservative Republican and liberal Democratic persuasions.

During a hot Washington August, while most of official Washington was seeking the cool of the seashore, Dowley worked with scholars at AEI and Brookings to assemble a balanced faculty for the tax retreat. (One of the authors, John Makin, participated in the Rostenkowski tax retreat. The details that follow are based on his recollections.) Considerable effort also went into the selection of a location for that retreat, Patrick Air Force Base, on the west coast of Florida, which could easily accommodate the military planes that the powerful members of the Ways and Means Committee employed for travel on official business. Patrick Air Force Base is not located in an unpleasant area, nor is it remote from golf courses. Rostenkowski also wanted to encourage relaxed discussion of some new ideas on tax policy among committee members, who have remarkably little time available to them in Washington for thoughtful discussions.

At the September 28–30 tax retreat, Jerome Kurtz, former commissioner of the Internal Revenue Service, expressed the fear that the tax code had become so riddled with loopholes that it was becoming impossible to administer. Middle-class Americans were beginning to suspect that their neighbors paid less in taxes than they did by virtue of tax shelters and tax loopholes. The growth of loopholes had seriously undermined the perception that the tax code was fair. Kurtz believed that tax compliance, already beginning to slip, would fall off even further unless the tax code was cleaned up.

Conservative economists like Michael Boskin, who became chairman of George Bush's Council of Economic Advisers, favored a consumption-based tax and tax breaks for investments, such as the investment tax credit. Boskin cleverly argued that a consumption tax was actually fairer than an income tax, since consumption was more stable than income and since use of consumption as the tax base amounted to a form of income averaging. Furthermore, because consumption was a better measure of an individual's ability to pay than income in any given year, it should replace income as the tax base.

The academic economists, like Boskin, presented arguments that were considered elegant by their academic colleagues, but in many cases fell wide of the mark with the Ways and Means Committee members, who actually had to vote on tax measures. They always pictured themselves trying to present an argument for or against a tax measure to a gathering of constituents who were primarily interested in the effect of reform on their taxes. That tax reform was required to be revenue-neutral—that is, to raise the same amount of revenue as the old tax code but in a different way—was small consolation to individual taxpayers, who tended to assume, with some justification based on experience, that tax reform really meant higher taxes.

REAGAN'S PROPOSAL

Despite the tax retreat and the Treasury's tax proposal, as 1984 came to a close, the betting was that the tax reform would certainly not move rapidly in the coming year. Deficit reduction would take the preeminent place in Washington fiscal politics. But the president and apparently the Ways and Means chairman were still committed to moving ahead. The first five months of 1985 were spent crafting the president's tax proposal for fairness, growth, and simplicity—growth having moved ahead of simplicity in the evolution from Treasury's proposal to the president's. Everyone awaited the official appearance of the president's tax-reform proposal to see if the advocates of investment incentives, homeowner incentives, lower tax rates, and other preferences in the existing code could influence the Treasury and the Reagan White House to modify Treasury's proposal to suit their ends. Finally, on May 29, 1985, the president's ideas on tax reform appeared.

His proposal, as opposed to Treasury's, showed the effects of political compromises. The master politician and strategist, James Baker, who had been White House chief of staff when the Treasury tax plan was released, had switched jobs with Treasury Secretary Donald Regan. Regan went to the White House, and Baker moved to Treasury. One of Baker's top priorities was implementation of the president's tax-reform program.

The Treasury's more elegant and economically accurate indexing for capital gains had been replaced by a differential, or lower tax rate of 17.5 percent. This placated traditional Republicans, who attached a mystical significance to a lower capital gains tax rate even though they might end up paying more tax than under Treasury's indexed proposal.

Gone too was Treasury's proposal to increase saving and to cut borrowing by indexing interest income and expense. The nation's borrowing-driven sectors, such as real estate and many corporations that were heavy users of debt, had mobilized squadrons of lawyers to convince the Treasury tax writers that indexing interest income and expense would create an economic disaster of some unspecified sort and would be far too complicated to implement. Few bothered to notice that the proposal could be implemented quite simply by the rough approximation of allowing half of interest expense to be deducted and taxing only half of interest income. The subsequent economic disasters largely involved curtailment of highly leveraged commercial real estate ventures that, since 1989, have been proved unwise, in view of the huge losses, for example, in savings and loan institutions, banks, and developers like Olympia and York.

The Treasury's attempt to end the bias against financing corporate activity by issuing stocks did not survive Baker's rewriting. Treasury had originally proposed excluding 50 percent of the dividends paid from corporate taxes. The Baker Treasury reduced the 50 percent exclusion to 10 percent. Baker probably wanted to keep the idea alive in case some of the leaders of corporate America came to their senses and realized that this was a tremendous break for corporations trying to finance newer, riskier undertakings. But as usual, a somnolent corporate America, fearful of the notion that it might actually be expected to pay dividends to shareholders, actively opposed the idea. Incentives for the decade's debt-for-equity swaps remained in place. Corporate raiders like T. Boone Pickens and Michael Milken continued to use junk bonds to buy up companies whose managers were sitting on piles of cash that should have been distributed as dividends or invested in expanding the business.

The health-care lobby weighed in with the Baker Treasury and succeeded in eliminating the ceiling on deductibility of health-care benefits. It was replaced by a floor on benefits that required all taxpayers to pay tax on the first twenty-five dollars of health-care benefits. Under this remarkably ill-designed provision, lower-income workers would pay a far higher tax on their health-care benefits than higher-income workers. The influence of the health-care lobby later persuaded Congress, which was already unhappy about this highly regressive measure, to eliminate it. Ultimately, health-care benefits remained fully exempt from tax under the final tax-reform bill that was adopted a year later and remained so when comprehensive health reform arose in 1993.

As is so often the case, a protected form of compensation becomes ever more popular. Employees recognized the value of tax-exempt benefits for health care and were negotiating harder and harder for health-benefit increases in salary packages. By 1988, companies were reeling under the effects of exploding health-care costs. The tax code continued to invite increased compensation through generous health-care benefits and pushed up the demand for health care and thereby the price. By 1989, health-care costs were rising at about twice the inflation rate.

Corporate America fared slightly better under the president's proposal than under Treasury's. The 33 percent top rate on corporate income taxes was retained; small business interests induced the Baker Treasury to add three lower rates for corporate income up to $75,000. A Texas favorite, no tax on intangible drilling costs, was restored in the president's proposal. Some accelerated depreciation was also restored to the president's proposal, but the investment tax credit was eliminated, as it had been in the first Treasury proposal.

The president's tax-reform proposal was less complete, less consistent, and therefore somewhat more intellectually and even politically fragile than Treasury's. By yielding on some special measures such as intangible drilling costs and accelerated write-offs, the president's proposal was vulnerable to the "Why not me?" argument from lobbyists representing special interests.

But the proposal still retained enough shape to be called fundamental tax reform. It cut the top personal tax rate from 50 percent to 35 percent and closed many loopholes to provide the funds to do so. Lower tax rates and loophole closing were consistent with the president's Jeffersonian rhetoric about intrusive government and the progressivity built into the final package fit the *Democratic* version of Jeffersonianism. His plan had considerable appeal for tax reformers, since it restored part of the corporate income tax. Under the president's proposal, individuals would pay 6 percent less in taxes over the remainder of the 1980s, while corporations would pay 25 percent more. These figures only recognized that the 1981 tax reform had almost eliminated the corporate income tax, thanks to the investment tax credit and accelerated-depreciation provisions. The president's proposal restored about half the corporate income tax. Still, corporate America was not happy with the prospect of returning to the tax rolls and, through its many lobbyists and representatives, protested loudly that the president's tax bill could produce not only a recession but also a collapse of investment in America.

Appropriately, the president released his proposal for fundamental tax reform on May 29. That day would have been the sixty-eighth birthday of John F. Kennedy, the first president to consider targeted changes in the tax law as a means to improve economic performance. He had first proposed the investment tax credit to stimulate investment and had proposed the lowering of top marginal tax rates from astronomical levels of more than 90 percent to 50 percent. Kennedy was also an early advocate of loophole closing. "The time has come when our tax laws should cease their encouragement of luxury spending as a charge on the federal treasury," Kennedy said in 1961. "The slogan, 'it's deductible,' should pass from our scene."

Unlike Reagan's, Kennedy's tax reforms did not get far. Congress did pass the investment tax credit but was not in those days interested in the fundamental tax-code reform that required the closing of favorite loopholes. The investment tax credit just opened another loophole and eventually led to a round of investment-incentive roulette, whereby the Congress enacted, canceled, and reenacted measures to spur investment spending with tax measures. The shifts regarding investment spending merely changed the timing of investment to make it coincide with the occasional tax benefits.

But Kennedy did establish the precedent of presidential leadership on the tax-reform issue. Ronald Reagan, by issuing a five-hundred-page document entitled "The President's Tax Proposals to the Congress for Fairness, Growth, and Simplicity," had declared himself squarely behind fundamental tax reform. At his side stood his treasury secretary, James Baker, an able negotiator who had good relations with Congress and especially with Ways and Means Chairman Rostenkowski, another advocate of tax reform.

REACTIONS

The initial reaction of economists to the president's tax proposal ranged from lukewarm to hostile. The Treasury's proposal had embodied more characteristics of an idealized income tax than did the president's. Many economists regretted the removal of savings incentives like the indexing of interest income and expense from the proposed tax reform. They knew that if the president did not support them at the start, such measures would never be restored during congressional deliberations, where compromises had to be made and the interests of lobbyists would be powerfully represented.

Perhaps the sharpest split within the economics profession concerned the removal of investment incentives, especially the investment tax credit. On June 11, 1985, testifying along with five other leading economists on the economic impact of the president's tax proposal, Martin Feldstein began his testimony with a warning: "Eliminating the investment tax credit in January 1986 as proposed by the administration would cause a recession in 1986." He qualified his statement by suggesting that perhaps the elimination could be put off until January 1987. It became clear as the tax-reform debate intensified in later months that Feldstein was adamantly opposed to elimination of the investment tax credit and willing to predict severe economic damage from its removal. He also opposed the president's proposal to increase the personal exemption from $1,080 to $2,000 as "a huge, $40 billion annual revenue loss" that "would disproportionately benefit higher income groups and would discourage work effort." Feldstein's arguments about the regressivity of the president's proposal were too subtle for most of the Ways and Means Committee members to follow. But their actions reflected his basic point; the final tax reform bill, although it retained a $2,000 exemption for most households, phased out the exemption for high-income individuals. This phaseout of the personal exemption and other benefits in the tax law that finally emerged created a bubble: the marginal tax rate rose to 33 percent for individuals or households with incomes in the $70,000-to-$150,000 range and then dropped back to 28 percent for incomes above that level. The technical reality that the highest average tax rates were still paid by the individuals with the highest incomes, even with the bubble, has consistently eluded most analysts and apparently many in Congress who voted on the tax bill. Dissatisfaction with the bubble persisted, and the bubble was largely eliminated in 1990—predictably, by raising tax rates on incomes over $150,000.

Shortly after its release, the president's tax plan was in serious trouble. Tax reformers seeking an idealized income tax, like that outlined by the Treasury's original plan, were lukewarm about the president's. Meanwhile, its opponents were on the warpath to kill it, or any other major revision of the current tax system. The intense opposition was no surprise. The tax system in effect in 1985 heavily favored some sectors of American industry. The investment tax credit and accelerated depreciation measures meant negative tax rates on acquisition of equipment by the manufacturing sector: the government was actually paying American companies to buy equipment rather than taxing the returns from use of the equipment at some modest rate.

PROVISIONS FOR HOMEOWNERSHIP

From a tax reformer's point of view, both the Treasury plan and the president's fell short of the ideal by refusing, for political reasons, to alter the major tax provisions affecting homeownership. These special provisions, such as full deductibility of interest expense, deductibility of property taxes, and shelter from taxation of capital gains on housing, amounted to massive tax shelters (which happened to enhance the real wealth of the middle class). Some $50 to $75 billion in lost revenue was tied up with tax breaks for housing. If tax rates were to be lowered in a revenue-neutral setting, one where the "reformed" tax system yields the same amount of revenue as the unreformed one, the only way to make up enough lost revenue was to rescind investment incentives and disallow deductibility of state and local taxes. These expedients concentrated much of the burden of base broadening on two powerful constituencies—manufacturing industries and high-tax states —which could then ask, with some justification, "Why pick only on us?"

A second problem arising from special treatment of owner-occupied housing was the incentive it created to begin dismantling provisions for indexing the tax code to inflation. The Treasury's original proposal indexed interest income and expense for tax purposes, removing a large subsidy to borrowers and a tax on lenders that was implicit in the current system. Under the untouchable status of owner-occupied housing, however, mortgage interest was exempt from interest indexing. This had produced a gaping loophole for highly leveraged homeownership. In the president's plan, however, instead of simply closing the loophole for homeownership, the whole interest-indexing provision would be dropped altogether and the large subsidy to owner-occupied housing continued in the tax code. The president's proposal amounted to worrying that the cows might get through a hole in the fence and deciding to knock down the fence instead of mending the hole. Once indexing interest income and expense, along with the opportunity to lower interest rates, was lost, other important indexing provisions affecting depreciation, capital gains, and inventories fell by the wayside at various stages of the tax-reform process.

The sanctity of owner-occupied housing within the tax code is usually related by politicians to the need to provide affordable housing and to underwrite the "dream" of every American to own a home. Although housing tax incentives are good for those who already own homes, they push homeownership further and further out of reach of those who do not. A tax break on mortgage interest simply raises the price that people are willing to pay for homes. Almost every homebuyer remembers stretching the budget to buy the most house, with the pain softened by the real estate agent's reminder that all that interest was deductible. Under the old tax law prevailing before 1987, Uncle Sam picked up 40 to 50 percent of the interest payments for most homebuyers: they could thus afford to pay more for a home, and the price of housing was pushed up.

Oddly enough, tax advantages for homeowners are often most favored by liberal Democrats in the name of fairness. They fail to recognize that the incentives for homeownership favor high-income taxpayers over low-income taxpayers. That is, they are regressive. The benefit of tax deductibility is directly related to tax bracket. Those in the 50 percent bracket had Uncle Sam paying 50 percent of their mortgage-interest costs, while those low-income individuals in the 15 percent bracket, if they even bothered to itemize —as most do not—had the government paying only 15 percent of their mortgage-interest costs.

Despite the regressivity of tax breaks for homeownership, the idea of encouraging homeownership through the tax system or encouraging other kinds of "desirable behavior" dies hard. The intense debate over tax reform clearly revealed that many blue-collar workers, including those who did not itemize or who did not own homes, were resentful of all tax breaks for homeownership. Many first-time homebuyers also began to recognize that tax breaks for homeownership meant tax breaks for those who already owned homes and a tax disadvantage for those who were trying to acquire them. But most taxpayers were already homeowners and feared the implications of major changes in the one tax break available to them.

Ultimately, tax reform did undermine tax breaks for homeownership simply by lowering the top tax rate. A top rate of 33 percent meant that Uncle Sam would pay only a third of the bill on mortgage interest, rather than half the bill, as under the old tax system. Those in the 33 percent bracket, however, still benefited more from the deductibility of mortgage interest and of other expenses attached to housing than the lower-income taxpayers in the 15 percent or 25 percent brackets. And the inexorable push for higher top marginal rates would ultimately increase the disparity yet again.

RESCUING REFORM

Initial testimony on the president's tax proposals before the Ways and Means Committee came with a barrage of criticism from corporations opposed to the increase in corporate taxes and from other special-interest groups, like real estate, which opposed lower tax rates. These critics convinced the president and his able strategists at the Treasury, James Baker and Richard Darman, that the tax-reform proposal faced an uphill struggle. Baker and Darman knew that they had no chance to push forward with tax reform without solid support from Rostenkowski and the members of his committee. They also knew that Rostenkowski wanted to move ahead with tax reform but that most of the members of the committee were either indifferent or firmly opposed to the measure. Both liberal Democrats and conservative Republicans on the committee were strongly opposed: the liberal Democrats did not like the cut in the top tax rates on the "rich," while the conservative Republicans did not like the removal of breaks for investment and for higher taxes on corporations. In their own way, both factions wanted to use the tax code as an instrument of social policy, while the president's proposal represented the new tendency among the reformers to make government assume a more neutral stance toward taxpayers' behavior.

The White House, the Baker-Darman Treasury, and Chairman Rostenkowski all knew that decisive action would be required to rescue the tax reform. Recalling the retreat at Patrick Air Force Base ten months earlier, Rostenkowski hit on the idea of another retreat to keep tax reform alive. This time, in addition to the members of the Ways and Means Committee, he included Treasury Secretary Baker, Deputy Secretary Darman, and key members of their staff. Along with the Treasury and Ways and Means members, Rostenkowski decided to include other experts, among them Martin Feldstein, who was by then adamantly opposed to what he saw as the anti-capital-formation bias of the president's tax plan.

The preparations for the September Retreat, called a taxation seminar by the Ways and Means Committee, were much more intense than the preparations for the earlier tax retreat. Rostenkowski knew that the retreat would be his only chance to get all the committee members together outside Washington to think over their reaction to the president's tax proposals. He also knew that many committee members were not enthusiastic about the president's bill—or about any other major tax reform.

The seminar included ten tax specialists. They were all either university professors or members of a research institute, except for Jerome Kurtz, former IRS commissioner. Four of them had already proclaimed their belief, either in testimony before the Ways and Means Committee or in public statements during the summer that the president's proposal was an improvement over the current tax law. Two others were also strongly supportive, two had not stated a position, and two were leaning against.

The notion that the Ways and Means Committee was going off into the country to rewrite the tax code with a select group of experts, out of the reach of lobbyists, caused consternation among the industries that stood to be powerfully affected by tax-code changes. The timber industry, for example, was deeply concerned about changes in the tax treatment of valuable forests. Many manufacturing companies were alarmed about the proposal to eliminate the investment tax credit and to moderate accelerated-depreciation schedules. Capital gains provisions were of considerable interest to venture capitalists and other investor groups.

A howl of protest went up among these and other groups on the grounds that they were not being represented at Rostenkowski's tax seminar. Participants were bombarded with position papers put together by industry groups that wanted them to "understand" how important certain tax provisions were to the health of the American economy. Some of the experts were tracked down by high-ranking corporate officials, who entreated them to understand how important it was not to change certain provisions of the tax code.

But Rostenkowski stood his ground and, on August 23, 1985, announced the September 7–8, 1985, seminar, at Airlie House, outside Warrenton, Virginia. Rostenkowski did not say that Treasury Secretary Baker and Deputy Secretary Darman would also attend the seminar. The decision to include Baker and Darman was a bold one both for Chairman Rostenkowski and for the Treasury and the White House. Since the purpose of the seminar was to discuss the president's tax proposal, the president's primary representatives on tax policy needed to be present. The presence of Baker and Darman at Airlie House established working ground rules that were to serve both Rostenkowski and the president well in the long, arduous road to the final achievement of a tax bill more than a year later.

Secretary Baker's presentation was a highlight of the two-day meeting both because of its specificity and because of the spirited discussion it permitted between the treasury secretary and individual committee members. Baker's message was simple. There were four fundamental points on which the president would not concede. He called them "lines drawn in the sand," but they were more like lines drawn in cement. The first of these basic nonnegotiable principles was *revenue neutrality:* the tax plan had to leave the deficit unaffected, neither gaining nor losing revenue relative to current law. In addition, *the highest tax rate had to be no higher than 35 percent, the poor had to be off the income tax rolls,* and, finally, *the mortgage-interest deduction, so precious to homeowners, had to be preserved.*

These four conditions taken together were far more stringent than they sound individually. Retaining the mortgage-interest deduction eliminated a major revenue source from loophole closing. Setting the top rate at 35 percent and eliminating low-income taxpayers from the tax rolls also required much loophole closing. The president's proposal gained a tremendous amount of revenue by eliminating the deductibility of state and local taxes, but that proposal was unacceptable to Ways and Means Committee members from high-tax states such as California and New York. Some inflexible battle lines were being drawn over the issue of state and local taxes.

Nevertheless, Baker's presentation of the president's four unyielding positions left some room to maneuver. Baker said nothing about the income levels at which the president's proposed three tax brackets of 15 percent, 25 percent, and 35 percent were set. A great deal of revenue could be gained by having a 35 percent rate start at lower income levels. Clearly, the investment tax credit and accelerated depreciation provisions, so favored by some corporations, would have to be rescinded to meet the four conditions outlined by Baker. Feldstein understood this and so argued that the president's tax plan would hurt the economy and should be put aside in favor of alternative fundamental tax-reform proposals.

The most important session of the Airlie House tax retreat was a two-hour discussion session on September 8. No invited experts or Treasury personnel were at the members' discussion; Rostenkowski made a personal appeal to the members to consider real tax reform. He emphasized the need for reform and the existence of a fleeting chance to make the tax code more equitable. Writing about Rostenkowski's emotional presentation to the Ways and Means Committee, Jeffrey Birnbaum and Alan Murray of the *Wall Street Journal* in their book *Showdown at Gucci Gulch* described him with tears in his eyes as he described his daughter's struggles to get started and make ends meet while paying more taxes than some millionaires. Overlooking, for a moment, the awkward reality that his Ways and Means Committee had passed much of the tax law responsible for his daughter's predicament, Rostenkowski said that "we have an opportunity to etch what little we can in the history books. It's not going to be easy, but it's doable."

A few weeks later, back in Washington, many of the members of the Ways and Means Committee, while touched by Rostenkowski's sincere appeal for tax reform, were facing immense pressure from lobbyists and special interests, most of it reinforcing their own doubts about the desirability of staying with the president's plan. Eventually, Rostenkowski managed to hammer out a House version of tax reform that, to build a majority coalition, included a 38 percent top rate, a violation of one of the president's four conditions, and went further in watering down the Treasury's original 1984 proposal. The Ways and Means compromises were too much for some supporters of the president's plan. It was obvious to any tax reformer that the tax bill completed by the Ways and Means Committee in the wee hours of the morning of November 23, 1985, was tax revision, not reform. It was more of the same tax-code roulette that was likely to be followed by yet another unsubstantial "tax reform" bill in a few years.

By the end of 1985, many members of the Ways and Means Committee were convinced that tax reform was dead. They believed the 38 percent rate would force the president to abandon his pursuit of tax reform. The committee members also knew that the Senate was even less predisposed to tax reform than they had been. The next step in the process, early in 1986, was for the Senate to draft its version of a tax-reform bill. At holiday parties late in 1985, most of the tax lobbyists who had been trying to kill tax reform since November 1984, when the Treasury's first proposal appeared, toasted the success of their efforts and happily banked the fat bonus checks they had received at year's end for doing just that. Their celebrations and the bonuses were premature.

THE GROUNDSWELL FOR REFORM

Only nine months later, on September 25, 1986, the house passed a major tax-reform bill by a vote of 292 to 136. On September 27, the Senate passed the bill by a vote of 74 to 23 and sent it to the president. On October 22, President Reagan signed the Tax Reform Act of 1986 in a ceremony on the south lawn of the White House to which all major participants in the tax-reform debate were invited.

After the bill became law, the people who had been involved in the controversy surrounding it were in a reflective mood. How did the bill pass? Some attributed passage of the tax bill to the leadership of the president and the adept maneuvering of Baker and Darman. Others attributed it to mistakes by lobbyists, such as revealing their greed by cheering outside the tax-writing committee rooms when a key piece of the tax reform legislation was defeated during the low points in 1985 and 1986. Rostenkowski must be given credit, because tax legislation started with his Ways and Means Committee and the process would never have taken off without his commitment.

Beyond the powerful appeal of tax rates at 20 to 29 percent, deeper forces fed the process of tax reform and the events in Washington between 1984 and 1986. In 1968, the Treasury Department had reported on 154 taxpayers with incomes of $200,000 or more ($750,000 or more in 1990 dollars) who paid no tax—and did so legally within the tax code. Studies like that and endless anecdotal evidence convinced more and more taxpayers, most of whom did not even itemize, that rich people, with all the privileges that money bestowed, did not even pay taxes. How, people began to wonder, could individuals facing tax rates of 70 percent avoid paying taxes?

Real tax reform, ironically, came to life at just the point it appeared that watered-down tax reform was dead. The source of rejuvenation was just as ironic—Senator Robert Packwood, the chairman of the Senate Finance Committee, who had early on declared himself a skeptic on sweeping tax reform, noting the many benefits that come with using the tax system to target social and economic policies.

Packwood became a convert to the basic principles of tax reform, but he was also motivated, to be sure, by the desire to succeed, and to avoid being labeled as the force behind tax reform's demise. In the end, the ardent desire by a majority of lawmakers to avoid the responsibility and blame for killing tax reform was as responsible for reform's success as the drive of the most ardent reform proponents. This was combined, however, with the skill of people like Bill Bradley and Ronald Reagan at convincing journalists and voters that lower rates, fewer loopholes, and a broader base were the first principles of reform.

Packwood's crucial role began in April 1986. He and his Finance Committee chief of staff, Bill Diefenderfer, were commiserating one afternoon about the dead end reached by the bill when they came up with a brilliant idea. They found a way to set the top tax rate at 27 percent by increasing the number of people in the top bracket. Making some changes to set the top rate at a level in the twenties provided a breathtaking illustration of the basic appeal of tax reform: drastically lower tax rates—a 27 percent top rate instead of a 50 percent top rate—in exchange for loophole closings. Once the twenty-something top rate was seen as reachable, tax reform could not be stopped. Even though the final bill contained a 28 percent top rate with the 33 percent bubble, it gave the members of Congress who voted for it a prize to offer their skeptical constituents and convinced most citizens that such a sharp drop in tax rates meant that their tax bills would go down. The drop in individual tax bills, however, was due largely to higher corporate tax bills, which ultimately were paid by individuals.

During the 1970s, when inflation pushed people into higher and higher tax brackets, the middle class began to play the same tax-avoidance games as the upper class. Organizations of lawyers and accountants prepackaged tax shelters that were sold in little chunks to middle-class taxpayers who sometimes cared nothing about the intrinsic value of the investment but only about lower federal taxes. Concentration by thousands of investors on the tax aspects of investment proposals, instead of their intrinsic economic worth, wasted an immense amount of investment. That was why genuine tax reformers who were committed to promoting growth and efficiency in the economy wanted the tax code to ensure that economic decisions would be made, as far as possible, without regard to their tax consequences.

Oddly enough, Ronald Reagan's first tax bill, the Economic Recovery Tax Act of 1981, may have contributed most to tax reform by focusing public opinion on tax breaks for corporations. In an effort to stimulate investment, the act had given investment tax credits and accelerated depreciation to corporations. So generous were the tax breaks that some corporations could not use them all. Many companies in 1982 were having a bad year and had low taxable income: the government-allowed offsets against taxable income were useless to them. But in the 1981 act, Congress had made tax breaks salable among corporations. A company that had invested heavily in new equipment and thereby received a tax break that it could not use because its taxable income was too low could sell the tax break to another, more prosperous company. This practice was called safe-harbor leasing, and as a result of it, some highly profitable American corporations paid no federal income tax for a number of years after 1981 (despite its repeal in 1982). The idea that huge corporations like General Electric could completely avoid federal taxes was repugnant to most Americans. And it did not make them feel any better to know that General Electric had paid for the tax shelters that it had bought through the safe-harbor leasing plan.

The perception that rich people and corporations did not pay taxes had been building for two decades. Senator Packwood stumbled onto a way to dramatize this fact by pointing out that loophole closing could cut the top tax rate to 27 percent. It was not hard to understand then that if the top tax rate could be cut in half without losing any revenue, someone had been getting generous tax breaks under the old system. Working people assumed that rich people and corporations were the culprits. With an outraged middle class, reformers believed, tax reform could not be stopped. Reform was also beginning to seem more logical to responsible members of Congress like Rostenkowski, who for years had been coming to the realization that a system with high tax rates invites a search for loopholes. This search eventually leads to a tax law that hurts the economy and all the middle- and lower-income taxpayers who cannot afford to play the loophole game. Beyond that, the whole process of the annual game called the tax bill was beginning to exhaust the members of the tax-writing committees.

By the 1980s, American businesses had divided into two groups: one that tended to business and another that focused a large share of its energies on round after round of tax breaks. Part of the latter focus meant hiring lobbyists to represent their interests every time a tax bill came up. As hearings on the tax bill came around every year, members of Congress, especially members of the tax-writing committees, were spending more and more time with more, and more persistent, lobbyists who were seeking tax breaks to keep businesses afloat. Ultimately, many members of the tax-writing committees were simply sick of the process. If a tax bill would lower tax rates and make loopholes less attractive so that they could get on with other business before the committee, they were for it.

IN THE RIGHT DIRECTION

Ultimately, a plan not too different from the president's proposal was adopted. Despite the warnings of the hired lobbyists, the feared collapse in investment did not materialize in 1987 or 1988, after the 1986 enactment of tax reform. In 1985, U.S. net domestic investment was 5.8 percent of net national product. In 1986, still under the old tax law, net national investment fell to 5.3 percent of the net national product. In 1987 and 1988, under the new tax law, net national investment was 5.3 percent and 5.4 percent of the net national product, respectively. Meanwhile, the personal savings rate that was supposed to fall under the president's tax proposal was 3.3 percent of the net national product in 1988—exactly equal to the 3.3 percent level in 1986 and close to the 3.5 percent level in 1985. It rose to more than 5 percent in 1989 and more than 6 percent in 1990.

The Tax Reform Act of 1986 did not completely stop the lobbyists' circus, but it was a step in the right direction. The question that has been neglected in the years since is, what is the next step? Looking at changes in the tax system provides a basis for the consideration of its future direction. Some suggestions may also be in order.

Undoubtedly, the Tax Reform Act of 1986 represented a watershed. The accelerating trend since the 1930s toward more and more loopholes to exploit high marginal rates was reversed with a decisive movement toward lower tax rates and fewer tax loopholes. From January 1, 1987, the U.S. economy became less of a tax-motivated economy. Providers of tax shelters sharply curtailed their activities, while investors began looking more at the intrinsic economic value of investments than at their tax-sheltering properties. Shopping centers and historic preservation projects, heavily subsidized under the pre-1987 tax code, began to dry up as investment projects.

By 1990, there had been little retrogression to tax-code tinkering, with the notable exception of proposals to restore a differential lower tax rate for capital gains. Although the tax rate on capital gains was not a major tax issue, it was part of the tax package that George Bush promised along with his "no new taxes" pledge.

The tax treatment of capital gains is probably more important as a political symbol than as an economic tool. Only 7 percent of all taxpayers even report capital gains on their returns, and while capital gains are probably more widespread among the middle class than is commonly supposed, tax treatment of capital gains is not an unambiguous economic issue. The economy has performed both well and poorly under many capital gains tax rates. Tax writers have learned that threatening either to raise the capital gains tax rate, as was done in 1986, or to lower the capital gains tax rate, as was proposed in 1989, provides additional revenues. Threatening to raise the capital gains tax rate causes accelerated realization of gains in the year before the rate rises, which happened late in 1986. Putting forth the possibility of a lower capital gains tax rate usually reduces tax revenues during the year when the change in the tax rate is under consideration, as taxpayers hopefully await more advantageous lower rates. If the lower rates materialize, there is an initial surge of activity, as investors realize gains that they have deferred and push up revenues, but once the surge is over, a normal flow of capital gains is taxed at a lower rate. Arguments about the net effect on tax revenues rage on endlessly, but the most likely effect is close to zero.

Representing as it does a tax break for the rich at least symbolically, a lower tax rate on capital gains causes an emotional reaction among liberals. Typically, they propose a trade-off and couple a capital gains measure, if it must be acceded to, with a higher top marginal rate. There were some rumblings on the Ways and Means Committee during the 1989 deliberations that a 33 percent tax rate for all high-income individuals would be part of the price to be paid for any tax breaks on capital gains. Interestingly, the final measure adopted by the House did not include such a tax increase for all high-income taxpayers, although the same proposal resurfaced during the 1990 discussion of tax measures (and, of course, reappeared in the Clinton plan in 1993).

Most liberal tax specialists would probably like to see some increase in top marginal tax rates. Their judgment is that rates of 35 percent or 38 percent would garner more income from high-income taxpayers without being high enough to set off another frantic search for loopholes and for tax shelters, which was characteristic of the period before 1981, when marginal tax rates were between 50 percent and 90 percent.

These specialists may be right, but the political feasibility of tinkering with the rate structure of the 1986 law depends on what most taxpayers think about the new tax system. There was some risk of taxpayer dissatisfaction initially because to make the tax reform revenue-neutral, some revenue gains were needed for the first year. The tax-rate cuts were therefore phased in only partially in 1987, while most of the loophole closings became effective immediately. As a result, many individuals, especially those in the highly vocal group making between $50,000 and $100,000 a year, found their taxes higher in 1987. But 1988 brought fully phased-in lower rates and lower tax bills for most Americans.

By the beginning of the 1990s, most people neither warmly endorsed nor condemned the new tax law. There was no new groundswell for further tax reform from the public. At the same time, the tax system remained a useful thermometer for official Washington in testing the political waters. In 1989, Democratic strategists were initially ecstatic that President Bush was prepared to push his capital gains tax measure. They thought that it would be very easy to portray a Republican president as the cynical author of a tax break for the country club friends who helped to get him elected. But many Democratic strategists did not count on the capital-gains tax revolt led by a conservative southern Democrat, Ed Jenkins. Many families in the Midwest or South who run farms or small businesses have a strong attachment to a preferential tax treatment of capital gains. When liberals and tax reformers start talking about taxing capital gains drastically, these constituencies become active, and members of the tax-writing committees, who are always attuned to political liabilities, pay attention.

But the need for deficit-reduction revenue, and the ideological drive to hit the rich in the name of fairness and make the tax code more progressive, moved President Clinton and Congress in 1993 to push the top marginal rate sharply higher. Breaching the 40 percent barrier for the top rate meant profound future changes in the tax code, with a sharp jump in the drive to shelter income and push for new loopholes, but it met with surprisingly little resistance from Congress. Tax-reform proponents held their breath that the 1993 changes would not open Pandora's loophole box.

Many tax reformers believe that a single exception to the Tax Reform Act of 1986, such as one on capital gains, would open the door to a stampede of special interests and cause the Tax Reform Act to unravel. Certainly, a cut in the capital gains tax would excite new efforts for special provisions like investment tax credits, accelerated depreciation, and special provisions for real estate. But unlike a preferential rate for capital gains, such tax breaks demonstrably cost huge amounts of tax revenue. Their advocates face the problem that these measures would increase the deficit unless they are prepared to seek higher tax rates or the removal of other loopholes—something they are unlikely to do. Capital gains is a special case, because although the debate over its revenue effects is intense, specialists on both sides of the issue suggest that the revenue loss is ultimately too small to cause a major rupture in efforts at deficit reduction.

Any change in the current system for the better would come in further moves in the same direction. Some provisions in the tax code still allow huge revenue losses from the nontaxability of expenditures on health-care coverage and on most items related to homeownership, such as deductibility of mortgage interest.

In a fundamental way, the Tax Reform Act of 1986 both stabilized the tax code and reduced the value of special tax breaks simply by virtue of the act's lower tax rates. An effective top tax rate of 28 percent means that tax breaks are not as valuable as they were when the top tax rate was 50 percent. Indeed, the value of tax breaks is directly proportional to the level of the top tax rate for the taxpayers who make most intensive use of special tax provisions. To corporations, the value of tax breaks is proportional to the corporate income-tax rate, which was set at 34 percent under the Tax Reform Act of 1986— down from 48 percent under the pre-1986 tax law.

One of the most remarkable effects of the recent tax reform was the significant reduction, by virtue of lower rates and loophole closing, in the power of the tax-writing committees that made tax reform a reality. Because of lower tax rates and the loophole closing that was required to pay for them, members of the Ways and Means and Finance committees had fewer special tax breaks to distribute, and those that they did distribute were worth less than when tax rates were higher. Why would politically attuned members of the tax-writing committees vote to undercut their own power? Part of the reason may have been a recognition that the process of seeking tax breaks was getting out of control. Probably more fundamental was the growing fear that a loophole-ridden tax code that seemed to favor the rich and corporations over average American taxpayers was becoming a political liability. The members of the tax-writing committees decided to be prudent. After all, under the Tax Reform Act of 1986, they still control immense resources. But there was a limit to how much time they wanted to spend deciding whether or not to dole out special tax breaks that led only to calls for more tax breaks. And once they broke that cycle, further reform began to seem possible— although moving back to higher marginal rates and more deduction-based distortions was more likely.

TWO FUTURE PATHS

After 1986, the tax code could follow two paths toward additional reform. One would move toward more radical income-tax reforms, or a consumption-based tax system as was proposed in 1976 in the Treasury's blueprints for tax reform. Having been rejected during the tax deliberations between 1984 and 1986, the future of a consumption-tax path became more cloudy. An add-on variant of a consumption tax, a value-added tax or a national sales tax, however, remains high on the list of priorities of those in Congress who seek a large new source of revenue for the federal government instead of just a change in the manner in which a given amount of revenue is collected, which has been the formula for tax reform thus far.

Every 1 percentage point of a national sales tax levy could yield about $20 billion for federal coffers. A 3 percent national sales tax would yield $60 billion, enough to make up a large part of any future budget deficit. There are, however, a number of major impediments to the implementation of a national sales tax. First, conservatives fear that such a powerful revenue machine would provide the means by which the federal government's expenditures could grow from their current share of about 20 percent of GNP to 25 percent or 30 percent. Second, a national sales tax impinges on a major source of revenue for states and localities. A national sales tax would turn merchants into tax collectors for the federal government in addition to the role they already play as tax collectors for state and local governments. Considerable resistance to such a measure would be easily mobilized.

Many liberals object to a sales tax as a regressive tax. Since it is essentially a tax on consumption, it would probably fall more heavily on middle- and lower-income taxpayers than it would on upper-income taxpayers. The usual idea to dilute the effect of such a tax on lower-income taxpayers is to exempt essentials like food and medical care from a national sales tax. The administrative headaches involved in collecting a national sales tax on some things and not on others, however, are tremendous. Retailers have every incentive to try to make the goods they handle qualify for exemption under the sales tax. In the European experience, such administrative headaches greatly increase the cost of collecting the tax. If restaurant meals are taxed while food purchased at supermarkets is not, for example, many restaurants may attempt to sell takeout food as if it were supplied by a supermarket so patrons can avoid the tax. The European experience suggests that the best approach, should a value-added tax (VAT) or national sales tax, be employed, is to tax everything and to provide a tax credit for low-income taxpayers to protect them from the full burden of the national sales tax.

If tax reform is to move forward, probably the most likely path is the second option, further reform of an income-based tax, rather than a consumption-based tax system. One way to achieve a fairer, simpler, and more growth-oriented income-based tax system is to devalue remaining deductions in exchange for further cuts in tax rates. An across-the-board devaluation of tax breaks combined with lower tax rates would further encourage work, investment, and saving, while discouraging high-income itemizers and corporations from resuming the search for more tax breaks.

Whatever the outcome of the political and economic factors affecting, and affected by, the tax code, the prospect of change arises every year as part of the revenue side of the budget that the president must submit to Congress. The real question concerning the direction of the tax code concerns whether we return to the road toward a more neutral, reformed tax system or whether we revert to the higher tax rates together with the search for loopholes that characterized the period from 1945 to 1986. Both politically and economically, the system wherein individuals and corporations can make decisions based on their intrinsic desirability, rather than their effect on tax liabilities, is best for the country. But preconceptions about ways to tax the rich appropriately make higher marginal rates a near-irresistible lure for Jeffersonian liberals, while more tax breaks for business provide a comparable attraction for Hamiltonian conservatives. At the same time, the lure of shaping economic activity through the tax code, using "modern" economics, has appeal to both sides. And one other factor remains important: the decline in flexibility in the federal budget, caused by deficits and growing formula-based entitlements, makes manipulation of the tax code an alluring alternative for politicians to address social and economic problems.

Still, even if tax reforms in 1986 had the long-term effect of scraping the barnacles off the fiscal hull only to have them gradually reappear, it still remained a major political and economic accomplishment of the Reagan years, both by its very sweep and breadth, and by reaffirming basic economic verities through political action—all by uniting Hamiltonian and Jeffersonian principles and politicians in both parties.

PART FIVE

LESSONS

✦

· 11 ·

COPING WITH HISTORY:
FISCAL POLICY
AFTER REAGAN

Fiscal policy in the Reagan years ended up having far less impact on the size of government and the economy than was feared or expected by most observers. Reagan's largely fruitless effort to shrink the federal government by cutting taxes ultimately resulted in disputes with the Democratic Congress and created in Washington, at least for a time, a lingering sense of foreboding about the economic consequences of large budget deficits. But continued economic expansion and the resulting shrinkage of budget deficits as a share of GNP from a peak of 6.3 percent in 1983 to about a 4 percent average during 1987–1989 seemed to belie the fears of those who saw them as dangerous to the economy. After all, the deficits were not all that much higher than their average of 2.5 percent of GNP between 1962 and 1989. Nevertheless, continued large deficits became the symbol of Washington's "failure to govern." Many "responsible" Washington insiders—including George Bush—were haunted by lingering fears that such large deficits could not go on forever without serious economic harm resulting. In modern historical context, their fears were not surprising.

Official Washington has consistently demonstrated that it has few settled convictions about the relationship between budget deficits and the economy. In October 1990, President Bush and Congress joined hands in an attempt to reduce the budget deficit, even including some tax increases for the good of the economy. A year later, the president and Congress flirted with the idea that a tax cut would be good for the economy. Clearly, views on the budget deficit are determined by some larger political vision that is often colored by some dubious economic theory. This political coloring is further shaded by the fact that economists have failed to provide a consistent and coherent analysis of the economic effects of budget deficits. The testimony from economists and businessmen to the National Economic Commission, established in 1989, on the relationship between budget deficits and the economy reveals a range of opinions sufficiently wide to provide solace for any action that politicians may wish to take—or not to take—regarding the budget deficit.

Both major political parties are, after all, heirs to a long tradition of cynicism about budget deficits. During much of the nineteenth century, Republicans talked about balanced budgets as a means to justify high tariffs that actually were aimed at protecting American industries from foreign competition. Under the aegis of their big-government policies, generous pork-barrel spending programs were devised by Republicans, especially after the Civil War, to buy off resistance to the high tariffs. Eventually, the revenue requirements of the government programs that grew up after 1870 outran the revenue-generating potential of tariffs, and despite their best efforts to prevent it, Republicans had to yield to an income tax. This was a much more efficient and broad-based system of revenue collecting, but it represented a new power to expand greatly the scope of the federal government. Faced with the income tax, Republicans suddenly became worshipers of spending limits to constrain the expansion of spending that could be financed by the income tax, and to try to limit the growth of the tax itself.

Democrats adhered to the balanced-budget orthodoxy through and including Presidents Franklin Roosevelt and Harry Truman. Roosevelt, the last Jeffersonian Democrat, abandoned fiscal orthodoxy in the face of an overwhelming political necessity for action in a serious prolonged depression. The Depression and World War II resulted in budget deficits and an accumulation of national debt that had never been dreamed of in normal times and that, had they been foreseen, would have been taken to be sure signs of impending economic disaster. Actually, the debt that accumulated by 1945, although it was unequaled in the history of the nation even when deflated by GNP, was easily managed during the Truman and Eisenhower years by an effective bipartisan commitment to balanced budgets and a surge of real economic growth.

The Kennedy administration, with some trepidation of its own and considerable resistance from Congress, began the first experiments with fiscal policy as a direct means to increase economic growth. Because of Kennedy's willingness to discuss and even to propose measures like an investment tax credit, initially decried and condemned by the business community, such measures were eventually enacted. By 1965, the Kennedy-Johnson fiscal program and the coincident surge of economic growth had convinced White

House economists that tax policy could push the long-run average growth rate to more than 4 percent a year, while mitigating, if not altogether eliminating, business cycles. The surge in the economic growth rate between 1961 and 1967 to 4.9 percent a year, well above the long-term average of about 3 percent, created an unjustified optimism in Washington about the ability of the economy to support both the Great Society and the Vietnam War.

The Kennedy-Johnson experiment with fiscal policy was not so much concerned with budget policy, though it adhered to the balanced-budget rhetorical orthodoxy, as it was with the structure of tax policy. The belief was that if tax measures gave business the right incentive to invest, then a persistent higher level of investment would lead to the creation of more jobs and to faster economic growth, and the budget would take care of itself.

There was a difference between Kennedy's view and Johnson's view of the implications of higher growth for social policy. In Kennedy's more neo-Jeffersonian view, expanded social programs were conditional on higher economic growth. In Johnson's neo-Hamiltonian view—once he became totally enamored of the Great Society—these programs were so important that Americans would come to love them and would be willing to pay to finance them.

Richard Nixon, while adhering to fiscal orthodoxy and a stated belief in balanced budgets, did little as a practitioner of big government to resist the expansion of the social programs begun by Lyndon Johnson. Far more significant, however, he allowed huge increases in Social Security benefits as part of his struggle with Wilbur Mills, the Democratic presidential hopeful, who chaired the House Ways and Means Committee. The generous expansion of Social Security benefits and their indexing to inflation in 1976 coincided with a burst of inflation and rapid growth in the over–sixty-five population. The massive increase in the cost of Social Security that resulted had by 1983 bankrupted the system. The Social Security rescue package passed in that year provided for further increases in payroll taxes to maintain the high levels of spending on Social Security and other entitlements established in the 1970s and set the budget on its rigidifying path for the 1990s.

The reasons why large budget deficits persisted during the 1980s and into the 1990s are both political and economic, and the responsibility for them is bipartisan. The Kennedy-Johnson experiment with supply-side cuts for business generated a belief among economists in Washington that the U.S. economy could sustain economic growth of about 4 percent a year. That conviction together with the politics surrounding the Great Society programs and the growth of entitlements during the Nixon administration resulted in legislated increases in government spending that continued regardless of the actual performance of the economy. These entitlements, together with mandatory payments of interest on the debt, have come to make up nearly 70 percent of total government spending, and they are not subject to normal deficit-reduction negotiations. Laws would have to be changed to alter the level of spending on entitlements, and throughout all of the budget negotiations since 1985, there has never been a successful effort mounted to reduce significantly the growth of spending on entitlements.

LEADING UP TO THE NINETIES

Other things being equal, had the economy continued to grow after 1967 at the annual average rate of 4 percent then supposed possible by many politicians and economists, there would be no budget deficit today. Indeed, if economic growth had proceeded at 4 percent between 1967 and 1990 along with the average inflation rate of about 6 percent, the 19.4 percent share of GNP that federal revenues represented in 1990 would have produced total revenues of $1,406 billion. That would have meant a federal budget surplus of $153 billion given FY 1990 outlays of $1,253 billion. It could be argued that 4 percent growth, rather than the 2.67 percent actually achieved, would have meant slower inflation, less in outlays for deposit insurance, and therefore less in cuts of discretionary spending of the sort that occurred during the 1980s. Nevertheless, much of the deficit problem of the 1990s is simply the result of government spending programs that have been legislated permanently against the background of a transient surge of economic growth during the 1960s.

The Reagan era with its supply-side tax cuts, defense-spending increases, and relentless growth of entitlement spending caused the political and economic debate about the budget deficit to heat up by 1985. Reagan threw a monkey wrench into the accepted fiscal orthodoxy with his willingness to cut taxes, and especially to cut tax rates, and to provide special investment incentives, even in the face of large budget deficits.

Reagan's Jeffersonian philosophy of limited government seemed impossible to act on without an abandonment of Republican orthodoxy on budget deficits once it became clear that tax cuts could not be matched with spending cuts. But whatever the economic consequences of that abandonment, it brought him political success by disconcerting the Democratic opposition. Democrats had never got past their hopes for faster growth as a means to finance the ambitious spending programs begun under the Great Society.

Now they found themselves forced to subordinate their natural urge to increase spending to their new and unwanted role as defenders of fiscal conservatism by default, joined in an unholy alliance with more traditional GOPers.

Reagan's economic advisers deflected criticism about the prospective budget deficits by assuming a high rate of inflation in their forecasts for the next few years. High inflation rates pushed taxpayers into higher and higher tax brackets and inflated tax revenues. From 1976 to 1981, the surge in inflation pushed tax revenues from a low of about 17.5 percent of GNP in 1976 to more than 20 percent of GNP in 1981. Reagan's economic advisers found that with the right inflation assumptions and by a careful postponement until 1985 of the indexing of tax brackets that would largely eliminate bracket creep, they could predict a budget surplus in a few years.

The Reagan fiscal revolution spawned numerous myths, while simultaneously offering many useful lessons about the relationship between taxes, budget, and the economy. Simultaneously with its introduction of the Economic Recovery Tax Act of 1981, the Reagan administration joined forces with Paul Volcker, chairman of the Federal Reserve Board, in a program of inflation control that reduced inflation well below the forecast of budget experts. That happy result had an unhappy, unintended consequence: an increase in the budget deficit from around 2.6 percent of GNP during the 1981 recession to a 5.4 percent of GNP during 1985, a year of rapid growth.

The sharp rise in the deficit and the national debt between 1981 and 1985 was alarming enough, given the orthodox view among economists that rising deficits were bad for the economy, to prompt the Congress to begin to cut spending. Ronald Reagan's successful advocacy of tax cuts as being good for the economy broadly precluded discretionary tax increases as an avenue for Congress to use to close the deficit gap. Payroll taxes to finance entitlement programs rose steadily throughout the Reagan years, and the additional burden on most American households gave rise to numerous articles about the gap between the rhetoric of Reagan tax cuts and the reality. What Ronald Reagan did was to cap increases in the individual income tax and to lower tax collections from corporations by an amount that roughly offset the huge increases in payroll taxes. During the eight years of the Reagan administration, from 1981 through 1988, total revenues were actually $140 billion higher than they would have been with the ratio of tax revenues to the GNP that prevailed between 1973 and 1980. After 1982, when the Reagan tax measures had taken effect, individual income taxes held steady relative to the pre-Reagan years, while the corporate income taxes averaged about $40 billion less per year than they would have under the tax regime of the 1970s. Meanwhile, 1981–1988 payroll tax collections were $350 billion *above* levels that would have flowed from 1973–1980 payroll tax rates.

Reagan's ability to hold the line on income taxes coupled with congressional concern about budget deficits led to steep reductions in rates of nondefense discretionary spending—including most social programs left over from the Great Society. From 1981 to 1988, nondefense discretionary spending was $300 billion less than it would have been if the spending rates in the eight years before the Reagan administration had prevailed. Meanwhile, the same calculation for entitlements and other mandatory spending showed an increase for 1981 to 1988 of $360 billion, along with an increase in national defense spending of $270 billion above what it would have been. Another category of mandatory spending, net interest on the debt, was $422 billion higher during 1981–1988 than it would have been at the expenditure rates of the eight years before the Reagan administration. Reagan had cut social programs and increased defense spending on the margins of a budget process dominated by spending over which he had little or no control. To do this while continuing to look presidential, he had had to cultivate an indifference toward the budget deficit, which marked a new era in the Republican political approach to fiscal responsibility.

In the nineteenth-century era of high tariffs, the Republicans had the opposite problem: spending enough to justify embarrassingly high tax revenues. Now that they were in the position of having to find revenue enough to justify embarrassingly high spending, they adopted a bold new strategy. If a popular president cut taxes and the Congress continued to believe that deficits were bad, eventually spending had to come down. But because 70 percent of the budget was devoted to such seemingly uncontrollable outgoings as entitlements and interest payments, there was not enough left to be cut from nondefense discretionary spending. The only hope of deficit reduction, Congress was thus reluctantly forced to conclude, lay in attacking popular middle-class entitlement programs like Medicare, Medicaid, and Social Security. Would Congress's fear of deficits prove more exigent than its fear of the wrath of older, politically active middle-class voters?

The first major test came in 1985, when a courageous group of Republican senators fashioned a deficit-reduction program that included some modest caps on the *growth* in Social Security benefits. During the critical eleventh hour of negotiations, Ronald Reagan sided with the Democratic House Majority Leader Tip O'Neill to abandon the package in favor of a more cosmetic approach that left entitlements untouched. Had Reagan supported his own party in Congress in 1985, House Democrats would have been compelled to go along, and the growth of entitlements would have been curbed, budget deficits would have been far below those that actually occurred, and the great Reagan fiscal experiment of cutting taxes and still reducing the budget deficit might well have succeeded.

The president's desertion of his own party on control of entitlements occurred after he had been elected to a second and last term as president and need not have feared the wrath of the voters. To achieve an agreement on the budget package, the Republicans then in control of the Senate took a terrific political risk. By abandoning the Republican senators who had supported a budget package that included caps on the growth of entitlement spending, the president, they were convinced, doomed many of them to defeat in the 1986 congressional elections. Indeed, the Republicans lost control of the Senate, which they had held since 1981.

A plausible explanation for the president's failure to follow through with measures that could have achieved his goal of controlling federal spending was the loss of focus of the administration during its second term. Reagan was preoccupied with foreign policy in 1985, but that hardly makes more comprehensible his apparent lack of any strategy to force entitlement cuts. The golden opportunity presented to him in that year was simply lost, and apparently without regret, amid intense discussions about whether he should have visited a German cemetery at Bitburg.

Some Washington observers argue that the president's unwillingness to agree to a package that limited the growth of entitlements went back to 1981, when he had been buffeted by the reaction to a proposal for limits on the growth of Social Security outlays. The president's popularity plummeted, although it later recovered. Another explanation for his action in the summer of 1985 may be that he did not wish to expend political capital on the issue of the budget. Whatever the reason, the president's abandonment of his own party drove home to politicians in both parties the painful lesson that any effort to limit even the *growth* of spending on popular entitlement programs was political suicide.

The indexation of benefits was a critical element. It had led to the widespread public view that automatic increases were a part of the promise—the "entitlement." Indexation coincided with the institutionalization of the term "entitlement" for the series of programs that transferred money to citizens under formulas for eligibility. The origins of the term for governmental purposes are not entirely clear, but probably go back to the Social Security program. In the early years, politicians referred to Social Security benefits as "earned entitlements"—people earned money, put a portion into the Social Security trust fund—and then drew back what they had "earned."

By the 1970s, as many eligibility standards were relaxed and the connection blurred between taxes paid in and benefits taken out, the modifier of "earned" faded, and the term "entitlement" per se came into more common, and official, usage. It appears to have first been used in the 1974 Congressional Budget and Impoundment Control Act, which defined "entitlement authority" thusly:

> To make payments, the budget authority for which is not provided for in advance by appropriations acts, to any person or government if under the provisions of the law containing such authority, the United States is obligated to make such payments to persons or governments who meet the requirements established by laws.

The *Congressional Quarterly* used the term "entitlement programs" in its description of the act, but throughout the Ford and Carter administrations, "entitlement" in any form was used irregularly. By the time of the Reagan administration, however, the term took hold. In March of 1981, GAO released its third edition of the *GAO Glossary*, in which "entitlement" (by itself) is defined as "government programs that make payments to people or business that meet a criteria set in law"—perhaps the first "official" definition of the term.

On April 9, 1981, *U.S. News & World Report* referred to the "revolution" in "entitlements" when writing about the increased spending on social programs; in a feature on transfer programs a month earlier, the term was not used. Also in April, the Brookings Institution's annual volume, *Setting National Priorities—1982* used the word "entitlement" to refer to programs that provide benefits to the "retired, unemployed, sick and poor people."[1] And on June 24, President Reagan, who had always used the term "Social Security net" to describe these programs during the campaign, referred to them as "entitlements" in a speech at a U.S. Jaycee convention in San Antonio.

Later in the year, *Time, Business Week,* and other magazines also used the term; most of the publications put the word in quotes the first time it was used, indicating its novelty, but not thereafter.

Today, although OMB indicates that the word "entitlement" has no "official definition" in the agency, it is commonly used as a synonym for social-assistance programs, and is defined as such in recent Webster's and Random House dictionaries.

Language is important; moving from being defined as programs like all others to being defined as entitlements has changed the meaning and the political dynamic behind them. Mary Ann Glendon, in *Rights Talk*, notes that if the United States, unlike most European nations, lacks constitutional protection for the well-being of citizens, many programs, now called entitlements, have come to substitute for them. The language of entitlement suggests rights, which "tend to be presented as absolute, individual, and independent of any necessary relationship to responsibilities."[2] The choice of terms, she says, "has a powerful effect on how we imagine the role and the ends of government."[3]

Thus the ability to cut back on the growth of these social programs, or to alter their formulas, has been sharply constrained by the widespread public view that these are entitlements, that the recipients are "entitled" to them, and that any cutbacks are thus illegitimate. In consequence, it was politically, if not arithmetically, inevitable that the budget-deficit problem would not go away. Even the sharp reductions in the growth of defense spending that began to be enacted in 1985 were not enough.

THE POST-REAGAN ERA

Between 1985 and 1990, spending on mandatory programs like entitlements and interest on the debt was growing at a rate of 7.2 percent a year—nearly twice the 3.75 percent annual growth rate of spending on discretionary programs, including defense. Adjusted for inflation, spending on discretionary programs including defense actually *fell* at an annual rate of 3.4 percent between 1985 and 1990, while spending on mandatory programs rose at an annual inflation-adjusted rate of about 1.8 percent. The latter figure was approximately equal to the modest growth rate of the real economy.

By the time the Bush administration confronted the FY 1991 budget at the October 1990 budget summit, the options for reducing the budget were limited indeed. The ad hoc 1981 strategy—cutting taxes to control spending—had, after all, been abandoned by Reagan himself in 1985 and was no longer an option. Spending that Congress could allocate had already been cut nearly as much as was politically possible. In that environment and with the help of President Bush's more orthodox views on deficits, Democratic rhetoric that spoke of a "need" to raise taxes to reduce the budget deficit gained sway—despite the president's repeated, unconditional pledge of "no new taxes." The president was forced to concede some modest tax increases as part of a budget agreement with the Democrat-controlled Congress designed to eliminate the deficit within five years.

Unfortunately, at least for the promises made under the budget agreement, the October 1990 deficit-reduction package offered little deficit reduction until after the 1992 election. Even then, it relied heavily on optimistic economic assumptions to project the elimination of budget deficits by 1995. The perceived need to reduce the budget deficit caused Congress and the president to agree to a nominal deficit-reduction package that included spending cuts and tax increases as the economy headed into a recession. The notion that a fiscal policy that implies less burdensome taxes is good for the economy had obviously been forgotten sometime between 1985 and 1990. Meanwhile, in October 1990, Washington budgeteers were left with nothing but wishful thinking as they displayed a remarkable lack of interest in an anticyclical budget policy. The Keynesian principle of avoiding tax increases or spending cuts as the economy is slowing down had been accepted even by Republicans steeped in balanced-budget orthodoxy since the Eisenhower tax cuts in the 1950s but was somehow discarded in the October 1990 deficit-reduction package—or at least rationalized by the argument that monetary policy could compensate.

Without any sound conviction about appropriate budget and tax policy, both the Republican president and the Democratic lawmakers became the object of criticisms by ideologues on the Right and on the Left. In February 1991, the conservative Cato Institute published a study by Stephen Moore entitled "The Profligate President: A Mid-Term Review of Bush's Fiscal Policy." Wrote Moore:

> Midway through his presidency, George Bush is mired in a fiscal policy crisis worse than anyone could have envisioned when he entered the Oval Office two years ago. This crisis is the resurgence of record fiscal deficits. The crisis has been caused by an explosion of new domestic spending under Bush. Between the time that Reagan left the White House in 1989 and the next year (FY 1992), domestic spending will have climbed by $300 billion—from $670 billion to $970 billion. Since 1989 the federal government's domestic outlays adjusted for inflation have grown by an enormous 10 percent per year. Domestic spending is expanding at a faster clip under Bush than it did under other recent presidents typically labeled as big spenders, including Lyndon Johnson, Richard Nixon, and Jimmy Carter. Incredibly, Bush is on the way to being the biggest champion of domestic spending since Franklin Roosevelt.[4]

Its historical inaccuracy regarding FDR's views on spending aside, the Cato analysis is representative of the extreme disaffection with Bush from the conservative side of the political spectrum after his agreement to small tax increases during the 1990 budget summit. Cato's attack on the spending side was hardly substantiated by the facts. The increase in spending during FY 1991 was principally accounted for by a 17.4 percent jump in mandatory outlays, including a tremendous amount of new money for deposit insurance, while discretionary spending rose by only 5.4 percent—virtually a zero increase in inflation-adjusted terms.

Just eight months later, in October 1991, Democratic Senators Lloyd Bentsen and Bill Bradley were taken to task by Jeff Faux, president of the liberal Economic Policy Institute, for proposing middle-class tax relief and a reduction in the capital gains tax as a means to jump-start the economy. Faux's criticism was based on the recognition that if the tax cuts had to be matched by spending cuts, there would be no net stimulus left with which to jump-start. Faux went on to ask:

> What if Bentsen's or Bradley's tax cuts were not matched by spending cuts elsewhere in the budget? Wouldn't that stimulate the economy in the short run? The answer is yes, just as Ronald Reagan's tax cut driven deficits stimulated the economy in the early 1980s. The result then was the string of damaging fiscal deficits. Investment in the human, physical and technical capital needed to support America's competitiveness in the new global economy was squeezed out of the federal budget. Politically, Democrats were denied the resources to support broad-based domestic programs for their traditional constituencies.[5]

Faux's recommended method of stimulating the economy was to increase the budget deficit by extending unemployment benefits and to have the federal government provide emergency revenue sharing to distressed states and cities. The latter measure would amount to some restoration of the cuts in domestic nondefense discretionary spending that had been effected over the previous decade. He did not specify his economic rationale for the claim that such measures, presumably financed by higher taxes, would boost the economy.

It has become clear that in the 1990s, as in the earlier two-hundred-year history of the nation, fiscal policy has been largely driven by politics. With budget deficits nominally more than $300 billion, conservatives are reluctant to talk about tax cuts but feel free to complain about increases in spending— even when they are not under the control of the president or Congress. Meanwhile, Democratic leaders like Lloyd Bentsen, late in the Bush term, talked about potential tax relief financed by cuts in defense spending, or if push came to shove and the economy got really weak, by a countercyclical increase in the federal budget deficit. Talk of tax cuts by Democrats—especially the unforgivable mention of a capital gains tax cut by Bentsen—enraged commentators from the Left like Faux, who wanted to see the "peace dividend" devoted to restoring the cuts in domestic discretionary spending that resulted from the pressure of Ronald Reagan's tax cuts and congressional fears of deficit spending. Few cared to note that the defense buildup was financed by a buildup of debt: decriers of debt ought logically to wish to use freed-up defense dollars to pay down debt.

If policy makers in Washington, including President Bush, were caught up in the struggles over the deficit, and in the wash generated by the 1990 budget agreement, not much of the Washington concern was reflected on the 1992 presidential campaign trail. Bill Clinton, for example, launched his campaign in October of 1991 with an appeal to middle-income voters that said nothing about deficits or budget agreements:

> Middle-class people are spending more hours on the job, spending less time with their children, bringing home a smaller paycheck to pay for health care and housing and education.[6]

He coupled this message with an attack on the spendthrift and selfish 1980s, and with an appeal for personal responsibility, proposing a two-year limit on welfare, an expanded earned-income tax credit to help the working poor, and "microenterprise" grants for low-income people starting small businesses.[7]

In November 1991, Clinton focused more directly on an economic plan, which included a string of program proposals and a broader, thematic look at the global economy, but which again largely ignored the Washington debate on debt and taxes, except indirectly, via his attack on gridlock and business as usual in Washington. Clinton called for a "New Covenant for economic change that empowers people, rewards work and organizes our country to compete and win again." Clinton rapped both Bush and Congress, and said America needs to move "in a radically different direction" economically in order to meet the global competition of the 1990s.

He defined his radically different direction by first criticizing Democrats' traditional tax-and-spend policies, then calling for a middle-class tax cut averaging $350 per family; a higher ceiling on FHA mortgage guarantees, passage of a highway bill and accelerated spending on infrastructure funds; lower credit-card interest rates; full funding of Head Start; funding for job-training and education programs for high-school graduates; and a domestic GI Bill to pay for college, to be repaid through a program of national service.[8]

To be sure, Clinton's new program was not the opposite of tax-and-spend, as Reagan's program had purported to be—namely, tax cut and spending cut; rather, it was tax cut and spend. But he and several of his Democratic-candidate counterparts did break with the usual liberal party rhetoric and stress new themes. The focus of candidates like Bob Kerrey, Paul Tsongas, and Clinton on restoring economic growth and addressing the concerns of middle-class voters, as opposed to redistributing income to promote fairness, and stressing the needs of the underprivileged and poor, were a significant departure from contemporary Democratic orthodoxy and a return to neo-Kennedyism. As Robert Shapiro of the Progressive Policy Institute described it, this thrust represented "a new awareness for Democrats that the central goal of economic policy is the betterment of economic conditions for working Americans who earn average incomes. The center of economic policy is not those who are outside the economic mainstream."[9]

Clinton and Tsongas were probably the strongest proponents of this new Democratic thrust, agreeing that "economic growth is the best social program, that government spending should be tilted toward investment in the future rather than income support, and that free trade, not protectionism, best serves the economy." But Clinton coupled his "New Democrat" theme with a middle-class tax cut, which Tsongas both rejected and derided, saying "I'm no Santa Claus"; Tsongas, almost alone among the candidates, instead stressed the deficit, and the need to restrain federal spending, not push costly new government spending initiatives and tax breaks for the middle class.[10]

The middle-class tax cut, of course, was an attempt by Clinton and others to appeal to the economic mainstream, stressing that change would bring good things, not just more sacrifice on the part of voters. The idea was advocated by Clinton, Doug Wilder, and Bob Kerrey throughout the primary campaign; it had popular support and made for a good campaign issue, but it had little credibility among the policy and economic elite. Tsongas and Harkin both opposed the middle-class tax cut, but on different grounds—Harkin to sharpen his appeal on the left to the disadvantaged, Tsongas to identify himself as a nonpolitician who would speak the truth to voters no matter how unpleasant the reality.

In spite of the criticism from Tsongas and others, Clinton made the middle-class tax cut the centerpiece of his campaign in New Hampshire. In his first TV ad, he asked the rich to "pay their fair share" and promised to cut middle-class taxes by 10 percent. He planned to pay for the cut by raising taxes on those making over $200,000.[11] While Clinton eventually conceded that such a tax cut offset by an increase on the wealthy was not likely to increase overall revenues, he said it had merit on the sheer virtue of fairness.

Clinton's economic focus in the campaign did reflect a larger theme of investment. Besides his short-term antirecession spending proposals, he advocated an investment tax credit, a targeted capital gains tax cut for investments in new businesses which were held more than five years, and more government spending on civilian research, along with a civilian DARPA (Defense Advanced Research Projects Agency) to pinpoint and support productive industries, and more federal investment in education, children's health, environmental technology and infrastructure, and basic research and development.

In order to pay for all of this, Clinton proposed a 3 percent across-the-board cut in all government administrative expenses and further cuts in defense spending. He also talked about dividing the federal budget into two components—investment and consumption—and limiting growth in the consumption budget to the percent increase in personal income.

Clinton did not totally ignore the question of getting the federal budget under control; he spoke, generally in vague terms, about cutting medical expenditures as the key to the budget deficit. But his focus was far more on investment and spending than on taxing or deficit reduction. He spent very little time talking about the budget deficit.

If Clinton was criticized, by his rivals and by the press, for promising too much to too many, he was not alone in stressing economic ideas other than deficit reduction. With the striking exception of Tsongas, the other Democratic candidates used the deficit only as a foil, to criticize George Bush and, more generally, Washington. There were some bold fiscal-policy ideas, particularly Jerry Brown's call for a flat tax, but neither he nor his plan were taken seriously by any except a small fraction of the electorate. At least in their zeal to capture primary voters, most of the Democratic candidates saw no particular political payoff in stressing classical themes like a balanced budget or spending restraint.

Tsongas was different. The deficit was at the center of his political and economic approach. In economic terms, reflecting the views of Peter Peterson, he saw large continuing federal deficits as a disastrous hindrance to future economic growth and to American competitiveness. Although he discussed the issue in general terms, not through specific and pointed proposals, he also saw the key to deficit reduction coming through control of entitlement spending.

In political terms, Tsongas framed his appeal as distinct from all the other candidates precisely because he was willing to talk about the uncomfortable in ways that standard-issue, blow-dried politicians were not. By using the refrain "I'm no Santa Claus" and stressing his recovery from near-fatal cancer, he tried to set himself off as one concerned less about his own ambitions and more about the future of his children, and the country, and as one willing to tell the truth, even if unpleasant, to voters used to politicians' lies.

As much because of his personal appeal as a nontypical politician as because of the deep and specific voter concern about the deficit, Tsongas was able to garner more voter support than the traditional liberal Tom Harkin, "New Democrat" Bob Kerrey, and iconoclastic Jerry Brown. In the process, he gave additional legitimacy to the goal of deficit reduction, and to tax increases combined with spending cuts as means to that end.

Democrats were not the only ones discussing the economy, debt, and taxes in the early stages of the 1992 campaign. In the midst of the battle over the New Hampshire primary, under challenge from conservative Pat Buchanan in a depressed New England state, President Bush used his State of the Union message to present his own blueprint for the faltering economy—and debt and deficits were not prominent focal points. Short- and long-term investment spending, along with tax cuts, dominated the Bush scheme:

- By executive order, Bush ordered a ninety-day moratorium on any new regulations that might retard economic growth and an adjustment to tax-withholding tables to give workers a slight increase in take-home pay.
- The central component of Bush's effort to stimulate the economy in the short term was a renewed effort to cut the capital gains tax rate from 28 to 15.4 percent. In addition, the president proposed tax credits of up to $5,000 for first-time homebuyers, withdrawals from IRAs for a first-time home purchase, a passive-loss provision for commercial real estate developers, and accelerated business depreciation for certain plant and equipment purchases.
- For the longer term, Bush called for passage of the North American Free Trade Agreement (NAFTA), passage of his New American Schools program, a permanent research-and-development tax credit, increased research-and-development spending, increased funding for Head Start, and regulatory and tax relief for businesses that invest in poor neighborhoods.

A number of gestures by the president were geared to the middle-class voters being wooed by both Pat Buchanan and the Democrats: accelerating tax withholding, offering incentives for first-time homebuyers, making interest on student loans deductible, and allowing penalty-free withdrawals from IRAs for medical and educational purposes.[12] There was no hint of pain in the proposals.

Early 1992 brought additional bad news, when CBO economic projections revealed, once more, that the deficit would continue to present a major challenge and headache to the president and the Congress in the years to come. The figures showed that while the deficit was projected to shrink to $178 billion by 1996, it would then begin to climb again and would reach some $407 billion by the year 2002. The increase would be due primarily to growth in entitlement spending, left unchecked, yet again, by the 1990 budget summit agreement.

THE PEROT CANDIDACY

In February of 1992, Ross Perot began to toy with the idea of running for president. In an appearance on "Larry King Live," Perot suggested that he would consider running if his supporters around the country managed to get his name on all fifty states' ballots. While he claimed not to want the job, Perot said he would accept it for the good of the country. In an appearance on "This Week with David Brinkley" shortly after the Larry King appearance, Perot said, "I have no desire to be president. My personal feelings are anybody intelligent enough to be able to do the job would not want the toughest, dirtiest, most thankless job in the world, that is absolutely brutal on your family and everybody you love." But when asked if he would take it, he said, "It's up to the people."[13]

By March, a Draft H. Ross Perot for President National Committee had filed papers with the Federal Election Commission and set up shop in Washington to coordinate efforts to get Perot's name on ballots around the country. Volunteer groups formed throughout the nation, and early polls indicated a Perot candidacy might garner a fair bit of support.[14]

While the Perot candidacy was met with skepticism by many Washington insiders, he did receive a modicum of praise for his clear focus on the federal budget deficit. Early on, Perot started talking about the need to curb entitlement spending and end military subsidies to Europe and Japan. Liberal commentator Michael Kinsley said of Perot in late April 1992, he "has been slightly better than Clinton and miles ahead of Bush in conveying the essential message of no gain without pain."[15]

Perot shied away from offering any detailed plans or proposals during the early months of the campaign. In early May, he decided to cut back on his interviews and TV appearances in order to focus on "finalizing a strategy and developing carefully thought-out positions on each of the major issues." The *Washington Post*'s Dan Balz described a Perot appearance on "Meet the Press" early in May:

> Perot acknowledged that his deficit-reduction plan, which he has described repeatedly over the past two months, was flawed and needed additional study. When confronted with evidence that he would have to eliminate Social Security and Medicare for everyone making more than $40,000 to save $20 billion, Perot said, "Well, if your numbers are correct, then, you know, basically I got bad information from a man whose name is a household word."[16]

Shortly thereafter, Perot assembled a small group of experts, headed up by John White, former deputy director of OMB in the Carter White House, to help him come up with a platform for dealing with the nation's most pressing issues.

On the issue of taxes, Perot waffled in the early months of the campaign. At one point, he claimed to be "absolutely against raising taxes." Later he said he would be willing to raise taxes for spending on education. When asked about raising taxes on the wealthy, he said, "You know I believe it." Generally, he called for tax fairness and progessivity in the system.[17] Perot's ambiguity on the issue of taxes was typified by this statement:

> Let's assume that we're just unable to pay our bills, unable to meet our obligations, we have to raise our taxes. That's it. We have to pay our bills as a country. Deficit spending is addictive. We've got to stop this practice as a country. I'm saying that in an emergency, if we have to raise taxes to keep our country solvent, then you would have to raise taxes. But if there is such an emergency, it's because we create it as a people by being unwilling to face our obligations. Right now, we want everything, but we don't want to pay for it.[18]

Although the outlines of Perot's economic plan remained relatively vague, his campaign did begin to pick up momentum going into the summer months. When the bipartisan team of Ed Rollins and Hamilton Jordan joined the campaign in early June, Perot's candidacy seemed to gain more legitimacy with the Washington establishment—most of it centered on the expectation that he, alone among candidates, was willing to confront the deficit dilemma. Jordan expressed the hope he saw in the Perot candidacy:

> While there are real policy differences between Bush and Clinton, those traditional partisan differences are moot as long as the federal budget deficit persists and grows. Government today at every level is preoccupied with debt management. The federal debt has come to represent in both real and symbolic terms the failure of our system and our leadership to develop national consensus and to solve problems. Traditional partisan arguments about how to divide the pie are moot when there is no pie left to divide.[19]

As the summer wore on, Perot began to give some indication of how he would govern if elected president. He said he would focus intently on the economy, "on rebuilding our cities, focus on rebuilding our infrastructure, focus on rebuilding our job base, focus on re-industrializing America." In turn, he would spend little time dealing with divisive social issues such as abortion, gay rights, sex education, or gun control.[20]

Perot's public support soared in May and June, but began to falter some in July, when allegations about his personal behavior, including claims that he had associates and family members followed, and their phones tapped, created some doubts about his candidacy in the public. Still, his support was well over 20 percent in major polls when he abruptly withdrew his candidacy on July 16.

Even out of the race, however, and with his public approval having plummeted to 7 percent, Perot continued to move forward with the development of his deficit-reduction plan. As the details of Perot's plan began to emerge, it became apparent that many of the steps necessary to put a real dent in the deficit were politically unsalable.

The plan, drafted by John White, called for approximately $700 billion in deficit reduction over five years, to be achieved through spending cuts, tax increases, and other means. The plan included a ten-cents-a-gallon gasoline tax hike per year for five years, higher taxes on alcohol and tobacco, the elimination of various tax subsidies, and higher user fees for such things as use of federal lands and airports for private airplanes. Spending cuts included a 10 percent across-the-board reduction in administrative costs of federal agencies, deep cuts in various spending programs such as the space station and rural electrification, as well as massive cuts in defense spending. Perot's plan also included limits on cost-of-living increases for Social Security and other government pension programs. In an effort to spur investment, Perot proposed numerous tax incentives for business.

House Budget Committee Chairman Leon Panetta commented on Perot's plan by saying,

> They [the Perot campaign] were obviously trying to put together a plan that is credible. But as the administration and Congress have found out, these steps involve some political land mines.[21]

The Perot plan called for $364 billion in tax increases over five years, along with $415.8 billion in spending cuts, $267.8 billion of them coming from entitlements, $108 billion from cuts in domestic discretionary spending, and $40 billion in cuts (beyond the Bush budget) from defense—touching a lot of land mines. Perot's enthusiastic promotion of his plan, including its publication as a paperback book, did sensitize the public more about the need for deficit reduction, but his impact, especially on specific policy alternatives, was limited when he was private citizen Perot instead of presidential candidate Perot.

Perot reentered the presidential race on October 1. Throughout the fall, he took his economic plan to the airwaves. He aired numerous television "infomercials" designed to explain in elementary terms (e.g., "It's pretty simple" and "Let's raise the hood and go to work") how the nation's budget deficit hurts America and what should be done about it. In the ads, Perot assailed the trickle-down economics of the Reagan-Bush era and railed against the perks and privileges of Washington politicians. Interestingly, Perot scarcely mentioned the painful fiscal measures advocated in his economic plan.

While most experts shuddered at the thought of Perot as president, many conceded that his message was a real service to the American public. In endorsing Bill Clinton, Felix Rohatyn said of Perot:

> He can play a good role in spreading this message about fiscal integrity, and helping people understand taxes are a respectable part of any economic plan. He can help maintain a movement to keep fiscal discipline, and get it through Congress.[22]

Other budget experts praised Perot's plan. Congressional Budget Office Director Robert Reischauer said, "It's a clear plan with beef in it. It's real."

Former CBO Director Alice Rivlin commented, "It's a balanced plan with lots of things in it that a number of us have supported for a long time."

Fueled less by the specifics of his plan and more by his articulate, earthy, and pointed performances in the fall presidential debates, Perot's public support rose sharply before the election, before faltering again in late October. In the end, of course, he captured 19 percent of the popular vote, the best showing for an independent candidate for president since Teddy Roosevelt of the Bull Moose party in 1912. But if he raised public consciousness about the deficit problem, he did little to build a public consensus around any painful policy choices.

MOVING TOWARD THE FALL

By June 1992, Bill Clinton had gained enough distance on his rivals for the Democratic nomination that his victory was secured; as he moved forward toward the party convention in New York, Clinton released his own detailed economic blueprint for his first term as president. While deficit reduction had been at least an integral part of Clinton's overall approach to the economy early on in the campaign, this revised program, with clear priorities of economic stimulus and economic growth, did not reflect that. CQ Weekly Report described the plan this way:

> Budget-balancing rhetoric may have swept the capital, but it has not found a toehold in the presidential campaign of Democrat Bill Clinton.[23]

To be sure, Clinton did discuss the deficit in his plan, saying it would cut the deficit in half by 1996, with half the reduction coming from the economic growth resulting from his proposed stimulus plan, and the rest coming from savings from a massive overhaul of the health-care system. His plan focused largely on dealing with the nation's health-care crisis and spurring public and private investment. Clinton's advisers dismissed criticisms leveled at the plan by Washington experts and budget experts, saying their message was aimed at the voters.

The twenty-two-page plan, dubbed "Putting People First," seemed to indicate a shift on Clinton's part away from the centrist position he had held at the outset of the campaign and toward a more traditional Democratic program of federal spending, calling for nearly $220 billion in new spending over four years. Most observers agreed that Clinton's proposed tax increases and spending cuts would pay for the increased spending, but would do little or nothing to reduce the debt. Nonetheless, many groups slated to benefit from the new spending initiatives, including big-city mayors and the National Association of Manufacturers, applauded aspects of the plan.

The plan's new spending and investment proposals included:

- $20 billion a year for a Rebuild America Fund to help finance the building of bridges, roads, high-speed railways, and a fiber-optic information network
- an expanded earned-income tax credit, full funding of Head Start, and the WIC (Women's, Infants', and Children's feeding) program
- a tax credit for middle-class families with children (those without children would still receive the promised middle-class tax cut)
- additional funding for education, urban aid, worker-education and -training programs, and apprenticeship programs, along with a new national service corps
- tax breaks for manufacturers and small businesses, including an expanded research-and-development credit

The Clinton plan was to be financed by a combination of tax increases and spending cuts; the taxes, $150 billion over four years, were to come from the wealthy ($92 billion from those earning over $200,000) and from corporations, especially by recovering underpayment of taxes from foreign corporations. A nearly equal amount in spending cuts were to come from defense and from unspecified cuts in administrative costs.

The *Congressional Quarterly Weekly Report* characterized the Clinton plan this way:

> Drawing on promises rarely heard since the Reagan administration, Clinton says his broader economic policies would produce significant growth and consequent budgetary savings. His plan runs contrary to conventional Washington wisdom that program eliminations, massive cuts in entitlement spending and tax increases would be needed to erase the federal budget's red ink.[24]

The economic plan became the centerpiece of the Clinton presidential campaign. In accepting the Democratic nomination in July, he blamed the nation's current economic problems on twelve years of failed Republican policies, and made his plan the alternative.

In the fall campaign, the Clinton effort became synonymous with the sign tacked up in the "war room" at campaign headquarters: IT'S THE ECONOMY, STUPID. But in many ways, the watchword became not "deficit," "debt," "competitiveness," or even "economy," but "jobs." Clinton focused again and again on finding ways to create and sustain high-paying jobs, saying the country's current economic troubles went beyond a mere recession and involved major structural problems in the U.S. economy.

Indeed, both Bush and Clinton focused on job creation in their campaign rhetoric and each had his own plan. Bush's plan, called "Agenda for American Renewal," centered around tax incentives and training programs and relied heavily on market forces. The primary goal was to reduce taxes on profits (i.e., reduce the capital gains tax rate), assuming that businesses would then invest more heavily in new plants and equipment and in turn hire more workers. The Bush plan also included money for worker-training programs and "skill grant vouchers" of up to $3,000 per worker.

The Clinton plan involved a more active role for government in creating jobs, with massive federal spending on infrastructure projects (cited above), targeted tax credits for new plant and equipment investments, and a targeted capital gains tax cut.[25]

The dialogue in the fall of 1992 did involve more than the two major party presidential candidates, and for others, including Ross Perot, the deficit and debt became much more central. Although Perot withdrew as an official candidate in the presidential race on July 16, he remained an important player in the campaign and a visible figure on the national media. His economic plan, released as a paperback book which he promoted heavily, received a great deal of attention. The plan, an expansion of his campaign's proposal, was designed to balance the federal budget by 1998 through significant tax increases and spending cuts. Perot continued to advocate a fifty-cents-a-gallon gasoline tax and massive cuts in entitlements, including cuts in Medicare and Medicaid, reduced cost-of-living adjustments for federal retirees, reduced farm subsidies and agricultural tariffs, and higher taxes on Social Security benefits. But neither Perot nor his book stressed the painful quality of governmental choices to restrain government or reduce the deficit; rather, the focus was on waste, fraud, abuse, and corruption in Washington, and on the role of political reform in reducing or eliminating the waste and corruption.

Another group focusing on the deficit was led by two respected centrist senators, via a bipartisan, blue-ribbon commission. Senators Sam Nunn and Pete Domenici led a group of lawmakers, scholars, and budget experts in drafting a ten-year budget-balancing plan that included roughly $2 trillion in deficit reductions, many through tough cutbacks in all areas of federal spending, including entitlements. The most-discussed feature of their plan was a radical restructuring of the tax system, moving from an income tax to a consumption-based tax. They did not shrink from the tough aspects of their plan—but a blue-ribbon commission commanded none of the broad attention accorded a billionaire folk hero and erstwhile presidential candidate.

A third alternative was promoted by House Budget Committee Chairman Leon Panetta. Panetta proposed an alternative to Gramm-Rudman, prescribing an annual net amount of deficit reduction, leaving it up to Congress and the president to work out the details. Through a program of cuts in entitlement spending and increases in taxes, Panetta also aimed to balance the budget by 1998.

Perot's theme, if not his specific ideas and alternatives, received a lot of public and press attention; the Nunn-Domenici and Panetta plans received a lot of attention within the policy community in Washington.[26] But both George Bush and Bill Clinton chose to put their efforts and focus elsewhere; Bush, on optimistic growth forecasts as the route to a balanced budget, and Clinton, on economic growth, job creation, investment, and tax fairness for the middle class as the top economic priorities.

George Bush captured only 38 percent of the popular votes cast on November 3, indicating a massive rejection of the status quo. But Bill Clinton captured only 70 percent of the anti–status quo vote, the rest going to Ross Perot. The anti-Bush vote was fueled primarily by dissatisfaction with the economy, but unhappiness over the economy was more complicated than usual.

Some voters were unhappy with unemployment and current economic performance. But that clearly was not the whole story; the economy had come out of the recession, and while growth was sluggish, unemployment was not strikingly high, and inflation and interest rates were strikingly low.

When George Bush, in the fall presidential debates, said to voters about the economy, "It's not nearly as bad as you think it is," he was right. But many voters were unhappy because of their sense of unease about the economy's future—in a post–Cold War world dominated by a global economy in which America's control over its own economic future was less, and where policy makers seemed incapable of responding to worldwide change. Yet other voters were unhappy about budget deficits, both on economic grounds and, more generally, as a symbol of government ineptitude, indifference, and inertia.

In the latter group were concentrated Perot voters, but Ross Perot managed to capture wider support. Still, Bill Clinton won enough voter support to win a landslide electoral-vote victory. His activist, Hamiltonian approach to governance helped, as did a detailed program that at least showed he had a plan for the country's economic future.

The Clinton strategy, though not the policy direction, was not dissimilar to Ronald Reagan's in the 1980 election campaign. Reagan, too, had a Hamiltonian, activist plan—domestic budget cuts, deep tax cuts, and steep defense-spending increases. By focusing especially on the tax cuts, Reagan emphasized the pleasurable aspects of his plan and deemphasized the painful parts. Clinton's campaign focused on the pleasurable spending increases and a middle-class tax cut, and deemphasized the pain that serious deficit reduction would entail.

But both men found the situation changed after the election: Reagan, soon after his plan was enacted, found the necessity, in every year of his presidency after 1981, of confronting policy options that were unpleasant and politically unpalatable; for Clinton, the reality of deficit reduction became clear early in his first year in the White House.

Once elected, Clinton promised to focus "like a laser beam" on the economy. He was faced immediately with the challenge of reviving a sluggish economy without stirring fears of inflation and thereby sending the financial markets into a panic and interest rates soaring. While he succeeded in calming the immediate fears of the financial markets, he would soon find a greater challenge and bigger dilemma ahead—namely, dealing with a Congress and an attentive public anxious to get to work on serious deficit reduction. The climate in fact had changed through the campaign, and reflected public anxieties different in key ways from those Clinton had emphasized in his own speeches and messages. As the *Congressional Quarterly Weekly Report* described Clinton's environment in November, shortly after the election:

> When he gets to Washington, he will meet a Congress that is itching to take some action on the deficit—now. Revved up by the anti-deficit campaign of independent candidate Ross Perot and teeming with new members who got here by promising to start balancing the budget, the incoming Congress will be looking for some way to prove to constituents that its members take the deficit seriously.[27]

Clinton vowed initially that he had no intention of changing the economic plan he put forward during the campaign. In a November 12 news conference, he said, "I'm going to pursue my course, which is increased investment, gradual but disciplined reduction of the deficit, and we'll see if it works." He outlined a two-phase strategy for economic recovery: a modest, short-term stimulus plan and long-term policies designed to increase productivity and spur economic growth.[28]

At the same time, congressional leaders were exerting subtle pressure on Clinton to place more emphasis on deficit reduction. Tom Foley reassured incoming Democratic freshmen shortly after the election that "there will be more emphasis on deficit reduction than the Clinton administration has yet acknowledged."[29]

In December, Clinton began putting together his economic team. By appointing Lloyd Bentsen to be treasury secretary and Leon Panetta to head up OMB, Clinton demonstrated an understanding of the primacy of politics in launching his ambitious economic plan. He selected members of Congress who were not only expert on budgetary matters but who were also highly regarded by their colleagues. But these appointments, along with those of Alice Rivlin as deputy director of OMB and Robert Rubin to be economic coordinator, also signaled a new policy emphasis and direction: a more genuine interest in deficit reduction than had been apparent during the campaign, and a greater concern with the nation's long-term economic health than with the short-term effects of the recession.

In outlining his broad plans for the economy, Clinton moved further and further away from the emphasis in his earlier proposals to stimulate the economy in the short term. While he did not rule out short-term deficit spending, he began to argue that any short-term measures would also have to bring long-term benefits for the economy. The proposal for a middle-class tax cut went onto the back burner, with a promise to revive it later, when the deficit was under control.

Leading up to his inauguration, Clinton still seemed wedded, at least in part, to his earlier plans for investment in the nation's infrastructure as a means of stimulating the economy and creating jobs in the short term. Clinton faced a clear dilemma: whether to stick with his plan of spending $20 billion annually on infrastructure projects or, in light of improving economic conditions, to focus on the deficit problem.

To focus public attention on his plans for the economy, and to build support from economic elites, Clinton hosted an economic summit in Little Rock in mid-December. There, the president-elect reemphasized his desire to move away from the central tenet that guided the nation's fiscal policy for the past decade, namely that new spending initiatives must be paid for immediately by offsetting spending cuts or tax increases. He reiterated a campaign idea that the federal budget should be separated into a capital budget and a consumption budget, whereby "investment" on capital improvements would not be counted toward the deficit.[30]

AFTER THE INAUGURATION

The first signal that Clinton would not find it easy to live up to the lofty goals he had set forth for the economy during the presidential campaign and the transition came when he delayed the release of an economic plan he had pledged would be unveiled the day after his inauguration. In mid-January, he conceded that it would be several weeks before his plan was finished.

Clinton faced a clear dilemma attempting to put together an economic package that would encompass deficit reduction, short-term stimulus, and long-term investment and growth: could he be taken seriously as a deficit fighter if his first major proposal included a multibillion-dollar spending initiative? Clinton's advisers recognized this dilemma and early on began to indicate that any stimulus package proposed by the administration would be significantly smaller than what had originally been suggested.[31]

In their Senate confirmation hearings, Clinton's top economic advisers emphasized deficit reduction as a major priority of the administration. Leon Panetta went so far as to say that deficit reduction was more important than a middle-class tax cut or a short-term economic-stimulus program.

Treasury Secretary-designate Lloyd Bentsen, among others, suggested that newly released OMB figures, which placed the deficit much higher than earlier estimates, were forcing Clinton to abandon the proposed middle-class tax cut and consider deeper cuts in government spending, as well as additional taxes. At the same time, many Republicans and Democrats in Congress were beginning to speak with a new sense of urgency about the need to reduce the deficit and were growing increasingly skittish about a stimulus package of any kind.[32]

The president's first official action on economic policy came on January 21, forced by the 1990 budget agreement; Clinton decided to stick with floating deficit targets instead of exercising his option under the terms of the 1990 agreement to revert to the Gramm-Rudman–like alternative—fixed targets and the threat of a year-end, across-the-board spending cut to enforce them. While some Republicans slammed Clinton for backing away from earlier commitments to cut the deficit, most Democrats and independent observers supported the action as recognition that the 1990 agreement's fiscal discipline had in fact been greater than previous experiences under Gramm-Rudman.[33]

For three weeks after that initial economic-policy decision, the focus of the Clinton administration moved away from economic and budget policy; gays and the military, and personnel decisions like the choice of an attorney general, dominated public and press attention. But on February 17, the agenda shifted dramatically back to debt and taxes. Clinton used the State of the Union message to unveil the broad outlines of his long-awaited economic plan to a joint session of Congress. Clinton's plan called for nearly $500 billion in deficit reduction over five years, part of that coming from deep spending cuts but most to be raised through massive tax increases, aimed first at wealthy Americans, but also touching middle-income taxpayers and Social Security beneficiaries. In addition, the plan called for a multibillion-dollar short-term economic-stimulus program designed to create jobs and ensure long-term economic growth.

As the *Congressional Quarterly Weekly Report* described it, the plan contained three separate components:

1. A *Stimulus Package:* Included $16.3 billion in new budget authority, $3.24 billion in transportation-trust-fund spending and $3.3 billion in loans for fiscal 1993; also included $12 billion in tax cuts for businesses in 1993 and 1994. As a whole, the package was designed to create 500,000 new jobs and help shore up the economic recovery already under way. Once promoted as a "jobs bill," this package was presented as "a down payment on the administration's long-run investment program."
2. *Investment Spending:* Nearly $160 billion in spending programs and tax breaks proposed over four years, designed to stimulate business investment and place a renewed emphasis on infrastructure, education, child care, job training, and other areas neglected during twelve years of Republican rule.

These two aspects taken together were designed, in theory, to help the public and members of Congress accept the shared sacrifice required by deficit reduction.

3. A *Deficit-Reduction Plan:* Designed to cut the federal deficit by $493 billion over four years, $247 coming from spending cuts and $246 coming from tax increases, nearly a one-to-one ratio of tax increases to spending cuts. (This alleged ratio quickly became a focal point for critics of the plan, many of whom said the ratio was actually more like 4 to 1 or 5 to 1 of tax increases to spending cuts.)[34]

By nearly all accounts, the president's State of the Union speech itself was brilliant and well received, bringing substantial public support to the plan overnight. Reactions to the plan from political, business, and investment professionals were mixed. Alan Greenspan strongly endorsed the broad outlines of Clinton's plan, saying, "It is a serious proposal, its baseline economic assumptions are plausible and it is a detailed program-by-program set of recommendations as distinct from general goals." Ross Perot held his fire initially, calling the plan "a good first step," but adding, "the devil is always in the details." Paul Tsongas was pleasantly surprised by Clinton's plan, describing it as "much more effective and realistic than anyone watching last summer's presidential campaign would have expected."

Congressional Republicans reacted with skepticism and even contempt to Clinton's proposed program. Senator Phil Gramm said, "This is a bad package, and I intend to fight it hard." And Senator Domenici stated, "This is not a program to create jobs, this is a program to dramatically increase taxes."

Many lawmakers, Republicans and Democrats alike, were cautious in reacting to Clinton's plan, waiting to see how the public responded before going on record or casting any difficult votes. Initially, the public did react positively, as Clinton and his cabinet set off on a campaignlike blitz to drum up support for the program.

Clinton's plan signaled his rejection of the philosophy that had governed Ronald Reagan and, to a lesser extent, George Bush. By proposing sizable tax increases and aiming the bulk of the taxes at corporations and the wealthy, Clinton made clear his belief that the Reagan-Bush approach aimed at stimulating economic growth by cutting taxes came at too great a price and that a growing federal deficit could no longer stand. But the Clinton plan was not simply or even primarily root-canal politics, or traditional austerity. Tax increases and spending cuts were mixed in with substantial spending increases, some for new programs like national service, others for more traditional social programs like Head Start and highways. Still, the attack on twelve years of Republican economics was clear:

> Clinton has embarked on a politically explosive path of reversal, one
> that largely uses new taxes to cut the deficit and to generate money for
> new government spending to stimulate a sluggish economy. His pitch to
> roll back the Republican approach was overt and points up his belief
> that he can convince the American public—and a critical majority of
> Congress—that the economic expansion of the 1980s was a shallow boon
> with negative consequences in the long run.[35]

The attack was on more than GOP economics—it also hit the principles of 1986's tax reform. The major components of Clinton's tax plan included the following:

- *Individual Income Taxes:* A new top rate of 36 percent for taxable income above $140,000 for couples and $115,000 for individuals, along with a 10 percent surtax for people with taxable income over $250,000; maximum capital gains rates continued at 28 percent.
- *Earned Income Tax Credit:* Broader eligibility designed to help offset other tax increases for families making up to $30,000.
- *Social Security:* A tax increase for higher-income Social Security recipients; would tax up to 85 percent of benefits on couples with incomes higher than $32,000 and individuals with incomes higher than $25,000.
- *Energy Tax:* A comprehensive energy tax based on the heat content of various forms of energy measured in British thermal units, or BTUs; would also make permanent a 2.5-cent gas tax scheduled to expire in 1995.
- *Corporate Income Tax:* A new top rate of 36 percent for corporations with taxable income above $10 million, plus a 3 percent surtax on corporations with taxable income above $15 million.
- *Corporate Deductions:* Would end deductions for club dues and add a new $1 million cap on deductions for an individual executive's pay; would also eliminate deduction for expenses associated with lobbying.
- *Payroll Taxes:* Would make all wages subject to the Medicare payroll tax, removing the existing $135,000 cap.
- *Investment Tax Credit:* Would institute a 7 percent ITC that would expire in 1994, applied only to spending above a firm's base level; businesses with gross receipts of less than $5 million would qualify for a permanent ITC that would apply to their entire qualified investment spending.
- *Enterprise Zones:* Creation of fifty enterprise zones in economically distressed areas, which would qualify for tax breaks and other federal assistance.
- *Other Tax Provisions:* Permanent extension of the research-and-development tax credit, the low-income housing tax credit, the tax exemption for small-issue manufacturing bonds and for mortgage revenue bonds, the 25 percent deduction for health insurance costs of the self-employed, the targeted jobs tax credit, and the tax break for employer-provided educational assistance.[36]

Shortly after the budget plan was unveiled, Clinton moved to revise the schedule for votes on the Hill. Before members would be asked to vote on

Clinton's $16.3 billion stimulus bill, a vote would be taken on the budget resolution. Many members were nervous about voting for new spending initiatives before having the opportunity to vote for the more popular proposed spending cuts.

In the meantime, the stimulus bill, which took the form of a supplemental appropriations bill for the current fiscal year, sailed through the appropriations subcommittees with relative ease. The bill was then put on hold, so that the House could first vote on the overall budget outlines.

As Clinton's budget plan worked its way through the budget committees in the House and Senate, conservative Democrats began demanding more spending cuts in return for their support. Republicans, while united in their opposition to the Clinton plan, were having a hard time reaching consensus on an alternative. Individual House and Senate Republicans began releasing their own plans, all aimed at reducing the deficit without raising taxes.

On March 10–11, the House and Senate budget panels approved slightly modified versions of Clinton's budget plan on straight party-line votes. In the House, committee leaders bowed to conservative Democrats by adding approximately $63 billion in spending cuts to Clinton's original proposal. The Senate Budget Committee plan also included an additional $63 billion in deficit reduction, with a third of that coming from tax increases and the rest from spending cuts. The show of Democratic unity was impressive, as committee Democrats held together to defeat a series of proposed GOP amendments, some of which held great popular appeal. The question remained, however, whether this unity would hold up as the budget plan was transformed from a vague set of guidelines into a set of very specific and politically painful tax increases and spending cuts.

On March 18–19, the House passed both the Fiscal 1994 budget resolution and the economic-stimulus package, giving President Clinton back-to-back victories on his economic plan. The budget resolution passed on a largely party-line vote, with Democrats limiting House Republicans to votes on two broad substitutes for the entire Clinton package. The resolution called for $496 billion in deficit reduction over five years, evenly divided between tax increases and spending cuts; the budget as adopted was unchanged from the version passed earlier by the House Budget Committee.

The stimulus package, though a fraction of the size of the overall budget, stirred much more controversy. Conservative Democrats threatened to jump ship unless the package was cut back. However, aggressive lobbying by the administration—and in many cases by the president himself—kept most of them in check. When Charles Stenholm of Texas and Tim Penny of Minnesota, leading fiscal conservatives, threatened to disrupt the process, the House, at the urging of the administration, adopted a restrictive rule designed to prevent consideration of amendments aimed at cutting or otherwise changing the stimulus package. Penny explained the dilemma he and others faced this way:

> None of us come from safe Democratic districts, and we have to explain every vote we cast. If we're here for deficit reduction, then we have to explain how a stimulus package fits that overall theme. There has to be some consistency to what's being proposed. [37]

The Senate passed the budget resolution on March 25, 54 to 45. Again, the Democrats exercised impressive party loyalty, voting down a series of GOP amendments designed to chip away at Clinton's proposed tax increases. While the Democrats supported the broad outlines of the Clinton budget, however, many expressed reservations over some of Clinton's specific proposals, casting doubt over the continued smooth sailing of the plan through the reconciliation process. The Senate budget resolution, as passed, included $502 billion in deficit reduction over five years (virtually identical to the House-passed version).

A final version of the budget resolution passed the House and Senate on March 31 and April 1, the earliest time Congress has completed work on the president's budget since the budget process was created in 1974. The resolution was adopted with no support from Republicans and very few defections by Democrats. The compromise budget included $496 billion in deficit reduction over five years, leaving Clinton's original proposal largely intact, while adding some $50 billion in additional spending cuts as a concession to conservative lawmakers who advocated deeper cuts than those proposed by Clinton.

But the president's success on the budget resolution proved deceptively easy. Even as it moved through both houses, Clinton was encountering real problems with the stimulus plan in the Senate. While support from liberal and moderate members, as well as outside liberal interests, remained strong, support from conservative-to-moderate Democrats began to wane. Two of them, Senators John Breaux and David Boren, floated an amendment which would have split the stimulus package in two pieces, with money for projects designed to create jobs to be allocated immediately and the rest to be placed in trust until after a budget reconciliation bill had been passed; the amendment was designed to reassure fiscal conservatives worried that the spending increases would pass and take effect while the promised spending cuts, absent the lure of new programs to balance their pain, never would. The president rejected that approach, believing he could swing enough votes without it to win on the stimulus package in the Senate. His gamble failed.

The failure occurred for a number of reasons. One was tactical. In an effort to thwart Democratic and Republican opposition to the stimulus package, its floor leader, Senate Appropriations Committee Chairman Robert Byrd, used a series of parliamentary maneuvers to protect the bill against amendments from either side of the aisle. The rarely utilized procedural move, which guaranteed that no amendments offered by Republicans could possibly be successful, infuriated Republicans, who moved to a retaliatory filibuster that eventually killed the package in the Senate.

The Republican filibuster might not have been tried were it not for the collapse of the Breaux-Boren compromise, and Byrd's parliamentary ploy. It might not have succeeded, once tried, were it not for the fact that President Clinton, after several weeks of intense public campaigning for his economic package, put the issue aside to deal with foreign-policy crises and other, less immediate domestic issues. With the public focus off deficit reduction and the Clinton plan, the agenda could be changed, away from the appeal that Clinton had used—that there were two alternatives, the Clinton plan, or inaction and continued economic decline. The GOP framed the issue differently, adding a third alternative—changing the Clinton plan by removing unnecessary spending.

While Republicans were at first leery about appearing to be the agents of gridlock, they eventually settled, with perfect party unity, on a strategy of stiff opposition, hoping that they could convince the public that their opposition was to larger deficits, and not simply a partisan ploy to create more gridlock. Republicans accused Clinton of old-fashioned pork-barrel spending, and argued that most of the projects included in the stimulus plan were routine and thus did not come under the heading of "emergency" spending. Democrats responded by labeling the stimulus package a vital jobs bill and a crucial element of a continued economic recovery. But experts, seeing an economy that seemed to be buoyant, did not give the Clinton stimulus plan much support, and the public was not moved. The $16 billion plan, only 1 percent of the federal budget and one-quarter of 1 percent of the economy, was more symbolic than real; its very lack of depth made it that much harder for the president to build public enthusiasm or create outrage at Republican tactics.

Only belatedly recognizing that his plan was in trouble, the president tried to rally public support—and failed. After four unsuccessful attempts to invoke cloture and end the GOP filibuster, the stimulus plan was scrapped on April 21, handing President Clinton a major and embarrassing defeat which sharply slowed the momentum of his economic plan and his presidency as a whole.[38]

With the stimulus package gone, the president tried to refocus on the remaining core of his economic program. On April 8, a week after Congress approved the 1994 budget resolution, President Clinton provided more details of his economic plan by submitting his 1994 budget proposal. While the budget held few surprises, it provided actual numbers for Clinton's proposed tax increases and spending cuts.

Clinton's plan was heralded by its supporters as bold and honest, and slammed by its opponents as classic "tax-and-spend liberalism." One important and sadly familiar point was acknowledged by both sides: if Clinton's budget did provide for substantial deficit reduction over a five-year period, long-term projections revealed that the deficit would hit a low in 1997 and then begin to climb again, fueled largely by explosive growth in Medicare and Medicaid, the health-related entitlements. Once again, heroic efforts to eliminate budget deficits would at best provide a temporary solution.

Built into Clinton's plan was the assumption that health-care costs would be brought under control prior to 1997, bringing further major deficit reduction. Thus, implicitly, the Clinton health-care reform, billed simply as health-care reform, became Stage II of the Clinton deficit-reduction plan, even though it was not explicitly portrayed as such. That underlying reality underscored how difficult the budget problem had become; real, enduring budget discipline required policy changes going far beyond simple fiscal policy.

But for Clinton, the first goal was to get some economic plan in place. The budget resolution moved in April into the House and Senate tax-writing committees, where the solid Democratic unity exhibited during the votes on the budget resolution would surely be tested. At the outset, some moderate and conservative members were calling for deeper spending cuts, particularly in entitlements, while liberal members remained firmly opposed to any additional cuts in areas other than defense. The reconciliation bill which ultimately emerged from this process was designed to account for roughly two-thirds of the $496 billion in deficit reduction proposed by Clinton; the remaining third coming from the thirteen regular appropriations bills.

The House Ways and Means Committee, under the tough and determined leadership of Chairman Dan Rostenkowski, reported out a bill with relative dispatch, and the twelve other panels dealing with the bill met or exceeded the five-year savings targets set in the budget resolution. However, Clinton was forced to accept a compromise on his business-tax proposals. Ways and Means members were unwilling to accept Clinton's proposed top tax rate of 36 percent, opting for a less drastic 35 percent rate. The committee also revised Clinton's proposed energy tax by refining the collection points, in an effort to ease the tax burden on businesses. All in all, though, Clinton had to be pleased with what emerged. The bill included income-tax increases on wealthy Americans, a broad-based energy tax, and higher taxes on the Social Security benefits of upper-income retirees. Again the Democrats exhibited strong party cohesion, voting down every attempt by the Republicans to alter the plan. As the bill gained momentum, however, liberal support began to wane, especially among members of the Congressional Black Caucus who felt that provisions directed at helping the poor and underprivileged were not generous enough, and that cuts in them had been bargained away too easily to appease energy state lawmakers.

Clinton's package was met with stiffer resistance in the Senate. On May 20, a bipartisan collection of four senators—Democrats David Boren and Bennett Johnston and Republicans John Danforth and Bill Cohen—announced their own alternative to Clinton's plan. Boren, a member of the Senate Finance Committee, which had only an 11-to-9 Democrat to Republican party ratio, could easily tilt the delicate balance of power on the Senate's tax writing committee—especially since it was clear that there would be no GOP votes on the panel for any plan. The four senators proposed scrapping Clinton's energy tax and capping entitlement spending to produce a better than 2-to-1 ratio of spending cuts to tax increases. This plan went nowhere, but it did signal widespread dissent in the Senate and served as a springboard for Senator Boren to cause interminable headaches to the administration and his colleagues. Ultimately, to appease Boren and Breaux, and get the eleven committee votes necessary, the BTU tax was scrapped in the Senate, and a tax on transportation fuels—primarily, a 4.3 cent increase in the gasoline tax, was substituted. To make up the nearly $50 billion shortfall left by the diluted energy levy, the Finance Committee plan relied more heavily on cuts in Medicare than had Clinton's original plan, and it eliminated some of the tax breaks for the poor and for businesses proposed by Clinton, steps which infuriated the Black Caucus and other House liberals.

The House voted on the reconciliation bill on May 27, and it passed by a dangerously close margin. Conservative Democrats were brought into the fold less than twenty-four hours before the vote by a compromise deal designed to provide a modicum of control over spending for entitlement programs. This compromise brought Stenholm and Penny on board, and some of their conservative colleagues followed suit. Other members were swayed by administration promises that major changes in the controversial energy tax and additional entitlement cuts would be forthcoming once the Senate took up the measure in June.[39]

In the Senate, Clinton adopted a somewhat different strategy than he had in the House, distancing himself from the day-to-day negotiations and horse-trading and simply enunciating a set of broad principles. "I'm promoting the principles, these guys are going to work it out," he told reporters the week of June 7. Those principles included the following: the tax burden must fall more heavily on those with high incomes; the plan must include a regionally balanced energy tax; it must also include investment provisions designed to give tax breaks to businesses, poor families, and urban areas; finally, the plan must meet the goal of roughly $500 billion in deficit reduction over four years.

After the stimulus package debacle in the Senate,

> for Clinton, the details were less important than simply getting the bill out of committee and to the full Senate. . . . Assuming Senate leaders can drum up enough Democratic votes to pass the measure, Clinton hopes to reassert control when the final drafting occurs in a joint House-Senate conference later this summer.[40]

On June 25, the Senate passed the reconciliation bill, 50 to 49, with Vice President Gore casting the tie-breaking vote. The bill was opposed by all GOP Senators, as well as six Democratic members. Many members voting for the bill supported it only reluctantly, warning that if significant changes were to come out of the conference committee they might jump ship.[41] But in the House, liberal and conservative Democrats issued their own warnings —acceding to the Senate plan would jeopardize their votes.

In the Senate, prodded by charges that they were doing no more than voting for gridlock, the Republicans did offer an alternative, relying on no tax increases and upon freezes on all entitlements, save Social Security, to equal Clinton's projected $500 billion net in deficit reduction in four years. That the GOP even mentioned the dread word "entitlement" was an advance in political dialogue, but calling for a simple and undetailed freeze begged the question of how program formulas and specific policies would be changed to accommodate massive cuts in projected growth. Senate Republicans refused to offer any specifics, indicating once again how serious the dilemma was, and how sensitive the politics of deficit reduction, and especially entitlement reduction, had become.

CLINTON'S BUDGET NEGOTIATIONS

On July 15, over two hundred House and Senate budget negotiators convened to work out a compromise and draft a plan that could achieve final passage in both houses of Congress. They had three weeks to work out a deal on the $500 billion package of tax increases and spending cuts, pass it in both bodies, and send it to Clinton—amid a tension- and dissension-filled atmosphere and sharp partisan division. Even among rank-and-file Democrats who had voted for the initial plan there were objections to the size of the package and to the fact that it contained an energy tax that would hit middle-class voters.

Democratic leaders in Congress quickly voiced their support for the energy tax and the half-trillion-dollar target for the overall package, but even they each had specific views and preferences on the details. Senate Finance Committee Chairman Daniel Patrick Moynihan (D-NY) would consider raising the fuels tax several cents higher but said he would draw the line below ten cents a gallon, and he ruled out expanding the tax to include electricity or other items. His House counterpart, Ways and Means Committee Chairman Dan Rostenkowski (D-IL), on the other hand, favored a new energy tax proposal that could be combined with the fuels tax to bring in more revenue. Even the Democrats opposed to the energy levy itself were far from agreeing on an appropriate alternative. Representative David R. Obey (D-WI) wanted the revenue replaced by raising other taxes, while Representative Charles Stenholm (D-TX) called for deeper spending cuts.[42]

The Republicans from the outset refused to take part in a bill that they claimed would hurt the economy and kill jobs; consequently, they had almost no voice in the conference. Since every Republican in Congress had voted against the plan in June, Democrats had no incentive to negotiate across party lines. The onus for passage of the package rested entirely in the hands of Democrats, where nervousness and divisions were evident.

During the first week of the conference, the Democrats concentrated on areas where they could find consensus and work out compromises. But they remained divided on issues such as the energy tax, the final size of the package, and which low-income spending incentives to include or how generous to make them. They faced another headache as they tried to lure recalcitrant lawmakers on board; Senate Republicans threatened to use their one form of influence: the Byrd rule, which allows senators to strike any provision unrelated to deficit reduction from a budget-reconciliation bill. In this way, Republicans could negate any provisions that conference leaders added to win liberal Democratic support, thus making any compromise much more difficult.

Starting with only a six-vote Democratic margin in the House and a tie in the Senate as the conference began, the president had virtually no leeway to lose votes. The administration was forced to consent to most demands, even from members who were not on the conference committee; some of the most distinctive were freshman senator Diane Feinstein's (D-CA) call for broader tax credit for research and development, and freshman senator Russell Feingold's (D-WI) demand for a ban on the use of growth hormones on cows. The Congressional Black Caucus, with thirty-eight Democratic members in the House, also proved a powerful voice and was assured that tax credits for inner cities and the working poor would be included.

The White House lobbied extensively, meeting with freshmen, women lawmakers, minorities, and Democratic opponents, and urging state discussions from members as well as White House staff. Clinton pressured the Democrats to reach a consensus: "We have come this far. This is no time to turn back. We have been bold. This is no time to be timid. We have faced this crisis squarely. This is no time to blink."[43]

Adding to the Congressional confusion, the Office of Management and Budget released a preliminary estimate that projected a current-year deficit of $285 billion, $42 billion below the fiscal 1993 deficit projected by the Bush administration; the former director of the House Post Office claimed involvement by Chairman Rostenkowski, a strong voice for the plan, in an alleged embezzlement scheme; amd Ross Perot appeared on national news programs speaking out against the conferees' program.

At the end of the second week of negotiations, Democrats still appeared short of the fifty votes in the Senate that could force a tie that Vice President Al Gore could then break. That shortfall in turn forced House leaders, against their better judgment, to adopt some of the Senate provisions it had bitterly fought in order to capture a handful of marginal votes in the Senate. Most significantly, the conferees were compelled to cut back even more the increase in the gasoline tax to mollify a few Democratic senators; they cut back even more, to a mere 4.3 cents a gallon, when liberal Herb Kohl of Wisconsin indicated that he would vote against the package if it were even a tenth of a cent higher.

Cutting back on the gas tax meant a shortfall in revenue, and a renewed dilemma: how to make up the shortfall without alienating even more Democrats who might turn to opposition. Senator David Boren, who had earlier been a vocal critic of the process but had still voted to send it to conference, attacked the emerging compromise on July 27 and called on conferees to start fresh, working out an alternative through a budget summit. Though his call for a summit was easily rejected, his action further destabilized the Democrats and reinforced the notion that the power and pique of any one member could negate all his or her colleagues' efforts.

Still, the pressure to come up with a plan of some sort was great enough to drive the conferees to a compromise. It came on August 2, three days after their self-imposed deadline. Although the final bill did differ in many key details from Clinton's original proposal, it retained the central elements of increased taxes on the wealthy, decreased defense spending, some form of energy tax, and a $500 billion deficit reduction over five years.

The conference package went first to the House, for tactical reasons. But the original six-vote margin in the House had evaporated over disgruntlement with senators' blackmail and nervousness about the 1994 elections. On August 5, as the hour of the House vote quickly approached, passage was still questionable; there were threatened defections from both liberals and conservatives.

To secure support from wavering conservatives who wanted more spending cuts, congressional leaders and Clinton acquiesced to a second round of cuts, via a promised spending-cut bill in the fall, which would give conservatives one more opportunity to reduce entitlement and discretionary spending. Just before the House vote, Foley made one last appeal to his colleagues: "Tonight is the time for courage. Tonight is the time to put away the old, easy ways. Tonight is the time for responsibility. Tonight is the night to vote."

As the fifteen-minute deadline for the roll call unfolded, it became clear that the votes were still not there. Finally, with the Democrats still short of the votes needed to secure a majority and out of time on the electronic voting box, the decisive vote was left to Marjorie Margolies-Mezvinsky (D-PA). The freshman who had voted no the first time around and had announced to her constituents that she would maintain her stance, slowly made her way toward the well of the House and voted yes. The House passed the $496 billion, five-year deficit-reduction package with the smallest possible margin of 218–216. Not a single Republican supported the plan, and forty-one Democrats voted no. Only one more would have killed it and inflicted a damaging blow to the Clinton presidency.

The drama moved the next day to the Senate, which also remained dicey.

Days earlier, a still unsatisfied Boren, despite the series of steps that had been taken to mollify him and meet his demands, announced that he would reverse his earlier support and vote against the package. This would kill the bill unless one of the six Democrats who voted no in June converted and countered Boren's defection—and no more Democrats joined Boren in jumping to the other side.

After days of lobbying and concessions, including a promise of a deficit-reduction trust fund, by party leaders and by Clinton himself, Dennis De-Concini (D-AZ) announced on August 4 that he would vote yes. Another mini-crisis emerged with a last minute decision to make up the revenue lost over the gas tax by making the income-tax increases on individuals and corporations retroactive to January 1. That decision created serious dissent until the terms for payment were made more lenient.

But another crisis emerged over the open indecisiveness of former presidential candidate and erstwhile plan supporter Bob Kerrey of Nebraska. Kerrey had voted yes when the Senate passed the bill in June, but had voiced strong skepticism since. Kerrey believed that this was the best opportunity in years to make serious cutbacks in spending, an opportunity that was being forfeited. He agonized publicly for days, until it became clear that his vote was the only remaining one in question, and the one that would make the difference. It was not until a few hours before the final balloting that he announced to a hushed chamber that he would support the plan.

Clinton's deficit-reduction package passed in Congress without a single vote in either chamber from the opposition party, and without a vote to spare in either chamber. Some key provisions:

TAXES

INDIVIDUALS

Personal Income: Top tax rate raised from 31 percent to 36 percent for individuals with taxable incomes in excess of $115,000 a year and couples with taxable income over $140,000, retroactive to January 1, 1993.

Social Security: Taxable portion of benefits increased from 50 to 85 percent for individuals whose income exceeds $34,000 and couples with incomes above $44,000.

Itemized Business Deductions: Reduced to 50 percent the portion of meals and entertainment outlays that can be deducted from income as business expenses. Elimination of business deductions for club dues, including country-club memberships, and many federal lobbying expenses.

Medicare: Eliminated the cap on wages subject to Medicare.

Energy: Federal gasoline tax increased by 4.3 cents on October 1.

Luxury: Repealed the 10 percent luxury tax on boats, furs, jewelry, and aircraft.

CORPORATE

Corporate Income Tax: Raised the top corporate income tax rate from 34 to 35 percent for taxable income exceeding $10 million, retroactive to January 1, 1993.

Puerto Rico: Scaled-back tax breaks for certain corporations with operations in U.S. territories.

Deductions: Eliminated business deduction for lobbying expenses. Publicly traded companies not able to deduct salaries in excess of $1 million for each of their top five executives.

Small-Business Incentives: Increased the amount from $10,000 to $17,500 that small businesses may write off on the cost of equipment and machinery in the year of a purchase. Introduced a highly modified capital gains tax cut: investors buying newly issued stock in small businesses and holding it for at least five years would receive a 50 percent cut in the capital gains tax on the profit from the sale of the stock.

SPENDING

Medicare: Payments to providers restrained by $56 billion over five years. Medicaid expenditures held down by about $7 billion.

Empowerment Zones: Created nine empowerment zones and provided aid to ninety-five other communities to stimulate investment in depressed urban and rural areas.

Earned Income Tax Credit: Increased for low-income families by $21 billion. By 1996 it will be worth up to $3,554 for families with two or more children and $2,050 for families with one child. Workers making less than $9,000 with no children would qualify for a $300 credit. Families making more than $23,760 are ineligible.

Immunization: Created a $500 million program to immunize all children.

Food Stamps: Spending increased by $2.5 billion.[44]

Although Ronald Reagan's economic plans had been forced regularly to go through a Democratic congressional gauntlet, he was always able to capture a core group of Democratic votes, usually from the conservative lawmakers known informally as boll weevils. Bill Clinton had no such luck or skill persuading Republican counterparts. For the first time in modern congressional history, the majority party had passed major legislation with no support from the opposition.[45] As President Clinton signed the bill into law at a White House ceremony August 10, many Republicans watched smugly. For even though it had passed, the success of the plan, at either sharply reducing the deficit or stimulating the economy, remained questionable.

Democrats were relieved that they had helped their president secure a victory, but they in turn were anything but ebullient. Many of those who voted for the plan worried about its political implications; others saw the victory as providing Clinton with little if any of the political boost or infusion of political capital that Reagan's comparable victory in August of 1981 had provided for him.

Regardless of Republican carping, Clinton and Democratic leaders claimed victory. Indeed, on the broad outlines of the package, they were right. But the details did show that the budget was nowhere near the major reform originally intended. Reductions in domestic spending were marginal, and organizational reforms and program eliminations were avoided. The bulk of projected savings were expected to come from Medicare, but the Medicare cuts were not adequate to bring about real restraint on entitlements and were clearly going to be complicated by the forthcoming health-care reform.

Senator Bob Kerrey, who had grudgingly voted yes at the eleventh hour, responded, "It is impressive in its honesty, but there is none of the radical change in structure that needs to occur. It is the same old stuff, in my judgment, in that it allows bureaucracies to continue to grow and doesn't make the kinds of spending cuts that everyone who walks around up here knows we need."[46]

The White House image did receive a boost from the Office of Management and Budget, which issued a surprisingly positive report on the plan on

September 1. It put the five-year deficit-reduction package at $504.8 billion, $9 billion more than the $496 billion congressional Democrats had claimed. It also projected the deficits through the 1994–98 period to be almost $96 billion lower than the congressional Democrats' August forecast. The September OMB numbers were also significantly lower than its own April projections.

The Congressional Budget Office issued its new estimate a week later. Although it contained more conservative figures, as expected, the report was still quite positive. It concluded that the deficit-reduction package would reach only $433 billion, falling about $63 billion short. Although much of the difference between the CBO and OMB figures lay in accounting procedures, the CBO did attribute their smaller numbers in part to Congress's failure to provide necessary funds for the continuing savings-and-loan problem, and to projections in the growth of spending for Medicare and Medicaid.[47]

But the new numbers met at least some negative response. Budget experts noted that the rosier projections depended upon a continued healthy economy, which would not be easy for Clinton and Congress to generate. Also, Republicans stressed CBO's smaller deficit-reduction figures as a way of proving that the Democrats' claims were falsely inflated all along—and noted that out-year projections showed deficits rising significantly yet again, driven by projected increases in the growth of entitlements, especially Medicare and Medicaid.

Overall, Clinton welcomed both figures. Even if the overall package was deflated by the CBO, both CBO and OMB still supported the rapid rate at which Clinton and congressional Democrats claimed deficits would drop over the next five years. Further, the two figures were less than $20 billion a year apart over that period, which experts say is an almost insignificant difference.

The struggle to produce a balanced budget, however, was and is still far from over. As of August 7, 1993, Leon Panetta, director of OMB, already had his office working on the priorities for next year's budget with much more focus on reorganization of the system as it now operates. Then in September, Vice President Gore released his much-publicized plan to "reinvent government," which calls for major streamlining initiatives. Republicans announced a willingness to work toward the administration's goals on the condition that any savings go directly toward deficit reduction. Democratic interest groups, however, pressured the White House to put all savings back into the programs from which those savings were gained.

Panetta then suggested combining appropriations cutbacks with cost-cutting pieces of the "reinventing government" package in the fall spending-cut bill to be offered by the White House in October. Many senators, including Senator Robert C. Byrd (D-WV), opposed this idea. But, majority leader George Mitchell said it "sounds like a reasonable proposal."[48]

The fall spending-cut proposal underscored yet again how difficult and controversial further deficit reduction would be. Long before any specific cuts were recommended by the administration, it was clear that some of the appropriations cutbacks would come from the fiscal 1994 appropriations bills just passed by Congress—cuts made in the face of a widespread feeling on the part of lawmakers that appropriations have already been cut as far back as possible, after the release of OMB figures showing that discretionary spending in 1994 would drop significantly from 1993—and with a "hard freeze," meaning no adjustment for inflation, pledged on the appropriations side for the next several years.

The alternative, of course, was to aim at the entitlements, but that had its own dilemma attached; with the fastest-growing entitlements being the health-related ones like Medicare and Medicaid, would it be either feasible or desirable to alter these programs radically before considering them as part of the overall health-care reform package? That question disguised another key question: should savings from Medicare and Medicaid go toward deficit reduction, or should they finance comprehensive health-care reform? To President Clinton, cutting health entitlements in the fall of 1993, when massive health-care reform was scheduled for 1994, put the cart before the horse —but it also underscored the age-old tension over governmental priorities that had underlaid the budget debate throughout the 1980s and 1990s.

For years, the lack of sharp movement on deficit reduction and sharp change in budget policy was blamed on divided government and a lack of public concern about deficits. But in 1993, unified party government reigned, and public concern was sharply higher, fueled no doubt in part by Ross Perot, and in part by Bill Clinton's stirring State of the Union message. But policy movement did not easily follow. Trapped by public unwillingness to focus on entitlement restraint, continued partisan tactical maneuvering, self-centered actions by individual lawmakers, and political miscalculation on the part of the new president, Congress was unable to take forceful action. The slow and painful route appeared to be the model for the future.

· 12 ·

AN ECONOMIC PRIMER:
THE DEFICIT IN CONTEXT

Although the approach of the 1992 presidential election with a lingering recession in the background inevitably led to talk of tax cuts by both Democrats and Republicans, those who have followed the deficit debate over the past decade must wonder whether there are any objective standards by which to judge budget and tax policies and their relationship to the performance of the economy. There are three such guidelines. First, there is a broad analytical framework focused on the sustainability of fiscal policy and deficits that emerged during the budget discussions in the mid-1980s. Second, some comparison with the budget and tax experience of other industrial countries is instructive. Third, the federal government's balance sheet and income statements regarding debt and interest costs may be compared with those of typical corporations in the private sector to see if the government is managing debt in a manner that would be judged to be prudent by investors who invest in corporate bonds. With these three perspectives in mind, we might arrive at an accurate and dispassionate judgment of U.S. budget policy.

SUSTAINABILITY OF BUDGET DEFICITS

Some objectivity is required when discussing the "dangers" to the economy that can arise from a large budget deficit. A particularly good example of the need for objectivity arose during the autumn of 1991. The economy appeared to be slipping back into recession after a brief recovery spurred by the end of the Gulf War. Monetary policy had not been effective in stimulating the economy because heavily indebted households were wary of borrowing, even at lower interest rates, while commercial banks were wary of lending to households both because of the need to reduce the size of their balance sheets to compensate for heavy losses on real estate loans and because of concerns about the creditworthiness of heavily indebted households.

The only instrument left with which to stimulate the economy—so the argument went at the time—was fiscal policy, either through tax cuts or through increases in government spending. In an election year, the preference was for tax cuts. But tax cuts meant lower revenues and larger deficits. Would tax cuts that put more money in the pockets of households stimulate the economy? Or would the larger budget deficits that resulted from them push up interest rates enough to cut spending, so that there would be no net stimulus or perhaps even contractionary pressure on the economy?

Whether a tax cut can be stimulative when the deficit is large depends on how much the tax cut enlarges the deficit and causes interest rates to rise. Extensive empirical research has not fully resolved the relationship between deficits, the national debt, and interest rates, but some conclusions point to a useful criterion for determining whether deficits are sustainable and whether they result in upward pressure on interest rates.

Broadly speaking, deficits raise interest rates and thus become unsustainable if they result in a rapid increase in the ratio of the national debt to GNP. The national debt held by the public, currently nearly $4.0 trillion, is the sum of all past deficits and represents the outstanding liabilities of the federal government to the public at home and abroad. That figure is well over half of the $6.2 trillion GNP. Some empirical evidence indicates that a rapid rise in the ratio of debt to GNP, such as occurred between 1982 and 1986 when the debt-to-GNP ratio jumped from 29 percent to 42 percent, puts upward pressure on real interest rates. Investors worldwide must be compensated for holding a larger share of U.S. government securities in their portfolios, and a rise in real (inflation-adjusted) interest rates is the natural way for that to happen. Further, higher real interest rates make it more attractive to save rather than to spend the money today. To take an extreme example: if the real interest rate on U.S. government securities were 20 percent, far higher than it is today, every dollar spent today would mean forgoing an expenditure worth 20 percent more, or $1.20, a year hence. Higher real interest rates of that magnitude would probably persuade many American consumers to put off expenditures for a year to earn such an attractive rate of return.

Still, even the theoretical effect of real interest rates on current versus future consumption is ambiguous. The higher real interest rates make savers better off and thereby increase their income and spending.

To slow the economy, budget deficits must be large enough to push up the ratio of debt to GNP (that is, make debt rise faster than GNP). Beyond that, the rise in the ratio of debt to GNP has to be rapid enough to push up real interest rates, and the net effect of higher real interest rates on spending must be negative. None of these conditions is satisfied so easily as is often assumed by critics of stimulative tax or spending measures.

Suppose we take a conservative tack and assume that higher real interest rates will reduce spending by American households and investment by American corporations. Questions about whether a larger deficit can be stimulative then come down to questions of the effect of the deficit on the debt-to-GNP ratio and the effect of the debt-to-GNP ratio on real interest rates.

If a given deficit does not raise the debt-to-GNP ratio, and if the ratio is at normal levels relative to other industrial countries, then cutting taxes or raising spending can probably stimulate the economy. It is therefore important to know the determinants of the debt-to-GNP ratio.

Change in the debt-to-GNP ratio comes about as a result of the difference between the growth rate of debt and the growth rate of GNP. The deficit, the change in debt, determines the growth rate of debt. The deficit has two basic parts: the first is the difference between government spending on goods and services and tax revenues and is called the primary deficit; the second consists of interest payments on the debt. Interest payments on the debt must be made: the discretionary portion of the deficit for policy purposes is the primary deficit.

The ratio of debt to GNP provides a constant reminder that economic growth is one of the ways to deal with the deficit problem. If, over a decade, deficits are large enough to push up the national debt by 50 percent, the burden of the debt relative to national income or GNP will not be increased if GNP also rises by 50 percent.

GNP can increase either through real growth or through inflation. Inflation that has not been anticipated by investors actually reduces the burden of national debt. In the mid-1970s, when most investors expected U.S. inflation to hover between 3 and 4 percent, they were willing to lend to the federal government at an interest rate of 6 to 7 percent, thereby receiving an after-inflation or real interest rate of about 3 percent. When, by 1980, inflation rates had risen to more than 10 percent, investors who had lent to the federal government at 7 percent were earning a −3 percent real rate of return. The unanticipated increase in inflation thereby lowered the real burden of the debt accumulated by the government during a period of unanticipated inflation.

Under these circumstances, investors eventually learn to adjust their expectations and must be convinced that lower inflation is likely in the future before they will again lend to the government at lower interest rates. In the past decade, the federal government has made considerable progress in convincing investors that the high inflation of the late 1970s and early 1980s will not be repeated. As a result, interest rates have gradually fallen from 1982 through 1991, and the borrowing cost to the federal government has been reduced below what it would have been if high interest rates and high inflation had persisted.

Besides interest rates and growth, the other variable in the calculation of the sustainability of debt is the primary deficit, that is, the portion of the deficit that excludes interest on the debt. Any change in the debt-to-GNP ratio depends on the size of the primary deficit and the effect of interest on the debt. That effect is calculated as the difference between the growth of GNP and the interest rate on the debt. If GNP grows at a rate above that of the interest rate on the debt, interest payments become less burdensome, and the debt-to-GNP ratio for a given primary deficit falls. When the economy slows down, if growth drops more than interest rates, then the debt-to-GNP ratio rises.

Finally, debt burden calculations have recognized that the difference between the growth rate of GNP and nominal interest rates can be further broken down into two components: the difference between the real interest rate and the real growth rate of GNP, and the difference between actual and anticipated inflation. The Organization for Economic Cooperation and Development (OECD) has used this framework to define countries' sustainability of fiscal policy. If, over some period, say three years, the sum of the primary deficit, the difference between the real interest rate and the real growth rate, and the difference between actual and expected inflation is close to zero, so that the debt-to-GNP ratio can be expected to be about constant, then a fiscal policy is said, under the OECD criterion, to be sustainable.

On average, actual and anticipated inflation are about equal. While some governments facing a fiscal problem are tempted to push up the inflation rate as rapidly as possible above the expected level as a means of dealing with the debt problem, the success rate of such exercises is poor. Investors who acquire government securities yielding 7 percent when they expect 4 percent inflation will, on discovering that the government is prepared to engineer 10 percent inflation, demand higher interest rates and thereby preclude the inflation route from reducing the burden of government debt. The equality on average between actual and expected inflation reduces the determinants of the debt-to-GNP ratio to two: the primary deficit and the difference between real interest and growth rates.

The second determinant, the gap between real interest and growth rates, provides a reminder of the sources of serious debt problems. If government debt becomes so large that real interest rates must be pushed up to 5 or 6 percent, they will exceed typical real growth rates of around 3 percent. That in turn will push up the debt-to-GNP ratio, which can feed back to produce further increases in real interest rates because of the increase in demand for capital. Such a negative spiral toward unsustainability of fiscal policy occurred in several Latin American countries in the early 1980s. These countries eventually were unable to provide debt-service payments on their outstanding debt, a circumstance that caused real interest rates to rise to levels higher than any possible real growth rate.

If the real interest rate is approximately equal to real growth rates over a three-year span, then the key determinant of the sustainability of fiscal policy is the behavior of the primary deficit. The primary deficit is approximately equal to zero, and therefore sustainable, if the total deficit is about equal to interest on the debt. This notion of sustainability, where the primary deficit is about equal to zero, can accompany situations where the deficit measured in dollars is quite large.

The case of the United States from 1983 to 1989—the heart of the Reagan years—is illustrative. The least sustainable U.S. fiscal policy, measured by the debt-to-GNP ratio, occurred in 1983, when the budget deficit was $207.8 billion. But three years later, when the budget deficit was even higher, at $221 billion, the index of sustainability had actually improved considerably, because the primary deficit had come down, while a larger portion of the deficit was interest on the debt. Part of the reason for the unsustainability of the 1983 budget deficit was that it had grown so rapidly—from a $79 billion deficit in 1981 to $128 billion in 1982 to $207 billion in 1983. Since sustainability is related to the rate of increase in the deficit relative to the growth of GNP and since, during 1982–1983, GNP growth was outstripped by the growth of the deficit and thus of the national debt, during that period the debt was becoming unsustainable.

But by 1991, the U.S. budget deficit, although high in nominal terms at about $270 billion, was much more sustainable by the OECD criterion. To measure the primary deficit, the $270 billion must be adjusted downward by the amount of interest on the debt, $196 billion. Moreover, about $75 billion of the increase in the deficit was due to lower tax revenues associated with the recession during 1991, and that amount should not be added to the long-run deficit. These adjustments left the primary deficit adjusted for the business cycle at −$1 billion during a year when nominal GNP growth was only about one-half the level of the nominal interest rate. A final adjustment for outlays on rescue operations for savings and loan institutions equal to $77 billion could also be subtracted from the primary deficit, because those outlays represent a transfer from the government insurance funds necessary to prevent losses of that amount by holders of deposits in S&Ls. Had the transfer not been made, depositors in S&Ls would have lost that amount. The transfers from the insurance fund therefore served only to keep aggregate demand constant and did not represent upward pressure on real interest rates. That final adjustment left the adjusted deficit at −$78 billion in FY 1991, a year when the economy experienced persistent recession.

GLOBAL PERSPECTIVE ON U.S. BUDGET DEFICITS

In addition to making such adjustments to the nominal U.S. federal budget deficit, we have another method of determining its true significance. This is to compare the U.S. budget deficits with those of other advanced industrial countries. This comparison is best made by looking at budget deficits of general government, that is, the aggregate deficit of all jurisdictions in a country, including federal, regional, state, and local governments, since the importance of the central, or federal, government varies from country to country. The deficit or surplus of general government gives a more comprehensive picture of the demands placed by governments on a nation's savings.

The Organization for Economic Cooperation and Development compiles statistics on general government financial balances for the so-called Group of Seven countries: the United States, Japan, Germany, France, Italy, the United Kingdom, and Canada. These statistics on general government financial balances running from 1971 to the present suggest a number of broad conclusions. What stands out most clearly about American deficits in relation to those of the other countries is their sharper increase as a share of GNP from the 1970s to the 1980s and their especially low levels during the 1970s. Between 1971 and 1980, U.S. budget deficits averaged 1 percent of GNP, which was well below the G-7 average of 2 percent. Between 1981 and 1990, U.S. budget deficits averaged 2.6 percent of GNP—exactly the average level for G-7 countries. Between the beginning of the 1970s and the end of the 1980s, the United States changed from being a country with deficits well below the average for industrial countries to one with average deficits. Deficits of industrial countries rose on average less sharply—from 2 percent of GNP to 2.6 percent.

There were significant shifts in the relative size of budget deficits among the G-7 governments during the 1980s. In 1980, for example, the U.S. general government budget deficit, was 1.3 percent of GNP, while Japan's was 4.4 percent, the United Kingdom's was 3.3 percent, and Germany's was 2.9 percent. The average for G-7 countries was 2.7 percent of GNP. By 1985, the U.S. general government deficit had risen to 3.3 percent of GNP, while Japan's had fallen dramatically to 0.8 percent. Deficits for the United Kingdom and Germany had fallen as well, to 2.8 percent and 1.1 percent respectively, while the average for G-7 countries of 3.2 percent of GNP was almost identical to the U.S. general government deficit.

During the late 1980s, general government financial balances were improving in most industrial countries. By 1989, the U.S. deficit had dropped to 1.7 percent of GNP, while Japan and Germany had achieved surpluses of 2.5 percent and 0.2 percent of GNP, respectively. The United Kingdom had moved into surplus of 1.2 percent of GNP. The average general government deficit for G-7 countries, at 1 percent of GNP, represented a significant improvement over the 3.2 percent of GNP for the United States in 1985. Although the United States had achieved significant improvement as well, falling from a 3.3 percent general government deficit in 1985 to a 1.7 percent deficit in 1989, it had not improved as much as typical G-7 countries, whose experience was dominated by the dramatic reductions in deficits and the movement into surplus by Japan and the United Kingdom.

The Group of Seven's general government financial balances moved slightly further into deficit in the 1990s. Several countries accounted for the increase in the general government deficit from 1 percent of GNP in the G-7 in 1989 to 2.3 percent in 1991. The U.S. general government financial deficit rose during the same period from 1.7 percent of GNP to 2.8 percent. This increase in the U.S. deficit reflected, as we have seen, a slowdown in the economy that not only reduced the revenues of the federal government but severely increased the budget deficits of state and local governments, which are also counted in the OECD measure.

The biggest fiscal swing in the industrial world occurred for Germany. In 1989, its general government financial balance was a surplus of 0.2 percent of GNP. By 1991, that balance had shifted to a deficit of 5.2 percent of GNP, largely a reflection of the immense costs of unification with East Germany. Japan's fiscal picture seemed brightest, as it registered a surplus of 2.7 percent of GNP in 1991, the largest among the G-7 countries (although its overall economic condition was much shakier). Meanwhile, the general government financial balance of the United Kingdom went from a surplus of 1.4 percent of GNP in 1989 to a deficit of 1.7 percent in 1991. Beginning in 1991, the United Kingdom has experienced a deep recession, largely as a result of tight money policies associated with its effort to join the exchange-rate mechanism of the European monetary system.

Over the next several years, the U.S. general government financial balances will probably remain in deficit. The OECD forecast a 3.8 percent deficit for the U.S. general government balance in 1992 against an average of 3.0 percent for the G-7 countries with only modest improvement in 1993 and 1994. After 1993, the total U.S. government balance will probably return to a level equal to that of the average among the advanced industrial countries, or about 2.5 percent of GNP. Of course, additional major political changes that affect the level of either government spending or revenues, including more budget cuts or health-care reform, could alter the picture, perhaps even sharply.

But looking at government finances only in terms of changes in government debt without considering government assets does not provide a complete financial picture. Whenever a household or a corporation seeks to borrow money, the lender is most interested in the assets of the prospective borrower, because he needs to obtain some collateral against the loan and a complete financial context. The household with substantial assets can borrow more than a household with few assets, even if the economic prospects of the latter are good. Net assets or net debts are what matter.

An examination of the assets and liabilities of governments has been undertaken by the OECD to obtain a measure of net public debt—that is, the excess of total government debt over its immediate assets. Consideration of government's assets improves considerably the debt picture for most countries, including the United States. In 1989, for example, the OECD estimates that the net public debt of the United States was about 30 percent of GNP. If the assets of the government were excluded, the ratio of debt to GNP would be well over 50 percent. Even so, the OECD estimate of the assets of the U.S. government is incomplete, excluding as it does the value of the U.S. weapons arsenal.

The difficulties in measuring the value of a military arsenal are legion. Changes in military technology can render the most expensive weapons systems virtually worthless on the battlefield. Alternatively, some weapons systems, such as the sophisticated electronic warfare arsenal of the United States that proved so effective in the 1991 Gulf War may have a value far above their dollar cost. Estimating the value of weapons systems is difficult because their usefulness depends so heavily on the accidents of history. The value of the military equipment that the United States was able to deploy in the Persian Gulf in 1990 and 1991 rose dramatically in August 1990, when

Iraq invaded Kuwait and U.S. military power was the only obstacle between the Iraqi forces and a far more extensive invasion of the oil-rich nations of the Middle East.

Even excluding the value of American military assets, the net public debt of the United States as a share of GNP has been virtually constant since 1986, rising from only 29.9 percent in that year to an estimated 31.3 percent in 1992. The average for the G-7 countries was 33.1 percent in 1986 and an estimated 28.8 percent in 1992. If we exclude the value of America's military assets, the real fiscal position of all governments in the United States, including federal, state, and local, deteriorated only slightly from 1986 to 1992, while the total position of other nations improved slightly. The average indebtedness among G-7 countries improved slightly, because Japan's net public debt fell from 26.4 percent of GNP in 1986 to only 2.4 percent in 1992. The United Kingdom also experienced a noticeable improvement—from 45.1 percent of GNP in 1986 to 27.4 percent in 1992.

Clearly, the most rapid fiscal improvement during the past decade has been experienced by Japan. Japan's stellar fiscal performance is the result primarily of three factors: a rapid growth rate, Draconian control of government spending initiated in the early 1980s to reduce deficits and debt, and the absence of the burden of heavy military spending. While the United States was investing heavily in modernizing its military equipment in the 1980s, Japan was continuing to spend barely 1 percent of GNP on defense. A significant part of that outlay was devoted to purchasing defense services from the United States. Japan's passive defense posture and willingness to accommodate U.S. military bases within its borders has helped the United States to maintain a major strategic presence in the Pacific. In return, Japan has benefited tremendously from the heavy American investment in military equipment that was part of the American defense umbrella over Japan during the Cold War. The collapse of the Soviet Union has led to the current reexamination of the strategic and military relationship between Japan and the United States.

Despite the tremendous attention that has been devoted to the deficits and debt of the U.S. government and the governments of other countries around the world, these figures represent an incomplete picture of deficits and debt for the total economy. In the United States, the government accounts for somewhere between a fifth and a fourth of gross national product, while its borrowing accounts for about a third of total borrowing. As American budget deficits rose during the 1980s without creating an economic calamity, analysts began to consider the effect of the deficit, or negative government saving, on the national savings rate—the amount devoted by the nation as a whole to provisions for economic growth. The sharp drop in the American national savings rate during the 1980s has alarmed many critics of U.S. budget policy. Much of the testimony before the National Economic Commission during its 1980 examination of U.S. budget deficits and their effects on the economy conceded that federal deficits per se were not large enough to cause an immediate crisis. Many analysts, however, focused their discussion on the contribution of the federal budget deficit to a comprehensive low level of national saving.

The two other players in determining the national savings rate, along with the government sector, are corporations and households. The major change affecting the national savings rate of the United States during the 1980s, in addition to larger federal budget deficits, has been the drop in the savings rate by U.S. households. During the 1970s, the net household savings rate tended to be between 7 and 9 percent. During the 1980s, it averaged between 3 and 5 percent, a swing of four percentage points, which was about $150 billion in 1991 dollars.

The national savings rate of the United States would not be viewed with alarm by many analysts if the federal budget deficit were equal only to the primary deficit of about $150 billion and if the national savings rate returned to its long-run average of 6.5 to 7 percent of disposable income. In that case, the increase in household saving would be sufficient to finance the primary deficit. Households would be allocating an additional $150 billion a year to acquiring government securities, which would, in turn, provide them with interest income over the life of the security.

The experience of the 1980s demonstrates that as long as U.S. federal budget deficits run at a level of around 3 to 4 percent of GNP and there is no recovery in the personal savings rate from 4 percent to the long-run average of about 7 percent of GNP, we will probably need to import foreign savings at a level of about 2 percent of GNP when the economy is growing. The importation of foreign savings and its mirror image—the acquisition of U.S. assets by foreigners—cannot go on forever without some adjustment. That adjustment began during the 1990s.

Although the decline in net savings in the 1980s at its most extreme was somewhat alarming, entailing as is it did the sale of U.S. assets to foreigners at a rate equal to 3.7 percent of GNP in 1987, like all economic phenomena, it was self-correcting. As foreign investors added more U.S. assets to their portfolios, the desire to continue acquiring those assets decreased. As a result, higher interest rates put pressure on U.S. borrowers to reduce their borrowing and to increase their rate of saving. Meanwhile, the debts already acquired by U.S. households and corporations as a result of past heavy borrowing began to result in pressure for reduced spending, as domestic and foreign borrowers displayed reluctance to continue the debt buildup.

The economy was slowing gradually when the Gulf crisis and then the Gulf War produced a high level of uncertainty, which caused spending to drop rapidly and precipitated a recession. This was naturally accompanied by some reduction of debt on balance sheets by households and corporations. Once that debt-reduction process was over, the economy at least sluggishly resumed growth, and the level of debt began to decline relative to income, as growth recovered.

DEBT MANAGEMENT BY THE GOVERNMENT AND BY THE PRIVATE SECTOR

The need to examine debt and deficits of households and corporations in order to obtain a comprehensive picture of national savings reminds us of the third way to judge the debt and deficits of the federal government. How does the debt and borrowing undertaken by the U.S. government over the past few decades compare with the debt and borrowing of corporations? Like the federal government, corporations must enter the market to borrow in order to finance their investments, but unlike the government, they lack the power to tax to ensure payment of interest on their debts.

The federal government's interest expense relative to revenues in 1991 was almost identical to that of a typical corporation in the private sector. Such a ratio may become a problem for a corporation because of a recession or because of some change in business conditions that reduces the demand for its products, but such risks are not faced by the federal government, which can always rely on tax revenues. Moreover, in a recession, companies face more difficult financing problems because of the risks of recession for the viability of the business, whereas recessions pose no particular risks for the federal government. Since federal liabilities become attractive in recessions as safe havens, the federal government has a built-in cushion for its interest costs, even when GNP and tax revenues are both falling.

Any concern expressed among businessmen about the fiscal health of the federal government may have more to do with the fact that its ratios of debt to assets and of interest expense to total revenues have risen more rapidly in the past twenty years than have similar ratios for corporations. But since such ratios are historically lower for government than for corporations, the federal government is still indistinguishable from a corporation with a conservative balance sheet. While its ratio of interest expense to tax revenue has risen to a level comparable to or slightly above that of typical American corporations, the far lower risk profile of the federal government more than compensates for a difference of one percentage point between its ratio of interest expense to revenue and that of typical corporations.

Historically, the U.S. government's ratio of interest expense to its revenues has been below the current level of about 20 percent, with some notable exceptions. Historical statistics suggest that, at the founding of the Republic in 1789, the ratio of interest expense to revenue for the fledgling U.S. government was 53 percent. At the end of the Civil War, the ratio was 25 percent, and at the end of World War I, it was 20.5 percent. By the end of World War II, the ratio had fallen to about 10 percent, partly because federal revenues had risen so rapidly and partly because patriotic Americans had lent money to their government at interest rates well below market levels. At the bottom of the Depression in 1933, the ratio of U.S. government interest expense to its revenues was 37 percent, but this was largely due to a collapse in revenues caused by a collapse in economic activity. Still, interest rates on federal debt fell at that time to their lowest levels in history, because the federal government was offering a riskless asset while the debt or equity of corporations was seen as highly risky.

Comparison of the fiscal health of the U.S. government with that of a typical private corporation helps to clarify why there has been no fiscal calamity despite the rapid increase in federal debt relative to GNP. If its debt and interest expense were to rise out of control, the federal government could pay its bills only by printing money, much as the Soviet Union did before its demise and as Germany was forced to do after World War I. The actual experience of the past decade, however, has been to the contrary. The Federal Reserve has steadfastly kept to a policy of bringing down the rate of inflation and has resisted the temptation to use inflation to reduce the burden of federal debt. That burden remains eminently manageable in terms not only of cash flow but also of interest expense relative to tax revenues and of the more fundamental ratio of federal debt to assets.

A political stalemate in Washington that leaves nominal deficits at levels above $200 billion a year frustrates Americans and constrains the federal government's ability to pursue countercyclical fiscal policy. While Congress and current and future presidents must continue to struggle with these problems, they are far from being as unmanageable or disastrous as many have suggested. It continues to be true that a few tough changes in budget priorities could make the problem move into the economically manageable category, but the changes inevitably must occur on the tax and entitlement parts of the ledger, requiring more political than economic pain.

CONCLUDING OBSERVATIONS

The 1980s will be seen as a time when both corporations and the federal government made more aggressive use of debt. The federal government's change in its use of debt was more radical than that of the private sector, but by the early 1990s, the federal government had reached a fiscal state far from the brink of imminent collapse. Rather, its fiscal problems, while manageable, had clearly identified sources. Decisions made previous to the 1980s to offer middle-class Americans generous entitlements in Social Security and health care, indexed to inflation, pushed up federal outlays beyond the level at which Americans were prepared to finance them by increasing current taxes. The accumulated debts will have to be serviced, and therefore either federal spending programs will eventually have to be reduced—as some, such as nondefense discretionary programs, were during the 1980s—or else taxes will have to be raised.

Part of the debt accumulated during the 1980s, a maximum of about $250 billion, was due to the defense buildup. That may have been a good investment if, as some have argued, it helped end the Cold War. International stability in a postsuperpower world would mean that American outlays on defense during the 1990s could be reduced significantly below the levels typical of the 1980s. America, as a mature, wealthy nation during the 1980s, elected to spend at a rate that required an increase in borrowing from newly emergent economic superpowers, particularly Germany and Japan, to finance government spending, private consumption, and investment. Nevertheless, the debt buildup is manageable; although like any other reduction of a national savings rate—such as that experienced by the United States during the 1980s—it means that the growth of future consumption will be slower than it would have been without the debt buildup.

The recession of 1990–1991 shows that when the U.S. economy is growing at a zero rate, the net importation of foreign loans can fall to zero. Part of the reason for the prolongation of this recession was that American households and corporations were rebuilding balance sheets and paying down debt. Simultaneously, American corporations reduced variable costs to a point where they could expect to be highly competitive in global markets.

In the rest of the 1990s, we will not see a debt buildup in the private sector comparable to what occurred in the 1980s. Nor are we likely to see again, after 1993, a deficit as high as 6 percent of GNP like that of 1983. The resumption of growth during 1993 moved the U.S. fiscal posture back to a sustainable path according to the criteria set forward by the OECD. If Americans tire of annual deficits in excess of $200 billion, then they will have to choose between higher taxes (about 10 percent higher than current levels) or a moderation in the growth of spending on entitlements. If experience is any guide, their choices will emerge only slowly and will be stated ambiguously.

· 13 ·

CONSTRUCTIVE
MANAGEMENT
OF AMERICA'S
DEBT AND TAXES

Dealing with debt and taxes has always been at the center of debate about what government can and should do in American society; central to the role and performance of government has been the ability to make coherent policy, and to exercise restraint in the exercise of political power over the purse. But rarely has the focus on policy making on debt and taxes been as intense or as negative as it has been for the past decade—among both policy makers and the public.

As we have seen, American history has been characterized by periods of ballooning debt, caused by a major war or economic reversal, followed by periods of adjustment to eliminate budget deficits and bring the debt down. Within that broad policy context, there have been three ongoing philosophical and political struggles beneath the macroeconomic policy surface. One has been the struggle over the overall size and scope of government. Each cycle of deficits from war or economic turmoil followed by debt reduction has resulted in an enduring enlargement of the size and scope of government as a factor in society and the economy—but not without the debate, in Hamiltonian and Jeffersonian terms, continuing fiercely.

A second struggle has been over who gets what in American society. Here, too, Hamiltonian and Jeffersonian philosophies have been brought to bear, but over time, in ways that cut across the two men's philosophies of allocation. Hamilton, who wanted an active and comparatively robust federal government managing federal debt to manage the economy, also favored the merchant and manufacturing classes. Jefferson, who feared a large government and the power it would wield, and who wanted to rein in the government by reining in deficits and debt, favored an agrarian society and small farmers, and sympathized with the less priviledged workers.

Of course, as government and society changed, especially in the late twentieth century, those who, in the tradition of Jefferson, favored workers over producers, the have-nots over the haves, have been more inclined to a Hamiltonian view of the size, scope, and power of government, and vice versa, complicating both the philosophical debate and the practical strategies of politics and policy making.

A third struggle is more institutional. How does a government in a democracy, faced with the need to capture favor from voters and with the insatiable demands of those voters, limit the growth of government and cope with the need, when deficits and debt do balloon, to keep them under control? Inside Congress, where the power over the purse was firmly lodged by the framers of the Constitution, this question has been addressed through periodic reforms and other structural changes, to variously strengthen or weaken appropriations committees or party leaders, to create a budget process to gain perspective on the total budget and priorities within it, or to build in procedures that enforce discipline where normal politics and economics do not demand it.

Another main venue for this struggle has been between the branches. From 1921 on, the executive branch, and the president specifically, have played a much greater role in deciding issues of debt and taxes. The larger and more direct role for the president was welcomed by Congress, which needed, in an industrialized, modern society, to have the prod of executive initiative, and the protection of the president against bureaucracies and outside interests, to fulfill its own responsibilities. But having a greater executive role has meant regular clashes and ongoing tensions over how great that role would be, and over differing priorities, both allocational and distributional, between the branches.

These interrelated struggles all have a familiar ring for the 1980s and 1990s. But there have been unique twists for this period. The struggles over deficits, including deep differences over priorities in allocation and distribution of resources, have occurred during an almost unprecedented era of sustained divided government, which has exacerbated partisan tensions and differences. The large budget deficits have not been generated in the typical and traditional ways—from a world or civil war, or via a deep economic depression. They emerged during both peace and economic prosperity, and continued regardless of economic conditions. And the ability to deal with the deficits was constrained by a federal budget increasingly difficult to control —especially because of programs underwritten not just by federal dollars but by solemn promises made by government to provide benefits to citizens and giving them the status of "rights" by calling them entitlements.

By 1992, the United States had been through a decade of outsized deficits, with no clear end to them in sight. Despite its staggering size, the deficit was no longer the dominating, immediate issue it had been through most of the decade, especially in 1990, for press, pundits, or politicians—much less for the general public. But the lack of palpable concern did not reflect a sense on anyone's part of either triumph or relief. Even those who believed that the worst of the problems were behind the country, and that it had overreacted to cries of deficit disaster, were not comforted by the performance of American governing institutions or confident about future fiscal stress. Fiscal policy had not been entirely futile; the 1986 tax reform was a major policy achievement. But even that reform, a historic example of dramatic policy change by a government that had not been forced into it, did little to bolster morale and, in fact, depressed it in some sectors of the economy, especially commercial real estate, which had become severely overbuilt under generous provisions of the pre-1986 tax law. The American public, seeing the policy change as unsettling and disruptive, reacted to tax reform more with skepticism and unhappiness than euphoria or satisfaction.

FAILURE AND FRUSTRATION

Indeed, the single most visible residue from the decade's experience with debt and taxes was a widespread sense of disappointment and distaste for politics and politicians, even among the politicians themselves. The midterm election in 1990 was dominated by the theme "throw the rascals out" and by movements in a number of states to limit the terms of legislators. The politics of the 1990 budget agreement was often cited as a reason for these feelings of discontent. Even though few lawmakers were ousted from office, the sense of public unhappiness with government's performance remained and was matched by high levels of frustration and dismay among the politicians—and no wonder. From their vantage point, continual good-faith efforts to solve this problem had led to nothing but repeated failure followed by public vilification. And the aftermath of this failure was a continuing sense of their own inability to act on other problems. Their capacity for purposeful action was limited both by the deficit straitjacket and by the cynicism it spread among the people about government's ability to do anything right. Nineteen ninety-two was more of the same, capped by George Bush's receiving only 38 percent of the vote in his reelection bid, and massive retirements from the House of Representatives.

For a decade, politicians in both parties had endlessly sought ways to resolve a problem that they themselves regularly and openly defined as the first order of government business: sound financial management of the federal government. From reconciliation to the Gang of Seventeen, from Gramm-Rudman I to Gramm-Rudman II to the 1990 budget agreement, there was a seemingly endless succession of procedural and structural measures which, it was hoped, would solve the deficit dilemma once and for all. Every one failed. Although procedural change had been a part of the response to previous budget crises, it could not produce a solution by itself, without any political consensus.

The worst embarrassment came after the excruciating, year-long negotiations that culminated in the budget agreement of 1990. After President Bush abandoned his campaign promise—"Read my lips, no new taxes"—to get the agreement, it was abruptly and decisively rejected by the House of Representatives. The initial agreement featured tougher reform in the budget process and more deficit reduction than any other in modern times, but it did not work. After the yearlong circus of negotiations, bargaining, reversal, and rhetoric had finally led to an agreement, the bottom line still projected even *higher* deficits than those a year earlier. As usual, the federal budget would be balanced some five years in the future if only the economy would grow more rapidly than anyone expected it would, while Congress refrained from continued rounds of "emergency" spending.

As we showed in the previous chapter, the objective record of U.S. fiscal performance over the decade, compared with that of other industrialized countries or to major corporations, was average—more accurately, respectably mediocre. Even more telling, the American political system, despite one of our most entrenched principles of conventional wisdom, managed to raise taxes four times in election years (1982, 1984, 1986, and 1990) while also managing repeatedly to exact politically painful cutbacks in discretionary domestic spending. Through reform and incremental budget action that all fit the traditional pattern of congressional action on budget deficits, the system worked just the way we might have expected it. But the budget deficit continued because Congress never touched the relentlessly growing programs for Social Security and medical care that had been placed outside the budget process. Fiscally, these programs had become like wars: uncontrollable outlays that added mightily to the national debt.

SYSTEMIC PROBLEMS

The budget actions taken by American lawmakers may have kept the deficit and debt problem of the 1980s and 1990s from becoming a crisis of monumental proportions. What could have been a fatal cancer proved to be only an annoying, persistent migraine headache for the economy. But general dissatisfaction that the patient had not been cured created political problems, including public unhappiness with politics and politicians. And the continuing psychological debilitation of politics and politicians who stand in the shadow of the deficit may prove threatening to the American political process. We are left with a budget heavily skewed toward payments to individuals and inclining more so, and a tax system more regressive and tilted away from the income tax and toward the payroll tax. Any possibility of change is limited by the inevitable outcry against any move that might be construed as "messing with Social Security."

In other words, the serious problems that remain differ in nature and scope from those confronted in previous bouts of deficit reduction. One difference frequently mentioned by observers and analysts is divided government. *Washington Post* columnist David Broder has been particularly harsh in his assessment of the deleterious impact on the budget process over the past decade and more of divided government, which he sees as having produced policy gridlock and destroyed political accountability.

But a systematic study of postwar policy making called *Divided We Govern* by David Mayhew of Yale University questions the gridlock thesis.[1] Mayhew argues that the policy decisions emanating from Washington are no less in number or significance in periods of divided government than in periods of united government. Under divided government, for example, the majority Senate Republicans in 1985, feeling that they would be held accountable for budget policy in the midterm elections of 1986, became the driving force for meaningful fiscal-policy change; they were thwarted not by the Democratic majority in the House of Representatives but by their own partisan ally, President Reagan.

Conceivably, without the heightened sense of political vulnerability generated by divided government, the plan forged by Senate Republicans would have been embraced by the president. But more plausibly, Reagan's own ideological beliefs and political instincts would have led him to the same decision—and would have kept him, both before and after 1985, from crafting or embracing any other sweeping deficit-reduction package that would have moderated the growth of spending on Social Security.

But if the structure of government did not make the 1980s different, three other factors did. First is the problem of inadvertent policy consequences, including the entitlement debacle and the tax dilemma. Second is the error of false expectations. Third is the impact of openness.

INADVERTENT POLICY CONSEQUENCES

"Public choice" economists, the most prominent being the Nobel laureate James Buchanan, have tirelessly promoted their theory that federal deficits are created by the need of politicians to secure reelection through more and more targeted domestic spending. But the evidence contradicts that theory. The most rabid growth in federal spending has come through programs no longer controlled by politicians; the areas of spending that can be targeted and controlled, where politicians can claim credit to win individual support from voters, have actually shrunk as a share of the budget.

The table below shows what has happened in the composition of federal outlays from 1957 to 1992. The traditional largest outlay, goods and services, has declined sharply, while transfer programs, grants to states, and interest have all grown. These last areas are often lumped together as uncontrollables —they are generally not changed through year-to-year appropriations, and most of them are set up to run through legislated formulas on automatic pilot. Entitlements make up the bulk of these, and their explosive growth can be observed in the table.

When lawmakers indexed entitlements in the early 1970s, they deliberately removed programs like Social Security and veterans' pensions from their own direct control—decisions they could have made every year and claimed credit for with voters. By forgoing that political advantage, as they supposed, to control runaway spending, the politicians disproved the public-choice-school theories of their motives—even though the consequences of their action were exactly the opposite of what they had intended. And when budget stress hit in the 1980s, politicians responded by cutting the programs they could get at directly—mostly discretionary domestic spending, which public-choice theorists see as most sacred to politicians. It was neither pure public-spiritedness nor sadistic zeal for cutting politically popular programs that led them to do so, however; it was simply because, given their abject failure when seen as "messing with Social Security," they found that they had few other targets. In the decade since, the perceived budget options available to lawmakers have continued to narrow, as uncontrollable costs have continued to expand.

Tax policy is another illustration of the impact of inadvertent consequences: The combination of Reagan's tax cuts of 1981, the sharp payroll-tax increases built into the Social Security reforms of 1983, and the Tax Reform Act of 1986 sharply tilted the bias of the tax system away from personal and corporate income taxes as the basis of federal revenue, and toward the payroll

Changes in the Composition of Federal Outlays,
Selected Years, 1957–1992 (percent)

Fiscal Year	Goods and Services	Transfer Payments	Grants to States	Net Interest	Net Subsidies
1957	63.3	21.5	4.9	7.0	3.4
1962	57.4	25.7	7.2	6.0	3.9
1967	55.0	25.2	9.4	6.1	2.7
1972	44.0	33.5	13.7	5.9	2.7
1977	35.0	40.8	15.8	6.8	1.6
1982	35.0	41.4	11.0	10.9	1.7
1987	35.4	38.8	9.7	13.1	2.9
1988	34.3	39.3	9.8	13.5	3.1
1989	34.0	39.4	9.9	14.3	2.4
1990	33.2	40.3	10.2	14.5	1.8
1991	33.3	39.7	11.0	14.7	1.4
1992	30.9	41.6	11.3	14.8	1.4

SOURCE: Allen Schick, *The Capacity to Budget*, p. 121, updated by authors from *The Economic Reports of the President*.

tax. For a full three-fourths of Americans, the payroll tax is the single largest share of their tax burden. As a consequence, the tax system has become more regressive than it was before 1980. The payroll tax is regressive in several ways: it is a flat-rate tax, it has an income cap, and it is a tax on wages, not on other sources of income like interest or capital gains. And because it is a dedicated tax, it is much harder to change in response to new economic or fiscal realities than the other major sources of tax revenue.

Policy makers did not intend this change toward regressivity in the tax code. The 1981 Kemp-Roth tax cuts were partly an attempt to promote economic growth in response to the difficult economic conditions of the time and partly an ideological effort to reduce the scope of the federal government. The 1983 Social Security reforms were undertaken to save the system from impending ruin and to respond to the long-term problem of an aging population. The 1986 tax reform was an attempt to change the income-tax system to make it fairer and more economically neutral. But at each stage of change to the tax code, there were profound unintended consequences that continue to shape the political universe.

FALSE EXPECTATIONS

Fiscal prudence and budget balancing have been preoccupations of American politicians for a long time. But never before has the issue of deficit reduction been such an obsession for policy makers. For most of the 1980s, dealing with the deficit became the overwhelming preoccupation of president, House, and Senate. Year after year, politicians set up the budget and its deficit reduction as the main goal of government—thus leading themselves, the press, and the public to expect them to solve the problem. President Reagan confidently pledged in 1982 that the budget would be balanced by the end of his first term.

When all these expectations were disappointed, lawmakers turned to dramatic procedural reform to bring about their predicted and desired outcomes. Gramm-Rudman was designed to force decisive action, setting into law an explicit timetable by which the deficit was to be reduced to zero by 1988. The deficit was not reduced to zero by 1988. Each year, a prudent goal was set. Each year, it was missed. Each year, the ultimate goal—a balanced budget—moved further away. One reason was the iron law of the unintended consequences of reform: the Gramm-Rudman process included incentives for politicians to meet the next year's targets on paper, but that meant in practice an even greater incentive for budgetary "ledger"demain—mostly in the form of shifting budget costs to the previous or the following year. After all, once the impending year's goal was met and the deadlines passed, there was no penalty for misestimates.

Only in 1987–1988 did the process appear to work satisfactorily. In the aftermath of the stock market crash of October 1987, the president and Congress did agree on a modest deficit-reduction package over two years to forestall panic in the markets. The agreement included an implicit understanding that the issue would not be reopened in the forthcoming presidential election year.

In 1988, as a consequence, all thirteen appropriations bills were enacted on schedule for the first time in fourteen years, and the budget deficit was not the central preoccupation of the policy process for the first time in six years. As another consequence, however, the tough issues that remained on the fiscal agenda were not addressed either in Congress or in the presidential campaign. That lack of focus on the country's urgent fiscal problems allowed George Bush's categorical pledge not to raise taxes to appear more plausible than it deserved to be. The temporary respite from budget embarrassment led only to the greater embarrassment over the budget process in 1990.

Deeply concerned about the long-term impact of large budget deficits, politicians struggled to eliminate the problem. Setting high expectations was one way to allay public concerns and to set a challenge for the political process to meet. But inevitably, those expectations were not met, and such highly public failure tended to breed further failure.

For politicians accustomed to a budget process that had changed only gradually, the changes called for each year in the 1980s and 1990s were considerably more far-reaching than the norm. These kinds of changes normally occur only during a crisis, or a perceived crisis. Neither condition prevailed in this era. At no point did as many as 10 percent of Americans in a major survey spontaneously identify the budget deficit as the single biggest problem facing the country. At no point did anything near a majority of Americans indicate a willingness to solve the deficit problem either by cutting programs or by raising taxes. Part of the reason for these reactions was excessively high expectations of the palliative measures that were taken.

And another problem of high expectations prevented budgeting decisions from being made in a timely fashion. High expectations meant high stakes, so that far-reaching decisions like budget cutbacks and tax increases could occur only after hard and tough bargaining by determined politicians—almost inevitably the endgame strategy of bargaining came into play. In the 1974 budget act, the fiscal calendar had been changed to give Congress more time to consider budgets; the start of the fiscal year moved from July 1 to October 1. Give lawmakers nine months instead of six months to consider the president's budget and pass appropriations bills, the reasoning went, and there will be no more problems with slipped deadlines, late appropriations bills, and continuing resolutions. The reasoning was faulty. The extra three months did not result in more timeliness but less. Within two years, the number of late appropriations bills was skyrocketing.

Reformers had failed to recognize that the growing delay in the budget process was a result of political bargaining, not calendars or timetables. Faced with tougher decisions and harder trade-offs, politicians were delaying decisions, hoping to use the timetable to their bargaining advantage. That same strategy was ever-present in the budget negotiations and decision making throughout the 1980s.

In their use of endgame technique, politicians are like high-priced, high-profile athletic superstars who tend to agree to new contracts only at the end of training camp, as the season is about to begin, or even well after it is under way. In this kind of bargaining with high stakes at risk, both sides try to use the calendar for leverage and turn to endgame negotiations.

But in politics, as in sports, the results of this tactical warfare are often deeply destructive. Players and teams look insensitive, disloyal, and greedy. Players miss crucial games and risk injury by reporting late and out of shape, while teams lose the services of their best players and still have to pay the salaries in the end. Politicians look as if they are more interested in gaining partisan advantage than in doing what is best for the economy. They leave other key policy decisions hanging fire for months on end, until the basic budget outlines are in place, and then, as the new fiscal year looms or even begins, scramble desperately to produce an agreement. Not surprisingly, such agreements often fail entirely or worsen the problem that they address. The bad faith of lawmakers who play the endgame has helped defeat efforts to reduce the budget deficit.

OPENNESS

If voters had not known or seen how these bargaining processes took place, and had seen only their results, they might not have been happy about them, but they would probably not have expressed the disgust and anger with the political process that was so common. After all, continuing deficits did not result in many direct and tangible adverse economic consequences. But the public saw not just the political results, but the year-by-year, day-to-day process by which they were arrived at. One of the major aims of governmental reform in the mid-1970s was to bring about open government. By 1980, virtually every committee meeting was open to the public, where a decade earlier nearly all had been closed. And since the advent of C-SPAN and CNN in the following decade, nearly all twists and turns in the dance of budget legislation have been covered minute to minute on national television.

The openness that has come to politics and government in Washington is one of the proudest and most valuable achievements of the reform movement, and it is here to stay. But it has had its costs. One of the most venerable truisms about legislatures is that one should never watch laws or sausages being made. The result of such unprecedented scrutiny has been public disgust. Failure, deadlock, and greed have been regularly magnified as the evil essence of budget negotiating, while the staples of all political decision making—bargaining, and logrolling—have been meticulously documented and widely condemned by editorialists, reporters, and government reformers.

At the same time, every meeting, negotiating session, and strategy caucus of White House and congressional officials, separately and together, have been covered, reported on, and highlighted, usually as another example of high-level ineptitude and failure. Policy makers themselves have made the situation worse, as they have consistently been quick to find the nearest microphone and camera to be the first to proclaim failure.

It is no surprise, then, that the message that has come through most insistently for a decade is one of failure and ineptitude by our governing institutions and representatives—a message that has been received and believed by the public.

LESSONS

Besides the unintended policy consequences that brought it about and the false expectations and unprecedented openness of government that exacerbated it, the fiscal crisis of the 1980s and 1990s is unusual in American history for its intractability. Wars and depressions tend to generate political consensus, which may be expected to linger long enough to help pay off the enormous debts that they also generate. The deficits of the 1980s and 1990s, however, have come about through a lack of consensus, which continues to prevent anyone from eliminating them. Nevertheless, the economic problem that they represent is not disastrous. Much more worrisome is the political problem—which expresses itself in cynicism and distrust of all politicians but does not stop there.

Another of the consequences is more regulation. Government, in essence, has three tools with which to shape public policy: spending, the tax system, and regulation. Spending more money is not an attractive option now, nor is raising taxes. But when public demands for government action are urgent, the easiest way to do something, but to avoid directly worsening the deficit or raising taxes, is to require somebody else to do it. Thus, we have seen in recent years a buildup of political pressure to mandate that business provide more benefits to workers, make fringe benefits portable, and clean up the environment, among other things. These expensive mandates, some of which amount to a rising tax on hiring American workers and all of which reduce the international competitiveness of the American companies, now constitute a serious negative by-product of the unwillingness of the federal government to curb the mandated spending it requires of corporations.

At the same time, the federal government has been reducing the amount of money given directly to state and local governments, while increasing the mandates imposed on states and requiring spending on education, welfare, health, safety, and the environment. Facing their own deepening fiscal crises, the states are indignant at having to accept these added burdens.

The political environment is putting a different kind of pressure on the Social Security and tax systems. Because additions to the Social Security trust fund are recorded as an offset to the budget deficit, the fund is an increasingly tempting target to politicians of both parties. If other programs, new or continuing, face the threat of the budget scalpel, why not redefine them to include them in the Social Security System? They could be placed under the aegis of the reserve fund with its large "surplus" of current receipts over current outlays.

The temptation is equally great to create more targeted taxes or user fees and to link them to trust funds so that individual spending programs can be protected from budget cuts. Up to a point, a targeted tax or user fee is an attractive way to make public policy, because it forces users of a program to pay for its benefits. But a trend of this sort increasingly isolates programs from rational decisions to set priorities. It makes even more of the budget uncontrollable and more of the revenue base inflexible, and it results in policies that continue inexorably on their path long after their usefulness has waned or disappeared.

We continued, for example, to pour large sums of money from the highway trust fund into building new highways, even long after it was clear to many policy makers that the transportation priorities of the country had changed and that the needs of mass transit had superseded those of new highways in national importance. Nevertheless, money has continued to pour into the trust fund from the gasoline tax, and the law for decades prevented it from being used for any purpose other than building new highways.

Political pressures have also led to movement to dismantle the 1986 tax reform. Top marginal rates were raised again as a part of the 1993 budget agreement, and there is talk again of introducing a series of new tax breaks to shape public behavior—many of them deductions, not credits—that would increase the temptation even more to raise marginal rates. This talk began in the Republican Bush administration, long before the Clinton White House began its own push to change the tax code. Reporter Steven Mufson, in the January 19, 1992, *Washington Post*, notes that tax reform

> was designed to discard much of the tangle of special tax breaks and loopholes accumulated over the years so that future investments would be based on economics, not political preferences. It was also designed to simplify the tax code and make it a mechanism for raising revenue rather than for making social or industrial policy.

The Bush Administration, by contrast, is turning to the tax code as

the main instrument of its economic, health and political agenda. . . .
Taxes have replaced the spending programs of the 1960s and 1970s as
the favored tools of government largess and policy.[2]

The Clinton administration's tax proposals and enactments have continued this trend.

WHAT TO AVOID

What should we do about all this? The first answer is what *not* to do. We
should not rush to implement the supposed panacea of structural reform. If
one idea has become clear over the past decade, it is that there is no easy
structural or institutional solution to whatever problems we have with debt
and taxes. Structures and rules do matter; the pay-as-you-go provisions of
the 1990 budget agreement, for example, have proved moderately effective
as a restraint on new spending and new taxing. Some reform of the budget
process may well make sense and could make a difference in policy, at least
at the margins.

But neither of the two most popular structural innovations—a constitutional amendment to balance the budget and a line-item veto for the president—would do anything to wipe away problems that all the resources and
good-faith efforts of our best policy makers have found just will not go away.
Neither reform would have kept policy makers from indexing entitlements,
cutting marginal income tax rates, or raising payroll tax rates. And these are
just the latest in a series of proposals that have been advanced with the
intention of cleaning up our deficit problems once and for all but have not
worked.

Congress has repeatedly responded to budget stress through internal reform, usually to centralize its own budget processes. For many decades, the
main institutional device that Congress relied on to limit deficits was the
requirement of periodic votes to increase the national debt limit. This device
was once expected to restrain spending and to force Congress to pay serious
attention to growing deficits. But driven by the demands of presidents and
limited by the constraints of public and interest-group pressure, Congress
has viewed the votes on the debt limit largely as nuisances. When, for any
reason, Congress has been unable to agree to increase the debt limit, a game
has ensued: government comes perilously close to being brought to a halt,
until, at the last minute, the limit is finally raised. Indeed, this device has
proved a wonderful way for many members of Congress to eat their cake and

have it, too. They vote consistently both against increases in the debt limit—so as to demonstrate to their constituents their concern for fiscal responsibility—and for programs and appropriations that increase federal spending, the debt, and the debt limit. A similar have-it-both-ways dynamic has been at play with all deficit-cutting initiatives: that is why the deficit has continued to grow.

The proposal for a constitutional amendment to balance the budget has served a similar purpose for many politicians. It enables proponents to show how deeply concerned they are about federal deficits without their having to propose or vote for the specific programs that might bring the budget into balance. Again, the purpose is to demonstrate fiscal responsibility without incurring the wrath of the large majority of Americans who are protecting most existing federal expenditures from the legislative scalpel.

Throughout the history of budgeting in America and everywhere else, a simple truth stands: the only way to eliminate a deficit—the difference between a flow of expenditures and revenues—is to reduce expenditures or raise revenues (taxes) or both until the two flows are equal. The approach of the federal government to this problem simply has not acknowledged this fact. Expected revenues have been set equal to expected expenditures; program costs have been estimated to understate outlays; tax receipts have been projected to rise; laws have been proposed to require that expenditures equal revenues. But always slippage has appeared either in the timing for the mandated equality of expenditure and revenues or in the definition of what is counted as an expenditure or what is counted as revenues. Meanwhile, after the fact, the deficit continues to be equal to the additions to the national debt measured as the difference between federal government expenditures and receipts.

Against this background, ideas for institutional reform have emerged from the conventional wisdom that lays the blame for outrageous deficits and uncontrollable spending entirely at the feet of a profligate Congress, thwarting the will of a penurious president. This line of reasoning often leads to a proposal for a line-item veto to enhance the power of the president by curtailing that of Congress.

President Reagan framed the issue in his 1984 State of the Union message:

Some forty-three of our fifty states grant their governors the right to veto individual items and appropriations bills without having to veto the entire bill. . . . It works in forty-three states. Let us put it to work in Washington for all the people.

It would be most effective if done by constitutional amendment. The majority of Americans approve of such an amendment, just as they and I approve of an amendment mandating a balanced federal budget. Many states also have this protection in their constitutions.

The main problem with the line-item veto is its basic premise that the president is better than Congress at controlling government spending. There is a fundamental flaw in this premise. Over time, any executive-centered political system will almost certainly spend more and enlarge the scope of government more than one with substantial legislative power. Compared with that of nearly all our European allies, which rely on parliamentary systems with strong executives and weak legislatures, the size of American government and taxation as a proportion of GNP is small indeed. Political scientist Michael Malbin, after a visit to France, made the point especially well:

> The French budget system clearly favors the executive. Party discipline rules out logrolling, and voting on the budget by department cuts down on localism. But one thing the system does not do, according to figures compiled by the Organization for Economic Cooperation and Development, is to produce a lower rate of government budgetary growth in France than in the United States. For fourteen of the twenty years from 1961 to 1981, under Presidents Charles deGaulle (1958–1969), Georges Pompidou (1969–1974), Valéry Giscard d'Estaing (1974–1981) and François Mitterrand, government spending went up at a faster rate, as a percentage of gross national product, than it did in the United States in the same period.[3]

The line-item veto is more a political ploy than a comprehensive proposal for reducing or eliminating deficits. For one thing, the veto as proposed aims exclusively at appropriations bills, while most spending is neither directly in the hands of the appropriations committees nor funneled through individual appropriations bills.

Take away the so-called uncontrollable expenditures that we discussed above, and what is left—the $200 billion or so in nondefense discretionary spending—is almost all the money available for trimming by line-item vetoes. The core is basically the general operating expenses of the federal government: the Central Intelligence Agency, the Federal Bureau of Investigation, the mint, the national parks, and so on. A small proportion of those expenses could be effectively vetoed if the president had the desire.

Most presidents, however, including Reagan, Bush, and Clinton, do not have that desire. Driven by the same political considerations as members of Congress, presidents generally support, even when they have an opportunity to veto, the kinds of programs that clearly stand out as wasteful federal spending. Consider Ronald Reagan and the subsidization of electric power in the West, Reagan's strongest political base and home to his closest supporters. Time after time, when bills calling for continued, large federal subsidies of power rates in Western states were sent to the president, he signed them without hesitation or protest—and with conservative Republican senators and congressmen at his side, he took credit for them. He did the same thing with subsidized grazing lands in Western states. No president, whatever his ideology, risks damage to his political base.

Nor was President Bush, the so-called education and environmental president, immune from the urge to be generous with domestic spending. He, too, supported the programs mentioned above, along with water projects, swollen farm subsidies and loan guarantees, and a bevy of other domestic programs. These are not the habits of a president who would wield the item-veto pen mercilessly.

The problem is not Ronald Reagan, George Bush, and Bill Clinton—it is presidents and Congress together. Every president wants to make his mark on the country. Some significant part of the president's success depends on proposing new programs and allocating the resources for them—and logrolling with members of Congress, with their own pet ideas and projects, to make them happen. Presidential power—in whatever form—is used to advance all presidential interests. Ironically, the line-item veto, over the long run, would probably *increase* spending, not cut it. Beyond doubt, if the line-item veto had been available to President Reagan in 1984, for example, when the MX missile was under fire in Congress, a number of calls would have been made from the White House to recalcitrant legislators suggesting that a favored dam or federal building would be item-erased if the lawmakers did not reconsider and support funding for the MX. We would have paid for all those dams and buildings—along with more MXs. President Clinton, in March 1993, would have used the line-item veto to get his stimulus package through the Senate, also leading to more, not less, spending.

Moreover, there is little to the claim that the item veto exists and has worked well in forty-three states. Even if we disregard the obvious differences between state and federal governments—for one thing, states have no responsibilities for foreign policy or defense—the promise of the line-item veto as an effective device for holding down the federal budget is not borne out by experience in the states. As writer Benjamin Zycher argued in the *Wall Street Journal*, per capita spending in the seven states whose governors lack line-item veto authority is no higher—and in some it is lower—than such spending in states with some form of line-item veto. After a systematic look at state and local spending patterns, Zycher concluded that the data "do not support the conclusion that the item veto power provides an effective constraint on government spending."[4]

LIMITED INSTITUTIONAL CHANGES

Not all suggestions for institutional change are misguided. Both the president and Congress should explore more frequent use of bipartisan commissions or informal working groups *early* in the budget season, to make it easier to seek a broad consensus on the rate of growth of big domestic programs and of defense as well as on any need for a tax increase. If some guidelines can be agreed on early in a process of give-and-take between both parties, both houses, and both branches, it will at least be somewhat easier to enact a budget that incorporates restraint in all spending and revenue areas.

Although we are skeptical about some of the more extravagant claims that are made for it, another institutional reform that may be of some efficacy is a two-year budget cycle. Certainly, the theory behind it is sound: it would be worthwhile if the budget process could move to a rhythm of one year spent on the hard budgeting decisions and one year spent on oversight and evaluation of those decisions. But as the experience of extending the beginning of the fiscal year from June to October suggests, it is not likely to work exactly in that way.

Currently, we make budget decisions based on economic projections from January for a fiscal year that begins in October and ends the following September 30: we rely on economic projections of nine to twenty-one months. The reconciliation process was originally crafted, in part, to provide a mechanism by which budget priorities could be adjusted to economic realities closer to the budget year. The best projections by the best forecasters are inexact, and projections off by 1 percent in inflation or interest rates can mean tens of billions of dollars' worth of difference in budget categories.

A two-year budget cycle would mean economic projections of nine to thirty-three months. The two-year budget cycle would likely be spent in constant tinkering with budget totals and priorities as new data came in. At the same time, the temptation to play political games with economic projections would expand, because the impact of a massaged inflation or interest-rate number would be even greater as it was extended.

There is another problem with believing that two-year budgeting would mean a more reasoned timetable of decision making. As we have shown, it is natural to expect purposeful, determined lawmakers to use whatever bargaining tools they can when important and contested decisions are being made. That is why the endgame has been so prevalent in tough budget decisions during the past decade, and why it would be just as prevalent and perhaps even more forceful with a two-year cycle. Finally, two-year budgeting would have to incorporate flexibility for countercyclical budget policy. A loose two-year budget undertaken to mitigate an expected weak economy would have to be tightened if the economy unexpectedly boomed, to avoid a jump in inflation.

None of this means that the idea should not be tried, only that it is unlikely to prove any more of a panacea than the other budget reforms that have been proposed or tried. The salient fact is that America's problem with budget deficits and an increasing debt load is not an institutional one: it is a political one. No institutional solution will solve a long-term deficit problem. A solution like the line-item veto, which would strengthen the executive at the expense of Congress, is likely to make it worse. A political problem requires a political solution: both Congress and the president must be involved. Our historical review makes it clear that despite Congress's constitutionally given power over federal money, it rarely, if ever, takes action requiring comprehensive policy initiatives without presidential pressure—or at least presidential concurrence. Opposition by the president to tax increases or budget cuts dooms them as surely as does congressional opposition.

For this reason, there can be no real solution to the budget problem without compromise and a degree of consensus between the executive and the legislature and, as things now stand, between the two parties in Congress.

Policy changes can occasionally be enacted without broad consensus, right after a dramatic election (1981), or when there is unified party control *and* a high level of party discipline (1993). But in neither case can tough and enduring constructive policy changes be implemented in a widespread way. Rather, what is needed is to alter some important and basic tax and substantive policies in fundamental ways that cut across usual partisan and ideological lines, while bringing more discipline and control to fiscal policy. If these changes were enacted, we could, before long, remove our obsession with debt and taxes and return to vigorous direct debates over the direction and size of government.

The political problems that must be addressed first are those of taxation,

Social Security, and health and housing policies, which must be reexamined in the light of the now-apparent consequences of policy choices that were made in the 1970s and 1980s. We devote our concluding section to some of the points for consideration in such a reexamination.

PRESERVING THE PRINCIPLES OF TAX REFORM

The federal tax system evolved over a long period of time into the progressive system, dominated by income taxes, that has dominated our lives. It was built on principles that fairness demanded progressivity, so that the rich would contribute a greater proportion of their income than the nonrich— which meant that the rich would pay via steeply higher marginal tax rates as their incomes rose.

The theory behind progressivity based on high marginal rates for the rich faltered some in the 1940s and 1950s, when top marginal rates approached the confiscatory level of 90 percent or more. But even with top rates at somewhat lower levels in the 1970s—50 percent for earned income, 70 percent for unearned income—the system's bulwark, fairness, came under attack because higher marginal rates increasingly came accompanied by additional deductions and exceptions—"loopholes" that enterprising taxpayers could utilize to reduce their tax loads.

The higher the marginal rates, the greater the incentive for wealthier citizens to seek ways to reduce their taxable incomes, sheltering parts of it from the IRS through investment strategies or tax-free bonds, or changing behavior to take advantage of deductions, from interest to charities, that were worth more to those paying higher rates.

By the mid-1980s, a system built on fairness was almost universally perceived as patently unfair—allowing the rich to take advantage of loopholes while leaving the less well off paying higher taxes, often via "bracket creep." Tax reform gained credence, legitimacy, and momentum as a system that built in fairness in a different way—reducing marginal rates in general, and reducing the disparity between top and bottom rates, and in return, broadening the base by erasing many of the deductions, exceptions, and loopholes.

Unfortunately, the principles of tax reform were forgotten in a hurry. By 1993, barely six years after the enactment of tax reform, the Clinton administration's tax plan involved higher taxes on the rich *by raising their marginal tax rates*, while at the same time restoring several deductions and loopholes that had been reduced or eliminated in 1986.

To many lawmakers, the only way to bring progressivity to the tax code, or to make the well-off pay their "fair share" is to increase their marginal rates. But this ideological article of faith is wrong. Higher marginal rates reduce the incentive to work and earn more, and have the perverse side effect of increasing regressivity in a key way—by making the value of deductions much higher for wealthier taxpayers than for their poorer counterparts. Consider a $10,000 yearly mortgage-interest deduction for taxpayers in the 39 percent bracket and in the 15 percent bracket. For the richer taxpayer, the deduction is worth $3,900; for the poorer taxpayer, only $1,500. More important, the higher the marginal rates, the more the incentive for well-to-do citizens to pressure Congress to add more targeted provisions that complicate the tax code and narrow its base, reducing its economic efficacy. Ultimately, reversing tax reform will lead to the level of public distrust and dissatisfaction that created the tax revolt in the early 1980s.

There is a better way to craft an income-tax system that is progressive but not destructive. That is to devalue deductions, taking away their regressive tilt, by allowing all taxpayers to apply them only at the lower marginal rate of 15 percent. This approach would raise substantial sums of revenue from the well-off and sharply reduce the impetus for higher and more differential marginal rates.

TRANSFORMING OLD-AGE FINANCES

Beyond procedural reforms in the budget process some major changes in spending priorities and the tax code would help to enhance saving and growth, while making the gradual elimination of the budget deficit possible in about ten years. Our recommendations could also slow the growth of health-care costs while helping to make housing more affordable.

There are two fundamental problems closely related to current tax and budget policy: the low level of saving by American households and the high cost of housing and health care. Each could be turned around by measures that would reduce the budget deficit both directly, by lowering outlays, and indirectly, by enhancing investment and growth. These measures, together with measures to reduce the bias against investment in the current U.S. tax system, would go far toward returning the long-run U.S. growth rate to about 3 percent, well above the minuscule average growth rate of roughly 1 percent that has persisted since 1989.

Some changes required to eliminate the bias of the tax code against investment would lose revenue in the short run, but over time, together with measures to moderate the growth of spending on entitlements, they would enhance growth enough to help to balance the budget. Taken altogether, these measures could achieve full employment in about a decade. Given the current status of the budget deficit, coupled with substandard economic performance, this is a fully adequate timetable. The time to begin is early in a new administration.

The moderation of growth in spending on entitlements, while apparently a major political problem, is simple to engineer with what are logical, if not politically appealing, arguments. First, we address Social Security, on which spending currently totals more than $300 billion per year, about one-quarter of total federal spending. Social Security was originally intended as a safety-net program to ensure against poverty among the elderly. Today, it would be considered radical to return the program to its primary original purpose. If it were possible to overcome the deep-seated public belief in the sanctity of the Social Security System as the bedrock of American policy, that goal could be achieved with a negative income tax, whereby those with low incomes over retirement age would receive a check from the federal government sufficient to keep them above the poverty level. The cost of such a program would be about one-fifth to one-quarter of the cost of the current Social Security program, because it would eliminate payments to middle- and upper-income Americans who currently receive benefits on the grounds that they were forced to make "contributions" to Social Security by the payroll tax.

In eliminating poverty for the elderly—also a less ambitious goal today than it was several decades ago, since the per capita income of those over sixty is now above that of the working-age population—a negative income tax could be phased in over twenty years. During that time, in exchange for relinquishing Social Security benefits, middle- and upper-income taxpayers and employers would see their Social Security payroll tax—currently 12.4 percent of wages—phased out. The negative income tax would be financed out of general revenues, and removal of saving disincentives in the tax code —to be detailed below—would capture most of the payroll taxes in increased household saving, which could in turn be channeled into enhanced investment opportunities.

A phaseout of the payroll tax would also help to keep job opportunities expanding in America. The payroll tax and mandated benefits constitute a prohibitive tax on hiring American labor for many types of manufacturing activity. That is one important reason why jobs in industries like clothing manufacturing, basic manufacturing, and even automobile production are being exported to Mexico and countries in Central America, Asia, and Eastern Europe with low labor costs. The burden of the payroll tax, driven by the promise of Social Security benefits to most Americans who would be better served if they could be relieved of the payroll tax, is a far more onerous by-product of our Social Security System than its impact on deficits.

As advocates of the Social Security System observe and as we have pointed out above, the Social Security System is currently "in surplus." This means simply that current payroll tax receipts exceed current outlays on Social Security. This is necessary to enable payment of currently mandated benefits to the numerous baby boomers now aged thirty to forty-five who, when they retire, will place a huge burden on the system, after having paid into it an ever larger amount to pay for their parents' benefits in addition to their own. Meanwhile, no one has mentioned that even with the current high payroll taxes, there will be nothing left for the children of baby boomers. By the time children born in 1983 and afterward reach age sixty-five, the Social Security System may well be bankrupt. Either taxes will have to be raised still further, benefits cut sharply, or a sensible alternative like the negative income tax will have to be found.

Even if we cannot replace Social Security with a more targeted system to provide a real safety-net pension for elderly Americans who need it, we can, more practically, make prudent, moderate, and sensible changes in the present system that will bring more fiscal restraint, eliminate the need to build large "surpluses" in the reserve fund that simply mask the size of overall budget deficits, and reduce the destructive impact of the payroll tax. Here are some proposals to deal both with today's budget deficits and tomorrow's Social Security System:

1. *Change the cost-of-living adjustment formula for Social Security recipients.* Any change in cost-of-living adjustments, or COLAs, is politically difficult, since voters consider COLAs a part of the sacred commitment of government to the elderly. To be sure, simply cutting back COLAs, in the face of inflation, would be widely perceived as unfair. There is a better and more sensible way. Since we initiated annual, automatic cost-of-living adjustments for Social Security in the early 1970s, we have used the consumer price index to measure inflation. But the CPI is not an accurate measure of inflation's impact on the elderly. The CPI assumes the regular purchase of houses and cars—not the sorts of things most elderly people do. The best pragmatic way to deal with COLAs is to change the formula, moving from the CPI to a new index that tracks the typical spending patterns of Social Security recipients. That would be fair and reasonable —and would also save some money in both the short and long terms.

2. *Tax Social Security recipients fairly.* The 1983 reforms applied taxation to 50 percent of the benefits of higher-income Social Security recipients. President Clinton proposed increasing the tax base to 85 percent of benefits, to make it comparable to other pension programs, covering the amount over and above what recipients themselves put in over the years. This is wise policy—it is fair, and breaks no promises, explicit or implied, made to recipients. Clinton succeeded, but more modestly than he proposed. In fact, the income base for taxation should be broadened to include all recipients whose non–Social Security income is above the poverty line—in return for which, the limits on outside earnings of Social Security recipients would be removed. In addition, the revenue from this process should go into the general revenue pot, not, as is now the case, into the Social Security reserve fund. The surplus is no such thing; we should do nothing to exaggerate it. Income-tax revenues belong with other income-tax revenues, not diverted into a reserve that is supposed to be funded by other sources.

3. *Extend the retirement age gradually to seventy, with early retirement coming at sixty-five, and the retiree receiving 60 percent of full benefits.* The 1983 reforms extended full retirement age from sixty-five, over time, to sixty-seven. That is not enough. If, over the next twenty years, the retirement age is moved to reflect more closely contemporary realities of life expectancy and working patterns, and early retirement is given less of a reward than the 80 percent of benefits now proffered, we will not need huge surpluses now to fund the program after 2015. For people now in their forties, the difference today between retiring at sixty-seven or seventy is not great, if in return they get some greater assurance that the system will be solvent when they retire.

4. *Change the payroll tax.* The payroll tax made sense back in the 1930s, when it was logical to tie a government-supplied pension to one's work, and when it was a tiny percentage of employer revenues and employee wages. It does not make sense now, at more than 12 percent—15.3 percent or higher when the Medicare portion is included—the single largest tax burden on three-fourths of Americans, a full 7 percent of gross domestic product, and a serious drag on job creation. In the short or long term, we ought to lower the payroll tax, as Senator Moynihan has long suggested. More broadly, we should move the revenue base of Social Security further away from a payroll tax and more toward a consumption tax—perhaps toward a fifty-fifty mix between the payroll levy and a value-added tax, or VAT. Taxing consumption is much more sensible, and fairer, than taxing

employment. The approach of the Concord Coalition and business leader Peter Peterson, to "means test" Social Security and other entitlements gradually, is a clever and commendable one. But it must be accompanied by payroll tax reform if it is to have real, lasting economic and social value.

Dealing with the budget deficit has become our top immediate national priority. Dealing with the problems in our Social Security System is a critical long-term goal. If we are both resolute and clever, we can move toward both goals simultaneously, without violating promises or alienating voters.

AFFORDABLE HEALTH CARE

The efforts by the federal government to make affordable medical care available for Americans have been counterproductive. By increasing sharply the demand for health care with deductible health benefits for American workers and subsidies to retired Americans—Medicare and Medicaid—government policies have increased the demand for health care without effecting any significant increase in the supply. The resulting surge in health-care costs now consumes a full one-seventh of the economy. The American approach to subsidizing only the demand for health care has created a situation akin to that concerning owner-occupied housing: those in the system are protected at exorbitant cost while those outside the system cannot hope to pay for even basic medical care.

If the Clinton administration has focused on the broader topic of universal health-care coverage and reform, it has also understood the importance of reducing overall costs. But it is less focused on finding ways to alter demand as well as supply. One big incentive for it: a solution to this problem could have the happy by-product of reducing the budget deficit. If health benefits provided by employers were taxed as ordinary income, while simultaneously American workers were provided with an income-tax credit equal to 20 percent of health insurance premiums, up to a ceiling of $335 per month for families and $135 per month for individuals, the 1993–1997 budget deficit would be reduced by $200 billion, about 20 percent of the 1993–1997 full-employment deficit, while health-care costs would rise less rapidly. (These figures in 1993 dollars are based on Congressional Budget Office estimates.) For lower- and middle-income families, there would be little change. Instead of receiving "free" medical benefits worth $335 monthly for a family, workers would see their pay increased by that amount. If employees elected to spend the $335 on health-care insurance, the tax credit would reduce their tax bill by $67 per month, or about the amount of taxes saved by having health-care benefits not counted in income.

Another more important effect of the tax-credit approach to health-care insurance would be the incentive for families to shop for health-care programs. They would discover that the primary factor affecting costs is the level of self-insurance, or deductibles, in programs. For paying the first $800 to $1,000 of yearly medical bills themselves, most households could realize a significant saving on routine health-care costs, since their health-insurance premiums would be only about one-fifth of premiums for coverage with no deductible. Savings would increase over time, as households responsible for routine medical bills became more attentive to charges for routine procedures like X-rays and physical exams. Medical care, food, clothing, or anything else costs more if we pay for it as an unvarying deduction from our pay with no incentive for shopping around.

Over the past several years, while inflation has dropped steadily for almost all goods and services and while prices of some are actually falling, medical-care costs have continued to increase 8 to 10 percent a year. The demand for such services rises automatically because of deductible health-care benefits, and with huge increases in federal outlays on Medicare and Medicaid, the price also increases. Controlling the growth of demand for health care would help to reduce the budget deficit, while making health care more affordable for everyone. The Clinton plan focused on the supply of insurance coverage and medical services, and on the control of costs via caps and managed care. Reducing the demand for medical services needs to be a serious component of reform—tax reform *and* health reform.

Taxing Medicare benefits not currently subject to tax would be roughly equivalent to taxing health insurance for workers and would add another $50 billion to deficit reduction over the next five years. Taxation of Medicare benefits for retirees, who are prime beneficiaries of federal retirement programs, while replacing deductible health-care premiums with tax credits, would reduce budget deficits by $250 billion over the next five years. At the same time, it would help slow inflation of health-care costs and the export abroad of American jobs. These two measures alone would by 1997 eliminate one-quarter of the basic budget deficit by cutting the projected 1997 standardized employment deficit by $59 billion to $175 billion, just 2.2 percent of projected 1997 gross domestic product, well below the average deficit burden of the past twenty-five years.

OPENING THE HOUSING MARKET

Similar to the problem of health-care costs, where government subsidies designed to help people pay for medical care actually made it less affordable by pushing up demand indiscriminately, are programs to subsidize owner-occupied housing. At the core of these programs is the deductibility of mortgage interest on owner-occupied housing. That cherished middle-class entitlement has enhanced the value of existing real estate. Together with the inflation surge of the 1970s, it meant that house prices rose dramatically until the late 1980s, thereby greatly enhancing the welfare of older, middle- and upper-income individuals, who own most of the valuable housing stock, at the expense of younger, less affluent baby boomers, who were trying to acquire a first home or trying to buy a larger home as their families grew.

The many special tax breaks for homeowners that add mightily to the budget deficit, about $50 billion per year from the mortgage-interest deduction alone, have, like tax breaks for medical insurance, increased the demand for housing but not the supply. The result has been a rapid increase in the cost of housing.

More broadly, the tax preference for mortgage-interest expense on owner-occupied housing has reduced saving by American households, while pushing too much investment into housing. During the 1970s and 1980s, Americans correctly viewed their homes as their major investment. House prices were increasing 20 to 30 percent per year at the height of the housing boom, so saving out of current income was deemed unnecessary by many households. If a $200,000 house was increasing by $30,000 to $40,000 in value each year, why save out of an income of $70,000, especially if rising payroll taxes were forcing savings anyway?

Unfortunately, like all other bubbles, the real estate bubble has burst since 1989. Prices of housing in many areas dropped at least 15 percent instead of rising 15 percent as many homebuyers in the late 1980s had expected. The bubble burst for a number of reasons, including some tax changes and effects of lower inflation. The main reasons for the end of the housing boom, however, were a combination of oversupply and slower growth of disposable income, related in turn to depressed levels of investment and buildup of household debt.

Now is the time to make housing more affordable and to increase household savings by ending the heavy borrowing subsidy and the tax on savings currently in the tax code. The method, a savings incentive that could also apply to business, simply allows only one-half (approximately the "real" noninflationary portion) of interest expense to be deductible, while taxing only one-half of interest income. The effect would be to reduce interest rates, since a lower subsidy to borrowing would cut the demand for credit, while a larger incentive to lending would increase the supply. The lower interest rates would compensate most households for the loss of half of mortgage deductibility, so that no major disruptions would arise in household budgets.

Housing prices would fall somewhat with the removal of a tax subsidy like deductibility of all interest expense. Lower-income, younger, prospective homebuyers would benefit temporarily at the expense of more wealthy, older homeowners. The effect—increased affordability of housing—would be a positive achievement consistent with the stated objective of most politicians and most Americans. The modest losses of owners of large or multiple homes could be mitigated by gradually phasing in the savings incentives over five years.

The longer-term effect of the savings initiative between generations of Americans would be immensely positive. Even if the prices of houses, the source of the major bequest of Americans to their children, fell, the modest negative effect on housing affordability even for wealthier Americans would be largely mitigated by the lower cost under the prosavings program of the housing children tend to buy with their bequests. Further, interest rates would be lower, so that half-deductible mortgage interest would leave after-tax mortgage-interest costs largely unaffected.

Higher household savings would contribute to higher national savings, which, in turn, would reduce the need to import capital from abroad to finance even what is now a subnormal level of American investment. It is no accident that Japan, like virtually all other advanced industrial countries from which America has borrowed heavily over the past decade, allows no deduction of mortgage interest and allows considerable accumulations of assets whose interest earnings are not taxed. Beyond the increased national savings, the savings incentive would reduce the federal budget deficit by about $20 billion per year largely by limiting the benefits to wealthy home-buyers of the generous interest-deduction provisions currently in effect.

ENCOURAGING INVESTMENT

Beyond a low level of national savings, America's slowdown in growth is related to some major disincentives to invest still embedded in the tax code. Income from capital is overtaxed because no allowance is made for the fact that inflation changes the tax base against which taxes on capital are levied without creating any real value that helps to carry the tax burden. If an investment of $1,000 reaches $2,000 over five years only because of inflation, no value has been created, but under current law a 28 percent capital gains tax would be due on realization of such gain. Likewise, the failure to adjust depreciation and inventory allowances for inflation creates an excessive tax burden on capital that, in turn, discourages investment and thereby slows the growth of productivity and, more broadly, of output.

The usual remedy to the inflation tax bias on capital is lowering the capital gains tax rate. This ad hoc measure has been taken at irregular intervals, thereby creating uncertainty among investors, while causing the expenditure of considerable skill and energy—better used elsewhere—to play the capital gains tax game. A better solution is simply to index taxes on capital, so that only real capital gains are taxed as ordinary income on realization of the gain. Deferral of capital gains taxes until realization creates an extra incentive to invest, probably desirable in view of America's need to catch up on capital formation.

The absence of past indexing could be compensated for by a two-year "tax window" within which realized capital gains would be taxed only at 15 percent. Such a tax window would result in a surge of capital gains realization, which would increase revenues collected under the capital gains provision. The revenue gains could be used to end one more antigrowth tax provision, the double taxation of dividends. Currently, dividend payments by corporations are not deductible from their earnings and are counted as taxable income of recipients. Such double taxation forces corporations to overrely on debt finance (for which interest is fully deductible), which, in turn, makes them overly vulnerable to cash-flow problems in an economic slowdown, like the 1991–1992 slowdown that created a wave of bankruptcies.

Indeed, the unequal tax treatment of debt and equity finance contributed to the wave of leveraged buyouts during the 1980s. Such buyouts were merely exercises aimed at substituting debt (junk bonds with deductible interest payments) for equity (with nondeductible dividend payments) on the liability side of a corporate balance sheet. If a corporation could pay $10 million in deductible interest on junk bonds, instead of $10 million in dividends on equity, the pre-1986 tax saving was $49 million per year, or about $49 million in increased value for corporate assets. No wonder leveraged buyouts were the rage. They went too far, eventually, with too much paid for corporations just to get the tax benefits of debt finance. And when the economy slowed and corporate tax rates fell late in the 1980s, the debt-service burdens of some corporations came to exceed cash flow, leading to bankruptcy or consolidation.

Dividends should be made deductible for corporations, so that they are tax-indifferent between debt and equity finance. Since dividends can be adjusted by corporations to account for inflation and its burden on income from capital, half or inflation-adjusted deductibility of interest expense—the same as that applied to households—would help to complete a package of measures to ensure tax-neutral treatment of income from capital.

CONCLUSION

Not one year of the past fifteen has gone by without budgets, budget deficits, and taxes being the issues dominating discourse in the nation's capital, and among opinion leaders outside the Beltway. If the end of the Cold War was a triumph for American values, and for the ability of the political system to develop and apply policies that worked over decades, those facts have not convinced most Americans to love their government. Rather, it is deficits and budget gridlock, the inability of the federal government to get a handle on spending, taxing, and debt, that has become the operative metaphor for the failure of American politics and government. These failures have been used by reformers and demagogues alike to pursue their own agendas for dramatic systemic change, from term limits to the line-item veto. And they have gripped politicians and policy makers in both parties, who have expended enormous amounts of energy and time to try to resolve these problems.

As this book shows, the obsession with debt, budgets, and taxes is not new in American politics. Nor is the reality that discussion of debt and taxes often disguises broader debates about the direction and priorities of both government and society.

The term "fiscal policy" is a modern one, but it is evident throughout this book that fiscal policy—how the federal government makes policy with regard to budgets, taxes, deficits, and debt—pervades theory and practice in American government throughout its history. Debt and taxes shaped the American Revolution and the founding of the Republic. Arguments over debt and taxes divided the major American thinkers in their conceptions of society and the proper role of government, especially Hamilton and Jefferson. Every major change in politics and policy throughout American history has had direct links to debates over debt and taxes. That continues to be the case.

But if debt and taxes frame and shape much of the political debate, and can drive many of the policies that emerge, they are far more often an independent variable, a pretext for other, bigger underlying elements. For

Hamilton and Jefferson, ways of managing debt and dealing with taxes were means to shape ends—and the ends were competing visions of society.

Over the decades, the competing means and ends became far more intertwined than they had been in the eighteenth century. Jeffersonianism and Hamiltonianism no longer can be identified as Democratic and Republican, respectively. Ronald Reagan used Hamiltonian means to try to achieve Jeffersonian ends; Bill Clinton, with his activist approach and vision of an assertive, engaged government shaping America's economy, society, and role in the world, is a Hamiltonian through and through in his fiscal vision.

Steven Schier, writing about how contemporary congressmen think about economics, has distinguished between *stabilization*—normal fiscal policy—*distribution*—where resources go in society—and *allocation*—the size of government. While a lot of the contemporary debate revolves around issues of stabilization—as lawmakers talk about deficits, debt, and taxes in fiscal terms, relating them to concepts like economic growth, inflation, savings, investment, and unemployment—what most members of Congress really think about are issues of distribution and allocation.[5] What has happened in part is that the links between these functions or goals, especially between distribution and allocation, have changed over time.

Thomas Jefferson believed that smaller government would achieve his ends, including enhancing the status of farmers and small-town businessmen and workers—the downtrodden and "middle-class" of his day. His Democratic party heirs do not see the connection in the same way. To them, a larger and more assertive government is necessary to achieve their distributional goals. Hamilton's partisan political heirs, on the other hand, break from Hamilton philosophically by seeing smaller government and a reduced government role as key to their philosophy, including the enhancement of business and a mercantilistic economy. To them, a smaller and more constrained government—Jefferson's vision—is key to achieving *their* Hamiltonian distributional ends.

On occasion, the differing objectives of contemporary partisans have led them to the same conclusion; the 1986 tax reform, for example, built a bipartisan coalition in large measure because Democrats, hitting the rich by closing their loopholes, satisfied their distributional goals, while Reagan and his Republican allies saw the reform as restraining the growth of future revenues and giving more freedom to market forces, satisfying their allocational goals. The result was a Jeffersonian compromise.

But such compromises have been rare in recent years. One major reason is that policy makers have to play on a field that is far different than it was in

Jefferson's day. A series of wars over two centuries have successively expanded the role and size of government. The rise of the welfare state has
institutionalized a large federal government in a different way. And the
social-scientific revolution has made fiscal policy itself a key instrument in
government policy.

Thus, although many of the debates have echoes back into political history, and many of the structures of government are essentially the same, the
policy dynamic today is indeed different in several key ways from that of
other eras in America's past. Coping with debt and deficits when they have
not been generated by a few years of dramatic war is different. Controlling a
federal budget that is 50 percent entitlements, which are based on formulas
written into law and indexed to inflation, and which have overwhelming
public support, is radically different. And making these decisions in a world
where economic policy is shaped by assumptions, projections, and scientific
principles that assume governments can control domestic economies and
shape the world economy creates expectations that cannot be filled, and a
policy agenda that often ignores the underlying ideological divisions over the
role of government per se. Increasingly, policy about debt, deficits, budgets,
and taxes has been dominated by decisions that have had little to do with
fiscal policy.

There is no magic way to resolve these differences in outlook and priorities,
or to return the policy debate to an earlier time, when America found ways,
albeit painful ones, to roll back huge mountains of debt generated by the
Civil War, the Spanish-American War, and the two world wars. Reforming
the process of decision making may be able to help at the margins, but
neither term limits nor a constitutional amendment to balance the budget
nor a line-item veto will bring consensus where none exists, or bring under
control parts of the budget that are currently uncontrollable.

Still, as our final chapter has demonstrated, there are some basic ways to
move fiscal policy back to a base where decisions do not lead inexorably to
dead ends or bigger problems, and where policies can more directly reflect
national priorities—fiscal and otherwise. If we can move even modestly toward that outcome, we might begin to satisfy the legacies of both Hamilton
and Jefferson.

APPENDIX:
GRAPHS AND CHARTS

SOURCES OF DATA IN CHARTS

Budget of the United States Government: Fiscal Year 1993. Executive Office of the President. Washington, D.C.: U.S. Government Printing Office, 1992.

The Economic and Budget Outlook: Fiscal Years 1994–1998. Congressional Budget Office. Washington, D.C., January 1993.

Facts & Figures on Government Finance, 1990 Edition. The Tax Foundation. Baltimore, Md.: Johns Hopkins University Press, 1990.

The Historical Statistics of the United States: Colonial Times to 1970. U.S. Department of Commerce, Bureau of the Census. Washington, D.C., 1975.

Historical Tables: Budget of the United States Government—Fiscal Year 1988. Executive Office of the President, Office of Management and Budget. Washington, D.C.: U.S. Government Printing Offices, 1987.

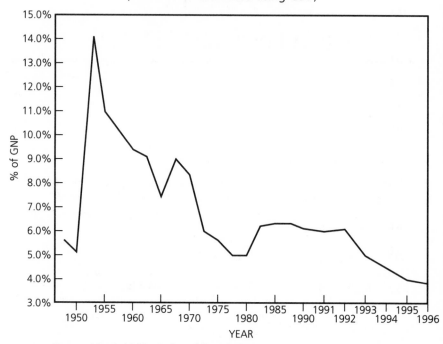

DEFENSE SPENDING AS A % OF GNP
(1993–1996 estimated using GDP)

Sources: *Historical Tables: Budget of the United States Government—FY 1988* (OMB), Table 6.2. *The Economic and Budget Outlook: Fiscal Years 1994–1998,* Table 1–4. *Budget of the United States Government: Fiscal Year 1993,* Table 2–3.

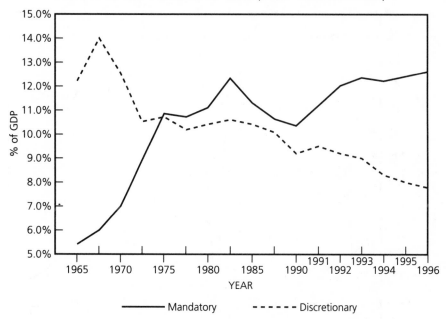

MANDATORY AND DISCRETIONARY SPENDING
AS A % OF GDP FROM 1965–1996 (1993–1996 estimated)

Source: *The Economic and Budget Outlook: Fiscal Years 1994–1998,* Table 2–4, Table E–5.

ANNUAL DEFICIT/SURPLUS AS A % OF GNP
(1993–1996 estimated using GDP)

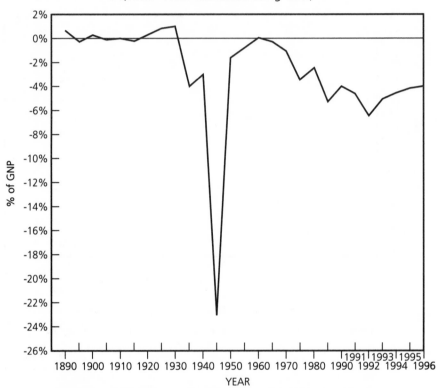

Sources: *The Historical Statistics of the United States: Colonial Times to 1970*, Series F 1–5,
Series Y 335–338. *Facts & Figures on Government Finance: 1990 Edition*, Table C5. *The
Economic and Budget Outlook: Fiscal Years 1994–1998*, Summary Table 3.

FEDERAL SPENDING AS A % OF GNP
(1993–1996 estimated using GDP)

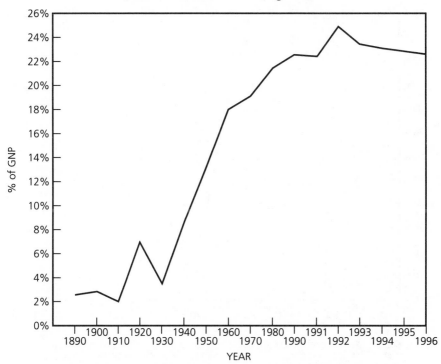

Sources: *The Historical Statistics of the United States: Colonial Times to 1970,* Series F 1–5,
Series Y 457–465. *Facts & Figures on Government Finance: 1990 Edition,* Table A31. *The
Economic and Budget Outlook: Fiscal Years 1994–1998,* Summary Table 3–1.

PUBLIC DEBT AS A % OF GNP
(1993–1996 estimated using GDP)

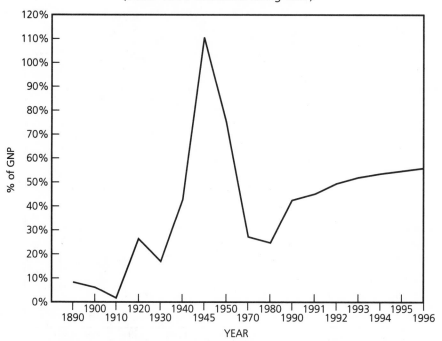

Sources: *The Historical Statistics of the United States: Colonial Times to 1970*, Series F 1–5, Series Y 493–504. *Facts & Figures on Government Finance: 1990 Edition*, Table C5. *The Economic and Budget Outlook: Fiscal Years 1994–1998*, Table 2-4.

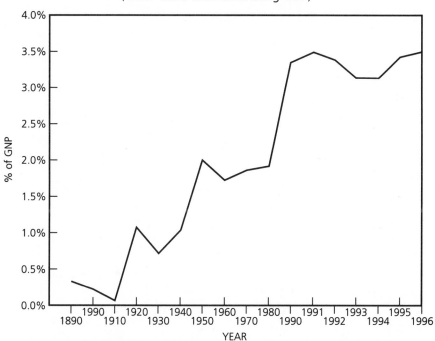

INTEREST ON THE DEBT AS A % OF GNP
(1993–1996 estimated using GDP)

Sources: *The Historical Statistics of the United States: Colonial Times to 1970*, Series F 1–5, Series Y 457–465. *Facts & Figures on Government Finance: 1990 Edition*, Table C5, Table C9. *The Economic and Budget Outlook: Fiscal Years 1994–1998*, Table 2–4.

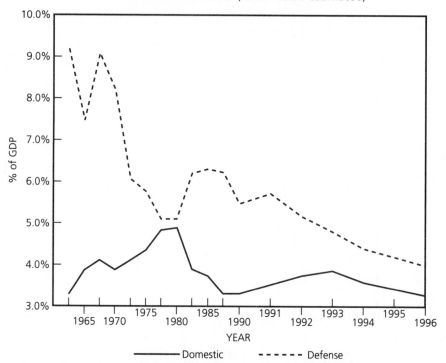

DISCRETIONARY AND DEFENSE SPENDING
AS A % OF GDP 1963–1996 (1993–1996 estimated)

Sources: *The Economic and Budget Outlook: Fiscal Years 1994–1998,* Table 1–4, Table E–9.
Budget of the United States Government: Fiscal Year 1993, Table 2–3.

RISING MEDICARE AND MEDICAID COSTS

Medicare and Medicaid are the government's fastest-growing entitlements. Medicare spending has slowed in the past few years but is expected to reach $395 billion by 2003. It cost $129 billion in 1992. Federal Medicaid costs doubled from $31 billion in 1988 to $68 billion in 1992 and are projected to reach $231 billion by 2003.

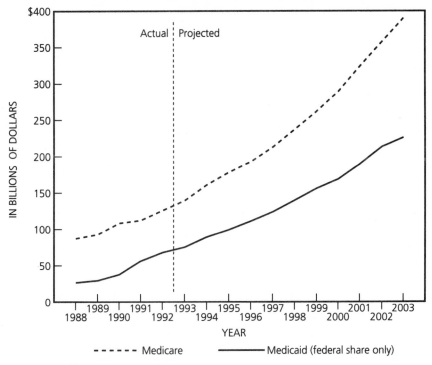

Source: Congressional Budget Office

✦ NOTES ✦

2. THE REAGAN REVOLUTION IN 1981

1. David Stockman, *The Triumph of Politics: How the Reagan Revolution Failed* (New York: Harper & Row, 1986), p. 97.
2. William Niskanen, *Reaganomics: An Insider's Account* (New York: Oxford University Press), p. 14.
3. Quoted in Albert R. Hunt, "The Campaign and the Issues," in Austin Ranney, ed., *The American Elections of 1980* (Washington, D.C.: American Enterprise Institute, 1981), p. 157.
4. David Stockman, "The Social Pork Barrel," and Jude Wanniski, "The Mundell-Laffer Hypothesis—A New View of the World Economy," *Public Interest*, no. 39 (Spring 1975).
5. Stockman, *The Triumph of Politics*, p. 31.
6. Stockman, "The Social Pork Barrel," p. 26.
7. Ibid., p. 30.
8. Wanniski, p. 31.
9. Paul Craig Roberts, *The Supply-Side Revolution: An Insider's Account of Policymaking in Washington* (Cambridge: Harvard University Press, 1984), p. 28; and Niskanen, p. 19.
10. Roberts, p. 28.
11. Ibid., p. 101.
12. See account by Roberts, pp. 19–20.
13. Ibid., p. 20.
14. Ibid., p. 86.
15. Stockman, *The Triumph of Politics*, p. 76.
16. "A Modest Program," *Wall Street Journal*, September 20, 1980, quoted in Martin Anderson, *Revolution* (San Diego: Harcourt Brace Jovanovich, 1988), p. 139.

17. Daniel P. Moynihan, *Came the Revolution: Argument in the Reagan Era* (San Diego: Harcourt Brace Jovanovich, 1988), p. 61.
18. Allen Schick, "How the Budget Was Won and Lost," in Norman J. Ornstein, ed., *President and Congress: Assessing Reagan's First Year* (Washington, D.C.: American Enterprise Institute, 1982), p. 28.
19. Ibid., p. 32.
20. Quoted in Laurence I. Barrett, *Gambling with History: Ronald Reagan in the White House* (New York: Penguin, 1984), p. 140.
21. Ibid., pp. 139–141.
22. Roberts, p. 110.
23. Schick, p. 32.
24. Barrett, p. 141.
25. Schick, p. 41.
26. Stockman, *The Triumph of Politics*, p. 8.
27. Ibid., p. 260.
28. Ibid., p. 250.
29. Ibid., p. 295.
30. Ibid., p. 284.
31. Ibid., p. 205.
32. Ibid., p. 289.

3. WHAT MAKES FISCAL POLICY?

1. For accounts of the lives and views of Alexander Hamilton and Thomas Jefferson, see Henry Cabot Lodge, *Alexander Hamilton* (New York: Chelsea House, 1980, reprint of 1898 edition); and Forrest McDonald, *Alexander Hamilton: A Biography* New York: Norton, 1982), along with the six-volume biography of Thomas Jefferson by Dumas Malone, *Jefferson and His Time: The Saga of Monticello* (Boston: Little, Brown), 1982.
2. For a look at realignments generally, see Walter Dean Burnham, "Party Systems and the Political Process," in William N. Chambers and Walter D. Burnham, *The American Party Systems: Stages of Political Development*, 2nd ed. (New York: Oxford University Press, 1975); and James L. Sundquist, *Dynamics of the Party System* (Washington, D.C.: Brookings Institution, 1973).
3. Sundquist, p. 5.
4. David Brady, *Critical Elections and Congressional Policymaking* (Stanford: Stanford University Press, 1988), p. 44.
5. Ibid., p. 49.
6. John Hughes, *The Governmental Habit Redux: Economic Controls from Colonial Times to the Present* (Princeton: Princeton University Press, 1991), p. 134. See also Douglas Higgs, *Crisis and Leviathan* (New York: Oxford University Press, 1987).
7. James Savage, *Balanced Budgets and American Politics* (Ithaca: Cornell University Press, 1988), p. 126.
8. Higgs, pp. 244–246.
9. As Susan Hansen notes, "This was not war legislation, but an effort to attract Republican presidential votes in the upcoming presidential election in protectionist states such as Pennsylvania, and to supplement revenue lost in the business panic of 1857." Susan B. Hansen, *The Politics of Taxation: Revenue Without Representation* (Westport, Conn.: Greenwood Press, 1983), p. 79.
10. Savage, p. 141.

4. ROOTS OF AMERICAN FISCAL POLICY

1. The discussion of the Dutch Rebellion comes largely from Barbara Tuchman, *The First Salute* (New York: Knopf, 1988), chap. 3.
2. Samuel Eliot Morison, Henry Steele Commager, and William E. Leuchtenburg, *The Growth of the American Republic*, vol. 1 (New York: Oxford University Press, 1980), p. 143.
3. Ibid., p. 143.
4. See Frank Bourgin, *The Great Challenge: The Myth of Laissez-Faire in the Early Republic* (New York: George Braziller, 1989); and Forrest McDonald, "The Constitution and Hamiltonian Capitalism," in Robert Goldwin and William Schambra, eds., *How Capitalistic Is the Constitution?* (Washington, D.C.: American Enterprise Institute, 1981).
5. McDonald, "The Constitution and Hamiltonian Capitalism," p. 70.
6. Ibid., p. 71.

5. FROM THE CIVIL WAR TO THE GREAT DEPRESSION

1. James Savage, *Balanced Budgets and American Politics*, p. 126.
2. De Alva Alexander, *History and Procedure of the House of Representatives* (New York: Lenox Hill, 1916), p. 237.
3. For discussions of the impetus behind these budget-process changes, see both Thomas Wander, "Patterns of Change in the Congressional Budget Process, 1865–1974," *Congress & the Presidency*, vol. 9, no. 2 (Autumn 1982); and John F. Cogan, "*Federal Budget Deficits: What's Wrong with the Congressional Budget Process*" (Stanford, Calif.: Hoover Institution, 1992).
4. For a solid account of America's deflation era, see Milton Friedman and A. J. Schwartz, *Monetary History of the United States, 1867–1960* (Princeton: Princeton University Press, 1963).
5. Savage, see p. 122.
6. See, for example, William E. Dodd, *Woodrow Wilson and His Work* (Garden City, N.Y.: Doubleday, 1927).
7. John Witte, *The Politics and Development of the Federal Income Tax* (Madison: University of Wisconsin Press, 1985), p. 110.
8. Sidney Ratner, James H. Soltow, and Richard Sylla, *The Evolution of the American Economy* (New York: Basic Books, 1979), p. 422.
9. John Hughes, *The Governmental Habit Redux*, p. 137.

6. FROM FDR TO EISENHOWER

1. Herbert Stein, *The Fiscal Revolution in America* (Chicago: University of Chicago Press, 1969), p. 27.
2. Ratner et al., *The Evolution of the American Economy*, p. 511.
3. Steven Schier, looking at how contemporary members of Congress think about budgets and fiscal policy, has noted that members are constantly addressing and juggling three elements of fiscal policy: *allocation*, meaning the provision of public goods by the government, including spending priorities and the overall size of government; *distribution*, meaning the distribution of income and wealth to achieve fairness; and *stabilization*, or the use of budget policy to provide employment, price stability, and economic growth. Rhetoric about stabilization usually disguises a more direct agenda of preferences about distribution or the size of

government, or both. (Steven E. Schier, "Deficits Without End: Fiscal Thinking and Budget Failure in Congress," *Political Science Quarterly*, vol. 107, no. 3 [1992], pp. 411–433.)

Schier's terms and context have some real relevance for earlier eras. Jefferson's passion about redistribution and fairness led him to push for a sharply restricted allocational policy, trying to restrain the size of the government through the use of fiscal-policy tools. Roosevelt adopted Jefferson's views on distribution, but believed that they could be achieved better through a more Hamiltonian, expansive allocational policy, and used fiscal-policy tools, and the panic of the populace over stabilization, to achieve his goals.

4. See E. Carey Brown, "Fiscal Policy in the Thirties: A Reappraisal," *American Economic Review*, December 1956, p. 864.
5. *The Literary Digest*, January 30, 1932, p. 13.
6. Morison et al., vol. 2, p. 474.
7. Ibid.
8. Charles Kindleberger, *The World in Depression, 1929–1939*, p. 101.
9. A. J. P. Taylor, *English History 1914–1945* (London: Oxford University Press, 1965), p. 267.
10. Ibid.
11. Ratner et al., p. 345.
12. John Witte, *The Politics and Development of the Federal Income Tax*, p. 117.
13. Higgs, *Crisis and Leviathan*, pp. 235–236.
14. Stein, p. 172.
15. Sherman Adams, *Firsthand Report: The Story of the Eisenhower Administration* (New York: Harper & Bros, 1961), p. 156.
16. Ibid.
17. Ibid., p. 163.
18. Stein, p. 342.
19. Ibid., p. 343.
20. Ibid., p. 344.

7. THE NEW PROMISE OF ECONOMIC GROWTH

1. William Manchester, *The Glory and the Dream* (Boston: Little, Brown, 1974). Manchester's characterization overlooks the experimentation with budget policy described in chap. 6.
2. As William Safire notes, the quote, widely repeated, is somewhat inaccurate. Wilson actually said, "For years I thought what was good for our country was good for General Motors, and vice versa," in a context that made the quote much less rigidly pro–big-business than it was characterized. See William Safire, *Safire's Political Dictionary* (New York: Random House, 1978), p. 787.
3. Manchester, p. 795.
4. Ibid.
5. John Kenneth Galbraith, *The Affluent Society* (Boston: Houghton Mifflin, 1957).
6. James Tobin, *Yale Law Review*, no. 3 (March 1958), pp. 321–344.
7. Herbert Stein, *The Fiscal Revolution in America*, pp. 375–378.
8. Ibid., p. 377.
9. Ibid., pp. 378–379.
10. From Kennedy's April 20, 1961, special message to Congress on taxation.
11. Ibid.

12. *New York Times*, April 21, 1961.
13. Quoted in Karl Schriftgiesser, *Business and Public Policy* (New York: Prentice-Hall), p. 97.
14. Stein, pp. 410–411.
15. Ibid.

8. The End of Jeffersonian Liberalism

1. Doris Kearns, *Lyndon Johnson and the American Dream* (New York: Harper & Row, 1976), p. 286.
2. Herbert Stein, *Presidential Economics*, 2nd ed. (Washington, D.C.: American Enterprise Institute, 1988), p. 115.
3. Ibid., p. 116.
4. Ibid., p. 117.
5. Lyndon B. Johnson, *The Vantage Point* (New York: Holt, Rinehart & Winston, 1971), p. 440.
6. Martha Derthick, *Policymaking for Social Security* (Washington, D.C.: Brookings Institution, 1979), pp. 4–5.
7. Ibid.
8. *Statistical Abstract of the United States 1990* (Washington, D.C.: U.S. Government Printing Office), Table 749.
9. Cruikshank quote from Natalie Spingarn, "Congress Debates Application of Billions in Social Security Funds," *National Journal*, April 29, 1972, p. 725.
10. Daniel P. Moynihan, *Politics of a Guaranteed Annual Income* (New York: Random House, 1973), p. 399.
11. Murray Seeger, "Reports and Comment," *Atlantic Monthly*, August 1971, pp. 6–13.
12. John Manley, *The Politics of Finance* (Boston: Little, Brown, 1970), p. 401.
13. Murray Seeger, p. 13.
14. Kent Weaver, *Automatic Government: The Politics of Indexation* (Washington, D.C.: Brookings Institution, 1988), pp. 74–75.
15. Derthick, p. 348.
16. Weaver, pp. 78–79.
17. Allen Schick, *Congress and Money* (Washington, D.C.: Urban Institute, 1983), pp. 43–46.
18. Stein, *Presidential Economics*, p. 207.
19. Ibid., p. 205.
20. Ibid., p. 214.
21. Edward R. Fried and Charles Schultze, "Overview," *Higher Oil Prices and the World Economy: The Adjustment Problem* (Washington, D.C.: Brookings Institution, 1975), pp. 66–67.
22. "Summit in Slump," *The Economist*, November 15, 1975, pp. 81–84.

9. Fiscal Policy in the Reagan Years

1. Joseph White and Aaron Wildavsky, *The Deficit and the Public Interest: The Search for Responsible Budgeting in the 1980s* (Berkeley: University of California Press, 1990), p. 183.
2. "Why Wall Street Worries," *Newsweek*, September 21, 1981.
3. "Reagan's Confidence Gap," *Newsweek*, September 21, 1981.

4. Ibid.
5. "Goodbye Balanced Budget," *Newsweek*, November 16, 1981.
6. *Congress and the Nation*, vol. VI, 1981–1984 (Washington, D.C.: Congressional Quarterly, 1985), p. 47.
7. Ibid., p. 48.
8. White and Wildavsky, p. 254.
9. Ibid., p. 277.
10. "President Reagan's Fiscal 1984 Budget Message," in *Congress and the Nation*, vol. VI, p. 1065.
11. White and Wildavsky, p. 361.
12. *Time*, February 7, 1983, p. 13.
13. *Congress and the Nation*, vol. VI, p. 53.
14. *Congressional Quarterly Weekly Report*, May 14, 1983 (hereafter *CQ Weekly Report*).
15. White and Wildavsky, p. 379.
16. "Tough Talk from Dole," *Time*, August 15, 1983.
17. "Taking the Easy Way Out," *Time*, September 26, 1983.
18. Quotes are from "The Reaganites' Civil War Over Deficits," *Fortune*, October 17, 1983.
19. *CQ Weekly Report*, November 26, 1983.
20. "Cowering Before the Deficit," *Time*, November 21, 1983.
21. Quotes are from "We're Unable to Act," *Time*, November 28, 1983.
22. "The Tough Issues Left Hanging," *Business Week*, December 5, 1983.
23. White and Wildavsky, p. 380.
24. "Taking the Easy Way Out," *Time*, September 26, 1983.
25. Hugh Heclo, "Executive Budget Making," in Gregory B. Mills and John L. Palmer, eds., *Federal Budget Policy in the 1980s* (Washington, D.C.: Urban Institute, 1984), p. 275.
26. Weaver, *Automatic Government*, pp. 206–207.
27. Richard Polenberg, "Roosevelt Revolution, Reagan Counterrevolution," in B. B. Kymlicka and Jean V. Matthews, eds., *The Reagan Revolution?* (Chicago: Dorsey Press, 1988), p. 52.
28. Michael Boskin, *Reagan and the Economy* (San Francisco: ICS Press, 1987), p. 62.
29. Murray Weidenbaum, *Rendezvous with Reality: The American Economy After Reagan* (New York: Basic Books, 1988), p. 34.
30. Niskanen, *Reaganomics*, p. 37.
31. James Pfiffner, ed., *The President and Economic Policy* (Philadelphia: Institute for the Study of Human Issues, 1986).
32. Estimates are from Boskin, p. 65.
33. *National Journal*, May 29, 1992, p. 944.
34. Ibid.
35. *CQ Weekly Report*, August 7, 1982, p. 1887.
36. *CQ Weekly Report*, December 14, 1985, p. 2604.
37. Boskin, p. 75.

10. Taxes and the Drive for Neutrality

1. John Adams, "If I Really Were a Rich Man," *Newsweek*, October 1, 1984, p. 14.
2. Quoted in *The New York Times*, November 28, 1984.

11. COPING WITH HISTORY: FISCAL POLICY AFTER REAGAN

1. Joseph A. Pechman, ed., *Setting National Priorities: 1982* (Washington, D.C.: Brookings, 1981).

2. Mary Ann Glendon, *Rights Talk* (New York: Free Press, 1991), p. 12.

3. Ibid., p. 100.

4. Stephen Moore, "The Profligate President: A Mid-Term Review of Bush's Fiscal Policy," *Cato Policy Analysis*, no. 147, February 4, 1991.

5. Jeff Faux, *Increasing Public Investment: New Budget Priorities for Economic Growth in the Post–Cold War World* (Washington, D.C.: Economic Policy Institute, 1991), p. 218.

6. Dan Balz, "Governor Clinton Enters Presidential Race," *Washington Post*, October 4, 1991.

7. Spencer Rich, "Clinton Vows to Honor Middle-Class Values," *Washington Post*, October 24, 1991.

8. Dan Balz, "Clinton Hits Both GOP, Democrats on Economy," *Washington Post*, November 21, 1991.

9. E. J. Dionne, "Economic Programs Help Define Players," *Washington Post*, February 5, 1992.

10. Steve Mufson, "Divergent Views on Economic Policy," *Washington Post*, March 9, 1992.

11. Howard Kurtz and E. J. Dionne, "Clinton Pushes Tax Cut in Debut Ad," *Washington Post*, January 10, 1992.

12. Details on the Bush proposals come from Chuck Alston, "Bush's Economic Recovery Plan Finds Few Democratic Buyers," *CQ Weekly Report*, February 1, 1992.

13. Quoted in *The Washington Post*, March 23, 1992.

14. Quoted in *The Washington Post*, April 22, 1992.

15. Quoted in *The Washington Post*, April 30, 1992.

16. Quoted in *The Washington Post*, May 6, 1992.

17. Quoted in *The Washington Post*, May 29, 1992.

18. Quoted in *The Washington Post*, July 1, 1992.

19. Quoted in *The Washington Post*, June 7, 1992.

20. Quoted in *The Washington Post*, July 1, 1992.

21. Quoted in *The Washington Post*, July 22, 1992.

22. Quoted in *The Washington Post*, October 2, 1992.

23. John R. Cranford, "Clinton Makes Priorities Clear in Revised Economic Plan," *CQ Weekly Report*, June 27, 1992.

24. *CQ Weekly Report*, June 27, 1992, p. 1901.

25. Michael Weiskopf, "Bush, Clinton Economic Plans Miss Some of Their Real-World Targets," *Washington Post*, September 25, 1992.

26. George Hager, "Five Campaign Season Plans May Point Way on Deficit," *CQ Weekly Report*, October 17, 1992.

27. George Hager, "Clinton, Congress, The Deficit: On a Collision Course," *CQ Weekly Report*, November 14, 1992.

28. *CQ Weekly Report*, November 14, 1992, p. 3634.

29. Ibid.

30. See *CQ Weekly Report*, December 19, 1992, for an account of the summit.

31. David S. Cloud, "Crafting an Economic Package: A Reality Check for Clinton," *CQ Weekly Report*, January 16, 1993.

32. George Hager and David S. Cloud, "Clinton Team's Similar Lines Focus on Deficit Reduction," *CQ Weekly Report*, January 16, 1993.
33. George Hager, "GOP Ready to Fight Clinton Over Economic Policy," *CQ Weekly Report*, January 23, 1993.
34. George Hager, "President Throws Down Gauntlet," *CQ Weekly Report*, February 20, 1993.
35. David S. Cloud, "Package of Tax Increases Reverses GOP Approach," *CQ Weekly Report*, p. 360.
36. *CQ Weekly Report*, pp. 362–363.
37. Quoted in *CQ Weekly Report*, March 20, 1993, p. 650.
38. Jon Healy, "Republicans Slam the Brakes on Economic Stimulus Plan," *CQ Weekly Report*, April 3, 1993.
39. David S. Cloud, "Dems. Pull Off Squeaker in Approving Clinton Plan," *CQ Weekly Report*, May 29, 1993.
40. *CQ Weekly Report*, June 19, 1993, p. 1542.
41. Eric Pianin and David S. Hilzenrath, "Senate Approves Budget Plan, 50–49," *Washington Post*, June 25, 1993.
42. George Hager and David S. Cloud, "Democrats Seek Wiggle Room as Conference Begins," *Congressional Quarterly*, July 17, 1993, p. 1853.
43. George Hager and David S. Cloud, "Negotiations Begin to Shape Deficit-Reduction Deal," *Congressional Quarterly*, July 24, 1993, p. 1935.
44. "Highlights of the Compromise Plan," *Washington Post*, August 3, 1993, p. A6; and David S. Cloud, "New Levies on Gas and the Rich Would Yield $240 Billion," *Congressional Quarterly*, August 7, 1993, pp. 2132–33.
45. George Hager and David S. Cloud, "Democrats Tie Their Fate to Clinton's Budget Bill," *Congressional Quarterly*, August 7, 1993, p. 2122.
46. Jonathan Rauch, "Stage Two," *National Journal*, August 7, 1993, p. 1964.
47. Eric Pianin, " '93 Deficit Outlook Has Improved, CBO Says," *Washington Post*, September 9, 1993, p. A8.
48. George Hager, "White House Offers Glimpse of New Spending-Cut Bill," *Congressional Quarterly*, September 18, 1993, p. 2441.

13. CONSTRUCTIVE MANAGEMENT OF AMERICA'S DEBT AND TAXES

1. David Mayhew, *Divided We Govern* (New Haven: Yale University Press, 1991).
2. Steven Mufson, "Bushwhacking the Reagan Tax Reforms: President's Election-Year Plan Would Undo Some '86 Changes," *Washington Post*, January 19, 1992.
3. Michael J. Malbin, "Plus Ça Change," *National Journal*, April 14, 1984, p. 729. Also see Gardner Ackley, "Leviathan Revisited: Macroeconomic Evidence on the Relative Size of Government," *Rackham Reports*, Fall 1984.
4. Benjamin Zycher, "An Item Veto Won't Work," *Wall Street Journal*, October 24, 1984.
5. Steven E. Schier, "Deficits Without End: Fiscal Thinking and Budget Failure in Congress," *Political Science Quarterly*, vol. 107, no. 3 (1992), pp. 411–433.

✦ INDEX ✦

ABOUT THE AUTHORS

JOHN H. MAKIN is director of fiscal policy studies at the American Enterprise Institute in Washington, D.C. He is a former consultant to the International Monetary Fund, the Federal Reserve, and the Treasury Department, and is the author of *The Global Debt Crisis: America's Growing Involvement.*

NORMAN J. ORNSTEIN is a resident scholar at the American Enterprise Institute. He is an election consultant to CBS News and other television programs, and a frequent contributor to "The MacNeil/Lehrer NewsHour," and writes and comments regularly on Congress, politics, and elections.